THIRD EDITION

KEYS TO
Effective
Learning

Carol Carter

Joyce Bishop

Sarah Lyman Kravits

EDITORIAL CONSULTANT

Richard D. Bucher

Professor of Sociology

Baltimore City

Community College

Prentice
Hall

Library of Congress Cataloging-in-Publication Data

Carter, Carol.
    Keys to effective learning / Carol Carter, Joyce Bishop, Sarah Lyman Kravits ; editorial consultant, Richard D. Bucher.— 3rd ed.
       p. cm.
    Includes bibliographical references and index.
    ISBN 0-13-061877-2
    1. Study skills. 2. Learning. 3. Cognitive styles. 4. Note-taking. 5. Test-taking skills. I. Bishop, Joyce (Joyce L.) II. Kravits, Sarah Lyman. III. Bucher, Richard D. IV. Title

LB2395.C27 2002
378.1'0281—dc21   2001036434

Vice President and Publisher: Jeffery W. Johnston
Acquisitions Editor: Sande Johnson
Assistant Editor: Cecilia Johnson
Production Editor: Holcomb Hathaway
Design Coordinator: Diane C. Lorenzo
Cover Designer: Thomas Borah
Cover Photo: Corbis/The Stock Market
Production Manager: Pamela D. Bennett
Director of Marketing: Kevin Flanagan
Marketing Manager: Christina Quadhamer
Marketing Assistant: Barbara Koontz

This book was set in Sabon by Aerocraft Charter Art Service. It was printed and bound by Banta Book Group. The cover was printed by The Lehigh Press, Inc.

Pearson Education Ltd., *London*
Pearson Education Australia Pty. Limited, *Sydney*
Pearson Education Singapore Pte. Ltd.
Pearson Education North Asia Ltd., *Hong Kong*
Pearson Education Canada, Ltd., *Toronto*
Pearson Educación de Mexico, S.A. de C.V.
Pearson Education–Japan, *Tokyo*
Pearson Education Malaysia Pte. Ltd.
Pearson Education, *Upper Saddle River, New Jersey*

10 9 8 7 6 5 4 3 2

ISBN 0-13-061877-2

Our Mission Statement

Our mission is to help students know and believe in themselves, take advantage of resources and opportunities, set and achieve goals, learn throughout their lives, discover careers that fulfill and support them, build fruitful and satisfying relationships with others, and experience the challenges and rewards that make life meaningful.

Brief Contents

Targeting Success in School

Creating Life Success

Contents

PART ONE

DEFINING YOURSELF AND YOUR GOALS   1

Becoming a Lifelong Learner   2   1

OPENING DOORS

Goal Setting and Time Management   32

MAPPING YOUR COURSE

Self-Awareness   58

KNOWING WHO YOU ARE AND HOW YOU LEARN

PART TWO

SETTING THE STAGE FOR LEARNING   91

Critical and Creative Thinking   92   4

BECOMING AN ACTIVE LEARNER

Reading and Studying 134
YOUR KEYS TO KNOWLEDGE

Listening and Memory 174
TAKING IN AND REMEMBERING INFORMATION

PART THREE

TARGETING SUCCESS IN SCHOOL   203

Note Taking and Research   204

LEARNING FROM OTHERS

8 Effective Writing   244
COMMUNICATING YOUR MESSAGE

9 Quantitative Learning   278
BECOMING COMFORTABLE WITH MATH, SCIENCE, AND TECHNOLOGY

Test Taking   306
SHOWING WHAT YOU KNOW

10

PART FOUR

CREATING LIFE SUCCESS   337

11 Relating to Others   338

APPRECIATING YOUR DIVERSE WORLD

12 Managing Career and Money   370

REALITY RESOURCES

Moving Ahead   404   13
BUILDING A FLEXIBLE FUTURE

Foreword

One of the greatest benefits of college is all of the doors that open to you. Opportunities arise to which you might never have ever been exposed. Activities from internships and co-ops to studying abroad are readily accessible. However, these opportunities can and sometimes do slip by because we, as students, are so engrossed in the activities with which we are already involved. As I read through this book, it hit me that if only I had come across *Keys to Effective Learning* earlier, I might have developed a better awareness of all of the opportunities surrounding me.

The greatest asset of this book is that it is an easy-to-follow guide to being successful in life. As it points out, there are several routes to achieving your goals. Not only does *Keys to Effective Learning* offer strategies to improve critical thinking, note taking, test taking, and listening skills, but it also teaches life skills such as the art of budgeting, creating a strategic job plan, and dealing with success and failure. The book covers these topics and more, all while providing important definitions, applicable exercises, and advice from our peers.

Right now you might be asking yourself: What am I going to do for the rest of my life? This and other questions might cross your mind over the next few years, as they have crossed mine. Right out of high school I was sure that I wanted to be an architect, but shortly after I began my undergraduate education at the University of Maryland I decided that it was not what I wanted for my lifelong career. Luckily, it didn't take me until I graduated to realize that. Although it took me a year and a half to decide, I have now chosen to major in communications.

As you pursue your education, you will have to make decisions that will affect you for the rest of your life. With *Keys to Effective Learning* you will be able to learn helpful strategies and gain the ability to make the best possible decisions. Never forget that success comes from within, and that knowledge is power.

Keys to Effective Learning has given me a second chance at getting all I can out of my college education and beyond. I hope that this resourceful book will help you enjoy your undergraduate experience and keep you from missing out on all the opportunities available in life. Good luck in all your endeavors!

Sammy Popat
Undergraduate student
University of Maryland

Preface

OWNER'S MANUAL
Please Read This First

You are living in a world of enormous change, a world where technology turns imaginative visions into reality, where people from every land and culture are in communication with one another, where new opportunities are created as quickly as old opportunities fade away. Your world may seem bright with promise, or it may seem to be a confusing array of choices—what to study, what career to pursue, what lifestyle to adopt, what to value, what to believe.

There are two essentials for getting where you want to go. The first is *awareness.* Only when you are aware of information, possibilities, and choices can you hope to take what you need from them. The second is *motivation.* Even the most aware person is only halfway there without the determination and drive to achieve goals. Both awareness and motivation are part of you right now—your job is to activate them as you pursue your future.

AWARENESS
Become Aware of the Ways This Text Can Help You Succeed

Keys to Effective Learning will help you maximize the time and effort you put into your education. Becoming aware of the keys of this text *before* you start reading will help you jump-start your drive toward success.

KEY #1: STUDY SKILLS. This edition contains updated study-skills chapters, with a brand-new chapter on quantitative thinking (math, science, and technology), as well as expanded coverage of reading, studying, and library and Internet research. Now there is even more information to help you take in, remember, and use what you learn in college.

KEY #2: AN EMPHASIS ON LIFELONG LEARNING. If what you study in this course only helped you read textbooks and pass tests, its usefulness would end at graduation, and you would have to start all over to learn how to deal with the real world. The ideas and strategies that help you succeed in school are the same ones that will bring success in your career and personal life. Therefore, this book focuses on success strategies as they apply to *school, work,* and *life,* not just the classroom.

KEY #3: SKILLS THAT PREPARE YOU TO LEARN. Success in any course depends upon your building a base of preparation that allows you to be the best student you can be. The following skills will fill the bill.

- *Thinking skills.* Being able to remember facts and figures won't do you much good at school or beyond unless you can put that information to work through clear and competent thinking. Chapter 4 will introduce you to the mind actions that enable you to use information to solve problems, make decisions, and plan strategically.
- *Learning styles.* There is no one "right" way or "wrong" way to learn—each person has a unique learning style with its own strengths and challenges. Chapter 3 will help you identify your learning style and formulate strategies to make it work for you.
- *Goal setting and time management.* Being able to identify priorities and go after your goals through effective time management often means the difference between success and immobility. You'll learn valuable goal setting and time management skills in Chapter 2.

KEY #4: DIVERSITY OF VOICE. The world is becoming increasingly diverse in ethnicity and race, culture, lifestyle, perspective, choices, and more. Because one point of view can't apply to everyone, many voices will speak to you from the following features on these pages:

- *Windows on the World,* a feature that appears in every chapter, involves real-life students asking questions that affect their lives. Experts and other students give advice to help the students meet their challenges.
- *Examples* throughout the text deal with the situations and stresses that various students face—working while in school, parenting, dealing with financial problems, and much more.
- Finally, a *summary word or phrase* from a non-English language at the end of each chapter will invite you to consider how an idea from another culture might apply to your own life.

Become Aware of the Exercises and Features That Will Help You Learn

As you scan each chapter, you will find the following features, each of which is designed to help you master chapter content and apply what you have learned to your own life and future:

- *Thinking It Through.* This exercise encourages you to evaluate your attitudes and knowledge *before* you read each chapter. Reviewing your completed checklist after you finish the chapter will help you pinpoint changes in your ideas and knowledge.
- *Thinking Back/Thinking Ahead.* This question-and-answer feature provides a quick review of what you just read in the first half of the chapter (Thinking Back) and a preview of what's to come in the remainder (Thinking Ahead).
- *Important Points to Remember.* To further solidify what you have read, a summary helps you focus on the critical information in each of the chapter's major sections.

- *End-of-Chapter Exercises: Building Skills for College, Career, and Life Success.* Today's graduates must be effective thinkers, team players, writers, and strategic planners. This exercise set will encourage you to develop the following valuable skills. The exercises include:
  - *Critical Thinking: Applying Learning to Life* encourages you to apply critical thinking to chapter content as the content relates to your personal needs and goals.
  - *Teamwork: Combining Forces* gives you an opportunity to interact and learn in a group setting, building your teamwork and leadership skills in the process.
  - *Writing: Discovery Through Journaling* gives you the chance to express your thoughts and develop your writing ability.
  - *Career Portfolio: Charting Your Course* helps you build a career portfolio by gathering evidence of your unique qualifications, experience, and progress. By the end of the semester, you will have a packet of information that will help you focus your career search to find a fulfilling job.

MOTIVATION

Now that you are aware of what is available to you within these pages, the next step depends on your motivation—your ability to get yourself moving toward your goal. In this case, being motivated means first reading and studying *Keys To Effective Learning* and then taking action to use what you have learned, so that you can create options and opportunity in your life.

You are responsible for your education, your growth, your knowledge, and your future. If you know yourself, choose the best paths available to you, and follow them with determination, you will earn the success that you deserve in school, the workplace, and your personal life. We can offer helpful suggestions, strategies, ideas, and systems, but ultimately it is up to you to use them. So start now. Take whatever fits your unique situations, needs, and wants, and create the life you want to lead. You've made a terrific start by choosing to pursue an education—now you can build the future of your dreams.

Acknowledgments

This book has come about through a heroic group effort. Many thanks to:

- Our student editor, Sammy Popat, and student reviewers Sandi Armitage, Marisa Connell, Jennifer Moe, and Alex Toth.

- Our reviewers: Glenda Belote, Florida International University; John Bennett, Jr., University of Connecticut; Ann Bingham-Newman, California State University-LA; Mary Bixby, University of Missouri-Columbia; Barbara Blandford, Education Enhancement Center at Lawrenceville, NJ; Jerry Bouchie, St. Cloud State University; Mona Casady, SW Missouri State University; Janet Cutshall, Sussex County Community College; Marie Davis-Heim, Mississippi Gulf Coast Community College; Valerie DeAngelis, Miami-Dade Community College; Rita Delude, NH Community Technical College; Judy Elsley, Weber State University in Utah; Kathie Erdman, South Dakota State University; Sue Halter, Delgado Community College in Louisiana; Suzy Hampton, University of Montana; Maureen Hurley, University of Missouri-Kansas City; Karen Iversen, Heald Colleges; Kathryn K. Kelly, St. Cloud State University; Nancy Kosmicke, Mesa State College in Colorado; Frank T. Lyman, Jr., University of Maryland; Jo McEwan, Fayetteville Technical Community College; Barnette Miller Moore, Indian River Community College in Florida; Rebecca Munro, Gonzaga University in Washington; Virginia Phares, DeVry of Atlanta; Brenda Prinzavalli, Beloit College in Wisconsin; Laura Reynolds, Fayetteville Technical Community College; Tina Royal, Fayetteville Technical Community College; Jacqueline Simon, Education Enhancement Center at Lawrenceville, NJ; Carolyn Smith, University of Southern Indiana; Joan Stottlemyer, Carroll College in Montana; Thomas Tyson, SUNY Stony Brook; Mary Walkz-Chojnacki, University of Wisconsin at Milwaukee; Rose Wassman, DeAnza College in California; Michelle G. Wolf, Florida Southern College.

- The instructors at Baltimore City Community College, Liberty Campus, especially college President Dr. Jim Tschechtelin, Co-ordinator Jim Coleman, instructors Stan Brown, Sonia Lynch, Jack Taylor, Peggy Winfield, and the late Rita Lenkin Hawkins. Thanks also to reps Alice Barr and Beth Harris.

- The instructors at DeVry, especially Susan Chin and Carol Ozee.

- Library research material reviewers Marjorie Freilich-Den, Sheri Garrou, Ross T. Labaugh of California State University at Fresno, and Bobbie Stevens of the University of Texas at Arlington.

- Those who worked on the instructors' manual: Todd Benatovich, University of Texas at Arlington; Amy Bierman, student, Old Dominion University; Jennifer Cohen; Jodi Levine, Temple University; Geri MacKenzie,

Southern Methodist University; Gene Mueller, Henderson State University; Tina Pitt, Heald College; Dan Rice, Iowa State University; Michael and Frances Trevisan, Washington State; Karen Valencia, South Texas Community College; Eve Walden, Valencia Community College; Don Williams, Grand Valley State University; William Wilson, St. Cloud State University; and Nona Wood, North Dakota State University.

• Editorial consultant Rich Bucher, professor of sociology at Baltimore City Community College, for his advice and consultation on diversity.

• Dr. Frank T. Lyman for his permission to use and adapt his Thinktrix system.

• Those who contributed stories for Windows on the World: Cherie Andrade, Beverly Andre, Stephen Beck, Edhilvia Campos, Shera Chantel Caviness, Peter Changsak, Rosalia Chavez, Maxine Deverney, Titus Dillard, Jr., Darrin Estepp, Ruth Ham, Jose L. Ivarez, Jr., Hiromi Kodakehara, Angela D. Kvasnica, Raymond Montolvo, Jr., Vernon Nash, Tim Nordberg, Morgan Paar, Richard Pan, Shyama Parikh, the Rev. Eric Gerard Pearman, Jo Anne Roe, Norma Seledon, and Anwar Smith.

• Amy Peltier for her work on the website and technology, Erica Thode for her work on symposium events, and Cecilia Johnson, Kate Lareau, Sue Bierman, Kathleen Cole, Jackie Fitzgerald, Jordan Austin, and Cynthia Nordberg for invaluable assistance.

• Publisher Jeff Johnston, Editor Sande Johnson, President of Education, Career, and Technology Robin Baliszewski, and co-President of Prentice Hall Gary June, for their interest, commitment, and leadership with the Student Success list.

• Our production team, especially Gay Pauley, JoEllen Gohr, Pam Bennett, and typesetters Aerocraft Charter Art Service.

• Our marketing gurus—especially Director of Marketing Kevin Flanagan and Marketing Manager Christina Quadhamer—and the Prentice Hall representatives and the management team led by David Gillespie.

• Our families and friends, for their support and encouragement.

• Special thanks to Judy Block, whose research, work, and editing suggestions on the text as a whole were essential and invaluable.

• Finally, thanks to the students and instructors who have shared their ideas, especially our current adopters, too many to name, whose candid feedback continues to fuel our improvements. Joyce in particular would like to thank the thousands of students who have allowed her, as their professor, the privilege of sharing part of their journey through college. We appreciate that, through reading this book, you give us the opportunity to learn and discover with you—in your classroom, in your home, on the bus, and wherever learning takes place.

About the Authors

Carol Carter is Vice President, Director of Student Services for the College Learning Network. She has also been Director of Faculty Development at Prentice Hall for the last six years. She has written *Majoring in the Rest of Your Life: Career Secrets for College Students* and *Majoring in High School.* She has also coauthored *Keys to Preparing for College, Keys to College Studying, The Career Tool Kit, Keys to Career Success, Keys to Study Skills, Keys to Thinking and Learning,* and *Keys to Success.* She has taught welfare-to-work classes, team taught in the La Familia Scholars Program at the Community College of Denver, and has conducted numerous workshops for students and faculty around the country. She is the host of the Keys to Lifelong Learning Telecourse, a 26-episode telecourse to help students at a distance prepare for college, career, and life success. In addition to working with students of all ages, Carol thrives on foreign travel and culture; she has been fortunate enough to have been a guest in 40 foreign countries. Please visit her website at www.caroljcarter.com.

Joyce Bishop holds a Ph.D. in psychology and has taught for more than 20 years, receiving a number of honors, including Teacher of the Year for 1995 and 2000. For five years she has been voted "favorite teacher" by the student body and Honor Society at Golden West College, Huntington Beach, CA, where she has taught since 1987 and is a tenured professor. She has worked with a federal grant to establish Learning Communities and Workplace Learning in her district and has developed workshops and trained faculty in cooperative learning, active learning, multiple intelligences, workplace relevancy, learning styles, authentic assessment, team building, and the development of learning communities. She is currently teaching online and multimedia classes, and training other faculty to teach online in her district and region of 21 colleges. She also coauthored *Keys to College Studying, Keys to Success, Keys to Thinking and Learning,* and *Keys to Study Skills.* Joyce is the lead academic of the Keys to Lifelong Learning Telecourse, distributed by Dallas Telelearning.

Sarah Lyman Kravits comes from a family of educators and has long cultivated an interest in educational development. She coauthored *Keys to College Studying, The Career Tool Kit, Keys to Success, Keys to Thinking and Learning,* and *Keys to Study Skills* and has served as Program Director for LifeSkills, Inc., a nonprofit organization that aims to further the career and personal development of high school students. In that capacity she

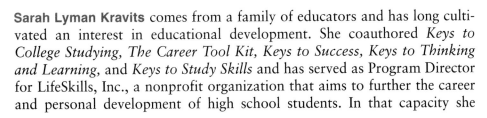

helped to formulate both curricular and organizational elements of the program, working closely with instructors as well as members of the business community. She has also given faculty workshops in critical thinking, based on the Thinktrix critical-thinking system. Sarah holds a B.A. in English and drama from the University of Virginia, where she was a Jefferson Scholar, and an M.F.A. from Catholic University.

Defining Yourself and Your Goals

PART ONE

I

Thinking It Through

Check those statements that apply to you right now:

- I doubt if I will learn anything new that can help me in my work or life after I finish school.

- I think that the most typical college student is an 18-year-old right out of high school.

- Sometimes school feels like a detour that's keeping me from moving ahead in my life.

- When I need help with school or personal issues, I know that there are places I can go, but I'm not sure how to find them.

- One moment I'm determined to suc-ceed, and then I turn around and I've lost all my drive.

- I'm not sure if there's any relationship between the self-esteem I have right now and my future success.

- I don't really see the point of learning to work together with others. What matters most is what I do on my own.

IN THIS CHAPTER,

you will explore answers to the following

questions:

- Why is lifelong learning important?
- Who is pursuing an education today?
- How does education promote success?
- What resources are available at your school?
- How can you strive for success?

Welcome—or welcome back—to your education. Whether you are right out of high school, returning to student life after working for some years, or continuing on a current educational path, you are facing new challenges and changes. Whether you feel excited or worried or both, you have taken an important step. By choosing to pursue the self-improvement, knowledge, and opportunity that an education can provide, you have given yourself a strong vote of confidence.

This first chapter will give you an overview of the need for lifelong learning, the relation between education and success, and the opportunities to begin on the road to success in college. You will explore specific success strategies that will help you maximize

Becoming a Lifelong Learner

your educational experience. You will also learn how building your self-esteem and focusing on teamwork can help you achieve your goals and how life success is linked to being open to change.

OPENING DOORS

WHY IS LIFELONG LEARNING IMPORTANT?

In his book *TechnoTrends—24 Technologies That Will Revolutionize Our Lives,* futurist Daniel Burns describes a tomorrow that is linked to continuing education: "The future belongs to those who are capable of being retrained again and again," he said. "Think of it as periodically upgrading your human assets throughout your career. . . . Humans are infinitely upgradeable, but it does require an investment" in lifelong learning.[1]

Today's trends showcase the enormous change taking place in your world. Here are some that will make lifetime learning a reality for you in the years ahead.

KNOWLEDGE IN NEARLY EVERY FIELD IS DOUBLING EVERY TWO TO THREE YEARS. That means that if you stop learning, for even a few years, your knowledge base will be woefully inadequate to keep up with all the changes in your career.

TECHNOLOGY IS CHANGING HOW YOU LIVE AND WORK. Experts can only guess at the ways in which the Internet will shape communications and improve productivity in the next 20 years. Technological advances, like those you are seeing today, will require continual learning and will be the mechanism through which learning takes place.

OUR ECONOMY IS MOVING FROM A PRODUCT AND SERVICE BASE TO A KNOWLEDGE AND TALENT BASE. Tomorrow's jobs will depend on what you know and your ability to learn more every day.

PERSONAL CHOICES ARE BECOMING MORE COMPLEX. The responsibility to make certain critical decisions is becoming yours alone. For example, years ago most companies provided employee pensions that guaranteed income after retirement. Now you probably have—or one day will have—an Individual Retirement Account (IRA), in which you make decisions for your own retirement based on your knowledge of investments.

These signs point to the need to become *lifelong learners*—individuals who embrace learning as a mechanism for improving their lives and careers. All of the material in this book is geared toward showing you how you can learn throughout your life as well as in school. You and millions of other students have taken an important step on the road to learning by enrolling in college.

WHO IS PURSUING AN EDUCATION TODAY?

It has long been accepted in the United States that a formal education is the right of all people regardless of race, creed, color, age, or gender. As a result, schools have become responsive to many different kinds of students. Although many students still enter college directly after high school, the old standard of finishing a four-year college education at the age of 22 no longer applies to many students. Some students take longer than four years to finish. Some students return to school later in life. The old rules no longer apply.

The student population in the United States has changed in significant ways since the 1980s. According to government statistics, developments include growth in the following populations:[2]

- Students over the age of 25
- Students working full-time while in school
- Female student population
- Students who are also parents
- Minority students
- Students in two-year schools
- Part-time students
- Students taking over four years to get a degree

The varying needs of an increasingly diverse student body have molded a new educational experience. Whether you require financial aid, help with child care, or scheduling flexibility to accommodate an unusual work schedule, you are likely to find a program that's right for you.

No school can force you to learn. You are responsible for seeking out opportunities and weaving school into the fabric of your life. Every student's life has its own individual set of challenges, and you may face one or more, such as single parenting, returning to school as an older student, adjusting to cultural diversity, having a physical or learning disability, or working while attending school. Your school can help you work through these and other challenges if you actively seek out solutions and help from available support systems around you. One way to motivate yourself is to consider how the hard work you put into your education will help you build the life you envision.

HOW DOES EDUCATION PROMOTE SUCCESS?

Education—the process of developing and training the mind—should be far more than the accumulation of credit hours. If you take advantage of all education has to offer, you will develop the skills and talents you need to succeed in your career and in life.

How can education help you succeed?

EDUCATION GIVES YOU TOOLS FOR LIFELONG LEARNING. You learn facts while you are in school, but more importantly, you learn how to think. Your ability to think will be useful always, in everything you do.

EDUCATION IMPROVES YOUR QUALITY OF LIFE. Income and employment get a boost from education. The *Digest of Education Statistics* reports that income levels rise as educational levels rise. Figure 1.1 shows average income levels for different levels of educational attainment. Figure 1.2, also from a report in the *Digest*, shows how unemployment rates decrease as educational levels rise.

FIGURE

1.1

Education and income.

Median annual income of persons with income 25 years old and over, by highest-degree attained and gender.*

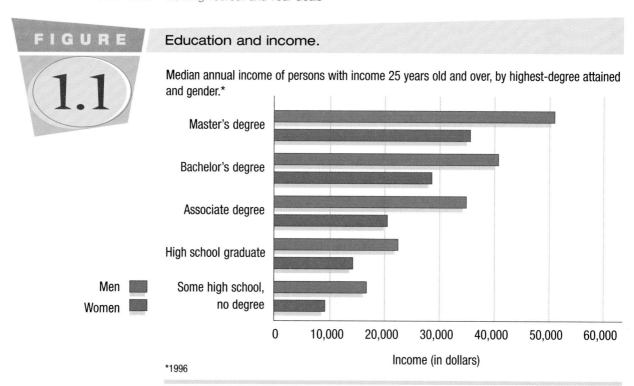

*1996

Source: U.S. Department of Commerce, Bureau of the Census, *Current Population Reports,* Series P-60, Monthly Income of Households, Families, and Persons in the United States: 1996.

EDUCATION EXPANDS YOUR SELF-CONCEPT. As you rise to the challenges of education, you will discover that your capacity for knowledge and personal growth is greater than you imagined. As your abilities grow, so do your accomplishments in class, on the job, and in your community.

EDUCATION ENLARGES YOUR POSSIBILITIES. When you take different courses, you learn about different careers and life goals. For example, while taking a writing class, you may learn about journalism careers, which may lead you to take a class in journalistic writing and reporting. Later, you may decide to work on a newspaper and to make journalism your career. In this case, an awareness of the path available, combined with an ability to follow it, could change the course of your life.

EDUCATION IMPROVES YOUR EMPLOYABILITY AND EARNING POTENTIAL. The skills you learn in college prepare you for the workplace. A college degree also tells prospective employers that you are motivated, ready, and able to meet your responsibilities.

EDUCATION BROADENS YOUR WORLDVIEW. As it introduces you to new ideas, skills, and attitudes, education increases your appreciation of areas with the potential to enrich the quality of your life. Among these areas are music, art, literature, science, politics, sociology, and economics.

EDUCATION AFFECTS BOTH COMMUNITY INVOLVEMENT AND PERSONAL HEALTH. Education prepares you for your role as a citizen by helping you understand the political, economic, and social conditions in your community and in the

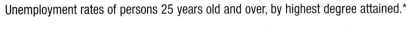

Education and employment.

FIGURE

1.2

Unemployment rates of persons 25 years old and over, by highest degree attained.*

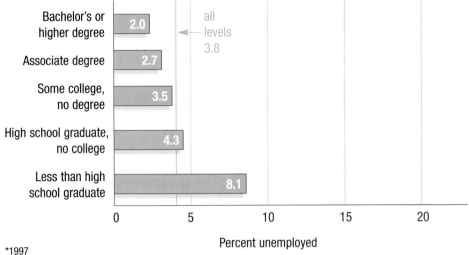

*1997

Percent unemployed

Source: U.S. Department of Labor, Bureau of Labor Statistics, Office of Employment and Unemployment Statistics, *Current Population Survey,* 1997.

world. Education also increases your ability to make wise health and financial decisions. The more education you have, the more likely you are to choose quality medical care, practice wellness, begin an early savings program, and avoid unnecessary debt.

Education is more than the process of going to school to earn a degree or certificate. Any program, no matter the length or the focus, is an opportunity to improve your mind and skills and to set and strive for goals. Education is also what you make of it. A dedicated, goal-oriented learner will benefit more than a student who doesn't try. If you make the most of your mind, your time, and your educational opportunities, you will realize your potential. Using available resources is part of that process.

WHAT RESOURCES ARE AVAILABLE AT YOUR SCHOOL?

Resources help you make the most of your education. As a student, you are investing money and time. Whether you complete your studies over the course of six months or 60 years, resources can help you get where you want to go. It is up to you to track down the resources that you need—as much as your school wants to help you, people may not always reach out to you directly. Be vocal in requesting services and diligent in finding resources.

Table 1.1 offers a general summary of resources, most or all of which can be found at your school. Helpful resources include people, student services, organizations, literature (course catalogs and student handbooks), and technology.

> **RESOURCES**
>
> People, organizations, or services that supply help and support for different aspects of college life.

TABLE 1.1   How resources can help you.

RESOURCE	ACADEMIC ASSISTANCE	FINANCIAL ASSISTANCE	JOB/CAREER ASSISTANCE	PERSONAL ASSISTANCE
Instructors	Choosing classes, clarifying course material, helping with assignments, dealing with study issues		Can tell you about their fields, may be a source of networking contacts	During office hours, are available to talk to you
Administrators	Academic problems, educational focus, problems with school services		Can be a source of valuable contacts	Can help you sort through personal problems with instructors or other school employees
Academic Advisors	Choosing, changing, or dropping courses; getting over academic hurdles; selecting/changing a major		Can advise you on what job opportunities may go along with your major or academic focus	
Personal Counselors	Can help when personal problems get in the way of academic success	Services may be free or offered on a "sliding scale," depending on what you can afford		Help with all kinds of personal problems
Financial Aid Office		Information and counseling on loans, grants, scholarships, financial planning, work-study programs	Information on job opportunities within your school environment (work-study jobs and others)	
Academic Centers	Help with what the center specializes in (reading, writing, math)		Perhaps an opportunity to work at the center	
Organizations and Clubs	If an academic club, can broaden your knowledge or experience in an area of study; can help you balance school with other enriching activities		Can help you develop skills, build knowledge, and make new contacts that may serve you in your working life	Depending on the club focus, can be an outlet for stress, a source of personal inspiration, a source of important friendships, an opportunity to help others
Wellness/ Fitness Center(s)		Usually free or low cost to enrolled students		Provides opportunity to build fitness and reduce stress; may have weight room, track, aerobic or dance classes, martial arts, team sports, exercise machines, etc.

How resources can help you, continued.

RESOURCE	ACADEMIC ASSISTANCE	FINANCIAL ASSISTANCE	JOB/CAREER ASSISTANCE	PERSONAL ASSISTANCE
Bulletin Boards	List academic events, class information, changes and additions to schedules, office hours, academic club meetings	List financial aid seminars, job opportunities, scholarship opportunities	List career forums, job sign-ups, and employment opportunities; offer a place for you to post a message if you are marketing a service	List support group meetings
Housing and Transportation Office		Can help find the most financially beneficial travel or housing plan		Can help commuters with parking, bus or train service, and permits; can help with finding on- or off-campus housing
Career Planning and Placement Office		Can help add to your income through job opportunities	Job listings, help with résumés and interviews, possible interview appointments, factual information about the workplace (job trends, salaries, etc.)	
Tutors	One-on-one help with academic subjects; assistance with specific assignments		If you decide to become a tutor, a chance to find out if teaching and working with people is for you	
Student Health Office		May provide low-cost or no-cost health care to enrolled students; may offer reduced-cost prescription plan		Wellness care (regular examinations), illness care, hospital and specialist referrals, and prescriptions
Adult Education Center	Academic help tailored to the returning adult student	May have specific financial aid advice	May have job listings or other help with coordinating work and classes	May offer child-care assistance and opportunities to get to know other returning adult students
Support Groups and Hotlines	If school-related, they offer a chance to hear how others have both stumbled and succeeded in school— and a chance to share your story			Personal help with whatever the hotline or support group specializes in; a chance to talk to someone whose job is to listen
School Publications	Academic news and course changes	News about financial aid opportunities or work-study programs	Job listings, information about the workplace and the job market	Articles and announcements about topics that may help you

People

Your school has an array of people who can help you make the most of your educational experience: instructors, administrative personnel, advisors and counselors, and teaching assistants. Their assistance is provided as part of your educational package. Take the opportunity to get to know them, and to let them get to know you. Together you can explore ways in which they can help you achieve your goals.

Instructors

Instructors are more than just sources of information during scheduled class time. They can clarify course material or homework, give advice on course selection in their departments, or pass on educational and career information. Most instructors keep office hours and will tell you the location and times. You are responsible for seeking out your instructor during office hours. If your schedule makes this impossible, let your instructor know, and perhaps you can schedule another time to meet. If your school has an electronic mail (e-mail) system, you may be able to communicate with your instructor via computer.

Some courses have teaching assistants as well as instructors. *Teaching assistants* may help with the course by teaching the smaller discussion or lab sections that accompany a large group lecture. They are extremely knowledgeable (often, they are studying to be instructors themselves) and are often more likely to be available than your instructor.

Administrators

The *administrators* of your school oversee your education and are responsible for delivering to you—the student consumer—a first-rate product. That product is the sum total of your education, comprising facilities, instructors, materials, and courses. Although students don't often have regular interaction with administrators, it is the business of the administrative personnel to know how the school is serving you. If you have an issue that you haven't been able to resolve on your own, such as a conflict with an instructor or an inability to get into a required class, schedule a meeting with your dean or department chair.

Advisors and Counselors

Advisors and counselors can help with both the educational and personal sides of being a student. They provide information, advice, a listening ear, referrals, and other sources of help. Generally, students are assigned academic *advisors* with whom they meet at least once a semester. Your academic advisor will help you with class selection, scheduling, and selecting a **major** when the time comes. Visit your academic advisor more than once a semester if you have questions or want to make changes.

Counselors, although not usually assigned, are available through student services or student health. Don't hesitate to seek a counselor's help if you have something on your mind. Your personal life influences the quality of your work in school. If you put some effort into working through personal

MAJOR

An academic subject chosen as a field of specialization, requiring a specific course of study problems, you will be more able to do your work well and hand it in on time. Occasionally, an illness or family difficulty may interfere enough with your schoolwork to require special provisions for the completion of your classes. Most colleges are very willing to assist you during challenging times.

Student Services

Basic *services* offered by almost every school include advising and counseling, student health/wellness, career planning and placement, tutoring, and fitness/physical education. Depending on your school, you may also find other services: housing and transportation, adult education services (for adults returning to school), services for students with physical or learning challenges, academic centers (writing center, math center, etc., for help with these specific subjects), various support groups, and school publications that help keep you informed.

Often a school will have special services for specific populations. For example, at a school where most of the students commute, there may be a transportation office that helps students locate bus schedules and routes, find parking and sign up for permits, or track down car pools.

Organizations

No matter what your needs or interests are, your school probably has an *organization* that suits you. Some organizations are sponsored by the school (academic clubs), some are independent but have a branch at the school (government ROTC programs), and some are student-run organizations (Latino Student Association). Some organizations focus on courses of study (Nursing Club), some are primarily social (fraternities and sororities), some are artistic (Chamber Orchestra), and some are geared toward a hobby or activity (Runner's Club). Some you join to help others (Big Brothers or Big Sisters), and some offer help to you (Overeaters Anonymous).

> *A journey of a thousand miles begins with a single step.*
>
> LAOTZU

When you consider adding a new activity to your life, weigh its positive effects against the negative ones. Positive effects could be new friends, enjoyable activities, help, a break from schoolwork, stress relief, improved academic performance, increased teamwork and leadership skills, aid to others, and experience that can broaden your horizons. On the negative side, there may be a heavy time commitment, dues, inconvenient locations or meeting times, or too much responsibility. Explore any club carefully to see if it makes sense for you.

To find out about organizations, consult your student handbook, ask friends and instructors, or check the activities office or center if your school has one. Some schools, on registration days, have an area where organizations set up tables and offer information to interested students. Some organizations seek you out, based on your achievements. When you explore any organization, ask what is expected in terms of time, responsibility, and any necessary financial commitment. Talk to students who are currently involved. Finally, if you try an organization and it becomes more than you can handle, bow out gracefully. In the best of all possible worlds, your involvement in organizations will enrich your life, expand your network of acquaintances, boost your time-management skills, and help you achieve goals.

Literature

Two publications can help you find your way through course offerings, department and resource offices, and the campus layout—the college catalog and the student handbook. Most schools provide these materials as a standard part of their enrollment information.

The *college catalog* lists every department and course available at the school. Each course name will generally have two parts, for example, EN101 or CHEM205. The first part is one or more letters indicating the department and subject matter, and the second part is a number indicating the course level (lower numbers for introductory courses and higher numbers for more advanced ones). The catalog groups courses according to subject matter and lists them from the lowest-level courses to the most advanced, indicating the number of credits earned for each class. See Figure 1.3 for a segment of an actual college catalog from Baltimore City Community College.[3] A course book released prior to each semester will indicate details such as the instructor, the days the course meets, the time of day, the location (building and room), and the maximum number of students who can take the course.

Your college catalog may also give general school policies such as the registration process and withdrawal procedures. It may list the departments

FIGURE 1.3   College catalog segment.

Course Descriptions

BIO 112: Anatomy and Physiology II (4 credits)

45 lecture hours; 45 lab hours
Fall, Spring - day, eve

Prerequisites: MAT 81; ENG 80 and RDG 82 or appropriate ACCUPLACER scores

Lab fee

This course provides a continuation of BIO 111 designed to provide up-to-date principles of the cardiovascular, lymphatic, respiratory, digestive, excretory (urinary), and reproductive (male and female) systems. Embryology, genetics and immunology are included. A consideration of the effects of stress on normal anatomy and physiology is interwoven throughout the course.

BIO 115: Principles of Ecology (3 credits)

45 lecture hours

The science of ecology is introduced with the major components of an ecosystem examined. Energy, biogeochemical cycles, and ecosystem structures and relationships are studied in both lecture and field components. Current environmental issues are also considered.

BIO 199: Individual Study in Biology (3 credits)

BIO 212: Microbiology (4 credits)

45 lecture hours; 45 lab hours
Fall, Spring - day, eve

Prerequisite: 6-8 credits in biology and/or chemistry

Lab fee

This course includes topics in morphology, physiology, genetics, control, culture and identification of microorganisms, along with a separate unit focusing on immunology. Emphasis is placed on the role of microorganisms in health and diseases.

BIOTECHNOLOGY—BTC

BTC 101: Special Topics in Biotechnology I (2 credits)

30 lecture hours
Fall, Spring - day

Students are introduced to the field of biotechnology with a preview of basic research and development techniques, laboratory safety, and career awareness. Field trips, computer simulations, lectures, and guest speakers are used in this course.

BTC 102: Special Top

Windows on the World

How can I connect to my university community?

Ruth Ham, *Dallas Theological Seminary, Dallas, Texas, Education Major*

Before I came to Texas, I studied English in my native home of Bangkok, Thailand. Now that I am here I find that the classes I took there, such as English poetry, were interesting but not very practical. The language barrier has made it difficult for me to get to know people.

I am ashamed of my English. If someone asks me a direct question, I will answer the best I can, but I don't seek out conversations with English speaking students. I have found it very hard to make friends. Instead of seeing people as people, I am always aware that they are different. If a student sits next to me in class and doesn't greet me, I feel hurt. I know I could also say hello, but it's very hard for me to take

that first step. Sharing my ideas with other people is very hard for me, so I usually stay quiet during class discussions.

One thing that has helped is joining the international students club. I've met other students who are also struggling with feeling like they belong. We practice our English together. I've also found that my English has improved by writing my thoughts out in English in a journal. It would be nice to find an American friend who has the time to help me with my English. One thing I noticed here though is that people seem to always be in a hurry. I want to be more involved at school than just going to class. What else can I do to feel more a part of my school?

Hiromi Kodakehara, *University of Nebraska, Omaha, Nebraska*

I had to take English for six years in school in Japan, but I couldn't speak it well at all. When I got to the United States, I was ashamed of my English.

In my ESL (English as a Second Language) program in Omaha, not many Americans paid attention to me or to any international students. The only time I spoke English was when I was in class or when I was with my teachers.

One day, I realized: "I am Japanese, and of course I cannot speak English well. Why am I so worried about it? I can talk and act like I am an international student." This helped me to think positively and start reaching out to people. Fortunately, my school has a program called Conversation

Partners, established by American volunteers to help international students improve their English. My school also had a homestay program, which registered American families who would take international students in for two weeks. These two programs helped me improve my English and make some good friends. My friends told me that they respected my learning a foreign language. They would say, "Your English is much better than my Japanese."

I am sure your school has international student advisors who can help you find an organization that helps international students. There probably are also non-profit organizations in your city that want to help foreign students get used to American culture and people. Through their events and activities, you can make American friends, practice your English, and eventually feel more comfortable talking to Americans. There are, of course, some people who ignore international students, but there are also many friendly Americans who want to be friends but don't know how. Remember that you don't have to speak perfect English. You can be proud of living in the United States, taking regular classes with American students, and keeping up with them.

to show the range of subjects you may study. It may outline instructional programs, detailing core requirements as well as requirements for various majors, degrees, and certificates. When you have a question, consult the catalog before you look elsewhere.

Your *student handbook* looks beyond specific courses to the big picture, helping you to navigate student life. In it you will find some or all of the following, and maybe more: information on available housing (for on-campus residents) and on parking and driving (for commuters); overviews of the support offices for students, such as academic advising, counseling, career planning and placement, student health, financial aid, and individual centers for academic subject areas; descriptions of special-interest clubs; and details about library and computer services. It may also list hours, locations, phone numbers, and addresses for offices, clubs, and organizations.

Your student handbook will also describe important policies such as how to add or drop a class, what the grading system means, campus rules, drug and alcohol policies, what kinds of records your school keeps, safety tips, and more. Keep your student handbook where you can find it easily, in your study area at home or someplace safe at school. It can save you a lot of trouble when you need to find information about a resource or service.

Technology

Computers regulate your class schedule and keep a record of your tuition payments. Computer centers on campus provide an opportunity for students to type papers, work on assignments, take tests, log lab results, access the college library, and send **e-mail** to instructors and fellow students. You may even have your own personal computer on which you do schoolwork and manage your personal schedule or finances. Here are some tips for exploring how computers can help you in college.

E-MAIL

Mail sent from computer to computer (e-mail stands for electronic mail) through systems that provide the electronic connection.

KNOW WHAT YOU WANT FROM COMPUTERS. Some people want to know how computers operate and look forward to a career in programming or systems. Others only want to use computers as a tool to achieve a goal—for example, to write articles or to design graphics. Knowing what you want will help you discover how much computer knowledge you need.

GET TRAINING. Once you know what you need from computers, give yourself a chance to learn. Look for software training programs, school-sponsored short courses, or computer learning centers that will help you develop your skills. A typing course can be extremely useful.

INVESTIGATE YOUR SCHOOL'S COMPUTER NETWORK. Your school's computers are on a network that links students, instructors, administrators, and others to various databases. The network may allow you direct access to the library card catalog and online publications, to your grades and transcript, and other databases. Even if you have your own computer, you may at some point need to use the school's system. Find out about the availability of school-owned computers, software, and printers. Be clear about computer center hours and locations, and plan strategically to avoid busy times when it's tough to get a computer terminal—you don't want to be without access when you have a major assignment due the next day.

KNOW WHAT PROGRAMS YOU NEED AND WHAT THEY DO. The basics in computer use fall into four general categories: word processing (for papers and other written assignments), **databases** and **spreadsheets** (for organizing and storing large volumes of information and data), the Internet (a worldwide computer network that connects businesses, schools, governments, and people), and e-mail (Internet mail system over which you can send letters, memos, or assignments).

SAVE, BACK UP, AND BACK UP SOME MORE. First, save your work onto the hard drive or disk every few minutes; you never know when a power outage might mean that you lose everything you did in the last hour. Second, always back up (copy) your work in a location other than the computer hard drive, such as a standard diskette or a Zip disk. You can never be too safe.

Making the most of your resources is one way to strive for success. The next section offers other strategies for you to consider.

Using a separate sheet of paper, complete the following.

> **DATABASES**
>
> A collection of data, organized by computer so that one can quickly organize, store, and retrieve it.

> **SPREADSHEETS**
>
> A ledger layout, usually found in an accounting program, that allows the user to list and calculate numerical data.

Thinking Back

1. Explain two reasons why lifelong learning will almost certainly be part of your future.

2. List and describe four characteristics of today's college students.

3. Name two ways your education can help you succeed in life.

4. Briefly discuss how you might use three different resources at your school: a service, a person, and an organization.

5. Describe two ways in which you are likely to use computer technology during college.

Thinking Ahead

1. Name one idea or goal that motivates you to succeed.

2. List three commitments that you have made in the past year and evaluate your success in achieving them.

3. List three ways you intend to "act with integrity" during your college years. How do you define integrity?

4. How do you define "self-esteem" and how would you rate your personal self-esteem on a scale from 1 to 10?

5. Why do you think teamwork is important to your future success? How do you imagine that you will use your teamwork skills in college and your career?

HOW CAN YOU STRIVE FOR SUCCESS?

Success is a process in motion, not a fixed mark. A successful person is one who is consistently learning, growing, and working toward goals. College provides an opportunity for you to define your goals and work hard to achieve them. Tom Bradley, son of a Texas sharecropper, became the first African-American mayor of Los Angeles in 1973 and served five successive terms. More than 30 years after Ruth Bader Ginsberg was rejected as a Supreme Court clerk because Justice Felix Frankfurter didn't hire women, she became a Supreme Court justice herself. If you put your energies to the task, you can create any future you envision for yourself.

Striving for success takes effort. It requires motivation, commitment, responsibility, and acceptance of academic integrity standards. It also requires working on your self-esteem and embracing teamwork in a diverse world. Finally, achieving success depends on your ability to accept the constancy of change and to develop strategies to make change work for you.

Get Motivated

MOTIVATION

The process of being moved to action by a want or need (referred to as a motive or motivator).

Motivation is what drives you toward your goals. Some kinds of motivation are biological (food, shelter); some are psychological and social (achievement, connection with others, autonomy); some are external (money, power); some are internal (creativity, self-improvement, personal fulfillment).

Each person has her own unique set of motivators. Furthermore, what motivates any given person can change from situation to situation or even from day to day. For example, pressing financial needs might motivate you to choose a major that is linked to a lucrative career area. Later, as you progress in your major and find that you really like one particular area, a need for personal fulfillment might motivate you to specialize in that area. When a close family member experiences a health emergency, the need to stay connected with that person might even motivate you to put your academics on hold while you attend to your family situation.

Motivation is a key ingredient in fulfilling goals. It requires energy to build and maintain, and it can falter from time to time. How can you build motivation or renew lost motivation?

- *Spend time reflecting on why your goal is meaningful to you.* Remind yourself about what you wanted and why that goal is still important.

- *Make a decision to take one step toward your goal.* Sometimes feeling overwhelmed by the enormity of a goal immobilizes you. Focus on the specific actions you can take today.

- *Examine and deal with your obstacles.* What's getting in your way? Decide to examine and remove your obstacles. For example, if health issues are distracting you from your studies, schedule an appointment with your doctor.

- *Begin or begin again.* Open that book or start that assignment. If you can just get yourself started, you'll feel better. A law of physics, Newton's first law of motion, says that things in motion tend to stay in motion and things at rest tend to stay at rest. *Be a thing in motion.*

For example, to pass an early-morning writing class that you've already failed once, you decide to implement particular strategies. First, you promise yourself that you will go to every class and turn in your work on time. Second, you make a commitment to write daily in a journal. Finally, you promise yourself a reward if you get at least a B minus in the course. Your motivation centers around self-improvement and financial security: Passing this course is necessary to continue your education, and the writing skills you learn will help you get a good job when you graduate.

Make a Commitment

How do you focus the energy of motivation? Make a **commitment**. Commitment means that you do what you say you will do. When you honor a commitment, you prove to yourself and others that your intentions can be trusted. A committed person follows through on a promise.

> **COMMITMENT**
>
> (1) a pledge or promise to do something, or (2) dedication to a long-term course of action.

Commitment requires that you set goals that are *specific* and *realistic*. For example, a vague and far-reaching decision to ace every course in your major might intimidate you into staying motionless on the couch. A decision to get a B or above in a specific course, or to pass every course in a particular semester, might be more doable. Break any goal into manageable pieces, naming the steps you will use to achieve it. Chapter 2 will provide more information about successful goal setting.

How do you go about making and keeping a commitment?

- *State your commitment concretely.* It's hard to commit to something such as "I'm going to pass this course" because you haven't set yourself clear tasks. Be specific: "I'm going to turn in the weekly essay assignments on time."

- *Get started and note your progress.* The long road of a commitment can tire you out. Looking for improvements on the way, no matter how small, can keep you going.

- *Renew your commitment regularly.* You're not a failure if you lose steam after a few weeks or even a few days; it's normal. Recharge by reflecting on the positive effects of your commitment and what you have already achieved.

- *Keep track of your commitment.* Find ways to remind yourself of your commitments. Keep a list in your date book or computer. Talk about your commitments with friends and family.

For example, you might make this commitment: "I will write in my journal every night before going to sleep." You make journal entries for two weeks and then evaluate how this daily practice is affecting your writing. You boost your commitment by periodically sharing your writing with a partner or friend.

The very spring and root of honesty and virtue lie in good education. **PLUTARCH**

Making and keeping your commitments helps you keep a steady focus on your most important goals. It gives you a sense of accomplishment as you experience gradual growth and progress.

Be Responsible

Being responsible is all about living up to your obligations, both those that are imposed on you and those that you impose on yourself. Through action, you prove that you are responsible, or "response-able," able to respond. When something needs to be done, a responsible person does the work—as efficiently as possible and to the best of his ability.

RESPONSIBILITY

The quality of being reliable, trustworthy, and accountable for one's actions.

Responsibility has definite benefits. For one, you make a crucial impression on others. You earn the trust of your instructors, supervisors, relatives, and friends. People who trust you may give you increasing responsibility and opportunities for growth because you have shown you are capable of making the best of both. Trust builds relationships, which, in turn, feed progress and success. Even more important is the self-respect that emerges when you prove that you can live up to your promises.

When you complete class assignments on time or correct errors, you demonstrate responsibility. You don't have to take on the world to show how responsible you can be. Responsibility shows in basic everyday actions: attending class, turning in work on time, trying your best, and being true to your word.

Act with Integrity

Acting with **integrity** is part of your responsibility as a student. As a person with integrity, you make the decision to avoid unethical behaviors that cheat yourself and others. You apply the highest standards of honor to every aspect of your academic life—your classes, assignments, tests, papers, labs, projects, and relationships with students and faculty.

INTEGRITY

Adherence to a code of moral values; incorruptibility, honesty.

Most schools publish written standards of academic integrity (check your student handbook). Although the specific definition may vary from school to school, the general principle prohibits the following actions:

- Plagiarism (copying the words, ideas, or structure of another person's work and claiming it as your own)
- Cheating on tests by referring to materials or using devices that are not authorized by the instructor (e.g., looking at a test that a friend has taken in a section of a course that meets a few hours before your own)
- Submitting work that you have already submitted elsewhere, in another class or in a previous school
- Getting help with a project on which you are supposed to be working alone
- Altering your academic record without authorization
- Misusing library materials (taking materials without checking them out, keeping materials late, removing materials that are not permitted to be removed, or damaging materials)
- Ignoring copyright restrictions on computer software
- Providing unethical aid to another student by allowing your work to be copied, helping a student cheat on a test, aiding a student on an independent project, or selling your work or tests

Explore your school's specific requirements so you know what is expected of you. As a student enrolled in your school, you have agreed to abide by that policy. You have also agreed to suffer the consequences if you are discovered violating any of your school's policies.

Maintaining an image of academic integrity will certainly help you pass your classes and graduate. But the effects of living with integrity can be life altering and wide ranging, involving far more than a few good grades on tests and papers. Having academic integrity can help you:

- Develop a habit of playing fair
- Retain knowledge for later use instead of just long enough for the test
- Interact with others respectfully and with trust
- Build your positive feelings about yourself by acting honorably

The process of building and maintaining self-esteem isn't easy. It involves many ups and downs, steps forward and slides back, successes and disappointments. Remember that you are in control of your self-esteem because you alone are ultimately responsible for your thoughts and actions. If you can both believe in yourself and take action that anchors and inspires that belief, you will give yourself the best possible base on which to build a successful life.

Build Self-Esteem

Believing in your value as a person and your talents and strengths can help you achieve your goals. Belief, though, is only half the game. The other half is action that helps you feel that you have *earned* your self-esteem. Rick Pitino discusses the necessity of earning self-esteem in his book, *Success Is a Choice:* "Self-esteem is directly linked to deserving success. If you have established a great work ethic and have begun the discipline that is inherent with that, you will automatically begin to feel better about yourself."[4] Building self-esteem, therefore, involves both thinking positively and taking action.

Think Positively

Attitudes influence your choices and affect how you perceive and relate to others. A positive attitude can open your mind to learning experiences and inspire you to take action. One of the ways in which you can create a positive attitude is through **positive self-talk.** When you hear negative thoughts in your mind ("I'm not very smart"), replace them with positive ones ("It won't be easy, but I'm smart enough to figure it out"). Try to talk to yourself as if you were talking to someone you care a lot about. The following hints will help you put positive self-talk into action.

STOP NEGATIVE TALK IN ITS TRACKS AND CHANGE IT TO POSITIVE TALK. If you catch yourself thinking, "I can never write a decent paper," stop and say to yourself, "I can do better than that and next time I will." Then think about some specific steps you can take to improve your writing.

> **POSITIVE SELF-TALK**
>
> Supportive and positive-thinking thoughts and ideas that a person communicates to himself or herself.

REPLACE WORDS OF OBLIGATION—WHICH ROB YOU OF POWER—WITH WORDS OF PERSONAL INTENT. Words of intent give you power and control because they imply a personal decision to act. *I should* becomes *I choose to, I'll try* becomes *I will.*

NOTE YOUR SUCCESSES. Even when you don't think you are at your best, congratulate yourself on any positive steps. Whether you do well on a paper, get to class on time all week, or have fewer mistakes on this week's paper than last week's, each success helps you believe in yourself.

It can be very difficult to think positively. If you have a deep-rooted feeling of unworthiness, you may want to see a counselor. Many people have benefited from skilled professional advice.

Take Action

Although thinking positively sets the tone for success, it cannot get you there by itself. You need to give those positive thoughts life and support by taking action. Without action, positive thoughts can become empty statements or even lies.

Consider, for example, a student in a freshman composition class. This student thinks every possible positive thought: "I am a great student. I can get a B in this class. I will succeed in school." And so on. Then, during the semester, this student misses about one-third of the class meetings and turns in some of her papers late. At the end of the course, when she barely passes the class, she wonders how things went so wrong when she had such a positive attitude.

This student did not succeed because she did not earn her belief in herself through action and effort. You cannot maintain belief unless you give yourself something to believe *in.* By the end of a semester like this, positive thoughts look like lies. "If I am such a great student, why did I barely make it through this course?" Eventually, with nothing to support them, the positive thoughts disappear, and with neither positive thoughts nor action, a student will have a hard time achieving any level of success.

The greatest discovery of any generation is that human beings can alter their lives by altering their attitudes of mind.

ALBERT SCHWEITZER

Positive thoughts are like seeds. Don't just scatter them on the soil: take action—plant them, water them, and feed them, and they will grow and be fruitful. Here are some ways to get yourself moving:

- *Make action plans.* Be specific about how you plan to take action for any given situation. Figure out exactly what you will do, so that "I am a great student" is backed up by specific actions to ensure success. Then, once you decide on your action, use your energy to just do it.

- *Build your own code of discipline.* To provide a framework for the specific actions you plan to take, develop a general plan to follow, based on what actions are important to your success. Construct each day's individual goals and actions so that they help you achieve your larger objectives.

- *Acknowledge every step.* Even the smallest action is worth your attention because every action reinforces a positive thought and builds self-esteem.

The process of building and maintaining self-esteem isn't easy for anyone. Only by having a true sense of self-esteem, though, can you achieve what you dream. Make the choice to both believe in yourself and take action that anchors and inspires that belief.

Self-esteem is a large part of what enables you to relate to others comfortably and successfully. With a strong sense of self-worth, you will be able to develop productive relationships with the diverse people who are part of your world.

Build Teamwork Skills in a Diverse World

Think of the path of your accomplishments, and you will find that rarely do you achieve anything using your own efforts alone. Your success at school and at work depends on your ability to cooperate in a team setting—to communicate, share tasks, and develop a common vision—with people from diverse backgrounds.

- You deal with the challenges of day-to-day life in a *family/community* team with the help of parents, siblings, relatives, or friends.
- You achieve work goals in a *work* team with supervisors, coworkers, or consultants.
- You learn, complete projects, and pass courses as part of an *educational* team with instructors, fellow students, tutors, administrators, or advisors.

Teams gain strength from the diversity of their members. In fact, diversity is an asset in a team. Consider a study group for a particular course. Each person has a different style of note taking and a different perspective, but by combining their abilities the students can build a knowledge base that they would not have been able to achieve alone. The more diverse the team members, the greater the chance that new ideas and solutions will surface, increasing the chances of solving problems.

Throughout this book you will find references to a diverse mixture of people in different life circumstances. Note especially the "Windows on the World" feature in every chapter, which highlights people from different backgrounds who are making the effort to learn about themselves and their world. Chapter 11 will go into more detail about communicating across lines of difference and addressing the problems that arise when people have trouble accepting each other's differences. Diversity is not a subject that you study at one point in the semester and then leave behind. It is a theme that touches every part of your life.

Opening your mind to differences can benefit both you and those around you. You may consider goals like these as you define your role in the diverse world:

- *To accept diversity as a fact of life and an asset.* The world will only continue to diversify. The more you adapt to and appreciate this diversity, the more enriched your life will be.

- *To explore differences.* Open your mind and learn about what is unfamiliar around you.

- *To celebrate your own uniqueness, as well as that of others.* It's natural to think that your own way is the best way. Expand your horizons by considering your way as one good way and seeking out different and useful ways to which other people can introduce you.

- *To consider new perspectives.* The wide variety of ideas and perspectives brought by people from different groups and situations offers the possibility of finding solutions to tough and complex problems.

- *To continue to learn.* Education is one of the best ways to become more open-minded about differences. Classes such as sociology and ethics can increase your awareness of the lives and values of people in other cultures. Even though your personal beliefs may be challenged in the process, facing how you feel about others is a positive step toward harmony between people.

The focus on diversity is one aspect of the enormous changes going on today. Constant change is one of the few givens of modern life.

Embrace Change

As author Isaac Asimov said, "It is change, continuing change, inevitable change, that is the dominant factor in society today. No sensible decision can be made any longer without taking into account not only the world as it is, but the world as it will be."[5] Change will often throw you for a loop with little or no warning. You cannot stop change from happening, but you can embrace change through awareness and by making active, conscious choices about how to handle the changes that come your way. Be an *agent of change* so that you can benefit and grow from it rather than being trampled by it.

Being an agent of change means being aware of change, adjusting to what it brings, and sometimes even causing change yourself. Every choice now will affect what happens down the road—and, conversely, you can trace what happens to you back to actions taken (or not taken) in the past. Start now to be in charge of your choices.

For example, say that your school is planning to cancel a number of sections of a course that you need, which would result in your not being able to take the course on time for graduation. You could be a victim of change—you could take the class another time, figure you'll have to graduate later, and suffer other consequences of the change such as putting off full-time employment. On the other hand, you can be an agent of change by speaking to your academic advisor about using another class to fulfill this requirement, gathering students who need the class and petitioning to keep those sections open, or finding an internship that will substitute for the class.

As a student, aim for continual change and improvement in your education so that you will move forward toward your goals. Take to heart this quote from a student in Mississippi: "Without an education, we the people will be in serious trouble. Because now everything is moving forward fast and without an education you will be moving nowhere." Remember, as a lifelong learner, you're in charge of your present and your future. Make the most of every moment.

In Chinese writing, this character has two meanings: One is "chaos," the other is "opportunity." The character communicates the belief that every challenging, chaotic, and demanding situation in life also presents an opportunity. By responding to challenges in a positive and active way, you can discover the opportunity that lies within the chaos.

Let this concept reassure you as you begin college. You may feel that you are going through a time of chaos and change. Remember that no matter how difficult the obstacles, you have the ability to persevere. You can create opportunities for yourself to learn, grow, and improve.

IMPORTANT POINTS *to remember*

1. Why is lifelong learning important?

Lifelong learning is more important today than ever before because of the pace of change that affects every part of your life. An explosion of knowledge and new technologies characterizes the twenty-first century. By embracing lifelong learning, you will develop the skills you need to continually better yourself in your career and your life.

2. Who is pursuing an education today?

Today's students don't fit any universal mold. They are of all different ages, abilities, cultural backgrounds, and life stages. Many are in school part-time while working or raising a family. Many attend two-year or night programs, and many are taking longer to complete a degree. These different needs have resulted in a more diversified educational system. Your responsibility is to make your needs clear to your school and to ask for help when you need it.

3. How does education promote success?

Education gives you new knowledge, as well as the tools you need to absorb that knowledge, retain it, and build on it. It helps you grow and increase your potential, often showing you that you are capable of more than you imagined. It makes you more likely to get involved in community activism, practice personal health habits, and improve your quality of life through better jobs and higher wages. It gives you power to make choices and expands your horizons by preparing you to respond to art, science, politics, and other issues that affect human lives.

4. What resources are available at your school?

Offering resources is part of your school's goal to provide a comprehensive education for each student. People such as instructors, administrators, and advisors can advise and guide you. Services may include advising, health, tutoring, financial aid, and career planning. Various organizations offer opportunities to get involved outside of class. The college catalog describes course offerings, registration and withdrawal procedures, and other important school policies. The student handbook will help you address student life issues including housing, counseling, career planning, and where to find the offices of organizations and services. Your gateway to much of this information—and to your own education—is the computer. Spend time learning computer basics and becoming comfortable with accessing your school's computer network.

5. How can you strive for success?

A successful person is continually growing, learning, and changing. These actions will help you move ahead: Getting motivated, making a commitment, being responsible, and acting with integrity. Building self-esteem will also help you achieve your goals. The key is to first believe in yourself and then take action that helps you feel that you have earned that belief. You can think positively about yourself through different styles of positive self-talk. Then you can fulfill the promise of those positive thoughts through action plans, discipline, and effort.

Your success also depends on your ability to value those who are different from you. Accepting others without prejudice will help you interact successfully with people in your home, school, and work communities. Successful teamwork in all aspects of your life depends on your ability to value diversity. Finally, success depends on your ability to embrace change and to develop strategies for remaining flexible in its face.

CRITICAL THINKING

APPLYING LEARNING TO LIFE

IDENTITY AND SELF-ESTEEM. Where do you fit in today's student population? Make a brief "sketch" of yourself in words—describe your particular circumstances, opinions, and needs in a short paragraph. Here are some questions to inspire thought:

- How do you describe yourself—your culture, ethnicity, gender, age, lifestyle?
- What is your work situation, if you work?
- What is your current living situation?
- What do you expect out of your college experience?
- How long are you planning to spend in college?
- What qualities make you special?
- How would you describe your family?

_____

_____

_____

_____

_____

_____

_____

_____

Use the two aspects of building self-esteem to move yourself toward an important school-related goal for this semester. Make your goal as specific as possible, for example, "I want to find a job that allows me to work at night and still have time to study for my day classes."

Your goal: _____

_____

_____

BE POSITIVE. What positive thoughts about yourself and your abilities will help you achieve your goal? List them here.

_____

_____

_____

TAKE ACTION. Be specific about the actions you will take to back up your positive thoughts and achieve your goal. List them here.

_____

_____

_____

_____

The last step is up to you: Just do it.

TEAMWORK

COMBINING FORCES

WHO CAN HELP YOU? Every school is unique and offers its own particular range of opportunities. Investigate your school. Use the resource table as a guide, and explore your student handbook. Make a check mark by the resources that you think will be most helpful to you.

- ☐ Advisors and counselors
- ☐ Adult education center
- ☐ Library/media center
- ☐ Support groups/hotlines
- ☐ Instructors
- ☐ Career/job placement office
- ☐ Clubs/organizations
- ☐ Administration
- ☐ Bulletin boards
- ☐ Academic centers
- ☐ Student health center
- ☐ School publications
- ☐ Housing and transportation
- ☐ Tutoring
- ☐ Wellness/fitness centers
- ☐ Financial-aid office

Gather in small groups; or if you have a small class, work as one large group together. Each member of each group should choose one or more different resources (make sure no two people within a group explore the same resource). Be sure all resources on the grid on pp. 28–29 are accounted for. Then, each group member will investigate his or her resources and fill in the information on the grid, answering the questions listed across the top. Use the blank space at the bottom of p. 29 if you need to include a resource not listed here.

After each person has completed his or her investigation, meet again to exchange information and fill in the information on the grid. You now have a resource guide that you can refer to at any time. Write here how you will use the three resources that you feel will benefit you the most.

1. _____

_____

_____

2. _____

_____

_____

3. _____

_____

_____

WRITING

DISCOVERY THROUGH JOURNALING

To record your thoughts, use a separate journal or the lined page at the end of the chapter.

ACADEMIC INTEGRITY. What to you are the most important principles of academic integrity? Do you feel that acting with academic integrity will help you or not? Discuss how you feel about your school's academic integrity policy (you can probably find it in your student handbook or course catalog). In what two specific ways would you change this policy?

CAREER PORTFOLIO

CHARTING YOUR COURSE

MATCHING CAREER TO CURRICULUM. Your success in most career areas will depend in part on your academic preparation. Some careers, such as medicine, require very specific curriculum choices (e.g., you will have to take a number of biology and chemistry courses to be considered for med-

RESOURCE	WHO PROVIDES IT?	WHERE CAN YOU FIND IT?	WHEN IS IT AVAILABLE?	HOW CAN IT HELP YOU?	HOW DO YOU ASK FOR IT?	PHONE # OR OTHER KEY DETAILS
Administrative Help						
Instructor Advice						
Academic Advising						
Personal Counseling						
Financial Aid						
Academic Centers						
Organizations and Clubs						
Bulletin Boards						
Housing and Transportation						

RESOURCE	WHO PROVIDES IT?	WHERE CAN YOU FIND IT?	WHEN IS IT AVAILABLE?	HOW CAN IT HELP YOU?	HOW DO YOU ASK FOR IT?	PHONE # OR OTHER KEY DETAILS
Career Planning and Placement						
Tutoring						
Student Health						
Adult Education Center						
Fitness						
Support Groups/ Hotlines						
Disabled-Student Services						
English as a Second Language						

ical school). Some careers require certain courses that teach basic competencies—for example, to be an accountant, you will have to take accounting and bookkeeping. Other career areas—such as many business careers—don't have specific requirements, but employers often look for certain curriculum choices that indicate the mastery of particular skills.

Choose two of the career areas in which you are interested. For each, investigate the curriculum choices that would benefit you or that are required. Ask instructors, students on those career tracks, your career planning and placement office, people you know who are employed in these areas, and advisors. Create two lists—one for each career area—of recommended courses. To set off the courses that are absolutely required from those that are simply recommended, mark them with a star. Try to list the courses in the order you plan to take them.

 ## SUGGESTED READINGS

Baker, Sunny and Kim Baker. *College After 30: It's Never Too Late to Get the Degree You Need!* Holbrook, MA: Bob Adams (1992).

Evers, Frederick T., James Cameron Rush, and Iris Berdow. *The Bases of Competence: Skills for Lifelong Learning and Employability.* San Francisco, CA: Jossey-Bass (1998).

Jeffers, Susan. *Feel the Fear and Do It Anyway.* New York: Fawcett Columbine (1992).

Shields, Charles J. *Back in School: A Guide for Adult Learners.* Hawthorne, NJ: Career Press (1994).

Weinberg, Carol. *The Complete Handbook for College Women: Making the Most of Your College Experience.* New York: New York University Press (1994).

 ## INTERNET RESOURCES

Student Center: www.studentcenter.org

Student.Com—College Life Online: www.student.com/

 ## ENDNOTES

1. Cited in Colin Rise and Malcolm J. Nicholl. *Accelerated Learning for the 21st Century.* New York: Dell (1997), pp. 5–6.

2. U.S. Department of Education. *National Center for Education Statistics. Digest of Education Statistics 1998,* NCES 99-036. Thomas D. Snyder. Washington, D.C.: U.S. Government Printing Office (1999).

3. *Baltimore City Community College 1999–2000 Catalog,* Baltimore: Baltimore City Community College, Division of Planning and Advancement (1999), p. 158.

4. Rick Pitino. *Success is a Choice.* New York: Broadway Books (1997), p. 40.

5. Isaac Asimov. "My Own View," in *The Encyclopedia of Science Fiction,* John Clute and Peter Nicholls, eds. New York: St. Martin's Press (1995).

Journal

DATE

NAME

Thinking It Through

Check those statements that apply to you right now:

- ◉ I haven't thought much about exactly what my values are.

- ◉ I set goals but don't always feel that I achieve them.

- ◉ I feel that my priorities have changed since I entered college.

- ◉ I have a date book but I don't use it all that much.

- ◉ I know it doesn't help me, but I procrastinate.

IN THIS CHAPTER,

you will explore answers to the following

questions:

- What defines your values?
- How do you set and achieve goals?
- What are your priorities?
- How can you manage your time?
- Why is procrastination a problem?

Goal Setting and Time Management

People dream of what they want out of life, but dreams often seem too difficult to achieve or completely out of reach. When you set goals, prioritize, and manage your time effectively, you can develop the kind of "big picture" vision that will help you achieve what you dream. This chapter explains how taking specific steps toward goals can help you turn your dreams into reality. The section on time management will discuss how to translate your goals into daily, weekly, monthly, and yearly steps. Finally, you will explore how procrastination can derail your dreams and how to avoid it.

MAPPING YOUR COURSE

WHAT DEFINES YOUR VALUES?

Your personal **values**—for example, family togetherness, a good education, caring for others, and worthwhile employment—are the beliefs that guide your choices. The total of all your values is your value system. You demonstrate your particular value system in the priorities you set, how you communicate with others, your family life, your educational and career choices, and even the material things with which you surround yourself.

Choosing and Evaluating Values

VALUES
Principles or qualities that one considers important, right, or good.

Examining the sources of your values—family, friends, religion, media, school, or work—can help you define those values, trace their origin, and question the reasons why you have adopted them. Value sources, however, aren't as important as the process of considering each value carefully to see if it makes sense to you. Your individual value system is unique. Your responsibility is to make value choices based on what feels right for you, for your life, and for those involved in your life.

You can be more sure of making choices that are right for you if you try to periodically question and evaluate your values. Ask yourself: Does this value feel right? What effects does it, or might it, have on my life? Am I choosing it to please someone else, or is it truly my choice? Values are a design for life, and you are the one who has to live the life you design.

Life change and new experiences may bring a change in values. From time to time, try to evaluate the effects that each value has on your life and see if a shift in values might suit your changing circumstances. For example, after growing up in a homogeneous town, a student who meets other students from unfamiliar backgrounds may come to value living in a diverse community. Your values will grow and develop as you do if you continue to think them through.

How Values Relate to Goals

GOAL
An end toward which effort is directed; an aim or intention.

Understanding your values will help you set goals because any **goal** can help you achieve what you value. If you value spending time with your family, a related goal may be living near your parents. A value of financial independence while you are still in school may generate goals, such as working part-time and keeping credit card debt low, that reflect this value. If you value reaching out to others, you might make time for volunteer work or choose a career in social work or another "helping" profession.

Goals enable you to put values into practice. When you set and pursue goals that are based on values, you demonstrate and reinforce values by taking action. The strength of those values, in turn, reinforces your goals. You will experience a stronger drive to achieve if you build goals around what is most important to you.

HOW DO YOU SET AND ACHIEVE GOALS?

A goal can be something as concrete as buying a health insurance policy or as general as working to reduce your stress level. When you set goals and work to achieve them, you engage your intelligence, abilities, time, and energy in order to move ahead. From major life decisions to the tiniest day-to-day activities, setting goals will help you define how you want to live and what you want to achieve.

Paul Timm, an expert in self-management, believes that focus is a key ingredient in setting and achieving goals: "Focus adds power to our actions. If somebody threw a bucket of water on you, you'd get wet. . . . But if water was shot at you through a high-pressure nozzle, you might get injured. The only difference is focus."[1] Focus your goal-setting energy by defining a personal mission, placing your goals in long-term and short-term time frames, evaluating goals in terms of your values, and exploring different types of goals.

Identify Your Personal Mission

If you choose not to set goals or explore what you want out of life, you may look back on your past with a sense of emptiness. You may not know what you've done or why you did it. However, you can avoid that emptiness by periodically thinking about where you've been and where you want to be.

One helpful way to determine your general direction is to write a personal mission statement. Dr. Stephen Covey, author of *The Seven Habits of Highly Effective People,* defines a mission statement as a philosophy outlining what you want to be (character), what you want to do (contributions and achievements), and the principles by which you live. Dr. Covey compares the personal mission statement to the Constitution of the United States, a statement of principles that gives this country guidance and standards in the face of constant change.[2]

Your personal mission isn't written in stone. It should change as you move from one phase of life to the next—from single person to spouse, from student to working citizen. Stay flexible and reevaluate your personal mission from time to time.

The following personal mission statement was written by Carol Carter, one of the authors of this text.

> My mission is to use my talents and abilities to help people of all ages, stages, backgrounds, and economic levels achieve their human potential through fully developing their minds and their talents. I also aim to balance work with people in my life, understanding that my family and friends are a priority above all else.

A company, like a person, needs to establish standards and principles that guide its many activities. Companies often have mission statements so that each member of the organization clearly understands what to strive for. If a company fails to identify its mission, thousands of well-intentioned employees might focus their energies in just as many different directions, creating chaos and low productivity.

Here is a mission statement from Prentice Hall, the company that publishes this text:

> To provide the most innovative resources—books, technology, programs—to help students of all ages and stages achieve their academic and professional goals inside the classroom and out.

You will have an opportunity to write your own personal mission statement at the end of this chapter. Thinking through your personal mission can help you begin to take charge of your life. It can put you in control instead of allowing circumstances and events to control you. If you frame your mission statement carefully so that it truly reflects your goals, it can be your guide in everything you do.

Place Goals in Time

Everyone has the same 24 hours in a day, but it often doesn't feel like enough. Your commitments can overwhelm you unless you decide how to use time to plan your steps toward goal achievement.

If developing a personal mission statement establishes the big picture, placing your goals within particular time frames allows you to bring individual areas of that picture into the foreground. Planning your progress step-by-step will help you maintain your efforts over the extended time period often needed to accomplish a goal. There are two categories: long-term goals and short-term goals.

Setting Long-Term Goals

Establish first the goals that have the largest scope, the long-term goals that you aim to attain over a lengthy period of time, up to a few years or more. As a student, you know what long-term goals are all about. You have set yourself a goal to attend school and earn a degree or certificate. Becoming educated is an admirable goal that often takes years to reach.

Some long-term goals are lifelong, such as a goal to continually learn more about yourself and the world around you. Others have a more definite end, such as a goal to complete a course successfully. To determine your long-term goals, think about what you want out of your professional, educational, and personal life. Here is Carol Carter's long-term goal statement:

Great minds have purposes; others have wishes.

WASHINGTON IRVING

> To accomplish my mission through writing books, building exciting interactive websites, giving seminars, and developing programs that create opportunities for students to learn and develop. To create a personal, professional, and family environment that allows me to manifest my abilities and duly tend to each of my responsibilities.

For example, you may establish long-term goals such as these:

- I will graduate from school and know that I have learned all that I could, whether my grade point average reflects this or not.
- I will use my current and future school experience to develop practical skills that will help me get a satisfying, well-paying job.

Long-term goals don't have to be lifelong goals. Considering what you want to accomplish in a year's time will give you clarity, focus, and a sense of what needs to take place right away. When Carol thought about her long-term goals for the coming year, she came up with the following:

1. Develop programs to provide internships, scholarships, and other quality initiatives for students.
2. Allow time in my personal life to eat well, run five days a week, and spend quality time with family and friends. Allow time daily for quiet reflection and spiritual devotion.

In the same way that Carol's goals are tailored to her personality and interests, your goals should reflect who you are. Personal missions and goals are as unique as each individual. Continuing the example above, you might adopt these goals for the coming year:

- I will look for a part-time job with a local newspaper or newsroom.
- I will learn to navigate the Internet and research topics online.

Setting Short-Term Goals

When you divide your long-term goals into smaller, manageable goals that you hope to accomplish within a relatively short time, you are setting short-term goals. Short-term goals narrow your focus, helping you to maintain your progress toward your long-term goals. Say you have set the long-term goals you just read in the previous section. To stay on track toward those goals, you may want to accomplish these short-term goals in the next six months:

- I will make an effort to ask my coworkers for advice on how to get into the news business.
- I will write an assigned paper using information found on the Internet.

These same goals can be broken down into even smaller parts, such as the following one-month goals:

- I will have lunch with my office mate at work so that I can talk with him about his work experience.
- I will learn to conduct Internet research using search directories.

In addition to monthly goals, you may have short-term goals that extend for a week, a day, or even a couple of hours in a given day. Take as an example the Internet research goal. Such short-term goals may include the following:

- Three weeks from now: Research my topic using the two search directories that have the most helpful information.
- Two weeks from now: Experiment with search directories to see which ones will be most useful to me.
- One week from now: Read an Internet guide book to learn how to use search directories effectively.
- By the end of today: Find out what the major search directories are.

As you consider your long- and short-term goals, notice how all of your goals are linked to one another. As Figure 2.1 shows, your long-term goals establish a context for the short-term goals. In turn, your short-term goals make the long-term goals seem clearer and more reachable.

FIGURE

2.1

Linking goals together.

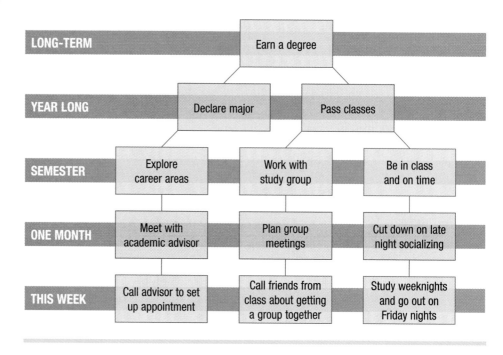

LONG-TERM	Earn a degree
YEAR LONG	Declare major / Pass classes
SEMESTER	Explore career areas / Work with study group / Be in class and on time
ONE MONTH	Meet with academic advisor / Plan group meetings / Cut down on late night socializing
THIS WEEK	Call advisor to set up appointment / Call friends from class about getting a group together / Study weeknights and go out on Friday nights

Link Goals with Values

If you are not sure how to start formulating your mission statement, look to your values to guide you. Define your mission and goals based on what is important to you. For example, if you value physical fitness, your mission statement might emphasize your commitment to staying in shape throughout your life. Your long-term goal might be to run a marathon, while your short-term goals might involve your weekly exercise and eating plans.

When you use your values as a compass for your goals, make sure the compass is pointed in the direction of your real feelings. Watch out for the following two pitfalls:

SETTING GOALS ACCORDING TO OTHER PEOPLE'S VALUES. Friends or family may encourage you to strive for what they think you should value. You may, of course, share their values. If you follow advice that you don't believe in, however, you may have a harder time sticking to your path. Staying in tune with your own values will help you make decisions that are right for you.

SETTING GOALS THAT REFLECT VALUES YOU HELD IN THE PAST. Life changes can alter your values. For example, a person who has been through a near-fatal car accident may experience a dramatic increase in how he or she values time with friends and family and a decrease in how he or she values material possessions. Keep in touch with your life's changes so your goals can reflect who you are today.

Focus on Different Kinds of Goals

People have many different goals, involving different parts of life and different values. Because school is currently a focus in your life, examine your educational goals.

Identifying Educational Goals

People have many reasons for attending college. You may identify with one or more of the following:

- I want to earn a higher salary.
- I want to build marketable skills in a particular career area.
- My supervisor at work says that a degree will help me move ahead in my career.
- Most of my friends were going.
- I want to learn.
- I am recently divorced and need to find a way to earn money.
- Everybody in my family goes to college; it's expected.
- I don't feel ready to jump into the working world yet.
- My friend loves her job and encouraged me to take courses in the field.
- My parent (or a spouse or partner) pushed me to go to college.
- I need to increase my skills so I can provide for my kids.
- I don't really know.

All of these answers are legitimate, even the last one. Whatever your reasons for being here, thinking about your educational goals—what you want out of being here—will help you make the most of your time. Consider what is available to you, for example, classes, instructors, class schedule, and available degrees or certificates. If you have an idea of the career you want to pursue, consider the degree(s), certificate(s), or test(s) that may be required. Don't forget to ponder what you want in terms of learning, relationships, and personal growth.

Goals in Your Career and Personal Life

Establish your long- and short-term goals for your other two paths—career and personal life—as well as for your educational path. Remember that all your goals are interconnected. A school goal is often a step toward a career goal and can affect a personal goal.

CAREER. Think of your career goals in terms of both job and financial goals.

- First, consider the job you want after you graduate—requirements, duties, hours, coworkers, salary, transportation, and company size, style, and location.
- Then, consider financial goals. How much money do you need to pay your bills, live comfortably, and save for the future? Compare your current financial picture to how you want to live, and set goals that will help you bridge the gap.

PERSONAL LIFE. Consider personal goals in terms of self, family, and lifestyle.

- First, look at yourself—character, personality, health/fitness, and conduct. Examine the difference between who you are and who you want to be.

- Then, consider your family goals. Do you want to stay single, be married, be a parent, or increase a family you've already started? Do you want to improve relations with a spouse or other family members?

- Finally, consider your ideal lifestyle—where you want to live, in what kind of space, and with whom. Consider goals that allow you to live the way you want to live.

Like learning a new physical task, setting and working toward goals takes a lot of practice and repeated efforts. As long as you do all that you can to achieve a goal, you haven't failed, even if you don't achieve it completely or in the time frame you had planned.

Achieving goals becomes easier when you are realistic about what is possible. Setting priorities will help you make that distinction.

WHAT ARE YOUR PRIORITIES?

When you set a **priority**, you identify what's important at any given moment. Prioritizing helps you focus on your most important goals, especially when the important ones are the most difficult. Human nature often leads people to tackle easy goals first and leave the tough ones for later. The risk is that you might never reach for goals that are crucial to your success.

> **PRIORITY**
>
> An action or intention that takes precedence in time, attention, or position.

To explore your priorities, think about your personal mission and look at your school, career, and personal goals. Do one or two of these paths take priority for you right now? In any path, which goals take priority? Which goals take priority over all others?

You are a unique individual, and your priorities are yours alone. What may be top priority to someone else may not mean that much to you, and vice versa. You can see this in Figure 2.2, which compares the priorities of two very different students. Each student's priorities are listed in order, with the highest priority at the top and the lowest priority at the bottom.

First and foremost, your priorities should reflect your goals. In addition, they should reflect your relationships with others. For example, if you are a parent, your children's needs will probably be high on the priority list. You may be in school so you can get a better job than you have now and give them a better life. If you are in a committed relationship, you may schedule your classes so that you and your partner are home together as often as possible. Even as you consider the needs of others, though, be true to your own goals and priorities so that you can make the most of who you are.

Setting priorities moves you closer to accomplishing specific goals. It also helps you begin planning to achieve your goals within specific time frames. Being able to achieve your goals is directly linked to effective time management.

Two students compare priorities.

FIGURE
2.2

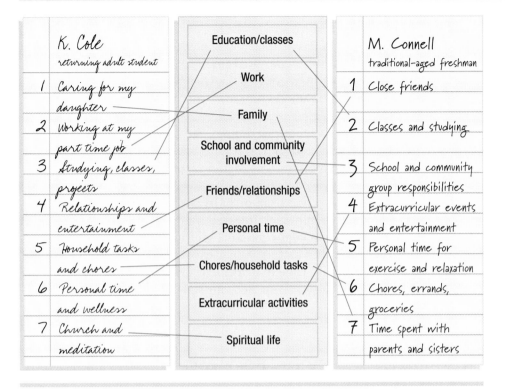

K. Cole
returning adult student

1 Caring for my daughter
2 Working at my part time job
3 Studying, classes, projects
4 Relationships and entertainment
5 Household tasks and chores
6 Personal time and wellness
7 Church and meditation

Education/classes

Work

Family

School and community involvement

Friends/relationships

Personal time

Chores/household tasks

Extracurricular activities

Spiritual life

M. Connell
traditional-aged freshman

1 Close friends
2 Classes and studying
3 School and community group responsibilities
4 Extracurricular events and entertainment
5 Personal time for exercise and relaxation
6 Chores, errands, groceries
7 Time spent with parents and sisters

Using a separate sheet of paper, complete the following.

Thinking Back

1. How can having a personal mission statement help you define your goals and priorities?

2. Why is it important to have both short-term and long-term goals?

3. Name a short-term goal that you hope to accomplish in the next six months, and name a one-month goal that is a step toward the six-month goal.

4. Name your top-priority educational, career, and personal goals.

5. What does it mean to prioritize your goals?

Thinking Ahead

1. What is your style of time management, and how would you rate yourself as a time manager?

2. What tools do you use that help you manage your time?

3. What kind of situation causes you the most difficulty in managing your time?

4. Do you ever put off things you know you should do? How does this behavior affect your life?

HOW CAN YOU MANAGE YOUR TIME?

Everyone has the same 24 hours in a day, every day; your responsibility and potential for success lie in how you use yours. You cannot change how time passes, but you can spend it wisely. Efficient time management helps you achieve your goals in a steady, step-by-step process.

People have a variety of approaches to time management. Your learning style (see Chapter 3) can help you understand how you use time. For example, students with strong logical-mathematical intelligence and Thinker types tend to organize activities within a framework of time. Because they stay aware of how long it takes them to do something or travel somewhere, they are usually prompt. By contrast, Adventurer types and less logical learners with perhaps stronger visual or interpersonal intelligences may neglect details such as how much time they have to complete a task. They can often be late without meaning to be.

Time management, like physical fitness, is a lifelong pursuit. Throughout your life, your ability to manage your time will vary with your stress level, how busy you are, and other factors. Don't expect perfection—just do your best and keep working at it. Time management involves building a schedule, taking responsibility for how you spend your time, and being flexible.

Build a Schedule

Just as a road map helps you travel from place to place, a schedule is a time-and-activity map that helps you get from the beginning of the day (or week, or month) to the end as smoothly as possible. Schedules help you gain control of your life in two ways: They allocate segments of time for the fulfillment of your daily, weekly, monthly, and longer-term goals, and they serve as a concrete reminder of tasks, events, due dates, responsibilities, and deadlines.

Keep a Date Book

Gather the tools of the trade: a pen or pencil and a date book (sometimes called a planner). A date book is indispensable for keeping track of your time. Some of you have date books and may have used them for years. Others may have had no luck with them or have never tried. Even if you don't feel you would benefit from one, give it a try. Paul Timm says, "Most time management experts agree that rule number one in a thoughtful planning process is: Use some form of a planner where you can write things down."[3]

Even if you're on the right track, you'll get run over if you just sit there.

WILL ROGERS

There are two major types of date books. The day-at-a-glance version devotes a page to each day. Although it gives you ample space to write the day's activities, it's harder to see what's ahead. The week-at-a-glance book gives you a view of the week's plans but has less room to write per day. If you write detailed daily plans, you might like the day-at-a-glance version. If you prefer to remind yourself of plans ahead of time, try the book that shows a week's schedule all at once. Some date books contain sections for monthly and yearly goals.

Another option is an electronic planner—a compact minicomputer that can hold a large amount of information. You can use it to schedule your days and weeks, make to-do lists, and create and store an address book.

Electronic planners are powerful, convenient, and often fun. However, they certainly cost more than the paper version, and you can lose a lot of important data if something goes wrong with the computer. Evaluate your options and decide what works best for you.

Set Weekly and Daily Goals

The most ideal time management starts with the smallest tasks and builds to bigger ones. Setting short-term goals that tie in to your long-term goals lends the following benefits:

- Increased meaning for your daily activities.
- Shaping your path toward the achievement of your long-term goals.
- A sense of order and progress.

For college students as well as working people, the week is often the easiest unit of time to consider at one shot. Weekly goal setting and planning allows you to keep track of day-to-day activities while giving you the larger perspective of what is coming up during the week. Take some time before each week starts to remind yourself of your long-term goals. Keeping long-term goals in mind will help you determine related short-term goals you can accomplish during the week to come.

Figure 2.3 shows parts of a daily schedule and a weekly schedule.

Daily and weekly schedules.

FIGURE 2.3

TIME	TASKS	PRIORITY
Monday, March 18		2002
7:00 AM		
8:00	Up at 8am — finish homework	*
9:00		
10:00	Business Administration	
11:00	Renew driver's license @ DMV	
12:00 PM		
1:00	Lunch	
2:00	Writing Seminar (peer editing today)	
3:00	↓	
4:00	check on Ms. Schwartz's office hrs.	
5:00	5:30 work out	
6:00	↳6:30	
7:00	Dinner	
8:00	Read two chapters for	
9:00	Business Admin.	
10:00	↓	
11:00		

Monday, March 18

8		Call: Mike Blair	1
9	BIO 212	Finanical Aid Office	2
10		EMS 262 *Paramedic	3
11	CHEM 203	role-play*	4
12			5
Evening	6pm yoga class		

Tuesday, March 19

8	Finish reading assignment!	Work @ library	1
9			2
10	ENG 112	(study for quiz)	3
11	↓		4
12			5
Evening		↓ until 7pm	

Wednesday, March 20

8		Meet w/advisor	1
9	BIO 212		2
10		EMS 262	3
11	CHEM 203 *Quiz		4
12		Pick up photos	5
Evening	6pm Aerobics		

Link Daily and Weekly Goals with Long-Term Goals

After you evaluate what you need to accomplish in the coming year, semester, month, week, and day to reach your long-term goals, use your schedule to record those steps. Write down the short-term goals that will enable you to stay on track. Here is how a student might map out two different goals over a year's time.

This year:	Complete enough courses to graduate. Improve my physical fitness.
This semester:	Complete my accounting class with a B average or higher. Lose 10 pounds and exercise regularly.
This month:	Set up study group schedule to coincide with quizzes. Begin walking and weight lifting.
This week:	Meet with study group; go over material for Friday's quiz. Go for a fitness walk three times; go to weight room twice.
Today:	Go over Chapter 3 in accounting text. Walk for 40 minutes.

Prioritize Goals

Prioritizing enables you to use your date book with maximum efficiency. On any given day, your goals will have varying degrees of importance. Record your goals first, and then label them according to their level of importance, using these categories: Priority 1, Priority 2, and Priority 3. Identify these categories by using any code that makes sense to you. Some people use numbers, as above. Some use letters (A, B, C). Some write activities in different colors according to priority level. Some use symbols (*, +, −).

PRIORITY 1 ACTIVITIES ARE THE MOST IMPORTANT THINGS IN YOUR LIFE. They may include attending class, picking up a child from day care, and paying bills.

PRIORITY 2 ACTIVITIES ARE PART OF YOUR ROUTINE. Examples include grocery shopping, working out, participating in a school organization, or cleaning. Priority 2 tasks are important but more flexible than Priority 1 tasks.

PRIORITY 3 ACTIVITIES ARE THOSE YOU WOULD LIKE TO DO BUT CAN RESCHEDULE WITHOUT MUCH SACRIFICE. Examples might be a trip to the mall, a visit to a friend, a social phone call, or a sports event. Many people don't enter Priority 3 tasks in their date books until they are sure they have time to get them done.

Prioritizing your activities is essential for two reasons. First, some activities are more important than others, and effective time management requires that you focus most of your energy on Priority 1 items. Second, looking at all your priorities helps you plan when you can get things done. Often, it's not possible to get all your Priority 1 activities done early in the day, especially if they involve scheduled classes or meetings. Prioritizing helps you set Priority 1 items and then schedule Priority 2 and 3 items around them as they fit.

Keep Track of Events

Your date book also enables you to schedule events. Think of events in terms of how they tie in with your long-term goals, just as you would your other tasks. For example, being aware of quiz dates, due dates for assignments, and meeting dates will aid your goals to achieve in school and become involved.

Note events in your date book so that you can stay aware of them ahead of time. Write them in daily, weekly, monthly, or even yearly sections, where a quick look will remind you that they are approaching. Writing them down will also help you see where they fit in the context of all your other activities. For example, if you have three big tests and a presentation all in one week, you'll want to take time in the weeks before to prepare for them.

Following are some kinds of events worth noting in your date book:

- Due dates for papers, projects, presentations, and tests.
- Important meetings, medical appointments, or due dates for bill payments.
- Birthdays, anniversaries, social events, holidays, and other special occasions.
- Benchmarks for steps toward a goal, such as due dates for sections of a project or a deadline for losing 5 pounds on your way to 20.

Take Responsibility for How You Spend Your Time

When you plan your activities with an eye toward achieving your most important goals, you are taking responsibility for how you live. The following strategies will help you stay in charge of your choices.

PLAN YOUR SCHEDULE EACH WEEK. Before each week starts, note events, goals, and priorities. Decide where to fit activities like studying and Priority 3 items. For example, if you have a test on Thursday, you can plan study sessions on the preceding days. If you have more free time on Tuesday and Friday than on other days, you can plan workouts or Priority 3 activities at those times. Looking at the whole week will help you avoid being surprised by something you had forgotten was coming up.

MAKE AND USE TO-DO LISTS. Use a to-do list to record the things you want to accomplish. If you generate a daily or weekly to-do list on a separate piece

Sample monthly calendar.

SUNDAY	MONDAY	TUESDAY	WEDNESDAY	THURSDAY	FRIDAY	SATURDAY
	1 WORK	2 Turn in English paper topic	3 Dentist 2pm	4 WORK	5	6
7 Frank's birthday	8 Psych Test 9am WORK	9	10 6:30 pm Meeting @ Student Ctr.	11 WORK	12	13 Dinner @ Ryan's
14	15 English paper due WORK	16 Western Civ paper—Library research	17	18 Library 6 p.m. WORK	19 Western Civ makeup class	20
21	22 WORK	23 2 p.m. meeting, psych group project	24 Start running program: 2 miles	25 WORK	26 Run 2 miles	27
28 Run 3 miles	29 WORK	30 Western Civ paper due	31 Run 2 miles			

APRIL

of paper, you can look at all tasks and goals at once. This will help you consider time frames and priorities. Some people create daily to-do lists right on their date book pages. You can tailor a to-do list to an important event, such as exam week, or an especially busy day. This kind of specific to-do list can help you prioritize and accomplish an unusually large task load.

POST MONTHLY AND YEARLY CALENDARS AT HOME. Keeping a calendar on the wall will help you stay aware of important events. Use a yearly or a monthly version (Figure 2.4 shows a monthly calendar), and keep it where you can refer to it often. If you live with family or friends, make the calendar a group project so that you stay aware of each other's plans. Knowing each other's schedules can also help you avoid problems such as two people needing the car at the same time.

SCHEDULE DOWN TIME. When you're wiped out from too much activity, you don't have the energy to accomplish as much. A little **down time** will refresh you and improve your attitude. Even half an hour a day will help. Fill the time with whatever relaxes you—reading, watching television, chatting

DOWN TIME

Quiet time set aside for relaxation and low-key activity.

online, playing a game or sport, walking, writing, or just doing nothing. Make down time a priority.

BE FLEXIBLE. Changes can result in priority shifts that jumble your schedule. On Monday, a homework assignment due in a week might be Priority 2; then, if you haven't gotten to it by Saturday, it becomes Priority 1. Perhaps more serious changes occur, such as a car problem or a job loss. Think of change as part of life, and you will be able to more effectively solve the dilemmas that come up. For some changes that occur frequently, you can think through a backup plan ahead of time. For others, the best you can do is to keep an open mind about possibilities and to remember to call on your resources in a pinch. Your problem-solving skills (see Chapter 4) will help you build your ability to adjust to whatever changes come your way.

> *Obstacles are what people see when they take their eyes off the goal.* —NEW YORK SUBWAY BULLETIN BOARD

No matter how well you schedule your time, you will have moments when it's hard to stay in control. Knowing how to identify and avoid procrastination and other time traps will help you get back on track.

WHY IS PROCRASTINATION A PROBLEM?

Procrastination is part of nearly every student's life at some point in time. People procrastinate for different reasons. If it is taken to the extreme, however, procrastination can develop into a habit that will cause problems at school, on the job, and at home. Jane B. Burka and Lenora M. Yuen, authors of *Procrastination: Why You Do It and What To Do About It,* say that habitual procrastinators create problems because "The performance becomes the only measure of the person; nothing else is taken into account. An outstanding performance means an outstanding person; a mediocre performance means a mediocre person. . . . As long as you procrastinate, you never have to confront the real limits of your ability, whatever those limits are."[4] For the procrastinator, the fear of failure prevents taking the risk that could bring success.

Following are some ways to fight your tendencies to procrastinate.

> **PROCRASTINATION**
>
> The act of putting off a task until another time.

WEIGH THE BENEFITS (TO YOU AND OTHERS) OF COMPLETING THE TASK VERSUS THE EFFECTS OF PROCRASTINATING. What rewards lie ahead if you get it done? What will be the effects if you continue to put it off? Which situation has better effects? Chances are you will benefit more in the long term from facing the task head-on.

SET REASONABLE GOALS. Plan your goals carefully, allowing enough time to complete them. Unreasonable goals can be so intimidating that you do nothing at all. "Pay off the credit card bill next month" could throw you. However, "Pay off the credit card bill in 10 months" might inspire you to take action.

How can I stay focused on my school goals?

Rosalia Chavez, *University of Arizona, Tucson, Arizona, Public Administration Major*

I married at 18 and didn't finish high school. My husband became a cocaine addict and grew very posses- sive of me. After our two sons were born, I decided to get my GED, but he didn't want me to. At this point I knew I had to start making opportunities for myself.

Shortly after I had begun to further my education, my husband overdosed on drugs. His death was very traumatic and difficult to deal with. I am now taking classes full time at the University of Arizona and I work part-time in the Chicano/Hispanic student affairs office. I don't feel I'm getting an education just for myself, but for future generations of Hispanic women. There's a view in traditional Hispanic families that women stay home and only the man provides. I

would like to empower women by telling them my story and letting them know that they deserve to follow their dreams.

Even though I feel blessed, I have to make daily decisions about priorities, such as, "Do I take this test or stay home with my sick child?" Recently I had to drop a class because my children were sick and I couldn't keep up. My son, who is 11, has ADHD (Attention Deficit Hyperactivity Disorder). He was on medication and under a doctor's care, but when I reapplied for state medical assistance I was denied. Now I can no longer afford his medicine. These situations hinder me as a student because I am so preoccupied. Can you offer suggestions about how I can keep focused on my school goals?

Norma Seledon, *Las Mujeres en Accion, Chicago, Illinois*

Your story is not atypical. Your taking control of your life is, however, exemplary. Setting and sticking to your goals is not easy, particularly when you have cultural, societal and even religious factors working against you. It is essential to maintain a balance. With many higher education programs designed for those without families, it is challenging to meet the demands of school and family. Your

desire to learn and grow not only for yourself, but for your family and for the community at large, will fuel your efforts.

I recognize some of your challenges. In my last year of college I had a newborn, was pregnant, worked full time and attended school full time. You must prioritize and pace yourself. It may help to speak to professors about your situation. My daughter was due at the midterm of my last semester, and some professors were flexible with my assignments. It can't hurt to try.

As director of an organization whose primary focus is Latina leadership and working with survivors of domestic violence, it is difficult being a mother of two preteens and a preschooler. My son is also diagnosed with ADHD. I demand periodic meetings with a team of school officials so that we may approach my son's education from a team perspective.

With patience and perseverance, you will achieve your current goals and set more for yourself. Continue to develop a support system and to share your story. We must all continue to figure out how to distill the beauty and strength of our culture and traditions and discard those elements that hinder women's development. Felicidades!

BREAK THE TASK INTO SMALLER PARTS. Look at the task in terms of its parts. How can you approach it step-by-step? If you can concentrate on achieving one small goal at a time, the task may become less of a burden. In addition, setting concrete time limits for each task may help you feel more in control.

GET STARTED WHETHER OR NOT YOU "FEEL LIKE IT." Going from doing nothing to doing something is often the hardest part of avoiding procrastination. The motivation techniques from Chapter 1 might help you take the first step. Once you start, you may find it easier to continue.

ASK FOR HELP WITH TASKS AND PROJECTS AT SCHOOL, WORK, AND HOME. You don't always have to go it alone. For example, if you avoid a project because you dislike the employee with whom you have to work, talk to your supervisor about adjusting tasks or personnel. Once you identify what's holding you up, see who can help you face the task.

DON'T EXPECT PERFECTION. No one is perfect. Most people learn by starting at the beginning and wading through plenty of mistakes and confusion. It's better to try your best than to do nothing at all.

Procrastination is natural, but it can cause you problems if you let it get the best of you. When it does happen, take some time to think about the causes. What is it about this situation that frightens you or puts you off? Answering that question can help you address what causes lie underneath the procrastination. These causes might indicate a deeper issue that you can address.

In Hebrew, the word above, pronounced *chai*, means "life," representing all aspects of life—spiritual, emotional, family, educational, and career. Individual Hebrew characters have number values. Because the characters in the word *chai* add up to 18, the number 18 has come to be associated with good luck. The word *chai* is often worn as a good luck charm. As you plan your goals, think about your view of luck. Many people feel that a person can create her own luck by pursuing goals persistently and staying open to possibilities and opportunities.

Consider that your vision of life may largely determine how you live. You can prepare the way for luck by establishing a personal mission and forging ahead toward your goals. If you believe that the life you want awaits you, you will be able to recognize and make the most of luck when it comes around. *L'Chaim*—to life, and good luck.

IMPORTANT POINTS *to remember*

1. What defines your values?

Values are beliefs and standards, stemming from sources such as parents and friends, that are important to you. Together, they make up your value system, and they guide your life choices. Consider values carefully, questioning and evaluating each to see if it makes sense. Make responsible choices, based on what feels right. Because life changes can result in changing values, reassess your values as time goes by. Values can also help you set goals because most goals that are ideal for you will help you achieve what you value. Goals help you put values into practice.

2. How do you set and achieve goals?

A goal is a target toward which you direct your efforts. Goals can be long term or short term. A personal mission statement helps you define your most important long-term goals and adjust to changing life circumstances. Placing goals within particular time frames—a week, a month, a semester—can help you plan how to pursue them, especially when short-term goals act as steps toward a long-term goal. If you link goals to your values, your goals will reflect what's important to you. Consider your goals in your educational life, your working life, and your personal life. Spend some time evaluating why you are in school and what you want to achieve.

3. What are priorities?

A priority is an action or intention that takes precedence in time or importance. When you set priorities, you focus your time and energy on what is important to you and leave less important tasks until later. Explore priorities by thinking about your personal mission and what is most important among your goals. Your priorities should reflect your goals, your values, and your relationships with others. Setting priorities helps you to plan to achieve goals within specific time frames.

4. How can you manage your time?

Effective time management will help you achieve your goals. Building a schedule is your main time-management task. This involves using a date book, setting daily and weekly goals, linking those goals to long-term goals, prioritizing, and keeping track of events. When you take responsibility for how you spend your time, you are more able to take steps toward your goals. Taking responsibility means planning each week's schedule, using to-do lists, posting monthly and yearly calendars, scheduling down time, and being flexible. Flexibility will help you handle the sudden schedule changes that will arise.

5. Why is procrastination a problem?

Procrastination, the habit of putting off tasks, can keep you from achieving your goals. Explore your reasons for procrastinating and take steps to overcome them. Strategies to fight procrastination include asking for help with tasks, weighing the positive and negative effects of procrastination, setting reasonable goals, breaking the task into parts, and avoiding perfectionism.

CRITICAL THINKING

APPLYING LEARNING TO LIFE

KNOWING AND PRIORITIZING YOUR VALUES. Begin to explore your values by rating the following values on a scale from 1 to 4, 1 being least important to you and 4 being most important. If you have values that you don't see in the chart, list them in the blank spaces and rate them.

VALUE	RATING	VALUE	RATING
Knowing yourself	1 2 3 4	Mental health	1 2 3 4
Physical health	1 2 3 4	Fitness/exercise	1 2 3 4
Spending time with family	1 2 3 4	Close friendships	1 2 3 4
Helping others	1 2 3 4	Education	1 2 3 4
Being well-paid	1 2 3 4	Being employed	1 2 3 4
Being liked by others	1 2 3 4	Free time/vacations	1 2 3 4
Enjoying entertainment	1 2 3 4	Time to yourself	1 2 3 4
Spiritual/religious life	1 2 3 4	Reading	1 2 3 4
Keeping up with news	1 2 3 4	Staying organized	1 2 3 4
Financial stability	1 2 3 4	Intimate relationship	1 2 3 4
Creative/artistic pursuits	1 2 3 4	Self-improvement	1 2 3 4
Lifelong learning	1 2 3 4	Facing your fears	1 2 3 4
	1 2 3 4		1 2 3 4
	1 2 3 4		1 2 3 4
	1 2 3 4		1 2 3 4
	1 2 3 4		1 2 3 4

Considering your priorities, write your top three values here:

1. _____

2. _____

3. _____

Now evaluate whether how you spend your time reflects your values. For three of the values listed above, list the activities that reinforce and reflect that value. Then, estimate how much time you spend on these activities.

1. Value: _____

Corresponding activities: _____

How much time is spent? _____

2. Value: _____

Corresponding activities: _____

How much time is spent? _____

3. Value: _____

Corresponding activities: _____

How much time is spent? _____

Look at what you have written. Is there any area where you feel you spent too little time reinforcing that particular value? If so, write it here. Why do you think that is?

_____

_____

_____

_____

_____

Finally, gather in a group of three or four people. Share your list of your top three values with the group. Each person should choose one value that he or she would like to spend more time on and write the value on a blank piece of paper. Then, each person should pass his or her paper to the person next to them, and all group members should write on the paper one idea about how to use time management or activities to focus on that value. Continue passing the papers around until each person has written an idea on each page. Each group member should receive his or her page back with the suggestions on it.

TEAMWORK
COMBINING FORCES

INDIVIDUAL PRIORITIES. In a group of three or four people, brainstorm long-term goals and have one member of the group write them down. From that list, pick out 10 goals that everyone can relate to most. Each group member should then take five minutes alone to evaluate the relative importance of the 10 goals and rank them in the order that he or she prefers. Use a 1 to 10 scale, with 1 being the highest priority and 10 the lowest.

Display the rankings of each group member side by side. How many different orders are there? Discuss why each person has a different set of priorities, and be open to different views. What factors in different people's lives have caused them to select particular rankings? If you have time, discuss how priorities have changed for each group member over the course of a year, perhaps by having each person re-rank the goals according to his or her needs a year ago.

WRITING
DISCOVERY THROUGH JOURNALING

To record your thoughts, use a separate journal or the lined page at the end of the chapter.

PERSONAL MISSION STATEMENT. Using the personal mission statement examples in the chapter as a guide, consider what you want out of your life and create your own personal mission statement. You can write it in paragraph form, in a list of long-term goals, or in the form of a think link. Take as much time as you need in order to be as complete as possible. Write a draft and take time to revise it before you write the final version. If you have created a think link rather than a verbal statement, attach it separately.

CAREER PORTFOLIO
CHARTING YOUR COURSE

CAREER GOALS AND PRIORITIES. The most reasonable and reachable career goals are ones that are linked with your school and life goals. First, name a personal long-term career goal.

_____

_____

Then imagine that you will begin working toward it. Indicate a series of steps you can take—from short term to long term—that you feel will help you achieve this goal. Write what you hope to accomplish in the next year, the next six months, the next month, the next week, and the next day.

TIME FRAME	CAREER GOAL
One Year	
Six Months	
One Month	
This Week	
Today	

Now, explore your job priorities. How do you want your job to benefit you? Note your requirements in each of the following areas.

Job title

Duties and responsibilities

Salary and benefits

(for entry-level position—e.g., health insurance, child-care center at the work site)

Hours

(part time vs. full time; conventional schedule vs. unconventional schedule, involving evening, night, or weekend work)

Job requirements

(e.g., travel, location, working primarily with people or as an independent contributor, working in an office or in the field)

Industry or field

Flexibility

Affiliation with school or financial aid program

(applies if you are still in school)

What kind of job, in the career area for which you listed your goals, might fit all or most of your requirements? List two possibilities here.

1.

2.

UGGESTED READINGS

Covey, Stephen. *The Seven Habits of Highly Effective People.* New York: Simon & Schuster (1995).

Emmett, Rita. *The Procrastinator's Handbook: Mastering the Art of Doing It Now.* New York: Walker & Co. (2000).

Gleeson, Kerry. *The Personal Efficiency Program: How To Get Organized to Do More Work in Less Time,* 2nd ed. New York: John Wiley (2000).

Lakein, Alan. *How to Get Control of Your Time and Your Life.* New York: New American Library (1996).

McGee-Cooper, Ann with Duane Trammell. *Time Management for Unmanageable People.* New York: Bantam Books (1994).

Sapadin, Linda and Jack Maguire. *Beat Procrastination and Make the Grade: The Six Styles of Procrastination and How Students Can Overcome Them.* New York: Penguin USA (1999).

Timm, Paul R. *Successful Self-Management: A Psychologically Sound Approach to Personal Effectiveness.* Los Altos, CA: Crisp Publications (1996).

 NTERNET RESOURCES

Mind Tools (section on time management): www.mindtools.com/page5.html

Top Achievement (goal setting and self-improvement resources): www.top achievement.com

 NDNOTES

1. Paul R. Timm, Ph.D. *Successful Self-Management: A Psychologically Sound Approach To Personal Effectiveness.* Los Altos, CA: Crisp Publications, Inc. (1987), pp. 22–41.

2. Stephen Covey. *The Seven Habits of Highly Effective People.* New York: Simon & Schuster (1989), p. 108.

3. Timm. *Successful Self-Management,* pp. 22–41.

4. Jane B. Burka and Lenora M. Yuen. *Procrastination: Why Do You Do It and What to Do About It.* Reading, MA: Perseus Books (1983), pp. 21–22.

DATE

NAME

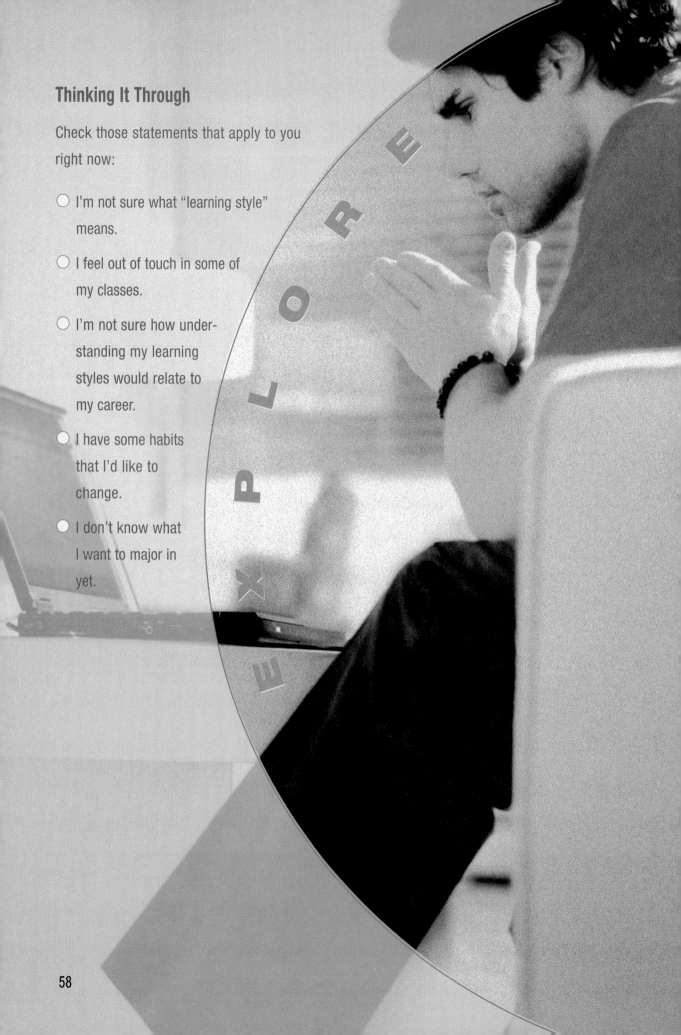

Thinking It Through

Check those statements that apply to you right now:

○ I'm not sure what "learning style" means.

○ I feel out of touch in some of my classes.

○ I'm not sure how understanding my learning styles would relate to my career.

○ I have some habits that I'd like to change.

○ I don't know what I want to major in yet.

IN THIS CHAPTER,

you will explore answers to the following

questions:

- What is a learning style?
- How can you discover how you learn?
- How can you identify and manage learning disabilities?
- How can you develop positive habits?
- How can you start thinking about choosing a major?

The ability to learn is much more than a college skill. Being a learner for life means that you will be able to keep pace with rapidly changing workplace technology, stay aware of world developments and how they affect you, and continue to grow as a person. To learn effectively, you need to understand how you learn. This chapter will help by introducing you to two different personal assessments—one focusing on how you take in information, and one that helps you determine how you

Self-Awareness

interact with others. You will then explore other important elements of self: your self-perception, interests, and habits. The more you know about your learning style, interests, and abilities, the better prepared you will be to choose a career that makes the most of who you are and what you can do.

WHAT IS A LEARNING STYLE?

Your mind is the most powerful tool you will ever possess. You are accomplished at many skills and can process all kinds of information. However, when you have trouble accomplishing a particular task, you may become convinced that you can't learn how to do anything new. Not only is this perception incorrect, it can also damage your belief in yourself.

Every individual is highly developed in some abilities and underdeveloped in others. Many famously successful people were brilliant in one area but functioned poorly in other areas. Winston Churchill failed the sixth grade. Abraham Lincoln was demoted to a private in the Black Hawk war. Louis Pasteur was a poor student in chemistry. Walt Disney was fired from a job and told he had no good ideas. What some might interpret as a deficiency or disability may be simply a different method of learning. People have their own individual gifts—the key is to identify them.

Although it may sometimes seem like there is one "best" **learning style**, there are actually many different and equally valuable ways to learn, each suited to particular topics and situations. The way each person learns is a unique blend of styles resulting from her distinctive abilities, challenges, experiences, and training. In addition, how you learn isn't necessarily set in stone—particular styles may develop or recede as your responsibilities and experiences lead you to work on different skills and tasks.

Understanding how you learn is one of the first steps in discovering who you are. Although it takes some work and exploration, this knowledge can benefit you in many ways—in your studies, the classroom, and the workplace.

> **LEARNING STYLE**
>
> A particular way in which the mind receives and processes information.

Study Benefits

Most students aim to maximize learning while minimizing frustration and time spent studying. If you know your strengths and limitations, you can use techniques that take advantage of your highly developed areas while helping you through your less developed ones. For example, say you perform better in smaller, discussion-based classes. When you have the opportunity, you might choose a course section that is smaller or that is taught by an instructor who prefers group discussion. You might also apply specific strategies to improve your retention in a large group lecture situation.

Following each of this chapter's two assessments, you will see information about study techniques that tend to complement the strengths and shortcomings of each intelligence or spectrum. Remember that you have abilities in all areas, even though some are dominant. Therefore, you may encounter useful suggestions under any of the headings. What's important is that you use what works. During this course, try a large number of new study techniques, eventually keeping those you find to be useful.

Classroom Benefits

Knowing your learning style can help you make the most of the teaching styles of your instructors. Your particular learning style may work well with the way some instructors teach and be a mismatch with other instructors. Remember that an instructor's teaching style often reflects his learning style. After perhaps two class meetings, you should be able to make a pretty good assessment

Teaching styles.

FIGURE 3.1

Lecture	Instructor speaks to the class for the entire period, little to no class interaction.
Group discussion	Instructor presents material but encourages discussion throughout.
Small groups	Instructor presents material and then breaks class into small groups for discussion or project work.
Visual focus	Instructor uses visual elements such as diagrams, photographs, drawings, transparencies.
Verbal focus	Instructor relies primarily on words, either spoken or written on the board or overhead projector.
Logical presentation	Instructor organizes material in a logical sequence, such as by time or importance.
Random presentation	Instructor tackles topics in no particular order, jumps around a lot, or digresses.

of teaching styles (instructors may exhibit more than one). Once you understand the various teaching styles you encounter, plan to make adjustments that maximize your learning. See Figure 3.1 for some common teaching styles.

Assess how well your own styles match up with the various teaching styles. If your styles mesh well with an instructor's teaching styles, you're in luck. If not, you have a number of options.

BRING EXTRA FOCUS TO YOUR WEAKER AREAS. Although it's not easy, working on your weaker points will help you break new ground in your learning. For example, if you're a verbal person in a math- and logic-oriented class, increase your focus and concentration during class so that you get as much as you can from the presentation. Then spend extra study time on the material, make a point to ask others from your class to help you, and search for additional supplemental materials and exercises to reinforce your knowledge.

ASK YOUR INSTRUCTOR FOR ADDITIONAL HELP. For example, a visual person might ask an instructor to recommend visuals that would help to illustrate the points made in class. If the class breaks into smaller groups, you might ask the instructor to divide those groups roughly according to learning style, so that students with similar strengths can help each other.

"CONVERT" CLASS MATERIAL DURING STUDY TIME. For example, an interpersonal learner takes a class with an instructor who presents big-picture information in lecture format. This student might organize study groups and in those groups, focus on filling in the factual gaps using reading materials assigned for that class. Likewise, a visual student might rewrite notes in different colors to add a visual element—for example, assigning a different color to each main point or topic, or using one color for central ideas, another for supporting examples.

Instructors are as individual as students. Taking time to focus on their teaching styles, and on how to adjust, will help you learn more effectively and avoid frustration. Don't forget to take advantage of your instructor's office hours when you have a learning style issue that is causing you difficulty.

Career Benefits

Because different careers require different abilities, there is no one "best" learning style. Specifically, how can knowing your learning style help you in your career?

YOU WILL PERFORM MORE SUCCESSFULLY. Your learning style is essentially your working style. If you know how you learn, you will be able to look for an environment that suits you best. You will perform at the top of your ability if you work at a job in which you feel competent and happy.

YOU WILL BE ABLE TO FUNCTION WELL IN TEAMS. Teamwork is a primary feature of the modern workplace. The better your awareness of your abilities and personality traits, the better you will be able to communicate with others and identify what tasks you will best be able to perform in a team situation.

YOU WILL BE MORE ABLE TO TARGET AREAS THAT NEED IMPROVEMENT. Awareness of your learning styles will help you pinpoint the areas that are more difficult for you. That has two advantages: One, you can begin to work on difficult areas, step-by-step. Two, when a task requires a skill that is tough for you, you can either take special care with it or suggest someone else whose style may be better suited to it.

Now that you know you have something to gain, look at some ways you can explore your particular learning style.

HOW CAN YOU DISCOVER HOW YOU LEARN?

Many different types of assessments are available to promote self-discovery. Each type provides a different means of exploring strengths and weaknesses, abilities and limitations. This chapter contains one each of two particular types—learning style assessments and personality assessments.

Learning style assessments focus on the process by which you take in, retain, and use information. Students may use learning style assessment results to maximize study efficiency and to choose courses that suit their styles. Personality assessments indicate how you respond to both internal and external situations—in other words, how you react to thoughts and feelings as well as to people and events. Employers may give such assessments to employees and use the results to set up and evaluate teams.

The learning styles assessment in this chapter is called Pathways to Learning and is based on the Multiple Intelligences Theory. It can help you determine how you best take in information as well as how you can improve areas in which you have more trouble learning. The second assessment tool, Personality Spectrum, is a personality assessment that helps you evaluate how you react to people and situations in your life. Pathways to Learning and the Personality Spectrum provide two different perspectives that together will give you a more complete picture of how you interact with everything you encounter—information, people, and your own inner thoughts.

> *To be what we are, and to become what we are capable of becoming, is the only end of life.*
>
> **ROBERT LOUIS STEVENSON**

Multiple Intelligences Theory

There is a saying, "It is not how smart you are, but how you are smart." In 1983, Howard Gardner, a Harvard University professor, changed the way people perceive intelligence and learning with his theory of Multiple Intelligences. Gardner believes there are at least eight distinct intelligences possessed by all people, and that every person has developed some intelligences more fully than others. Most people have at one time learned something quickly and comfortably. Most have also had the opposite experience: no matter how hard they try, something they want to learn just won't sink in. According to the Multiple Intelligences Theory, when you find a task or subject easy, you are probably using a more fully developed intelligence; when you have more trouble, you may be using a less-developed intelligence.[1]

Table 3.1 offers brief descriptions of the focus of each of the intelligences. You will find information on related skills and study techniques on page 68. The Pathways to Learning assessment will help you determine the levels to which your intelligences are developed.

INTELLIGENCE

As defined by H. Gardner, an ability to solve problems or fashion products that are useful in a particular cultural setting or community.

Personality Spectrum

One of the first instruments to measure psychological types, the Myers-Briggs Type Inventory (MBTI), was designed by Katharine Briggs and her daughter, Isabel Briggs Myers. Later, David Keirsey and Marilyn Bates combined the 16 Myers-Briggs types into four temperaments and developed an assessment based on those temperaments, called the Keirsey Sorter. These assessments are two of the most widely used personality tests, both in psychology and in the business world.

The Personality Spectrum assessment in this chapter can help you better understand yourself and those around you. Based on the Myers-Briggs and Keirsey theories, it adapts and simplifies their material into four personality types—Thinker, Organizer, Giver, and Adventurer—and was developed by Joyce Bishop (1997). The Personality Spectrum will give you

TABLE 3.1   Multiple intelligences.

INTELLIGENCE	DESCRIPTION
Verbal–Linguistic	Ability to communicate through language (listening, reading, writing, speaking)
Logical–Mathematical	Ability to understand logical reasoning and problem solving (math, science, patterns, sequences)
Bodily–**Kinesthetic**	Ability to use the physical body skillfully and to take in knowledge through bodily sensation (coordination, working with hands)
Visual–Spatial	Ability to understand spatial relations and to perceive and create images (visual art, graphic design, charts and maps)
Interpersonal	Ability to relate to others, noticing their moods, motivations, and feelings (social activity, cooperative learning, teamwork)
Intrapersonal	Ability to understand one's own behavior and feelings (self-awareness, independence, time spent alone)
Musical	Ability to comprehend and create meaningful sound (music, sensitivity to sound, understanding patterns)
Naturalistic	Ability to understand features of the environment (interest in nature, environmental balance, ecosystem, stress relief brought by natural environments)

KINESTHETIC

Coming from physical sensation caused by body movements and tensions.

a personality perspective on how you can maximize your functioning at school and at work. Each personality type has its own abilities that improve work and school performance, suitable learning techniques, and ways of relating in interpersonal relationships. Page 70 will give you more details about each type.

Using the Assessments

The two assessments follow this section of text. After each assessment you will find a page that details the traits of each dimension and offers strategies to help you make the most of that dimension's tendencies.

Complete both assessments, trying to answer the questions objectively—in other words, mark the answers that best indicate who you are, not who you want to be. The more closely you can see yourself today, the more effectively you can set goals for where you want to go from here. Then, enter your scores on page 71, where you will see a brain diagram on which to plot Personality Spectrum scores and boxes in which to enter your Pathways to Learning scores. This page is organized so that you can see your scores for both assessments at a glance, giving you an opportunity to examine how they relate to one another. Don't be concerned if some of your scores are low—that is true for most everyone. For Pathways to Learning, 21–24 indicates a high level of development in that particular type of intelligence, 15–20 a moderate level, and below 15, an underdeveloped intelligence. For the Personality Spectrum, 26–36 indicates a strong tendency in that dimension, 14–25 a moderate tendency, and below 14, a minimal tendency.

Knowing how you learn will help you improve your understanding of yourself—how you may function at school, in the workplace, and in your personal life. Keep in mind that these or any other assessments are intended not to label you but to be indicators of who you are. Your thinking skills—your ability to evaluate sources of information—will best enable you to see yourself as a whole, including both gifts and areas for growth. Your job is to verify and sift each piece of information and arrive at the most accurate portrait of yourself at this point in time.

Perspective on Learning Style

Both of the assessments in the chapter provide you with self-knowledge that can help you manage yourself in school, at work, and at home in the most effective way possible. However, no one assessment can give you the final word on who you are and what you can and cannot do. It's human to want an easy answer—a one-page printout of the secret to your identity—but this kind of quick fix does not exist. You are a complex person who cannot be summed up by a test or an evaluation.

Use Assessments for Reference

The most reasonable way to approach any assessment is as a reference point rather than as a label. There are no "right" answers, no "best" set of scores. Instead of boxing yourself into one or more categories, which limits you, approach any assessment as a tool with which you can expand your idea of yourself. Think of it as a new set of eyeglasses for a person with somewhat blurred vision. The glasses will not create new paths and possibilities for you, but they will help you see more clearly the paths and possibilities that already exist. They give you the power to explore, choose, and act with confidence.

You will continually learn, change, and grow throughout your life. Any evaluation is simply a snapshot, a look at who you are in a given moment. The answers can, and will, change as you change and as circumstances change. They provide an opportunity for you to identify a moment and learn from it by asking questions: Who am I right now? How does this compare to who I want to be?

Use Assessments for Understanding

Understanding your tendencies will help you understand yourself. Avoid labeling yourself narrowly by using one intelligence or personality type, such as if you were to say, "I'm no good in math" or "I'm never a thinker." Anyone can learn math; however, some people learn math more efficiently through intelligences other than logical–mathematical. For example, a visual–spatial learner may want to draw diagrams of as much of a math problem as possible. Everyone is a thinker; however, some people tend to approach life situations more analytically than others.

People are a blend of all the intelligences and personality types, in proportions unique to them. Most often one or two intelligences or types are dominant. When material is very difficult or when you are feeling insecure about learning something new, use your most dominant areas. When something is easy for you, this is an opportunity for you to improve your less developed areas. All of your abilities will continue to develop throughout your lifetime.

In addition, you may change which abilities you emphasize, depending on the situation. For example, an organizer-dominant student might find it easy to take notes in outline style when the instructor lectures in an organized way. However, if another instructor jumps from topic to topic, the same student might choose to use a think link. The more you know yourself, the more you will be able to assess any situation and set appropriate goals.

Elsewhere in the text you will see how your personality types and intelligences influence other skills and life areas. As you read, try to examine how your tendencies affect you in different areas—study techniques, time management, personal wellness, communication, and so on. Knowing your style can help you improve how you function in every area of your life.

Avoid Overreacting to Challenges

The assessments you complete reveal areas of challenge as well as ability. If you assume that your limitations are set in stone or let them dominate your self-image, you may deny yourself growth. Rather than dwelling on limitations (which often results in a negative self-image) or ignoring them (which often leads to unproductive choices), use what you know from the assessments to face your limitations and work to improve them.

In any area of challenge, look at where you are and set goals that will help you reach where you want to be. If a class is difficult, examine what improvements you need to make in order to succeed. If a work situation requires you to perform in an area that causes trouble for you, face your limitations head-on and ask for help. Exploring what you will gain from working on a limitation will help you gain the motivation you need to move ahead.

Knowing your learning style will move you ahead on the road to self-knowledge. Following the assessments, you will explore your habits and then you will begin to consider what majors may be right for you.

PATHWAYS TO LEARNING

Name _____   Date _____

Developed by Joyce Bishop, Ph.D., and based upon Howard Gardner's *Frames of Mind: The Theory of Multiple Intelligences.*[2]

Directions: Rate each statement as follows. Write the number of your response (1–4) on the line next to the statement and total each set of six questions.

① rarely ② sometimes ③ usually ④ always

1. _____ I enjoy physical activities.
2. _____ I am uncomfortable sitting still.
3. _____ I prefer to learn through doing.
4. _____ When sitting I move my legs or hands.
5. _____ I enjoy working with my hands.
6. _____ I like to pace when I'm thinking or studying.
   _____ **TOTAL for Bodily–Kinesthetic**

7. _____ I enjoy telling stories.
8. _____ I like to write.
9. _____ I like to read.
10. _____ I express myself clearly.
11. _____ I am good at negotiating.
12. _____ I like to discuss topics that interest me.
    _____ **TOTAL for Verbal–Linguistic**

13. _____ I use maps easily.
14. _____ I draw pictures/diagrams when explaining ideas.
15. _____ I can assemble items easily from diagrams.
16. _____ I enjoy drawing or photography.
17. _____ I do not like to read long paragraphs.
18. _____ I prefer a drawn map over written directions.
    _____ **TOTAL for Visual–Spatial**

19. _____ I like math in school.
20. _____ I like science.
21. _____ I problem-solve well.
22. _____ I question how things work.
23. _____ I enjoy planning or designing something new.
24. _____ I am able to fix things.
    _____ **TOTAL for Logical–Mathematical**

25. _____ I listen to music.
26. _____ I move my fingers or feet when I hear music.
27. _____ I have good rhythm.
28. _____ I like to sing along with music.
29. _____ People have said I have musical talent.
30. _____ I like to express my ideas through music.
    _____ **TOTAL for Musical**

31. _____ I need quiet time to think.
32. _____ I think about issues before I want to talk.
33. _____ I am interested in self-improvement.
34. _____ I understand my thoughts and feelings.
35. _____ I know what I want out of life.
36. _____ I prefer to work on projects alone.
    _____ **TOTAL for Intrapersonal**

37. _____ I like doing a project with other people.
38. _____ People come to me to help settle conflicts.
39. _____ I like to spend time with friends.
40. _____ I am good at understanding people.
41. _____ I am good at making people feel comfortable.
42. _____ I enjoy helping others.
    _____ **TOTAL for Interpersonal**

43. _____ I enjoy nature whenever possible.
44. _____ I think about having a career involving nature.
45. _____ I enjoy studying plants, animals, or oceans.
46. _____ I avoid being indoors except when I sleep.
47. _____ As a child I played with bugs and leaves.
48. _____ When I feel stressed I want to be out in nature.
    _____ **TOTAL for Naturalistic**

67

Adapted by Joyce Bishop, Ph.D., from *Seven Pathways of Learning*, David Lazear, © 1994.

SKILLS	STUDY TECHNIQUES
Verbal–Linguistic • Analyzing own use of language • Remembering terms easily • Explaining, teaching, learning, using humor • Understanding syntax and meaning of words • Convincing someone to do something	**Verbal–Linguistic** • Read text and highlight no more than 10% • Rewrite notes • Outline chapters • Teach someone else • Recite information or write scripts/debates
Musical–Rhythmic • Sensing tonal qualities • Creating or enjoying melodies and rhythms • Being sensitive to sounds and rhythms • Using "schemas" to hear music • Understanding the structure of music	**Musical–Rhythmic** • Create rhythms out of words • Beat out rhythms with hand or stick • Play instrumental music/write raps • Put new material to songs you already know • Take music breaks
Logical–Mathematical • Recognizing abstract patterns • Reasoning inductively and deductively • Discerning relationships and connections • Performing complex calculations • Reasoning scientifically	**Logical–Mathematical** • Organize material logically • Explain material sequentially to someone • Develop systems and find patterns • Write outlines and develop charts and graphs • Analyze information
Visual–Spatial • Perceiving and forming objects accurately • Recognizing relationships between objects • Representing something graphically • Manipulating images • Finding one's way in space	**Visual–Spatial** • Develop graphic organizers for new material • Draw mind maps • Develop charts and graphs • Use color in notes to organize • Visualize material (method of loci)
Bodily–Kinesthetic • Connecting mind and body • Controlling movement • Improving body functions • Expanding body awareness to all senses • Coordinating body movement	**Bodily–Kinesthetic** • Move or rap while you learn; pace and recite • Use "method of loci" or manipulatives • Move fingers under words while reading • Create "living sculptures" • Act out scripts of material, design games
Intrapersonal • Evaluating own thinking • Being aware of and expressing feelings • Understanding self in relationship to others • Thinking and reasoning on higher levels	**Intrapersonal** • Reflect on personal meaning of information • Visualize information/keep a journal • Study in quiet settings • Imagine experiments
Interpersonal • Seeing things from others' perspectives • Cooperating within a group • Communicating verbally and nonverbally • Creating and maintaining relationships	**Interpersonal** • Study in a group • Discuss information • Use flash cards with others • Teach someone else
Naturalist • Deep understanding of nature • Appreciation of the delicate balance in nature	**Naturalist** • Connect with nature whenever possible • Form study groups of people with like interests

STEP 1. **Rank order** all four responses to each question from most like you (4) to least like you (1). Use the boxes next to the responses to indicate your rankings.

1. I like instructors who
   a. ☐ tell me exactly what is expected of me.
   b. ☐ make learning active and exciting.
   c. ☐ maintain a safe and supportive classroom.
   d. ☐ challenge me to think at higher levels.

2. I learn best when the material is
   a. ☐ well organized.
   b. ☐ something I can do hands-on.
   c. ☐ about understanding and improving the human condition.
   d. ☐ intellectually challenging.

3. A high priority in my life is to
   a. ☐ keep my commitments.
   b. ☐ experience as much of life as possible.
   c. ☐ make a difference in the lives of others.
   d. ☐ understand how things work.

4. Other people think of me as
   a. ☐ dependable and loyal.
   b. ☐ dynamic and creative.
   c. ☐ caring and honest.
   d. ☐ intelligent and inventive.

5. When I experience stress I would most likely
   a. ☐ do something to help me feel more in control of my life.
   b. ☐ do something physical and daring.
   c. ☐ talk with a friend.
   d. ☐ go off by myself and think about my situation.

6. I would probably not be close friends with someone who is
   a. ☐ irresponsible.
   b. ☐ unwilling to try new things.
   c. ☐ selfish and unkind to others.
   d. ☐ an illogical thinker.

7. My vacations could be described as
   a. ☐ traditional.
   b. ☐ adventuresome.
   c. ☐ pleasing to others.
   d. ☐ a new learning experience.

8. One word that best describes me is
   a. ☐ sensible.
   b. ☐ spontaneous.
   c. ☐ giving.
   d. ☐ analytical.

STEP 2. Add up the total points for each letter.

TOTAL for a. ☐ Organizer   TOTAL for c. ☐ Giver

TOTAL for b. ☐ Adventurer   TOTAL for d. ☐ Thinker

STEP 3. Plot these numbers on the brain diagram on page 71.

THINKER

Personal strengths—You enjoy solving problems and love to develop models and systems. You have an abstract and analytical way of thinking. You love to explore ideas. You dislike unfairness and wastefulness. You are global by nature, always seeking universal truth.

Work/school—You work best when assigned projects that require analytical thinking and problem solving. You are inspired by futuristic ideas and potentials. You need the freedom to go beyond the established rules. You feel appreciated when praised for your ingenuity. You dislike repetitive tasks.

Relationships—You thrive in relationships that recognize your need for independence and private time to think and read. Stress can come from the fear of appearing foolish. You want others to accept that you feel deeply even though you may not often express it.

Learning—You like quiet time to reflect on new information. Learning through problem solving and designing new ways of approaching issues is most interesting to you. You may find it effective to convert material you need to learn into logical charts and graphs.

ORGANIZER

Personal strengths—You value the traditions of family and support social structures. You never take responsibility lightly. You have a strong sense of history, culture, and dignity. You value order and predictability. You dislike disobedience or nonconformity. You value loyalty and obligation.

Work/school—You enjoy work that requires detailed planning and follow-through. You prefer to have tasks defined in clear and concrete terms. You need a well-structured, stable environment, free from abrupt changes. You feel appreciated when you are praised for neatness, organization, and efficiency. You like frequent feedback so you know you are on the right track.

Relationships—You do best in relationships that provide for your need of security, stability, and structure. You appreciate it when dates that are important to you are remembered by others.

Learning—You must have organization to the material and know the overall plan and what will be required of you. Depending on your most developed Multiple Intelligences, organizing the material could include any of the following: highlighting key terms in text, rewriting and organizing notes from class or text, making flash cards.

GIVER

Personal strengths—You value honesty and authenticity above all else. You enjoy close relationships with those you love and there is a strong spirituality in your nature. Making a difference in the world is important to you, and you enjoy cultivating potential in yourself and others. You are a person of peace. You are a natural romantic. You dislike hypocrisy and deception.

Work/school—You function best in a warm, harmonious working environment with the possibility of interacting with openness and honesty. You prefer to avoid conflict and hostility. You thrive when your creative approach to your work is appreciated and praised.

Relationships—You thrive in relationships that include warm, intimate talks. You feel closer to people when they express their feelings and are open and responsive. You think romance, touch, and appreciation are necessary for survival. You blossom when others express a loving commitment to you and you are able to contribute to the relationship.

Learning—You enjoy studying with others and also helping them learn. Study groups are very effective for you to remember difficult information.

ADVENTURER

Personal strengths—Your strength is skillfulness. You take pride in being highly skilled in a variety of fields. Adventure is your middle name. A hands-on approach to problem solving is important to you. You need variety, and waiting is like "emotional death." You live in the here and now. It is your impulsiveness that drives everything you do. You dislike rigidity and authority.

Work/school—You function best in a work environment that is action-packed with a hands-on approach. You appreciate the opportunity to be skillful and adventurous, and to use your natural ability as a negotiator. You like freedom on the job so you can perform in nontraditional ways and in your own style. Keeping a good sense of humor and avoiding boredom on the job is important to you. You feel appreciated when your performance and skills are acknowledged.

Relationships—You function best in relationships that recognize your need for freedom. You thrive on spontaneous playfulness and excitement.

Learning—You learn exciting and stimulating information easiest, so pick classes and instructors care-fully. Study with fun people in a variety of ways and places. Keep on the move. Develop games and puzzles to help memorize terminology.

THINKER

Technical
Scientific
Mathematical
Dispassionate
Rational
Analytical
Logical
Problem Solving
Theoretical
Intellectual
Objective
Quantitative
Explicit
Realistic
Literal
Precise
Formal

ORGANIZER

Tactical
Planning
Detailed
Practical
Confident
Predictable
Controlled
Dependable
Systematic
Sequential
Structured
Administrative
Procedural
Organized
Conservative
Safekeeping
Disciplined

Directions: Place a dot on the appropriate number line for each of your four scores, connect the dots, and color each polygon. Write your scores in the four shaded boxes.

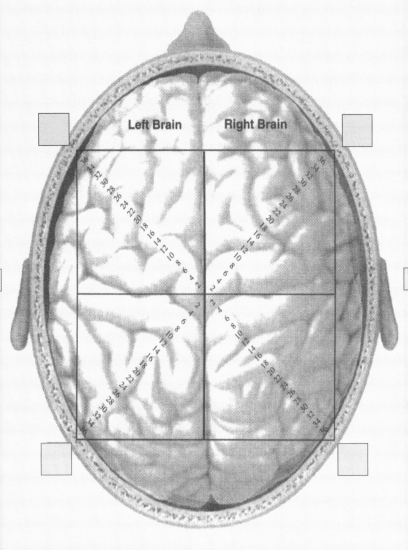

Left Brain   Right Brain

Source: Understanding Psychology, 3/e, by Morris, © 1996. Adapted by permission of Prentice-Hall, Inc., Upper Saddle River, NJ.

GIVER

Interpersonal
Emotional
Caring
Sociable
Giving
Spiritual
Musical
Romantic
Feeling
Peacemaker
Trusting
Adaptable
Passionate
Harmonious
Idealistic
Talkative
Honest

ADVENTURER

Active
Visual
Risking
Original
Artistic
Spatial
Skillful
Impulsive
Metaphoric
Experimental
Divergent
Fast-paced
Simultaneous
Competitive
Imaginative
Open-minded
Adventuresome

Pathways to Learning

From page 67, write your 8 Multiple Intelligences in the boxes, according to your total scores.

SCORES: 21–24 = HIGHLY DEVELOPED	15–20 = MODERATELY DEVELOPED	BELOW 15 = UNDERDEVELOPED

Using a separate sheet of paper, complete the following.

Thinking Back

1. Name your three most dominant intelligences (based on the Pathways to Learning assessment), and for each one, name a strength of yours associated with that intelligence.

2. Name your two most dominant areas from the Personality Spectrum, and for each, name a limitation associated with it.

3. What surprised you about your investigation of how you learn?

4. Name three study strategies that fit your needs, based on your learning styles assessments.

Thinking Ahead

1. If you feel that your work in school is complicated by a learning disability, ADD, ADHD, or any other disorder, name it and describe how you believe it affects your performance.

2. Name one habit of yours that you consider "good" and one that you consider "bad," and briefly tell why you would label them this way.

3. Name two areas of study or work that interest you. Then, name a major that corresponds to each.

4. Name two majors that you might consider based on your learning styles assessments—and indicate which intelligence or Personality Spectrum dimension corresponds to each major.

HOW CAN YOU IDENTIFY AND MANAGE LEARNING DISABILITIES?

Almost everyone has some measure of difficulty in some aspect of learning. Someone may be a brilliant writer, for example, who has trouble following driving directions, or an accounting whiz who makes frequent spelling errors. Almost anyone, if asked, can identify a personal stumbling block—for example, organization, math, visual and spatial knowledge, or relating to others.

Learning disabilities go beyond basic weakness in an area of ability. Because they can seem similar to other difficulties, however, they can be hard to identify. The following information will help. If you already have been diagnosed with a learning disability, some strategies follow that will help you manage your disability and stay positive about yourself.

Identifying a Learning Disability

The federal government, in Public Law 94–142, defines learning disabilities as follows: "Specific learning disability means a disorder in one or more of the basic psychological processes involved in understanding or in using language, spoken or written, which may manifest itself in an imperfect ability to listen, think, speak, read, write, spell, or to do mathematical calculations." A learning disability diagnosis results from specific testing done by a qualified professional, and may also involve documentation from instructors and family members.

The National Center for Learning Disabilities (NCLD) has published the important facts that will help you define and identify learning disability.[3]

- *A learning disability is a neurological disorder that interferes with one's ability to store, process, and produce information.* Learning disabilities can affect reading, writing, speaking, math abilities, areas of development, or social skills.

- *Learning disabilities do not include mental retardation, autism, or behavioral disorders.* Generally, learning disabled people are of average or above-average intelligence. The learning disability creates a "gap" that prevents them from performing according to their abilities.

- *Learning disabilities do not include impaired vision, hearing loss, or other physical disabilities.* The learning issue is separate from other physical issues that may be present.

- *Learning disabilities are lifelong.* You cannot be cured of a learning disability. However, you can use specific strategies to manage and even overcome areas of weakness.

- *Learning disabilities often run in families.* Although exact causes are not certain, researchers have found that heredity seems to play a significant role. Problems during pregnancy and birth, and incidents after birth, such as abuse or lead poisoning, may also contribute.

- *Learning disabilities must be diagnosed by professionals in order for the person with the disability to receive federally funded aid.* A professional will use a mix of interview, observation, and assessment tools to determine a diagnosis.

Now that you know a few facts, how can you determine if you should be evaluated for a learning disability? Although many people have one or more learning issues from time to time, a frequent problem with one or more might indicate that you should investigate further. The NCLD recommends you watch out for persistent problems with any of the following:[4]

- reading or reading comprehension
- math calculations, math language, and math concepts
- social skills or interpreting social cues
- following a schedule, being on time, or meeting deadlines
- reading or following maps
- balancing a checkbook
- following directions, especially on multi-step tasks
- writing, sentence structure, spelling, and organizing written work

If you feel that you would like to explore the possibility of an evaluation, contact your school learning center or student health center for a referral to a licensed professional, such as a psychologist or medical doctor. Evaluations may involve costs that may or may not be covered by your insurance or federal funding. Talk to any prospective evaluators to find out their credentials, what the evaluation involves, and what follow-up services will be provided.

An important note: Contrary to popular belief, ADD (Attention Deficit Disorder) and ADHD (Attention Deficit Hyperactivity Disorder) are not classified as learning disabilities. They do, however, often cause problems with learning, and a student may have ADD or ADHD in addition to particular learning disabilities.[5]

Although only a small percentage of the student population has a diagnosable learning disability, these students are as capable of success as any other student and deserve support. If you are diagnosed with a learning disability, read on to explore ways to get the help you need.

Managing a Learning Disability

If you have a learning disability, maintaining self-esteem may be your biggest challenge. You might feel like you are experiencing constant failure. You may compare yourself to others, labeling as failure anything that does not live up to the examples set by students around you. You can beat this **attitude**, though, by knowing and using strategies that address your specific issue. Table 3.2 shows some useful strategies for different learning disabilities and other conditions.

You will also benefit from becoming a strong advocate for your rights as a student with special needs, and by redefining failure and success in terms of your own accomplishments. Consider the following strategies.

ATTITUDE

A state of mind or feeling toward something.

BE INFORMED ABOUT YOUR DISABILITY. The more you know, the more able you will be to find the help you need. Use the library to find books on your learning disability. Search the Internet—you can find NCLD at **www.ncld.org** or LD Online at **www.ldonline.org.** You can also call NCLD toll-free at 1-888-575-7373. When you are diagnosed, you will receive an Individualized Education Program (IEP) that details your disability and the strategies recommended to manage it. Make sure you understand what's in your IEP.

SEEK ASSISTANCE FROM YOUR SCHOOL. If you are officially diagnosed with a learning disability, you are legally entitled to particular aid. Armed with your test results and IEP, speak with your advisor about how you can secure specific accommodations that will help you learn. Among the services mandated by law for learning disabled students are:

- extended time on tests
- note-taking assistance (e.g., having a fellow student take notes for you)
- assistive technology devices (e.g., tape recorders or laptop computers)
- modified assignments
- alternative assessments and test formats (e.g., having extended time)

Information on learning disabilities and other conditions.

DISABILITY/CONDITION	DESCRIPTION	HELPFUL STRATEGIES
Developmental writing disorders	Difficulties in composing complete sentences, organizing a writing assignment, or in translating thoughts coherently to the page	Take extra time with your work. Use visual organizers to map out your thoughts before you write. Be sure to include a delay between drafting and revising an assignment. Use spell check and grammar check. Have your work evaluated by a peer editor or tutor.
Dyscalculia (developmental arithmetic disorders)	Difficulties in recognizing numbers and symbols, memorizing facts, aligning numbers, and understanding abstract concepts like fractions	Estimate answers before you start work on problems. Work in groups so that you benefit from listening to others. Draw or graph problems if you are a strong visual learner. Ask someone to help you reword a problem so that it makes sense.
Dyslexia and related reading disorders	Problems with translating written language to thought or thought to written language (often involving problems with spelling, word sequencing, comprehension)	Find a tutor who can give you a multisensory experience of reading—teaching reading not just through sight but also through hearing, writing, and speaking. Approach reading by learning the sounds of letters and letter combinations systematically.
Speech and language disorders	Problems with producing speech sounds, using spoken language to communicate, or understanding what others say	Seek a therapist who knows how to address your particular disorder. Write or type when this will allow you to communicate more clearly than when speaking.
ADD/ADHD	Disorders involving consistent and problematic inattention, hyperactivity, or impulsivity	Structure will help; establish time structures, rules, and routines for academic, work, and personal situations. Ask instructors to clarify instructions when they aren't clear enough for you. List problematic behaviors and set rewards for yourself when you avoid them. Medication is sometimes prescribed based on a medical evaluation.
LD-related organizational issues	Difficulties in scheduling and in organizing personal, academic, and work-related materials	Structure and routine are key; establish regular modes of behavior (spending 10 minutes with your date book every morning, keeping a day planner program open on your computer screen at work). Find a "buddy" who can check in on you and keep you on track.
LD-related social issues	Problems in recognizing facial or vocal cues from others, controlling verbal and physical impulsivity, and respecting others' personal space	With a trusted friend, family member, or professional counselor or therapist, practice appropriate behavior. Look at past situations and evaluate the effects of your behavior.

Source: LD Online: Learning Disabilities Information and Resources, **www.ldonline.org/** accessed 1/6/01. © 2001 WETA.

Other services that may help learning disabled students include tutoring, study skills assistance, and counseling. Know, and ask for, what works best for you.

SEEK ASSISTANCE AT WORK. Employers are required by law to make accommodations for learning disabled employees as long as it does not impose an "undue hardship" to the company.[6] Such accommodations might include things like modified work schedules and interpreters. Employers also must not discriminate against learning disabled employees (such as in hiring, testing, salary, or benefits). Not all learning disabled employees need accommodations, but if you are a qualified employee who does, speak to someone whom you trust. It is in your employer's best interest to help you work to the best of your ability.

BE A DEDICATED STUDENT. Perhaps more than for other students, your focus and dedication will help you get where you want to go. Be on time and attend as many class meetings as you can. Read the assignments before class. Sit up front. Review your notes as soon after class as you can. Plan to spend extra time on assignments. Ask instructors for help.

BUILD A SUCCESSFUL ATTITUDE. See your accomplishments in light of where you were before and how far you have come. Keep a list of your successes and refer to it often to reinforce positive feelings. Rely on people in your life who support you and see you as a capable person. Focus on what you do well, not just on what causes you difficulty. Know that the help you receive at school is deserved—it will give you the best possible chance to learn and grow.

HOW CAN YOU DEVELOP POSITIVE HABITS?

> **HABIT**
>
> A preference for a particular action that you do a certain way, and often on a regular basis or at certain times.

Your personality and intelligences play an important role in the development of habits. A verbal learner might have a **habit** of reading the paper daily, while a visual learner may prefer to get the news from TV. An adventurer may habitually go out of town on the weekend, while an organizer may spend weekends getting things in order at home.

You may consider some habits "bad" and others "good." Bad habits earn that title because they can prevent you from reaching important goals. Some bad habits, such as chronic lateness, cause obvious problems. Other habits, such as renting movies three times a week, may not seem bad until you realize that you needed to spend those hours studying. People maintain bad habits because they offer immediate, enjoyable rewards, even if later effects are negative. For example, going out to eat frequently may drain your budget, but at first it seems easier than shopping for food, cooking, and washing dishes.

Good habits are those that have positive effects on your life. You often have to wait longer and work harder to see a reward for good habits, which makes them harder to maintain. If you cut out fattening foods, you won't lose weight in two days. If you reduce your nights out to gain study time, your grades won't improve in a week. When you strive to maintain good habits, trust that the rewards are somewhere down the road. Changing a habit can be a long process.

Evaluate your habits. Look at the positive and negative effects of each, and decide which help and which cause harm. Take the following steps to evaluate a habit and, if necessary, make a change (if the habit has more negative effects than positive ones). Don't try to change more than one habit at a time—trying to reach perfection in everything all at once can overwhelm you.

1. *Honestly admit your habit.* Admitting negative or destructive habits can be hard to do. You can't change a habit until you admit that it is a habit.

2. *Evaluate your habit.* What are the negative and positive effects? Are there more negatives than positives, or vice versa? Look at effects carefully because at times the trouble may not seem to come directly from the habit. For example, spending every weekend working on the house may seem important, but you may be overdoing it and ignoring friends and family members.

> *To fall into a habit is to begin to cease to be.*
>
> **MIGUEL UNAMUNO**

3. *If necessary, decide to change.* You might realize what your bad habits are but not yet care about their effects on your life. Until you are convinced that you will receive a benefit, efforts to change will not get you far.

4. *Start today.* Don't put it off until after this week, after the family reunion, or after the semester. Each day lost is a day you haven't had the chance to benefit from a new lifestyle.

5. *Reward yourself appropriately for positive steps taken.* If you earn a good grade, avoid slacking off on your studies the following week. If you've lost weight, avoid celebrating in an ice-cream parlor. Choose a reward that will not encourage you to stray from your target.

6. *Keep it up.* To have the best chance at changing a habit, be consistent for at least three weeks. Your brain needs time to become accustomed to the new habit. If you go back to the old habit during that time, you may feel like you're starting all over again.

Finally, don't get too discouraged if the process seems difficult. Rarely does someone make the decision to change and do so without a setback or two. Being too hard on yourself might cause frustration that tempts you to give up and go back to the habit. Take it one step at a time and use what you know from Chapter 1 to spur your motivation when you lose steam.

All of the self knowledge you are building will be very important for your educational decisions. Take what you know into account when thinking about your choice of major.

HOW CAN YOU START THINKING ABOUT CHOOSING A MAJOR?

Many students come to college knowing what they want to study, but many do not. That's completely normal. College is a perfect time to begin exploring your different interests. In the process, you may discover

How can I make the most of my learning style?

Anwar Smith, *Taylor University, Upland, Indiana, Christian Education Major*

Recently I took a multiple intelligences assessment. Some of it confirmed what I already knew, but some results were more surprising. I always knew I like to talk things out. I learn best through discussion. I also answered questions that showed I have a high degree of interpersonal intelligence, and I scored well in the verbal–linguistic category.

In addition to academics, I play football at Taylor and am managing to keep my GPA up. I'm trying to get all I can out of my education. When I graduate, I would like to go back to the inner city of Chicago where I grew up and help young people achieve their goals.

I am wondering how my learning style will affect what I want to do with my future. What do you think all this means regarding my study and work habits?

Rev. Eric Gerard Pearman, M. Div., *Ph.D. candidate at the University of Denver, Denver, Colorado*

First of all, I want to commend you on your vision and desire to return to the inner city of Chicago and help young people. Your verbal and interpersonal intelligences are well-suited for one who feels the "call" to reach out and meet the needs of youth in Chicago's inner city. Your verbal–linguistic results indicate that you like to talk things out and that you learn best in group discussions. Should you ever find yourself in a classroom setting that doesn't permit much discussion, find a classmate that you can talk with about the things you are learning.

Communication is key to solving the problems that affect inner-city children. We need people like yourself who will talk *to* them rather than talk *at* them and who will show them that they can achieve success rather than falling victim to the negative influences around them. We need people who will help them to help themselves rather than depending on others to help them.

I mention this because God has brought me from a single-parent home in the Ida B. Wells housing project on Chicago's south side through street gang activity and into a doctoral program with the desire to reach out to the "least of these" in my old neighborhood. My mother demanded excellence and provided me with the values that helped me make good choices during difficult moments. Participating in gang-related activity and seeing fellow peers killed during my adolescent years made me realize that I needed to explore another path in life. Positive influences at a church across the street reinforced the values that my mother taught and helped me to see that because I lived in "projects" did not mean that the projects had to live in me.

You obviously have a strong work ethic and deep concern for people. These skills, along with

your intelligences, might lead you to consider a seminary education. Seminary can give you an academic challenge and a chance to develop the skills needed for urban ministry. My 1990 Master of Divinity degree has given me opportunities from teaching to pastoral.

I challenge you to pursue a Ph.D. in the future, whether to teach, pastor, or work within some capacity of a youth-related ministry. Furthering your education will help you provide young people with an understanding and appreciation for educational achievement, and the benefits that will result from such hard studying and determination.

talents and strengths you never realized you had. For example, taking an environmental class may teach you that you have a passion for finding solutions to pollution problems, or you may discover a talent for public speaking and decide to explore on-camera journalism.

Although some of your explorations may take you down paths that don't resonate with your personality and interests, each experience will help to clarify who you really are and what you want to do with your life. Thinking about choosing a major involves identifying your interests, exploring potential majors, planning your curriculum, linking majors to career areas, being open to changing majors, and following your heart.

Identify Your Interests

The best majors and careers for you are ones that involve your interests. Look at your dominant intelligences and personality traits for clues. For example, a giver may be interested in service professions, an interpersonal learner may want to work with people, or a naturalistic learner might have nature as a primary interest.

Other ideas about your interests may come from asking yourself questions such as these.

- What areas of study do I like?
- What activities make me happy?
- What careers seem interesting to me?
- What kind of daily schedule do I like to keep (early riser or night owl)?
- What type of home and work environment do I prefer?

Interests play an important role in the workplace. Many people, however, do not take their interests seriously when choosing a career. Some make salary or stability their first priority. Some take the first job that comes along. Some may not realize they can do better. Not considering your interests may lead to an area of study or a job that leaves you unhappy, bored, or unfulfilled.

Choosing to consider your interests and happiness takes courage but brings benefits. Think about it: You spend hours attending classes and studying outside of class. You will probably spend at least eight hours a day, five or more days a week, up to 50 or more weeks a year as a working contributor to the world. Although your studies and work won't always make you deliriously happy, it is possible to spend your school and work time in a manner that suits you.

Here are three positive effects of focusing on your interests.

YOU WILL HAVE MORE ENERGY. When you're doing something you like, time seems to pass quickly. Contrast this with how you feel about disagreeable activities. The difference in your energy level is immense. You will be able to get much more done in a subject or career area that you enjoy.

YOU WILL PERFORM BETTER. When you were in high school, you probably got your best grades in your favorite classes. That doesn't change as you get older. The more you like something, the harder you work at it—and the harder you work, the more you will improve.

YOU WILL HAVE A MORE POSITIVE ATTITUDE. A positive attitude creates a positive environment and might even make up for areas in which you lack ability or experience. This is especially important for teamwork. Because businesses currently emphasize teamwork to such a great extent, your ability to maintain a positive attitude might mean the difference between success and failure.

Explore Potential Majors

The following steps will help you explore majors that interest you:

CONSIDER YOUR LEARNING STYLE. Many majors emphasize particular learning styles. For example, science and math curricula demand strength in analytical thinking, and education courses often involve extensive interpersonal interaction. Look at your stronger and weaker areas and see what majors are likely to make the most of what you do well. If you are drawn to a major that requires ability in one of your weaker areas, explore the major to see where you would need extra help and where your strengths would benefit you.

If you don't risk anything, you risk even more.

ERICA JONG

TAKE A VARIETY OF CLASSES. Although you will generally have core requirements to fulfill, use your electives to branch out. Try to take at least one class in each area that sparks your interest.

KNOW YOUR INTERESTS. The more you know about yourself, the more ability you will have to focus on areas that make the most of who you are and what you can do. Pay close attention to which areas inspire you to greater heights and which areas seem to deaden your initiative.

WORK CLOSELY WITH YOUR ADVISOR. Begin discussing your major early on with your advisor, even if you don't intend to declare right away. For any given major, your advisor may be able to tell you about the coursework and career possibilities. Consider a double major (completing the requirements for two different majors) if your school offers that possibility.

TAKE ADVANTAGE OF OTHER RESOURCES. Seek opinions from instructors, friends, and family members. Talk to students who have declared majors that interest you. Explore the course materials your college gives you in order to see what majors your college offers.

DEVELOP YOUR CRITICAL-THINKING SKILLS. Working toward any major will help you develop your most important skill—knowing how to use your mind. Critical thinking is the most crucial ingredient in any recipe for school and career success. More than anything, your future career and employer will depend on your ability to contribute to the workplace through clear, effective, and creative thinking.

Plan Your Curriculum

You won't necessarily want to plan out your entire college course load at the beginning of your first semester. However, you might find some advantages to thinking through your choices ahead of time. Planning your **curriculum** can help you feel more in control of your choices by giving you a clearer idea of where you are headed. It can also help you avoid pitfalls, such as not being able to secure a space in a course that you need to complete your major. When students wait until the last minute to register for the following semester, some courses they want have already been filled; as a result, they may have to take courses they would not necessarily have chosen.

> **CURRICULUM**
>
> The particular set of courses required for any degree.

Take advantage of the following ideas and strategies when working to plan your college curriculum.

CONSULT YOUR COLLEGE CATALOG. You will get the broadest idea of your possibilities by exploring everything your college offers. In addition, what is available to you may go beyond your college's doors. Check into "study abroad" programs (spending a semester or a year at an affiliated college in a different country) or opportunities to take courses at nearby schools that have arrangements with your school.

LOOK AT THE MAJORS THAT INTEREST YOU. Each major offered by your college has a list of required courses, which you will find online or in your catalog, or can get from an academic advisor. The list may also indicate a recommended order in which you should take the courses—certain courses your first year, others your second year, and so on. The list will help you determine whether you will like what you will be doing over the next few semesters if you choose a particular major.

BRANCH OUT. Even if you already have a pretty clear idea of your primary area of study, look into courses in other interesting areas that don't necessarily connect to your major. Enlarging the scope of your knowledge will help to improve your critical thinking, broaden your perspectives, and perhaps introduce you to career possibilities you had never even considered.

GET CREATIVE. Do you have a particular idea about what you want to major in but don't see it listed in your college catalog? Don't immediately assume it's impossible. Talk with your academic advisor. Some schools allow certain students to design their own majors with help and approval from their advisors. In such a case, you and your advisor would come up with a unique list of courses on your own.

Link Majors to Career Areas

The point of declaring and pursuing a major is to help you reach a significant level of knowledge in one subject, often in preparation for a particular career area. Before you discard a major as not practical enough, consider where it might be able to take you. Thinking through the possibilities may open doors that you never knew existed. Besides finding an exciting path, you may discover a path that is highly marketable and beneficial to humankind as well.

For each major there are many career options that aren't obvious right away. For example, a student working toward teaching certification doesn't have to teach in a public school. This student could develop curricula, act as a consultant for businesses, develop an online education service, teach overseas for the Peace Corps, or create a public television program. The sky's the limit.

Explore the educational requirements of any career area that interests you. Your choice of major may be more or less crucial depending on the career area. For example, pursuing a career in medicine almost always requires a major in some area of the biological sciences, whereas aspiring lawyers may have majored in anything from political science to philosophy. Many employers are more interested in your ability to think than in your specific knowledge; therefore, they may not pay as much attention to your major as they do to your critical-thinking skills. Ask advisors or people in your areas of interest what educational background is necessary or helpful to someone pursuing a career in that area.

Be Open to Changing Majors

Some people may change their minds several times before finding a major that fits. Although this may add to the time you spend in college, being happy with your decision is important. For example, an education major may begin student teaching only to discover that he really doesn't feel comfortable in front of students. Or, a student may declare English as a major only to realize that her passion is in religion.

If this happens to you, don't be discouraged. Changing a major is much like changing a job. Skills and experiences from one job will assist you in your next position, and some of the courses from your first major may apply—may transfer as credits—to your next major. Talk with your academic advisor about any desire to change majors.

Whatever you decide, realize that you do have the right to change your mind. Continual self-discovery is part of the journey. No matter how many detours you make, each interesting class you take along the way helps to point you toward a major that feels like home.

Follow Your Heart

Friends or parents may have warned you against certain careers, encouraging you to stay with "safe" careers that seem socially acceptable or that pay well. Prestige and money may be important—but they usually are not viable replacements for deep personal satisfaction. If for you the path of the heart diverges from the safe path, the choice may be very challenging. Only you can decide which is the best for you. Remember that this is your life, and you are the one who has to live with the choices you make. Make a choice that leads you toward the life you have dreamed of. Make a choice that makes the most of the real you.

Sabiduria

In Spanish, the term *sabiduria* represents the two sides of learning: knowledge and wisdom. Knowledge—building what you know about how the world works—is the first part. Wisdom—deriving meaning and significance from knowledge and deciding how to use it—is the second. As you continually learn and experience new things, the *sabiduria* you build will help you make knowledgeable and wise choices about how to lead your life.

Think of this concept as you discover more about how you learn and receive knowledge in all aspects of your life—in school, work, and personal situations. As you learn how your unique mind works and how to use it, you can more confidently assert yourself. As you expand your ability to use your mind in different ways, you can create lifelong advantages for yourself.

IMPORTANT POINTS *to remember*

1. What is a learning style?

A learning style is a particular way in which the mind receives and processes information. Each person has a particular learning style that best fits his capabilities. There is no one way to learn that's best for everyone—the key is to identify your particular gifts. Every individual has some highly developed areas and some underdeveloped areas of ability. How you learn may also change in response to training, life experience, and challenges. Knowing your learning style can help you improve your effectiveness at school, at work, and in life.

2. How can you discover how you learn?

Many assessments exist that can help you draw the picture of your learning styles. One is the Pathways to Learning inventory, based on Howard Gardner's Multiple Intelligences Theory. This theory says that people have varying degrees of development within eight different intelligences. Another is the Personality Spectrum, based on the Myers-Briggs assessment, which gives you a personality-based perspective on how you function at school and at work. Taking a reasonable approach toward learning styles involves using assessment results as a reference point rather than a label, a way to expand your idea of yourself instead of boxing yourself into a category.

3. How can you identify and manage learning disabilities?

Going beyond basic weakness in an area of ability, a learning disability is a neurological disorder that interferes with one's ability to store, process, and produce information. Generally, learning disabled people are of average or above-average intelligence. The disability prevents them from realizing their potential. Learning disabilities may involve problems with reading, math, organization, social interaction, and writing.

If you have a learning disability that is diagnosed by a professional, you are eligible to receive federally funded aid. You can help yourself by being informed about your disability and by seeking help at school and at work.

4. How can you develop positive habits?

A habit is a preference for a particular action performed in a particular way—often on a regular basis or at certain times. Bad habits prevent you from reaching important goals, while good habits have positive effects on your life. Trying to change a habit involves admitting the habit, evaluating the habit, deciding to change, starting right away, rewarding yourself, and keeping it up for at least three weeks.

5. How can you start thinking about choosing a major?

First, identify your interests. Then, take the time to explore different majors: take a variety of classes, look into majors that interest you, seek help from your advisor and other resources, and consider your learning style. Planning your curriculum ahead of time (by checking your course catalog and seeing what courses certain majors require) can help you see more clearly where you are headed. Link majors to career areas by looking at where a particular major might lead you in the working world. Finally, be open to changing majors if you declare a major that later doesn't seem to fit, and don't be afraid to follow your heart, even if it may not be what others think you should pursue.

CRITICAL THINKING

APPLYING LEARNING TO LIFE

LEARNING ABOUT HOW YOU LEARN. Your learning style profile can provide information that will help you make the best possible decisions about your future. List your four strongest intelligences.

_____

_____

Describe a positive experience at work or school that you can attribute to these strengths.

_____

_____

_____

_____

Name your four least-developed intelligences.

_____

_____

What challenge do you face that may be related to your least-developed intelligences?

_____

_____

_____

_____

Thinking about your strongest intelligences, name two majors that might make the most of those strengths.

_1._ _____

_2._ _____

For each major, name a corresponding career area you may want to explore.

1. _____

2. _____

Keep these majors and career areas in mind as you gradually narrow your course choices in the time before you declare a major.

TEAMWORK

COMBINING FORCES

IDEAS ABOUT PERSONALITY TYPES. Divide into groups according to the four types of the Personality Spectrum—Thinker-dominant students in one group, Organizer-dominant students in another, Giver-dominant students in a third, and Adventurer-dominant students in the fourth. If you have scored the same in more than one of these types, join whatever group is smaller. With your group, brainstorm four lists for your type: the strengths of this type, the struggles it brings, the things that cause particular stress for your type, and career ideas that tend to suit this type.

Strengths

  1.

  2.

and so on.

Struggles

  1.

  2.

Stressors

  1.

  2.

and so on.

Careers

  1.

  2.

If there is time, each group can present this information to the entire class to enable everyone to have a better understanding and acceptance of one another's intelligences. You might also brainstorm strategies for dealing with your intelligence's struggles and stressors, and present those ideas to the class as well.

WRITING

DISCOVERY THROUGH JOURNALING

To record your thoughts, use a separate journal or the lined page at the end of the chapter.

YOUR LEARNING STYLE. Discuss the insights you have gained through exploring your multiple intelligences. What strengths have come to your attention? What challenges have been clarified? Talk about your game plan for using your strengths and addressing your challenges both at school and in the real world.

CAREER PORTFOLIO

CHARTING YOUR COURSE

SELF-PORTRAIT. A self-portrait is an important step in your career exploration because self-knowledge will allow you to make the best choices about what to study and what career to pursue. Use this exercise to synthesize everything you have been exploring about yourself into one comprehensive "self-portrait." You will design your portrait in "think-link" style, using words and visual shapes to describe your learning style, habits, interests, abilities, and anything else you think is an important part of who you are.

A think link is a visual construction of related ideas, similar to a map or web, that represents your thought process. Ideas are written inside geometric shapes, often boxes or circles, and related ideas and facts are attached to those ideas by lines that connect the shapes. You will learn more about think links in the note-taking section in Chapter 7.

Use the style shown in the example in Figure 3.2, or create your own. For example, in this exercise you may want to create a "wheel" of ideas coming off your central shape, entitled "Me." Then, spreading out from each of those ideas (interests, learning style, etc.), you would draw lines connecting all of the thoughts that go along with that idea. Connected to "Interests," for example, might be "Singing," "Stock market," and "History." You don't have to use the wheel image. You might want to design a tree-like think link or a line of boxes with connecting thoughts written below the boxes, or anything else you like. Let your design reflect who you are, just as the think link itself does.

Sample self-portrait think link.

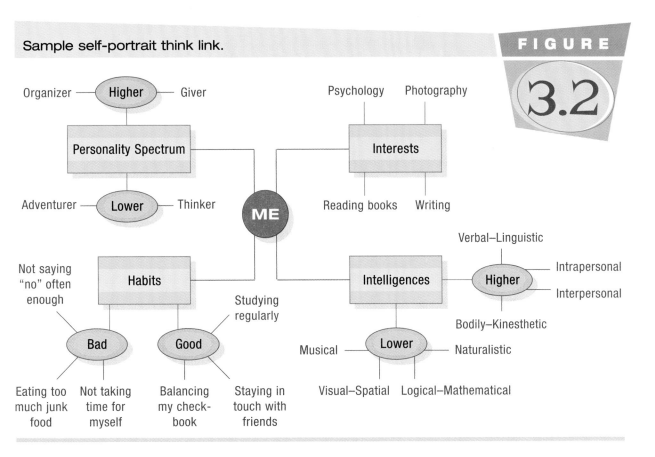

FIGURE 3.2

SUGGESTED READING

Barger, Nancy J., Linda K. Kirby, and Jean M. Kummerow. *Work Types: Understand Your Work Personality—How It Helps You and Holds You Back, and What You Can Do to Understand It.* New York: Warner Books (1997).

Cobb, Joyanne. *Learning How to Learn: A Guide for Getting Into College with a Learning Disability, Staying In, and Staying Sane.* Washington, D.C.: Child Welfare League of America (2001).

College Board, ed. *The College Board Index of Majors and Graduate Degrees 2001.* New York: College Entrance Examination Board (2000).

Gardner, Howard. *Intelligence Reframed: Multiple Intelligences for the 21st Century.* New York: Basic Books (2000).

Harrington, Paul, et al. *The College Majors Handbook: The Actual Jobs, Earnings, and Trends for Graduates of 60 College Majors.* Indianapolis, IN: Jist Works (1999).

Keirsey, David. *Please Understand Me II: Temperament, Character, Intelligence.* Del Mar, CA: Prometheus Nemesis Book Co. (1998).

Lewis, Erica-Lee and Eric L. Lewis. *Help Yourself: Handbook for College-Bound Students with Learning Disabilities.* New York: Princeton Review (1996).

Pearman, Roger R. and Sarah C. Albritton. *I'm Not Crazy, I'm Just Not You: The Real Meaning of the 16 Personality Types.* Palo Alto, CA: Consulting Psychologists Press (1997).

Phifer, Paul. *College Majors and Careers: A Resource Guide for Effective Life Planning,* 4th ed. Chicago: Ferguson Publishing (1999).

INTERNET RESOURCES

Keirsey Sorter and other Myers-Briggs information: www.keirsey.com
National Attention Deficit Disorder Association: www.add.org
National Center for Learning Disabilities: www.ncld.org

ENDNOTES

1. Howard Gardner. *Multiple Intelligences: The Theory in Practice.* New York: HarperCollins (1993), pp. 5–49.
2. Developed by Joyce Bishop, Ph.D., Psychology faculty, Golden West College, Huntington Beach, CA. Based on Howard Gardner, *Frames of Mind: The Theory of Multiple Intelligences.* New York: HarperCollins (1993).
3. National Center for Learning Disabilities. *Adult Learning Disabilities: A Learning Disability Isn't Something You Outgrow. It's Something You Learn To Master.* New York: National Center for Learning Disabilities (2000).
4. Ibid.
5. Ibid.
6. Ibid.

NAME

DATE

The Prentice Hall Supersite has a section entitled Majors Exploration. Go to www.prenhall.com/success and click on the Majors Exploration button. Choose one major that is of interest to you and use the site to answer the following questions on a separate sheet of paper. If you have time and are interested in more than one major, explore two or three.

1. Name and describe the major.

2. For what careers does this major prepare you?

3. What classes do students typically need to take in order to graduate with this major? If your school has a website, visit to determine what the specific course requirements are for this major at your school—and anything else you might need in order to be accepted into this major (such as a specific grade point average).

4. Describe how your learning style and personality make you a good candidate for this major.

5. Draw up a plan of short-term and long-term goals that would help you be successful in your major. Your plan might include:

   - courses you need to take as part of your major and your schedule for taking these courses during your time in college
   - grade point average needed in order to qualify for your major
   - meetings with academic advisors or instructors
   - organizations you could join that would be relevant to the major
   - internships to explore and apply for that would compliment this major
   - whether graduate school is a necessary step after graduating with this major

Setting the Stage for Learning

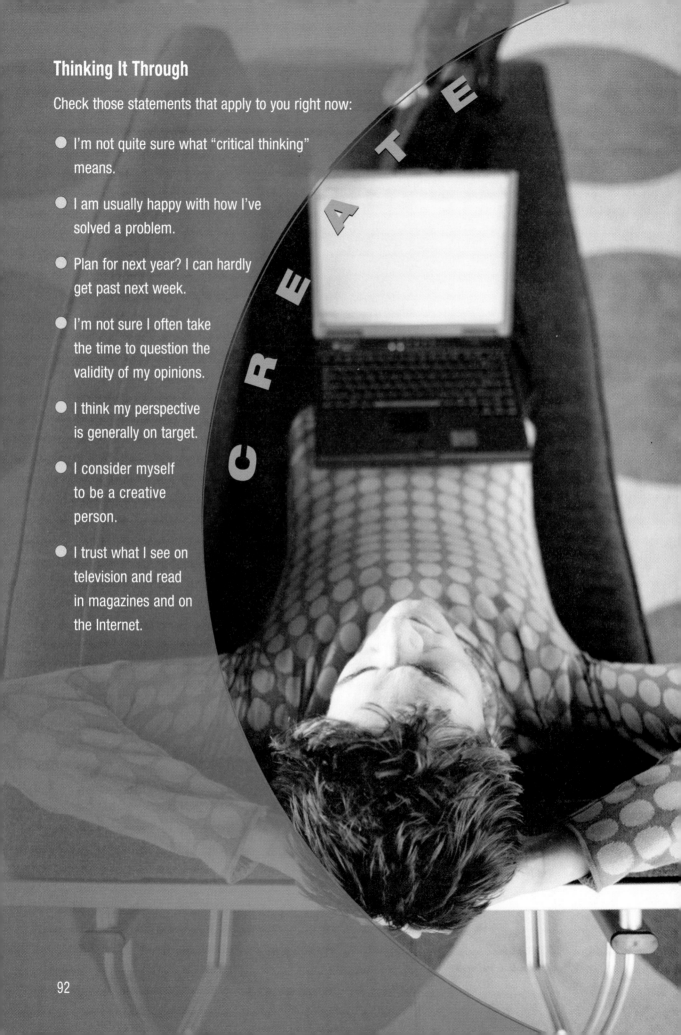

Thinking It Through

Check those statements that apply to you right now:

- I'm not quite sure what "critical thinking" means.

- I am usually happy with how I've solved a problem.

- Plan for next year? I can hardly get past next week.

- I'm not sure I often take the time to question the validity of my opinions.

- I think my perspective is generally on target.

- I consider myself to be a creative person.

- I trust what I see on television and read in magazines and on the Internet.

IN THIS CHAPTER,

you will explore answers to the following questions:

- What is critical thinking?
- How does critical thinking help you solve problems and make decisions?
- How do you construct and evaluate arguments?
- How do you think logically?
- Why should you explore perspectives?
- Why plan strategically?
- How can you develop your creativity?
- What is media literacy?

Critical and Creative Thinking

W hen you name 10 elements from the periodic table, that's thinking. When you consider how these elements interact chemically with one another to form new molecules, that's *critical* thinking. When you devise a lab experiment to demonstrate an interaction in an innovative way, that's *creative* thinking. Critical thinking is the core of active learning. Critical and creative thinking enable you to learn actively—to question, process, and create with the facts and ideas you encounter.

This chapter will help you understand how your mind works so that you can perform the essential critical-thinking task: asking important questions about ideas, information, and media. You will explore how being an open-minded critical thinker will promote your success in college, career, and life.

BECOMING AN ACTIVE LEARNER

WHAT IS CRITICAL THINKING?

Although you might figure that the word "critical" implies something difficult and negative, critical thinking is "critical" mainly in the sense of one particular dictionary definition of *critical*: "indispensable" and "important." You think critically every day, though you may not realize it.

Defining Critical Thinking

The following is one way to define critical thinking:

> Critical thinking is thinking that *goes beyond the basic recall of information* but depends on the information recalled. It focuses on the *important, or critical, aspects* of the information. Critical thinking means *asking questions.* Critical thinking means that you *take in information, question it, and then use it* to create new ideas, solve problems, make decisions, construct arguments, make plans, and refine your view of the world.

One way to clarify a concept is to consider its opposite. Not thinking critically means not examining important aspects through questioning. A person who does not think critically tends to accept or reject information or ideas without examining them. Table 4.1 compares how a critical thinker and a noncritical thinker might respond to particular situations.

Think about how you have responded to different problem situations. Are your responses more analytical and constructive when you use critical thinking than when you don't? Your analysis will help you begin to see the effect critical thinking can have on the way you live.

TABLE 4.1   Not thinking critically vs. thinking critically.

YOUR ROLE	SITUATION	NONQUESTIONING (UNCRITICAL) RESPONSE	QUESTIONING (CRITICAL) RESPONSE
STUDENT	Instructor is lecturing on the causes of the Vietnam war.	You assume everything your instructor says is true.	You consider what the instructor says, write questions about issues you want to clarify, go to the library to research the causes of the war, discuss what you learn with the instructor or classmates.
SPOUSE/ PARTNER	Your partner feels he/she does not have enough quality time with you.	You think he/she is wrong and defend yourself.	You and your partner brainstorm ways you can spend more time together.
EMPLOYEE	Your supervisor is angry with you about something that happened.	You avoid your supervisor or deny responsibility for the incident.	You talk with your supervisor about what happened and explore ways to ensure it will not happen again.

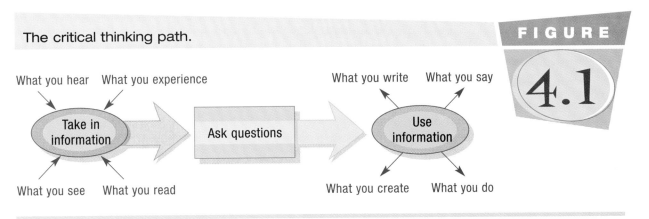

The critical thinking path.

FIGURE 4.1

The Path of Critical Thinking

Look at Figure 4.1 to see a visual representation of critical thinking. The path involves taking in information, questioning information, and then using information.

TAKING IN INFORMATION. Although most of this chapter focuses on questioning and using information, the first step of the process is just as crucial. The information you receive is your raw material that you will examine and mold into something new. If you take in information accurately and without judgment, you will have the best material with which to work as you think. Once you have the clearest, most complete information possible, then you can begin to examine its important aspects through questioning.

QUESTIONING INFORMATION. Questioning is the "action" in "active learning." A critical thinker asks many kinds of questions about a given piece of information, such as: *Where did it come from? What could explain it? In what ways is it true or false? How do I feel about it, and why? How is this information similar to or different from what I already know? Is it good or bad? What caused it, and what effects does it have?* Critical thinkers also try to transform information into something they can use. They ask whether information can help them solve a problem, make a decision, learn or create something new, or anticipate the future.

As an example of the questioning process, consider the following as your "information in": You encounter a number of situations—financial strain, parenting on your own, and being an older student—that seem to be getting in the way of your success at school. Whereas nonquestioning thinkers may assume defeat, critical thinkers will examine the situation with questions. Here are some you might ask:

"What exactly are my obstacles? Examples of my obstacles are a heavy work schedule, single parenting, being in debt, and returning to school after 10 years out." (recall)

"Are there other cases different from mine? I do have one friend who is going through problems worse than mine, and she's getting by. I also know another guy who doesn't have too much to deal with that I can tell, and he's struggling just like I am." (difference)

"Who has problems similar to mine? Well, if I consider my obstacles specifically, my statement might mean that single parents and returning adult students will all have trouble in school. That is not necessarily true. People who have trouble in school may still become successful." (similarity)

"What is an example of someone who has had success despite obstacles? What about Oseola McCarty, the cleaning woman who saved money all her life and raised $150,000 to create a scholarship at the University of Southern Mississippi? She didn't have what anyone would call advantages, such as a high-paying job or a college education." (idea to example)

"What conclusion can I draw from my questions? From thinking about my friend and about Oseola McCarty, I conclude that people can successfully overcome their obstacles by working hard, focusing on their abilities, and concentrating on their goals." (example to idea)

"Why am I worried about this? Maybe I am scared of returning to school. Maybe I am afraid to challenge myself. Whatever the cause, the effect is that I feel bad about myself and don't work to the best of my abilities, and that can hurt me and others who depend on me." (cause and effect)

"How do I evaluate the effects of my worries? I think they're harmful. When we say that obstacles equal difficulty, we can damage our desire to overcome them. When we say that successful people don't encounter obstacles, we might overlook that some very successful people have to deal with hidden disadvantages such as learning disabilities or abusive families." (evaluation)

Remember these types of questions. When you explore the seven mind actions later in the chapter, refer to these questions to see how they illustrate the different actions your mind performs.

The human mind is our fundamental resource.

JOHN F. KENNEDY

Using Information

After taking in and examining information through the questioning process, critical thinkers transform what they learn into decisions and solutions. This is where inventions happen, new processes are born, theories are created, and information interacts with your own thoughts to create something new.

The Value of Critical Thinking

Critical thinking will benefit you in many different ways, including the following.

YOU WILL INCREASE YOUR ABILITY TO PERFORM THINKING PROCESSES. Critical thinking is a learned skill, just like shooting a basketball or using a word-processing program. As with any other skill, the more you use it, the better you become. The more you ask questions, the better you think. The better you think, the more effective you will be in school, work, and life situations.

YOU CAN PRODUCE KNOWLEDGE, RATHER THAN JUST REPRODUCE IT. The interaction of newly learned information with what you already know creates new knowledge that can be applied in unique situations. For instance, it won't mean much for education students to quote the stages of child development on an exam unless they can evaluate children's needs when they begin working as teachers.

YOU CAN BE A VALUABLE EMPLOYEE. You won't be a failure if you follow directions. However, you will be even more valuable if you ask strategic questions—ranging from "Is there a better way to deliver phone messages?" to "How can we increase business?"—that will improve productivity. Employees who think critically are more likely to make progress in their careers than those who simply do what they are told.

YOU CAN INCREASE YOUR PROBLEM-SOLVING CREATIVITY. Asking critical-thinking questions will help you approach problems in creative ways—to see something you've seen a thousand times before from a different perspective. Creativity is essential in producing new ways to solve problems.

Your mind has some basic moves, or actions, that it performs in order to understand relations between ideas and concepts. Sometimes it uses one action by itself, but most often it uses two or more in combination. These actions are the blocks you will use to build the critical-thinking processes you will explore later in the chapter.

Learning How Your Mind Works

Identify your mind's actions using a system originally conceived by educators Frank Lyman, Arlene Mindus, and Charlene Lopez[1] and developed by numerous other instructors. Based on their studies of how students think, they named seven basic building blocks of thought. These actions are not new to you, although some of their names may be. They represent the ways in which you think all the time, the ways in which you learn actively.

Through exploring these actions, you can go beyond just thinking and learn *how* you think. This will help you take charge of your own thinking. The more you know about how your mind works, the more control you will have over thinking processes such as problem solving and decision making.

Following are explanations of each of the mind actions, including examples. As you read, write your examples in the blank spaces. Icons representing each action will help you visualize and remember them.

RECALL. *Facts, sequence, and description.* This is the simplest action. When you recall you name or describe facts, objects, or events, or put them into sequence. *Examples:*

- Naming the steps of a geometry proof, in order
- Remembering your best friends' phone numbers

Your example: Recall two important school-related events this month.

The icon: Capital R stands for recall or remembering.

SIMILARITY. *Analogy, likeness, comparison.* This action examines what is similar about one or more things. You might compare situations, ideas, people, stories, events, or objects. *Examples:*

- Comparing notes with another student to see what facts and ideas you both consider important
- Analyzing the arguments you've had with your partner this month and seeing how they all seem to be about the same problem

Your example: Tell what is similar about two of your best friends.

The icon: The Venn diagram illustrates the idea of similarity. The two circles represent the things being compared, and the shaded area of intersection indicates that they have some degree or element of similarity.

DIFFERENCE. *Distinction, contrast.* This action examines what is different about one or more situations, ideas, people, stories, events, or objects, contrasting them with one another. *Examples:*

- Seeing how two instructors differ—one divides the class into small groups for discussions; the other keeps desks in place and delivers lectures
- Contrasting a day when you combine work and school with a day when you attend class only

Your example: Explain how your response to a course you like differs from how you respond to a course you don't like as much.

The icon: Here the Venn diagram is used again, to show difference. The nonintersecting parts of the circles are shaded, indicating that the focus is on what is not in common.

CAUSE AND EFFECT. *Reasons, consequences, prediction.* Using this action, you look at what has caused a fact, situation, or event and/or what effects, or consequences, come from it. In other words, you examine what led up to something and/or what will follow because of it. *Examples:*

- Staying up late causes you to oversleep, which causes you to be late to class. This causes you to miss some material, which has the further effect of your having problems on the test.

- When you pay your phone and utility bills on time, you create effects such as a better credit rating, uninterrupted service, and a better relationship with your service providers.

Your example: Name what causes you to like your favorite class and the effects the class has on you.

The icon: The arrows, pointing toward one another in a circular pattern, show how a cause leads to an effect.

EXAMPLE TO IDEA. *Generalization, classification, conceptualization.* From one or more examples (facts or events), you develop a general idea or ideas. Grouping facts or events into patterns may allow you to make a general statement about several of them at once. Classifying a fact or event helps you build knowledge. This mind action moves from the specific to the general. *Examples:*

- You have had trouble finding a baby-sitter. A classmate even brought her child to class once. Your brother drops his daughter at day care and doesn't like not seeing her all day. From these examples, you derive the idea that your school needs an on-campus day-care program.
- Two of your friends, who work part-time for the same company, have told you that it's a good place to work. Believing that the company has a good reputation, you apply for a job there yourself.

Your example: Name activities you enjoy. From them, derive an idea of a class you want to take.

The icon: The arrow and "Ex" pointing to a light bulb on the right indicate how an example or examples lead to the idea (the light bulb, lit up).

IDEA TO EXAMPLE. *Categorization, substantiation, proof.* In a reverse of the previous action, you take an idea or ideas and think of examples (events or facts) that support or prove that idea. This mind action moves from the general to the specific. *Examples:*

- For a paper, you start with this thesis statement: "Computer knowledge is a must for the modern worker." To support that idea, you gather examples, such as the number of industries that use computers, the kinds of training employers are requiring, and so on.
- You talk to your instructor about changing your major, giving examples that support your idea, such as the fact that you have worked in the field you want to change to and you have fulfilled some of the requirements for that major already.

Your example: Name an admirable person. Give examples that show how that person is admirable.

The icon: In a reverse of the previous icon, this one starts with the light bulb and has an arrow pointing to "Ex." This indicates that you start with the idea and then move to the supporting examples.

EVALUATION. *Value, judgment, rating.* Here you judge whether something is useful or not useful, important or unimportant, good or bad, or right or wrong by identifying and weighing its positive and negative effects (pros and cons). Be sure to consider the specific situation at hand (a cold drink might be good on the beach in August, not so good in the snowdrifts in January). With the facts you have gathered, you determine the value of something in terms of both predicted effects and your own needs. Cause-and-effect analysis always accompanies evaluation. *Examples:*

- For one semester, you schedule classes in the afternoons and spend nights working. You find that you tend to sleep late and lose your only study time. From this harmful effect, you evaluate that it doesn't work for you. You decide to schedule earlier classes next time.
- Someone offers you a chance to cheat on a test. You evaluate the potential effects if you are caught. You also evaluate the long-term effects of not actually learning the material and of doing something ethically wrong. You decide that it isn't right or worthwhile to cheat.

Your example: Evaluate your mode of transportation to school.

The icon: A set of scales out of balance indicates how you weigh positive and negative effects to arrive at an evaluation.

You may want to use a *mnemonic device*—a memory tool, as explained in Chapter 6—to remember the seven mind actions. You can make a sentence of words that each start with a mind action's first letter, such as "Really Smart Dogs Cook Eggs In Enchiladas."

How Mind Actions Build Thinking Processes

The seven mind actions are the fundamental building blocks that indicate relations between ideas and concepts. You will rarely use one at a time in a step-by-step process, as they are presented here. You will usually combine them, overlap them, and repeat them, using different actions for different situations. For example, when a test question asks you to explain prejudice, you might give *examples, different* from one another, that show your *idea* of prejudice (combining difference with example to idea).

When you combine mind actions in working toward a goal, you are performing a thinking process. Following are explorations of six of the most important critical-thinking processes: solving problems, making decisions, constructing and evaluating arguments, thinking logically, recognizing perspectives, and planning strategically. Each thinking process helps to activate your critical thinking and direct it toward the achievement of your goals. Figure 4.6, appearing later in the chapter, reminds you that the mind actions form the core of the thinking processes.

HOW DOES CRITICAL THINKING HELP YOU SOLVE PROBLEMS AND MAKE DECISIONS?

Problem solving and decision making are probably the two most crucial and common thinking processes. Each one requires various mind actions. They overlap somewhat because every problem that needs solving requires you to make a decision. However, not every decision requires that you solve a problem (e.g., not many people would say that deciding what to order for lunch is a problem).

Although both of these processes have multiple steps, you will not always have to work through each step. As you become more comfortable with solving problems and making decisions, your mind will automatically click through the steps. Also, you will become more adept at evaluating which problems and decisions need serious consideration and which can be taken care of more quickly and simply.

Problem Solving

Life constantly presents problems to be solved, ranging from average daily problems (how to manage study time) to life-altering situations (how to design a child-custody plan during a divorce). Choosing a solution without thinking critically may have negative effects. If you use the steps of the following problem-solving process, however, you have the best chance of coming up with a favorable solution.

You can apply this problem-solving plan to any problem. Taking the following steps will maximize the number of possible solutions you generate and will allow you to explore each one as fully as possible.

STEP 1. IDENTIFY THE PROBLEM ACCURATELY. What are the facts? *Recall* the details of the situation. To define a problem correctly, focus on its causes rather than its effects. Consider the Chinese saying, "Give a man a fish, and he will eat for a day. Teach a man to fish, and he will eat for a lifetime." If you state the problem as "The man is hungry," giving him a fish seems like a good solution. Unfortunately, the problem returns—because hunger is an effect. Focusing on the cause brings a new definition: "The man does not know how to find food." Given that his lack of knowledge is the true cause, teaching him to fish will truly solve the problem.

Sample problem: A student is not understanding course material.

STEP 2. ANALYZE THE PROBLEM. Analyze, or break down into understandable pieces, what surrounds the problem. What *effects* of the situation concern you? What *causes* these effects? Are there hidden causes? Look at the causes and effects that surround the problem.

Sample problem: If some effects of not understanding include poor grades and lack of interest, some causes may include poor study habits, not listening in class, or lack of sleep.

> BRAINSTORMING

The spontaneous, rapid generation of ideas or solutions, undertaken by a group or an individual, often as part of a problem-solving process.

STEP 3. BRAINSTORM POSSIBLE SOLUTIONS. Brainstorming will help you think of examples of how you solved similar problems, consider what is different about this problem, and come up with new possible solutions (see p. 119 for more about brainstorming). Remember that to get to the heart of a problem you must base possible solutions on the most significant causes instead of putting a bandage on the effects.

Sample problem: Looking at his study habits, the student comes up with ideas like seeking help from his instructor or working with a study group.

STEP 4. EXPLORE EACH SOLUTION. Why might your solution work, or not? Might a solution work partially, or in a particular situation? *Evaluate* ahead of time the pros and cons (positive and negative effects) of each plan. Create a chain of causes and effects in your head, as far into the future as you can, to see where this solution might lead.

Sample problem: The student considers the effects of improved study habits, more sleep, tutoring, or dropping the class.

STEP 5. CHOOSE AND EXECUTE THE SOLUTION YOU DECIDE IS BEST. Decide how you will put your solution to work. Then, execute your solution.

Sample problem: The student decides on a combination of improved study habits and tutoring.

STEP 6. EVALUATE THE SOLUTION THAT YOU ACTED ON, LOOKING AT ITS EFFECTS. What are the positive and negative *effects* of what you did? In terms of your needs, was it a useful solution or not? Could the solution use any adjustments to be more useful? Would you do the same again or not? In evaluating, you are collecting data.

Sample problem: Evaluating his choice, the student may decide that the effects are good but that his fatigue still causes a problem.

STEP 7. CONTINUE TO EVALUATE AND REFINE THE SOLUTION. Problem solving is a process. You may have opportunities to apply the same solution again. Evaluate repeatedly, making changes that you decide make the solution better (i.e., more reflective of the causes of the problem). In this way an active learner makes connections that can be useful in similar problems later on.

Sample problem: The student may decide to continue to study more regularly but, after a few weeks of tutoring, could opt to trade in the tutoring time for some extra sleep. He may decide to take what he has learned from the tutor so far and apply it to his increased study efforts.

Using this process will enable you to solve school, work, and personal problems in a thoughtful, comprehensive way. The think link in Figure 4.2 demonstrates a way to visualize the flow of problem solving. Figure 4.3 shows how one person used this plan to solve a problem. It represents the same plan as Figure 4.2 but gives room to write so that it can be used in the problem-solving process.

Problem-solving plan.

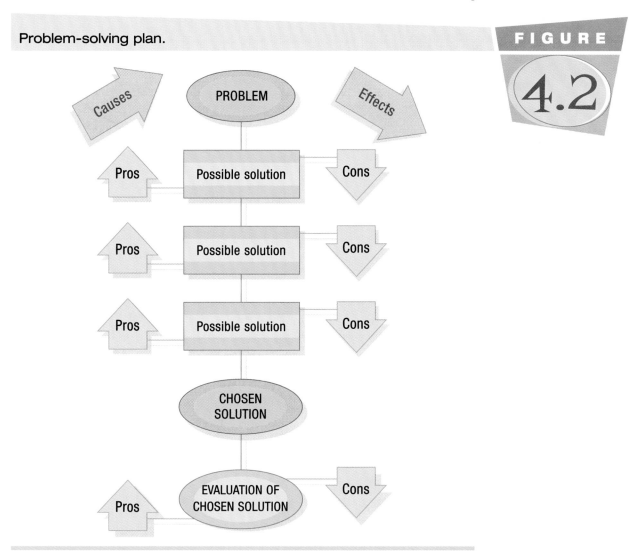

FIGURE

4.2

Decision Making

Although every problem-solving process involves making a decision (deciding on a solution), not all decisions involve problems. Decisions are choices. Making a choice, or decision, requires thinking critically through the possible choices and evaluating which will work best for you and for the situation.

Before you begin the process, evaluate the decision. Some decisions are little, day-to-day considerations that you can take care of quickly (e.g., what books to bring to class). Others require thoughtful evaluation, time, and perhaps the input of others you trust (e.g., whether to quit a good job). The following is a list of steps for thinking critically through the more complex kind of decision.

1. *Decide on a goal.* Why is this decision necessary? What result do you want from this decision, and what is its value? Considering the *effects* you want can help you formulate your goal.

    Sample decision: A student currently attends a small private college. Her goal is to become a physical therapist. The school has a good pro-

How one student walked through a problem.

LIST CAUSES OF PROBLEM:

Must go to school to take classes

Can't have child with me in class

No one else at home to watch
    child

LIST EFFECTS OF PROBLEM:

Missed exams and classes sometimes

Logistics take extra time, transport

Stress created for me and child

Lack of routine & comfort

STATE PROBLEM HERE:

Need some way to pro-
vide child-care while
I'm at school

Use boxes below to list
possible solutions:

List potential POSITIVE
effects for each solution:

Care is consistent

Reliable and familiar setting

Doesn't matter if child is sick

SOLUTION #1

Have a nanny at home

List potential NEGATIVE
effects for each solution:

Expensive

Hard to find someone to trust

Person must follow my schedule

Meet parents like myself

Child has playmates

Inexpensive

SOLUTION #2

Join child-care co-op

Must trust other parents

Sick child might get others sick

Close by to classes

Reliable care

No extra transport time

SOLUTION #3

Get school to provide
child care on campus

Costs school money

Need to find space and create facility

Restrictions & waiting lists

Now choose the solution you
think is best—and try it.

List the actual POSITIVE
effects of the solution:

CHOSEN SOLUTION

Join child-care co-op

List the actual NEGATIVE
effects of the solution:

Met some helpful people who understand me

My child likes the other three children

Low cost helps my budget

When it's my turn, I have to care for four children

Sometimes our schedules clash

Can't let a sick child participate

FINAL EVALUATION: Was it a good or bad choice?

All in all, I think this is the best I could do on my budget. There are times when I have to stay
home with a sick child, buy I'm mostly able to stay committed to both parenting and school.

gram, but her father has changed jobs and the family can no longer pay the tuition and fees.

2. *Establish needs. Recall* the needs of everyone (or everything) involved in the decision. Consider all who will be affected.

   Sample decision: The student needs a school with a full physical therapy program; she and her parents need to cut costs; she needs to be able to transfer credits.

3. *Name, investigate, and evaluate available options.* Brainstorm possible choices, and then look at the facts surrounding each. *Evaluate* the good and bad effects of each possibility. Weigh these effects and judge which is the best course of action.

   Sample decision: Here are some possibilities that the student might consider:

   - *Continue at the current college.* **Positive effects:** I wouldn't have to adjust to a new place or to new people. I could continue my course work as planned. **Negative effects:** I would have to find a way to finance most of my tuition and costs on my own, whether through loans, grants, or work. I'm not sure I could find time to work as much as I would need to, and I don't think I would qualify for as much aid as I now need.

   - *Transfer to the state college.* **Positive effects:** I could reconnect with people there that I know from high school. Tuition and room costs would be cheaper than at my current school. I could transfer credits. **Negative effects:** I would still have to work some or find minimal financial aid. The physical therapy program is small and not very strong.

   - *Transfer to the community college.* **Positive effects:** They have many of the courses I need to continue with the physical therapy curriculum. The school is close by, so I could live at home and avoid paying housing costs. Credits will transfer. The tuition is extremely reasonable. **Negative effects:** I don't know anyone there. I would be less independent. The school doesn't offer a bachelor's degree.

4. *Decide on a plan and take action.* Make a choice based on your evaluation, and act on it.

   Sample decision: In this case, the student might decide to go to the community college for two years and then transfer back to a four-year school to earn a bachelor's degree in physical therapy. Although she might lose some independence and contact with friends, the positive effects are money saved, opportunity to spend time on studies rather than working to earn tuition, and the availability of classes that match the physical therapy program requirements.

5. *Evaluate the result.* Was it useful? Not useful? Some of both? Weigh the positive and negative effects. If the student decides to transfer, she may find that it can be hard being back at home, although her parents are adjusting to her independence and she is trying to respect their concerns. Fewer social distractions result in her getting more work done. The financial situation is favorable. All things considered, she evaluates that this decision was a good one.

Making important decisions can take time. Think through your decisions thoroughly, considering your own ideas as well as those of others you trust, but don't hesitate to act once you have your plan. You cannot benefit from your decision until you act on it and follow through.

Using a separate sheet of paper, complete the following.

Thinking Back

1. Looking at the icons, write the name of each mind action.

2. Name one way you used a mind action to think critically this past week.

3. Name the steps in the problem-solving plan.

4. What decision do you have coming up for which you can use the decision-making process?

Thinking Ahead

1. In your papers or in verbal discussion, do you feel you get your point across effectively? Why or why not?

2. Name an assumption that you have heard someone make. Do you feel it is fact or opinion? Why?

3. Do you think you are a creative person? When are you most able to use your creativity?

4. Have you ever believed something you read or saw on television only to find out that it wasn't accurate? Briefly describe what happened.

HOW DO YOU CONSTRUCT AND EVALUATE ARGUMENTS?

In this case, "argument" refers to a persuasive case that you make to prove or disprove a point. It is a set of connected ideas supported by examples. Any time a statement is presented and supported—such as in textbook reading, newspaper articles, or lectures—an argument is taking place.

> **PERSUADE**
>
> To convince someone through argument or reasoning to adopt a belief, position, or course of action.

Constructing an Argument

You will often encounter situations in which your success depends on your ability to **persuade** someone, either verbally or in writing, to agree with you. You may need to write a paper persuading the reader that a particular historical event changed the world, for example, or you may need to persuade a prospective employer that you are the one for the job.

A sample argument.

FIGURE 4.4

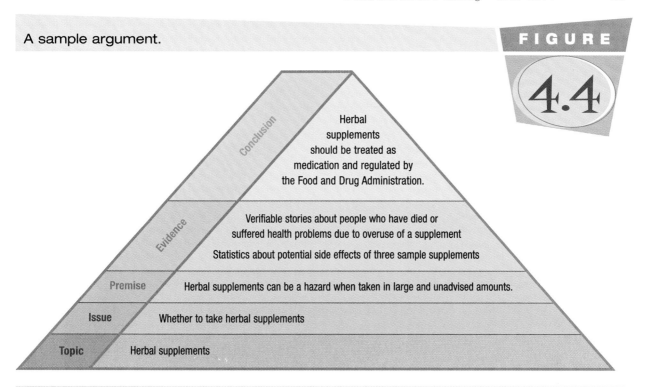

Conclusion
Herbal supplements should be treated as medication and regulated by the Food and Drug Administration.

Evidence
Verifiable stories about people who have died or suffered health problems due to overuse of a supplement
Statistics about potential side effects of three sample supplements

Premise
Herbal supplements can be a hazard when taken in large and unadvised amounts.

Issue
Whether to take herbal supplements

Topic
Herbal supplements

An argument is based on a particular topic and issue. It starts with an idea or **premise**, gives examples to support that premise, and finally asserts a conclusion. See Figure 4.4 for an example of an argument.

To construct an argument, follow these steps:

STEP 1. ESTABLISH THE PREMISE. Define what you want to argue. Establish the topic of your argument (the subject) and the issue at hand (the question that your argument will answer in a certain way).

STEP 2. GATHER EXAMPLES IN SUPPORT. Gather evidence that supports your premise, then put it into logical order. You might want to use "chain support"—a set of reasons that build on one another.

STEP 3. ANTICIPATE QUESTIONS AND POINTS AGAINST YOU. What might you be asked to explain? What could someone say that argues against you? Decide what you will say to address issues and opposing points.

STEP 4. DRAW A CONCLUSION. Formulate a conclusion that summarizes how this evidence supports your initial premise. Keep your goal in mind and make sure that your conclusion reflects that goal.

As an example, here is one way to present an argument for a raise and promotion at work.

- *Your topic:* Job status
- *Your issue:* What role you should have at this point in your career
- *Your premise:* You deserve a raise and promotion

PREMISE

Something supposed as a basis of argument; a preliminary assumption.

- *Your audience:* Your supervisor (who may or may not be receptive, depending on your relationship)
- *Your evidence, or examples, that support your idea:* You are a solid, creative performer. You feel that your experience and high level of motivation will have positive effects for the company.
  1. Questions you anticipate: "What have you achieved in your current position?" "What do you know about the position you want to take?" "What new and creative ideas do you have?"
  2. Potential counter-arguments: Your supervisor might say that you may not be able to handle the new position's hours because of your school schedule. In preparation, you could look into what it would take to reschedule classes and make adjustments in your other commitments.
- *Your conclusion:* Promoting you would have positive effects for both you and the company.

Above all, always work to remain flexible. You never know what turn a conversation will take, or how a written argument will be interpreted. Keep your mind active and ready to address any surprises that come your way, and watch out for errors in thinking—on your part or on the part of your audience.

Evaluating an Argument

It's easy—and common—to accept or reject an argument outright, according to whether it fits with one's own opinions and views. If you ask questions about an argument, however, you will be able to determine its validity and will learn more from it. Furthermore, critical thinking will help you avoid accepting opinions and assumptions that are not supported by evidence.

Thinking critically about an argument involves a two-part evaluation:

- Evaluating the quality of the evidence itself
- Evaluating whether the evidence adequately supports the premise

These two considerations will give you a pretty good idea of whether the argument works. If good quality evidence (true input) combines with good quality use of evidence (valid reasoning), you get a solid argument (true output).

Evidence Quality

Ask the following questions in order to see whether the evidence itself is valid.

- What type of evidence is it—fact or opinion?
- How is the evidence similar to, or different from, what I already believe to be true?
- Where is the evidence from? Are those sources reliable and free of bias? (Examples of sources include intuition, authorities, personal experience, and observation.)

Support Quality

Ask these questions to determine whether you think the evidence successfully makes the argument.

- Do examples logically follow from ideas, and ideas logically lead to given examples?
- Does the evidence show similarity to what I consider common sense?
- Are there enough pieces of evidence to support the conclusion well?
- Do I know of any competing views or pieces of evidence that differ from this evidence?
- Has the argument evaluated all of the positive and negative effects involved? Is there any unconsidered negative effect to what the conclusion is arguing? For whom, and why?

The more you read and listen to arguments, the more adept you will become at evaluating them. Read a newspaper and listen to public radio. Pay attention to the views of people around you. Make an effort not to take anything as true or false without spending some time asking questions about it first.

HOW DO YOU THINK LOGICALLY?

Logical thinking involves questioning the truth and accuracy of information in order to find out whether it is true or reliable. Logical thinking includes these two primary tasks: distinguishing fact from opinion and identifying and evaluating assumptions.

Distinguishing Fact From Opinion

Fact, according to the dictionary, is information presented as objectively real and verifiable. *Opinion* is defined as a belief, conclusion, or judgment and is inherently difficult, if not impossible, to verify. Being able to distinguish fact from opinion is crucial to your understanding of reading material and your ability to decide what information to believe and put to use. See Table 4.2 for some examples of factual statements versus statements of opinion. From the information in the table, observe that facts refer to the observable or measurable, while opinions involve cause-and-effect exploration.

Characteristics of Facts and Opinions

Following are some indicators that will help you determine what is fact and what is opinion.[2] Indicators of opinion are:

STATEMENTS THAT SHOW EVALUATION. Any statement of value—such as "Television is bad for children"—indicates an opinion. Words such as *bad, good, pointless,* and *beneficial* indicate value judgments.

STATEMENTS THAT PREDICT FUTURE EVENTS. Nothing that will happen in the future can be definitively proven in the present. Anything that discusses something that will happen in the future is an opinion.

TABLE 4.2   Examples of facts and opinions.

TOPIC	FACTUAL STATEMENT	STATEMENT OF OPINION
Stock market	In 1999 the Dow Jones Industrial average rose above 10,000 for the first time.	The Dow Jones Industrial average will continue to grow throughout the first decade of the twenty-first century.
Weather	It's raining outside.	This is the worst rainstorm yet this year.
Cataloging systems	Computer databases have replaced card catalogs in most college libraries.	Computer databases are an improvement over card catalogs.

ABSTRACT

Theoretical; disassociated from any specific instance.

QUALIFIER

A word that changes the meaning of another word or word group.

STATEMENTS THAT USE ABSTRACT WORDS. Although "one gallon" can be defined, "love" has no specific definition. **Abstract** words—*strength, misery, success*—usually indicate an opinion.

STATEMENTS THAT USE EMOTIONAL WORDS. Emotions are by nature unverifiable. Chances are that statements using words such as *delightful, nasty, miserable,* or *wonderful* will present an opinion.

STATEMENTS THAT USE QUALIFIERS. Absolute **qualifiers,** such as *all, none, never,* and *always,* can point to an opinion. For example, "All students need to work while in school" is an opinion.

Indicators of fact are:

STATEMENTS THAT DEAL WITH ACTUAL PEOPLE, PLACES, OBJECTS, EVENTS. If the existence of the elements involved can be verified through observation, chances are that the statement itself can also be proven true or false. "Former President Jimmy Carter was once a peanut farmer in Georgia" is an example of this principle.

STATEMENTS THAT USE CONCRETE WORDS OR MEASURABLE STATISTICS. Any statement that uses concrete, measurable terms and avoids the abstract is likely to be a fact. Examples include: "Thirty-six inches constitute a yard" and "There are 2,512 full-time students enrolled this semester."

It is important to separate the concepts of "fact" and "opinion" from those of "true" and "false." Neither a fact nor an opinion is automatically true or false. Actually, a fact can be false and an opinion can be true. The status of any statement as fact or opinion has to do with how it is presented, not the inherent truth or falsehood of what it says. Consider the following:

- *Facts can be wrong.* A fact is a statement presented as objectively real. Whether it is actually true is up to individual evaluation and investigation. For example, if someone tells you class is at 10:00, and you discover on checking the course catalog that it is actually at 11:00, that person has given you an incorrect statement of fact.

- *Opinions can seem like facts.* A statement of opinion can masquerade as fact. For example, an article may state, "Twenty to thirty minutes of vigorous exercise three to five times a week is essential for good health." That may sound like a fact. On examination, however, you realize that it is impossible to determine whether the same frequency and level of exercise would have the same effect on all people. To be safe, consider all statements opinions until proven otherwise.

When you find yourself feeling that an opinion is fact, it may be because you agree strongly with the opinion. Don't discount your feelings; "not verifiable" is not the same as "inaccurate." Opinions are not necessarily wrong even if you cannot prove them.

Using Questions to Investigate Truth and Accuracy

Once you label a statement as a fact or opinion, explore its degree of truth. Both facts and opinions require investigation through questioning. Critical-thinking experts Sylvan Barnet and Hugo Bedau state that when you test for the truth of a statement, you "determine whether what it asserts corresponds with reality; if it does, then it is true, and if it doesn't, then it is false."[3] In order to determine to what degree a statement "corresponds with reality," ask questions such as the following.

- What facts or examples provide evidence of truth?
- How does the maker of the statement know this to be true?
- Is there another fact that disproves this statement or information, or shows it to be an opinion?
- How reliable are the sources of information?
- What about this statement is similar to or different from other information I consider fact?

Another crucial step in determining the truth is to question the assumptions that you and others hold and that are the underlying force in shaping opinions.

Identifying and Evaluating Assumptions

"If it's more expensive, it's better." "You should study in a library." These statements reveal assumptions—evaluations or generalizations influenced by values and based on observing cause and effect—that can often hide within seemingly truthful statements. An **assumption** can influence choices—you may assume that you should earn a certain degree or own a car. Many people don't question whether their assumptions make sense, nor do they challenge the assumptions of others.

Assumptions come from sources such as parents or relatives, television and other media, friends, and personal experiences. As much as you think such assumptions work for you, it's just as possible that they can close your

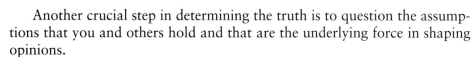

ASSUMPTION

An idea or statement accepted as true without examination or proof.

FIGURE
4.5

Questioning an assumption.

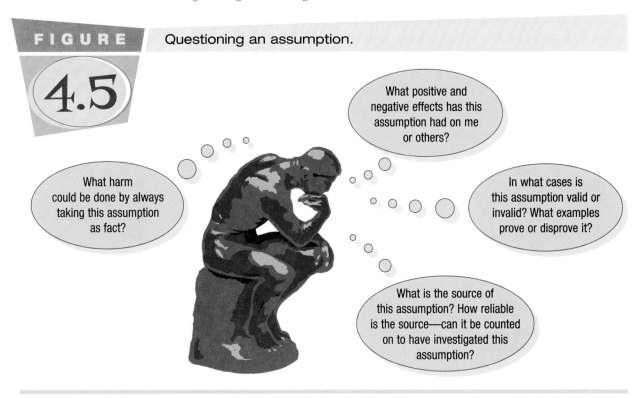

What positive and negative effects has this assumption had on me or others?

What harm could be done by always taking this assumption as fact?

In what cases is this assumption valid or invalid? What examples prove or disprove it?

What is the source of this assumption? How reliable is the source—can it be counted on to have investigated this assumption?

mind to opportunities and even cause harm. Investigate each assumption as you would any statement of fact or opinion, analyzing its causes and effects.

The first step in uncovering the assumptions that underlie a statement is to look at the cause-and-effect pattern of the statement, seeing if the way reasons move to conclusions is supported by evidence or involves a hidden assumption. See Figure 4.5 for questions you can ask to evaluate an assumption.

For example, here's how you might use these questions to investigate the following statement: "The most productive schedule involves getting started early in the day." First of all, a cause-and-effect evaluation shows that this statement reveals the following assumption: "The morning is when people have the most energy and are most able to get things done." Here's how you might question the assumption:

- This assumption may be true for people who have good energy in the morning hours. But the assumption may be not true for people who work best in the afternoon or evening hours.

- Society's basic standard of daytime classes and 8:00 A.M. to 5:00 P.M. working hours supports this assumption. Therefore, the assumption may work for people who have early jobs and classes. It may not work, however, for people who work shifts or who take evening classes.

- Maybe people who believe this assumption were raised to start their days early. Or, perhaps they just go along with what seems to be society's standard. Still, there are plenty of people who operate on a different schedule and yet enjoy successful, productive lives.

- Taking this assumption as fact could hurt people who don't operate at their peak in the earlier hours. For example, if a "night owl" tries to take early classes, he may experience concentration problems that would not necessarily occur later in the day. In situations that favor their particular characteristics—later classes and jobs, career areas that don't require early morning work—such people have just as much potential to succeed as anyone else.

Be careful to question all assumptions, not just those that seem problematic from the start. Form your opinion after investigating the positive and negative effects of any situation.

WHY SHOULD YOU EXPLORE PERSPECTIVES?

Perspective is complex and unique to each individual. You have your own way of looking at everything that you encounter, from your big-picture perspective on the world to your general opinion on ideas, activities, people, and places. However, seeing the world *only* from your perspective—and resisting any challenges to that perspective—can be inflexible, limiting, and frustrating to both you and others. You probably know how difficult it can be when someone cannot understand your point of view. Perhaps an instructor doesn't like that you leave early on Thursdays for physical therapy, or a friend can't understand why you would date someone of a race different from yours.

> **PERSPECTIVE**
>
> A mental point of view or outlook, based on a cluster of related assumptions, incorporating values, interests, and knowledge.

Evaluating Perspectives

The most effective way to evaluate perspectives involves taking in information, asking questions about it, and then acting on it in whatever way seems appropriate. Exploring perspectives critically will introduce you to new ideas, improve your communication with others, and encourage mutual respect.

Take in New Information

The first step is to take in new perspectives and simply acknowledge that they exist without immediately judging, rejecting, or even accepting them. It's easy to feel so strongly about a topic—for example, whether the government should allow capital punishment—that you don't even give a chance to anyone with an opposing view. Resist your own strong opinions and listen. A critical thinker is able to allow for the existence of perspectives that differ from, and even completely negate, her own.

Evaluate the Perspective

Asking questions will help you maintain flexibility and openness.

- What is similar and different about this perspective and my own perspective, and about this person and me? What personal experiences have led to our particular perspectives?
- What examples, evidence, or reasons could be used to support or justify this perspective? Do some reasons provide good support even if I don't agree with the reasons?

- What effects may come from this way of being, acting, or believing? Are the effects different on different people and different situations? Even if this perspective seems to have negative effects for me, how might it have positive effects for others, and therefore have value?
- What can I learn from this different perspective? Is there anything I could adopt that would improve my life? Is there anything I wouldn't do but that I can still respect and learn from?

Accept or Perhaps Take Action

On the one hand, perhaps your evaluation will lead you simply to a recognition and appreciation of the other perspective, even if you decide that it is not right for you. On the other hand, thinking through the new perspective may lead you to feel that it would be worthwhile to try it out or to adopt it as your own. You may feel that what you have learned has led you to a new way of seeing yourself or your life.

The Value of Seeing Other Perspectives

Seeing beyond one's own perspective can be difficult. Why put in the effort? Here are some of the very real benefits of being able to see and consider other perspectives.

IMPROVED COMMUNICATION. When you consider another person's perspective, you open the lines of communication. For example, if you want to add or drop a course and your advisor says it's impossible before listening to you, you might not feel much like explaining. But if your advisor asks to hear your perspective, you may sense that your needs are respected and be more ready to talk.

> *I have always thought that one man of tolerable abilities may work great changes, and accomplish great affairs among mankind, if he first forms a good plan.*
>
> BENJAMIN FRANKLIN

MUTUAL RESPECT. When someone takes the time and energy to understand how you feel about something, you probably feel respected and in return offer respect to the person who made the effort. When people respect one another, relationships become stronger and more productive, whether they are personal, workplace, or educational.

ACTIVE LEARNING. Every time you shift your perspective, you can learn something new and relate it to what you already know. There are worlds of knowledge and possibilities outside your experience. You may find different yet equally valid ways of getting an education, living as a family, or relating to others. Above all else, you may see that each person is entitled to his own perspective, no matter how foreign it may be to you.

The connection with others that you foster by being able to recognize perspectives may mean the difference between success and failure in today's world. This becomes more true as the information age introduces you to an increasing number of perspectives every day.

The wheel of thinking.

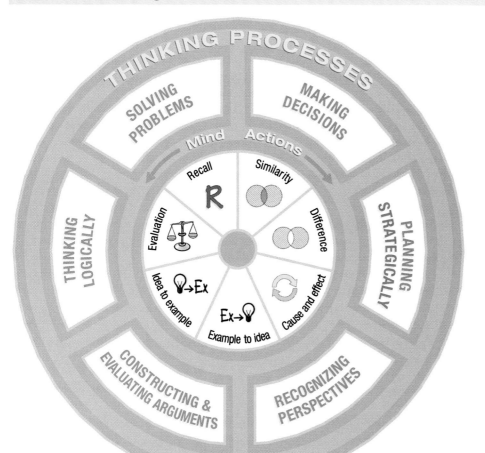

WHY PLAN STRATEGICALLY?

If you've ever played a game of chess, participated in a martial arts match, or made a detailed plan of how to reach a particular goal, you have had experience with strategy. Strategy is the plan of action, the method, the "how" behind any goal you want to achieve.

Strategic planning means looking at the next week, month, year, or 10 years and exploring the future positive and negative effects that current choices and actions may have. As a student, you have planned strategically by deciding that the effort of school is a legitimate price to pay for the skills and opportunities you will receive. Being strategic means using decision-making skills to choose how to accomplish tasks. It means asking questions.

> **STRATEGY**
>
> A plan of action designed to accomplish a specific goal.

Strategy and Critical Thinking

In situations that demand strategy, think critically by asking questions like these:

- If you aim for a certain goal, what actions may cause you to achieve that goal?

- What are the potential effects, positive or negative, of different actions or choices?
- What can you learn from previous experiences that may inspire similar or different actions?
- What can you recall about what others have done in similar situations?
- Which set of effects would be most helpful or desirable to you?

For any situation that would benefit from strategic planning, from getting ready for a study session to aiming for a career, these steps will help you make choices that bring about the most positive effects.

STEP 1. ESTABLISH A GOAL. What do you want to achieve? When do you want to achieve it?

STEP 2. BRAINSTORM POSSIBLE PLANS. What are some ways that you can get where you want to go? What steps toward your goal will you need to take 1 year, 5 years, 10 years, or 20 years from now?

STEP 3. ANTICIPATE ALL POSSIBLE EFFECTS OF EACH PLAN. What positive and negative effects may occur, both soon and in the long term? What approach may best help you achieve your goal? Talk to people who are where you want to be—professionally or personally—and ask them what you should anticipate.

STEP 4. PUT YOUR PLAN INTO ACTION. Act on the decision you have made.

STEP 5. EVALUATE CONTINUALLY. Your strategies might not have the effects you predicted. If you discover that things are not going the way you planned, for any reason, reevaluate and change your strategy.

The most important critical-thinking question for successful strategic planning is the question "how?" *How* do you remember what you learn? *How* do you develop a productive idea at work? The process of strategic planning, in a nutshell, helps you find the best answer to "how."

Benefits of Strategic Planning

Strategic planning has many important positive effects, including the following.

SCHOOL AND WORK SUCCESS. A student who wants to do well in a course needs to plan study sessions. A lawyer needs to anticipate how to respond to points raised in court. Strategic planning creates a vision into the future that allows the planner to anticipate possibilities and to be prepared for them.

SUCCESSFUL GOAL SETTING. Thinking strategically helps you see how to achieve goals over time. For example, a student might have a part-time job to work toward the goal of paying tuition.

KEEPING UP WITH WORKPLACE CHANGE. The speed of technological developments has created an ever-shifting working world where new areas of employment emerge and old areas fade away on a fairly regular basis. Thinking strategically about job opportunities may lead you to a broader range of courses or a major and career in a growing career area, making it more likely that your skills will be in demand when you graduate.

Strategic planning means using critical thinking to develop a vision of your future. Although you can't predict with certainty what will happen, you can ask questions about the potential effects of your actions. With what you learn, you can make plans that will bring the best possible effects for you and others.

HOW CAN YOU DEVELOP YOUR CREATIVITY?

Everyone is creative. Although the word may inspire images of art and music, **creativity** comes in many other forms. A creation can be a solution, idea, approach, tangible product, work of art, system, or program. Creative innovations introduced by all kinds of people continually expand and change the world. Here are some that have had an impact:

CREATIVITY
The ability to produce something new through imaginative skill.

- Jody Williams and her International Campaign to Ban Landmines have convinced nearly 100 countries to support a treaty that would end land mine production and sales.
- Harold Cohen, biology teacher at College of DuPage, helps his students gain hands-on experience by linking them up with aquariums and animal rehabilitation centers.
- Rosa Parks refused to give up her seat on the bus to a white person, setting off a chain of events that gave rise to the civil rights movement.
- Art Fry and Spencer Silver invented the Post-It™ note in 1980, enabling people to save paper and protect documents by using removable notes.

Even though these particular innovations had wide-ranging effects, the characteristics of these influential innovators can be found in all people who exercise their creative capabilities. Creativity can be as down-to-earth as planning how to coordinate your work and class schedules.

Characteristics of Creative People

Creative people respond to change with new ideas. "I've found that the hallmark of creative people is their mental flexibility," says creativity expert Roger von Oech. "Like race-car drivers who shift in and out of different gears depending on where they are on the course, creative people are able to shift in and out of different types of thinking depending on the needs of the situation at hand."[4]

Creative people combine ideas and information in ways that form completely new solutions, ideas, processes, uses, or products. See Figure 4.7 for some primary characteristics of creative people.

Enhancing Your Creativity

Following are some ways to enhance your natural creativity, adapted from material by J. R. Hayes.[5]

Characteristics of creative people.

CHARACTERISTIC	EXAMPLE
Willingness to take risks	Taking a difficult, high-level course
Tendency to break away from limitations	Entering a marathon race
Tendency to seek new challenges and experiences	Taking on an internship in a high-pressure workplace
Broad range of interests	Inventing new moves on the basketball court and playing guitar at open-mike night
Ability to make new things out of available materials	Making curtains out of bedsheets
Tendency to question norms and assumptions	Adopting a child of different ethnic background than the family
Willingness to deviate from popular opinion	Working for a small, relatively unknown political party
Curiosity and inquisitiveness	Wanting to know how a computer program works

Source: Adapted from T. Z. Tardif and R. J. Sternberg, "What Do We Know About Creativity?" in *The Nature of Creativity,* R. J. Sternberg, ed. (London: Cambridge University Press, 1988).

TAKE THE BROADEST POSSIBLE PERSPECTIVE. At first, a problem may look like "My child won't stay quiet when I study." If you take a wider look, you may discover hidden causes or effects of the problem, such as "I haven't chosen the best time of day to study," or "We haven't had time together, so he feels lonely."

CHOOSE THE BEST ATMOSPHERE. T. M. Amabile says that people are more creative and imaginative when they spend time around other creative folk.[6] Hang out with people whose thinking inspires you.

GIVE YOURSELF TIME. Rushing can stifle your creative ability. When you allow time for thought to percolate, or you take breaks when figuring out a problem, you may increase your creative output.

GATHER VARIED INPUT. The more information and ideas you gather as you think, the more material you have to build a creative idea or solution. Every new piece of input offers a new perspective.

Here are a few additional creativity tips from von Oech.[7]

DON'T GET HOOKED ON FINDING THE ONE RIGHT ANSWER. There can be lots of "right answers" to any question. The more possibilities you generate, the better your chance of finding the best one.

DON'T ALWAYS BE LOGICAL. Following strict logic may cause you to miss analogies or ignore your hunches.

BREAK THE RULES SOMETIMES. All kinds of creative breakthroughs have occurred because someone bypassed the rules. Women and minorities can vote and hold jobs because someone broke a rule—a law—many years ago. When necessary, challenge rules with creative ideas.

LET YOURSELF PLAY. People often hit upon their most creative ideas when they are exercising or just relaxing. Often when your mind switches into play mode, it can more freely generate new thoughts.

LET YOURSELF GO A LITTLE CRAZY. What seems like a crazy idea might be a brilliant discovery. For example, the idea for Velcro™ came from examining how a burr sticks to clothing.

DON'T FEAR FAILURE. Even Michael Jordan got cut from the basketball team as a high school sophomore in Wilmington, N.C. If you insist on getting it right all the time, you may miss out on the creative path—often paved with failures—leading to the best possible solution.

Brainstorming may combine many of these strategies. Use brainstorming for problem solving, decision making, writing a paper, or whenever you need to free your mind for new possibilities.

Learning to let yourself create is like learning to walk . . . Progress, not perfection, is what we should be asking of ourselves.

JULIA CAMERON

Brainstorming Toward a Creative Answer

You are brainstorming when you approach a problem by letting your mind free-associate and come up with as many possible ideas, examples, or solutions as you can, without immediately evaluating them as good or bad. Brainstorming is also referred to as *divergent thinking;* you start with the issue or problem and then let your mind diverge, or go in as many different directions as it wants, in search of ideas or solutions. Following are two general guidelines for successful brainstorming:[8]

DON'T EVALUATE OR CRITICIZE AN IDEA RIGHT AWAY. Write down your ideas so that you remember them. Evaluate later, after you have had a chance to think about them. Try to avoid criticizing other people's ideas as well. Students often become stifled when their ideas are evaluated during brainstorming.

FOCUS ON QUANTITY; DON'T WORRY ABOUT QUALITY UNTIL LATER. Generate as many ideas or examples as you can. The more thoughts you generate, the better the chance that one may be useful. Brainstorming works well in groups. Group members can become inspired by, and make creative use of, one another's ideas.

Remember, creativity can be developed if you have the desire and patience. Nurture your creativity by being accepting of your own ideas. Your creative expression will become more free with practice.

Creativity and Critical Thinking

Critical thinking is inherently creative because it requires you to use given information to come up with ideas or solutions to problems. For example, if you were brainstorming to generate possible causes of fatigue in afternoon classes, you might come up with lack of sleep, too much morning caffeine, or an instructor who doesn't inspire you. Through your consideration of causes and solutions, you have been thinking both creatively and critically.

Creative thinkers and critical thinkers have similar characteristics—both consider new perspectives, ask questions, don't hesitate to question accepted assumptions and traditions, and persist in the search for answers. You use critical-thinking mind actions throughout everything you do in school and in your daily life. In this chapter and in some of the other study skills chapters, you will notice mind-action icons placed where they can help you to understand how your mind is working.

One particularly important area in which you will benefit from thinking critically is in how you approach the media that you encounter on a daily basis.

WHAT IS MEDIA LITERACY?

Do you believe everything you read, see on television, or find on the Internet? Think about it for a moment. If you trusted every advertisement, you would believe that at least four fast-food restaurants serve "the best burger available." If you agreed with every magazine article, you would know that Elvis passed away many years ago and yet still believe that he was shopping for peanut butter last week in Oklahoma. It is impossible to believe it all without becoming completely confused about what is real.

If literacy refers to the ability to read, media literacy can be seen as the ability to read the **media**. Media literacy—the ability to respond with critical thinking to the media that you encounter—is essential for a realistic understanding of the information that bombards you daily. It means that instead of accepting anything a newspaper article, TV commercial, or Internet site says is fact, you take time to question the information, using your mind actions and critical-thinking processes.

The people who founded the Center for Media Literacy work to encourage others to think critically about the media. They have put forth what they call the "Five Core Concepts of Media Literacy."[9] Approaching what you read as an active learner means applying these concepts to any information you encounter through the media.

> **MEDIA**
>
> The agencies of mass communication—television, film, and journalism (magazines and newspapers).

How do I solve the problem of getting the classes I want?

Edhilvia Campos, *Parkland Community College, Champaign, Illinois, Microbiology Major*

Every semester it's a challenge to figure out what classes I will need. I am majoring in microbiology so I need a lot of science courses and the ones I want aren't always available. Also, I eventually want to transfer to the University of Illinois. The process for registering and figuring out what will transfer seems complicated.

When I came to the States for college, only a few of my math credits transferred because the math classes I had taken in high school in Venezuela

were not acceptable credits for college. My freshman year I took two algebra classes and later found out that they couldn't be applied to my major, which made me feel like I wasted my time. I also don't want to pay for class-

es that I don't need. Trying to regulate the number of classes you take isn't easy either. One thing I have learned to do is take at least one fun class each semester. Last semester I had to take chemistry and calculus so I decided to take music too, which was a nice break for me.

I may want to go back to Venezuela during the summers. I've considered taking classes then but the Venezuelan universities don't really have my major. Once again I'm trying to find out what classes are available that apply to my major. Do you have any suggestions for what I can do to make this process more efficient?

Shera Chantel Caviness, *University of Memphis, Early Childhood Education—Graduate Major*

First and foremost, hang in there. I know that things seem hard now, but it will pay off. Attending college is similar to a "micro" real world. Throughout col-

lege, you will have to face problems that must be resolved. I understand that you feel you wasted time and money taking certain classes. But some classes are not always transferable, and unfortunately extra money has to be utilized to take certain courses before entering a degree program.

To prepare to transfer, get acquainted with an academic counselor at the U. of Illinois (preferably one in your major) to help you. He or she can tell you what will transfer so you will not have to repeat or take unnecessary classes. While at Parkland, find an academic counselor in your field who can guide you toward appropriate courses for that degree. Use the undergraduate catalog to stay informed (and to inform your counselors) of the necessary classes for your major.

Get to know the professors in your field because they can help, and your interest will show the will to achieve. If some classes are not available

for one semester, gather at least 8 to 10 students to voice their concern abut opening a section for that class. The class schedule is done at the beginning of the previous semester, and professors are often unaware of the

demand for certain courses because students do not speak up.

If you plan to return to Venezuela for the summer, only take courses that will apply to your degree or take some general lower division classes that are transferable. Make sure you check with the counselors before signing up. All and all, keep your determination alive and do not let many things discourage you. Always find something valuable within each course you take because this will help you become more well-rounded. Remember to think positive; this is only a "micro" real world experience helping to prepare you for the R-E-A-L world.

ALL MEDIA ARE CONSTRUCTIONS. Any TV show or advertisement, for example, is not a view of actual life or fact but rather a carefully constructed presentation that is designed to have a particular effect on the viewer—to encourage you to feel a certain emotion, develop a particular opinion, or buy the product advertised. For example, an article that wants the reader to feel good about the president will focus on his strengths rather than his shortcomings.

MEDIA USE UNIQUE "LANGUAGES." The people who produce media carefully choose wording, background music, colors, images, timing, and other factors to produce a desired effect. When watching a movie, listen to the music that plays behind an emotional scene or a high-speed chase.

DIFFERENT AUDIENCES UNDERSTAND THE SAME MEDIA MESSAGE DIFFERENTLY. Individual people understand media in the context of their own unique experiences. For this reason people may often interpret media quite differently. A child who has not experienced violence in her life but who watches it on TV may not understand that violence brings pain and suffering. In contrast, a child who has witnessed or experienced violence first-hand may react to it with fear for her personal safety.

MEDIA HAVE COMMERCIAL INTERESTS. Rather than being driven by the need to tell the truth, media are driven by the intent to sell you something. Television programs, newspapers, magazines, and commercial Internet sites make sure that the advertisers who support them get a chance to convey a message to the consumer. Advertising is chosen so that it most appeals to those most likely to be reading or seeing that particular kind of media; for example, ads for beer and cars dominate the airwaves during major sports events.

MEDIA HAVE EMBEDDED VALUES AND POINTS OF VIEW. Any media product carries the values of the people who created it. For example, even by choosing the topics on which to write articles, a magazine's editor conveys an opinion that those topics are important. *Runner's World* thinks that how to stay warm on a winter run is important, for example.

The whole point of media literacy is to approach what you see, hear, and read with thought and consideration. Use your critical-thinking processes to analyze the media and develop an informed opinion.

ASK QUESTIONS BASED ON THE MIND ACTIONS. Is what you read in a newspaper similar to something you already know to be true? Do you evaluate a magazine article to be useful or not? Do you agree with the causes or effects that are cited?

EVALUATE THE TRUTH OF THE ARGUMENT. If a TV ad argues that a certain kind of car is the best on the road, evaluate this information the way that you would any argument. With what facts do they back up their claims? Are the claims opinion? Does assuming their claims to be true cause any harm? What strategies are they using to persuade you to adopt their idea?

RECOGNIZE PERSPECTIVE. It is just as important to avoid rejecting the media automatically as it is to avoid accepting them automatically. Any media offering has its own particular perspective, coming from the person or people who created it. Explore this perspective, asking what positive and negative effects it might have. For example, if a website encourages you to adopt the perspective that you should dislike a particular ethnic group, this may have harmful effects.

Becoming media literate will help you become a smart consumer of the media who ultimately is responsible for her actions. Don't let a TV ad or a web banner tell you what to do. Evaluate the message critically and make your own decision. Media literacy is a key to a responsible, self-powered life.

Krinein

The word "critical" is derived from the Greek word *krinein,* which means to separate in order to choose or select. To be a mindful critical thinker and active learner, you need to be able to separate, evaluate, and select ideas, facts, and thoughts.

Think of this concept as you apply critical thinking to your reading, writing, and interaction with others. Be aware of the information you take in and of your thoughts, and evaluate them with care. Critical thinking gives you the power to make sense of life by actively selecting how to respond to the information, people, and events that you encounter.

IMPORTANT POINTS *to remember*

1. What is critical thinking?

Critical thinking, at its heart, is questioning: when you think critically you take in information, question it, and then use what you have learned to create new ideas. The building blocks of critical thinking are seven mind actions: *recall, similarity, difference, cause and effect, example to idea, idea to example,* and *evaluation.* These mind actions, in various combinations, build the thinking processes that help you achieve your goals. Six of your mind's primary thinking processes are: solving problems, making decisions, constructing and evaluating arguments, thinking logically, exploring perspectives, and planning strategically.

2. How does critical thinking help you solve problems and make decisions?

Although not all decisions are about problems, every problem-solving process involves one or more decisions. Use the steps of the problem-solving process—identifying the problem, analyzing the problem, brainstorming solutions, exploring solutions, choosing and executing a solution, and evaluating the solution—to generate solutions and choose one. Decisions are choices that require an evaluation of possibilities. Evaluate a decision by using these steps: Decide on a goal; establish needs; name, investigate, and evaluate available options; decide on a plan of action and pursue it; and evaluate the result.

3. How do you construct and evaluate arguments?

An argument is a persuasive case that you make to prove or disprove a point. The following steps can help you make an effective argument: Establish the premise, gather examples that support it, anticipate questions and points against your argument, and draw a conclusion. It's important to remain as flexible as possible to handle unexpected twists in the conversation. When you evaluate an argument, look at both the quality of the evidence itself (e.g., whether it is fact or opinion, if it is from a reliable source) and the quality of the way in which the evidence supports the premise (e.g., degree of logic, whether there is enough evidence, whether the evidence concurs with common sense).

4. How do you think logically?

Logical thinking has two branches: Distinguishing fact from opinion and challenging assumptions. To distinguish fact from opinion, look for fact characteristics (e.g., actual people, places, objects, and events, and concrete words or measurable statistics) and opinion characteristics (e.g., evaluation, prediction of future events, abstract and emotional words). Ask questions to determine the truth of either a fact or opinion.

Assumptions—statements or ideas that people accept as true without proof—can shape important life decisions, and sometimes they can be problematic. Challenge your assumptions by asking when they are and aren't true, when they do and don't work, why someone may have made and communicated the assumption, and what harm the assumption can cause.

5. Why should you explore perspectives?

Perspective is a way of looking at the world. You have your own unique perspective, but seeing the world only from that perspective can be inflexible and limiting. Exploring perspectives will introduce you to new ideas, improve communication, and encourage mutual respect. To explore perspectives you take in new information, evaluate the perspective, and accept the perspective or perhaps even make it your own.

6. Why plan strategically?

Strategic planning means making long-range plans toward goals; that is, exploring the future effects of today's choices and actions. Strategic planning steps are establishing a goal, brainstorming possible plans involving your available resources, anticipating the effects of each plan, putting the plan into action, and evaluating continually. Strategic planning creates a vision of the future that brings school and work success through successful goal-setting and adjustment to change.

7. How can you develop your creativity?

Everyone has the ability to be creative. Actively creative people have such characteristics as flexibility, a willingness to take risks, inquisitiveness, and a broad range of interests. You can enhance your creativity by taking a broad perspective, spending time with creative people, gathering varied input, and letting yourself play. Brainstorming is a creative process that requires you to consider any ideas that come into your head and refrain from evaluating them right away.

8. What is media literacy?

Media literacy is the ability to respond with critical thinking to the media—radio, television, magazines, newspapers, and Internet materials—that you encounter. Thinking critically about the media will bring you to a more complete understanding of the information that comes your way. The five core concepts of media literacy are: Media are constructions; media use specifically chosen "languages"; different audiences understand the same media message differently; media have commercial interests; and media take particular points of view.

CRITICAL THINKING
APPLYING LEARNING TO LIFE

MAKE AN IMPORTANT DECISION. In this exercise you will use the seven mind actions and the decision-making steps. First, write here the decision you need to make. Choose an important decision that needs to be made soon.

Step 1: Name your goal. Be specific: What goal, or desired effects, do you seek from this decision? For example, if your decision is a choice between two jobs, the effects you want might be financial security, convenience, experience, or anything else that is a priority to you. Write down the desired effects that together make up your goal. Note priorities by numbering the effects in order of importance.

Step 2: Establish needs. Who and what will be affected by your decision? If you are deciding how to finance your education and you have a family to support, for example, you must take into consideration their financial needs as well as your own when exploring options.

List here the people, things, or situations that may be affected by your decision and indicate how your decision will affect them.

Step 3: Check out your options. Look at any options you can imagine. Consider options even if they seem impossible or unlikely; you can evaluate them later. Some decisions only have two options (e.g., to move to a new apartment or not; to get a new roommate or not); others have a wider selection of choices. For example, if you are a full-time student and the parent of a child you must coordinate your class schedule with the child's needs. Options could be the following: (1) put the child in day care, (2) ask a relative to care for the child, (3) hire a full-time nanny, or (4) arrange your class schedule so that you can balance the duties with another parent.

List three possible options for this decision. Then, evaluate the potential good and bad effects of each.

Option 1 _____

Positive effects _____
_____

Negative effects _____
_____

Option 2 _____
Positive effects _____
_____

Negative effects _____
_____

Option 3 _____
Positive effects _____
_____

Negative effects _____
_____

Have you or someone else ever made a decision similar to the one you are about to make? What can you learn from that decision that may help you?

_____
_____
_____

Step 4: Make your decision and pursue it to the goal. Taking your entire analysis into account, decide what to do. Write your decision here.

_____
_____

Next is perhaps the most important step: Act on your decision.

Step 5: Evaluate the result. After you have acted on your decision, evaluate how everything turned out. Did you achieve the effects you wanted to achieve? What were the effects on you? On others? On the situation? To what extent were they positive, negative, or some of both?

List three effects here. Name each effect, circle Positive or Negative, and explain that evaluation.

Effect _____

POSITIVE   NEGATIVE

Why? _____

Effect _____

POSITIVE   NEGATIVE

Why? _____

Effect _____

POSITIVE   NEGATIVE

Why? _____

Final evaluation: Write one statement in reaction to the decision you made. Indicate whether you feel the decision was useful or not useful, and why. Indicate any adjustments that could have made the effects of your decision more positive.

_____

_____

_____

_____

_____

TEAMWORK

COMBINING FORCES

GROUP PROBLEM SOLVING. As a class, brainstorm a list of problems in your lives. Write the problems on the board or on a large piece of paper attached to an easel. Include any problems you feel comfortable discussing with others. Such problems may involve school, relationships, jobs, discrimination, parenting, housing, procrastination, and others. Divide into groups of two to four with each group choosing or being assigned one problem to work on. Use the empty problem-solving flowchart to fill in your work.

1. *Identify the problem.* As a group, state your problem specifically, without causes ("I'm not attending all of my classes" is better than "lack of motivation"). Then, look at the causes and effects that surround it. Record the effects that the problem has. List what causes the problem. Remember to look for "hidden" causes (you may perceive that traffic makes you late to school, but getting up too late might be the hidden cause).

FIGURE **4.8**

Problem-solving flowchart.

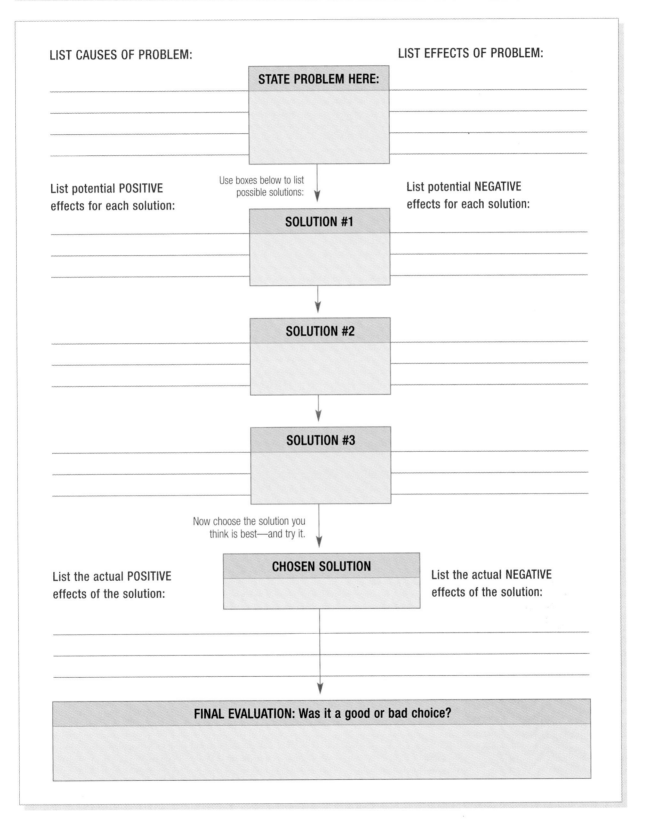

LIST CAUSES OF PROBLEM:

LIST EFFECTS OF PROBLEM:

STATE PROBLEM HERE:

Use boxes below to list possible solutions:

List potential POSITIVE effects for each solution:

List potential NEGATIVE effects for each solution:

SOLUTION #1

SOLUTION #2

SOLUTION #3

Now choose the solution you think is best—and try it.

CHOSEN SOLUTION

List the actual POSITIVE effects of the solution:

List the actual NEGATIVE effects of the solution:

FINAL EVALUATION: Was it a good or bad choice?

2. *Brainstorm possible solutions.* Determine the most likely causes of the problem; from those causes, derive possible solutions. Record all the ideas that group members offer. After 10 minutes or so, each group member should choose one possible solution to explore independently.

3. *Explore each solution.* In thinking independently through the assigned solution, each group member should (a) weigh the positive and negative effects, (b) consider similar problems, (c) determine whether the problem requires a different strategy from other problems like it, and (d) describe how the solution affects the causes of the problem. Evaluate your assigned solution. Is it a good one? Will it work?

4. *Choose your top solution(s).* Come together again as a group. Take turns sharing your observations and recommendations, and then take a vote: Which solution is the best? You may have a tie or combine two different solutions. Either way is fine. Different solutions suit different people and situations. Although it's not always possible to reach agreement, try to find the solution that works for most of the group.

5. *Evaluate the solution you decide is best.* When you decide on your top solution or solutions, discuss what would happen if you went through with it. What do you predict would be the positive and negative effects of this solution? Would it turn out to be a truly good solution for everyone?

WRITING

DISCOVERY THROUGH JOURNALING

To record your thoughts, use a separate journal or the lined page at the end of the chapter.

MEDIA LITERACY. Choose a magazine you read, an Internet site you visit, a TV program you watch, or any other media source with which you come into contact. Evaluate this media source according to what you know about media literacy. What effect does this media intend to have on you? Does it use particular language or images to create that effect? Is it trying to sell something? What values does it convey? And most importantly, how do you feel about its intentions and effects?

CAREER PORTFOLIO

CHARTING YOUR COURSE

INVESTIGATE A CAREER. Choose one career that interests you. Use your critical-thinking processes to think through all aspects of this career strategically. Be an investigator. Find out as many facts as you can and evaluate all opinions based on what you already know.

- What are the different kinds of jobs available in this career?
- What is the condition of the industry—growing, lagging, or holding steady?
- Does this career require you to live in a certain area of the country or world?
- Who can you talk with to find out more information about this career?
- What are the pros and cons (positive and negative effects) of working in this area?
- What types of people tend to succeed in this career, and what types tend not to do well?
- What are the opinions of those around you about this career?
- What preparation—in school and/or on the job—does this career require?

Then, write up your findings in a report. Use each question as a separate heading. Keep your research in your portfolio. Write a conclusion about your prospects in this career area based on what you learned in your investigation.

 ## UGGESTED READINGS

Bianculli, David. *Teleliteracy: Taking Television Seriously.* New York: Simon & Schuster (1994).

Cameron, Julia with Mark Bryan. *The Artist's Way: A Spiritual Path to Higher Creativity.* New York: G. P. Putnam's Sons (1995).

deBono, Edward. *Lateral Thinking: Creativity Step by Step.* New York: Perennial Library (1990).

Noone, Donald J., Ph.D. *Creative Problem Solving.* New York: Barron's (1998).

Postman, Neil and Steve Powers. *How to Watch TV News.* New York: Penguin (1992).

Sark. *Living Juicy: Daily Morsels for Your Creative Soul.* Berkeley, CA: Celestial Arts (1994).

von Oech, Roger. *A Kick in the Seat of the Pants.* New York: Harper & Row (1986).

von Oech, Roger. *A Whack on the Side of the Head.* New York: Warner Books (1998).

 ## NTERNET RESOURCES

Roger von Oech's Creative Think website: www.creativethink.com/
Center for Media Literacy: www.medialit.org/

**NDNOTES**

1. Frank T. Lyman, Jr., Ph.D. "Think-Pair-Share, Thinktrix, Thinklinks, and Weird Facts: An Interactive System for Cooperative Thinking." In *Enhancing Thinking Through Cooperative Learning,* ed. Neil Davidson and Toni Worsham. New York: Teachers College Press (1992), pp. 169–181.

2. Ben E. Johnson. *Stirring Up Thinking.* New York: Houghton Mifflin Company (1998), pp. 268–270.

3. Sylvan Barnet and Hugo Bedau. *Critical Thinking, Reading, and Writing: A Brief Guide to Argument,* 2nd ed. Boston: Bedford Books of St. Martin's Press (1996), p. 43.

4. Roger von Oech. *A Kick in the Seat of the Pants.* New York: Harper & Row Publishers (1986), pp. 5–21.

5. J. R. Hayes. *Cognitive psychology: Thinking and creating.* Homewood, IL: Dorsey (1978).

6. T. M. Amabile. *The Social Psychology of Creativity.* New York: Springer-Verlag (1983).

7. Roger von Oech. *A Whack on the Side of the Head.* New York: Warner Books, (1990), pp. 11–168.

8. Dennis Coon. *Introduction to Psychology: Exploration and Application,* 6th ed. St. Paul: West Publishing Company (1992), p. 295.

9. Center for Media Literacy, 1998.

Journal

NAME

DATE

Thinking It Through

Check those statements that apply to you right now:

- I find myself struggling to get through many of my texts.
- When I read rapidly, I have trouble understanding or remembering what I read.
- When I learn a new vocabulary word, I often don't remember the definition for long.
- When I study, I often have to read the same material over and over again to grasp it.
- When I learn something new, I rarely think about its relation to what I already know about the subject.
- When I study with a group of classmates, the whole group wastes a lot of time.

CHAPTER 5

IN THIS CHAPTER,

you will explore answers to the following questions:

- How can you set the stage for reading?
- What will help you understand what you read?
- How can you build a better vocabulary?
- How can you increase your reading speed?
- How can SQ3R help you own what you read?
- How can you respond critically to what you read?
- How and why should you study with others?

Your reading background—your past as a reader—may not necessarily prepare you for the new challenges of college reading. In the past, you may have had more time to read less material, with less necessity for deep-level understanding. In college, however, your reading will often be complex, and you may experience an overload of assignments. Even with study guides and other aids, college reading and studying require a step-by-step approach aimed at the construction of meaning and knowledge.

The material in this chapter will present techniques that can help you read and study as efficiently as possible, while still having time left over for other things. You will learn how you can overcome barriers to successful reading and why you should have a purpose each time you read. You will learn techniques for building a better vocabulary and for becoming comfortable with American English and increasing your reading speed. You will also explore the SQ3R study technique, see how critical reading can help you maximize your understanding of any text, and learn to use study groups to maximize your study time.

Reading and Studying

WHAT WILL HELP YOU UNDERSTAND WHAT YOU READ?

More than anything else, reading is a process that requires you, the reader, to *make meaning* from written words. This involves far more than interpreting the alphabet symbols on the page. When you make meaning, you connect yourself to the concepts being communicated. Your prior knowledge or familiarity with a subject, culture and home environment, life experiences, and even personal interpretation of words and phrases affect your understanding.

Because these factors are different for every person, your reading experiences are uniquely your own. For example, say your family owns a hardware store where you have worked from time to time. Although you may read a Retailing chapter in a business textbook in the context of what you observed while working, most of your classmates probably have no first-hand knowledge of how a retail business operates. Although your reading includes comparing text concepts to the methods your family used to run the store, your classmates are reading for basic vocabulary and concepts.

Reading *comprehension* refers to your ability to understand what you read. True comprehension goes beyond just knowing facts and figures—a student can parrot back a pile of economics statistics on a test, for example, without understanding what they mean. Only when you thoroughly comprehend the information you read can you make the most effective use of that information.

All reading strategies have the ultimate purpose of helping you to achieve greater understanding of what you read. Therefore, every section in this chapter will in some way help you maximize your comprehension. Following are some general comprehension boosters to keep in mind as you work through the chapter and as you tackle individual reading assignments.

BUILD KNOWLEDGE THROUGH READING AND STUDYING. More than any other factor, what you already know before you read a passage will influence your ability to understand and remember important ideas. Previous knowledge gives you a **context** for what you read.

> **CONTEXT**
>
> Written or spoken knowledge that can help illuminate the meaning of a word or passage.

THINK POSITIVELY. Instead of telling yourself that you cannot understand, think positively. Tell yourself: *I can learn this material. I am a good reader.*

THINK CRITICALLY. Ask yourself questions. Do you understand the sentence, paragraph, or chapter you just read? Are ideas and supporting examples clear? Could you explain the material to someone else? Later in this chapter, you will learn strategies for responding critically to what you read.

BUILD VOCABULARY. Lifelong learners consider their vocabulary a work in progress because they never finish learning new words. The more you know, the more material you can understand without stopping to wonder what new words mean.

HOW CAN YOU SET THE STAGE FOR READING?

On any given day during your college career, you may be faced with reading assignments like this:

- A textbook chapter on the history of South African apartheid (World History)
- An original research study on the relation between sleep deprivation and the development of memory problems (Psychology)
- Chapters 4–6 in John Steinbeck's classic novel, *The Grapes of Wrath* (American Literature)
- A technical manual on the design of computer antivirus programs (Computer Science—Software Design)

This material is rigorous by anyone's standards. To get through it—and master its contents—you'll need a systematic approach to reading.

If you have a reading disability, if English is not your primary language, or if you have limited reading skills, you may need additional support (see Chapter 3 for more on learning disabilities). Most colleges provide services for students through a reading center or tutoring program. Take the initiative to seek help if you need it. Many accomplished learners have benefited from help in specific areas. Remember that the ability to succeed is often linked to the ability to ask for and receive help.

Take an Active Approach to Difficult Texts

Because texts are often written to challenge the intellect, even well-written, useful texts may be difficult to read. Some textbooks may be written by experts who may not explain information in the friendliest manner for non-experts. And, as every student knows, some textbooks are poorly written and organized.

Generally, the further you advance in your education and your career, the more complex your required reading is likely to be. You may encounter new concepts, words, and terms that feel like a foreign language. Assignments can also be difficult when the required reading is from *primary sources*—original documents rather than another writer's interpretation of these documents—or from academic journal articles and scientific studies that don't define basic terms or supply a wealth of examples. Among the primary sources you may encounter are:

- historical documents
- works of literature (novels, poems, and plays)
- scientific studies, including lab reports and accounts of experiments
- journal articles

The following strategies may help you approach difficult material actively and positively:

- *Approach reading assignments with an open mind.* Be careful not to prejudge them as impossible or boring before you even start to read.
- *Know that some texts may require extra work and concentration.* Set a goal to make your way through the material, whatever it takes. If you want to learn, you will.
- *Define concepts that your material does not explain.* Consult resources—instructors, students, reference materials—for help.

To help with your make-meaning-of-textbooks mission, you may want to create your own mini-library at home. Collect reference materials that you use often, such as a dictionary, a thesaurus, a writer's style handbook, and maybe an atlas or computer manual (many of these are available as computer software or CD-ROMs). You may also benefit from owning reference materials in your particular areas of study. "If you find yourself going to the library to look up the same reference again and again, consider purchasing that book for your personal or office library," advises library expert Sherwood Harris.[1]

Choose the Right Setting

Finding a place and time that minimize outside distractions will help you achieve the focus and discipline that your reading requires. Here are some suggestions.

SELECT THE RIGHT COMPANY (OR LACK THEREOF). If you prefer to read alone, establish a relatively interruption-proof place and time, such as an out-of-the-way spot at the library or an after-class hour in an empty classroom. Even if you don't mind activity nearby, try to minimize distraction.

SELECT THE RIGHT LOCATION. Many students study at a library desk. Others prefer an easy chair at the library or at home, or even the floor. Choose a spot that's comfortable but not so cushy that you fall asleep. Make sure that you have adequate lighting and aren't too hot or cold. At home, you may want to avoid the distraction of studying in a room where a television is on.

SELECT THE RIGHT TIME. Choose a time when you feel alert and focused. Try reading just before or after the class for which the reading is assigned, if you can. Eventually, you will associate preferred places and times with focused reading.

Students with families have an additional factor involved in their decisions about when, where, and how to read. Figure 5.1 explores some ways that parents or other people caring for children may be able to maximize their study efforts. These techniques will also help after college if you choose to telecommute—work from home through an Internet-linked computer—while your children are still at home under your care.

Define Your Purpose for Reading

When you define your purpose, you ask yourself *why* you are reading a particular piece of material. One way to do this is by completing this sentence: "In reading this material, I intend to define/learn/answer/achieve. . . ." With a clear purpose in mind, you can decide how much time and effort to expend on various reading assignments. Nearly 375 years ago, Francis Bacon, the great English philosopher, recognized

Managing children while studying.

FIGURE
5.1

MANAGING CHILDREN WHILE STUDYING

Keep them up-to-date on your schedule.

Let them know when you have a big test or project due and when you are under less pressure, and what they can expect of you in each case.

Explain what your education entails.

Tell them how it will improve your life and theirs. This applies, of course, to older children who can understand the situation and compare it to their own schooling.

Find help.

Ask a relative or friend to watch your children or arrange for a child to visit a friend's house. Consider trading baby-sitting hours with another parent, hiring a sitter to come to your home, or using a day-care center that is private or school-sponsored.

Keep them active while you study.

Give them games, books, or toys to occupy them. If there are special activities that you like to limit, such as watching videos on TV, save them for your study time.

Offset study time with family time and rewards.

Children may let you get your work done if they have something to look forward to, such as a movie night, a trip for ice cream, or something else they like.

Study on the phone.

You might be able to have a study session with a fellow student over the phone while your child is sleeping or playing quietly.

SPECIAL NOTES FOR INFANTS

Study at night if your baby goes to sleep early, or in the morning if your baby sleeps late.

Study during nap times if you aren't too tired yourself.

Lay your notes out and recite information to the baby. The baby will appreciate the attention, and you will get work done.

Put baby in a safe and fun place while you study, such as a playpen, motorized swing, or jumping seat.

Some books are to be tasted, others to be swallowed, and some few to be chewed and digested; that is, some books are to be read only in parts, others to be read but not curiously; and some few to be read wholly, and with diligence and attention.

Achieving your reading purpose requires adapting to different types of reading materials. Being a flexible reader—adjusting reading strategies and pace—will help you adapt successfully.

Purpose Determines Reading Strategy

With purpose comes direction; with direction comes a strategy for reading. Following are four reading purposes, examined briefly. You may have one or more for any "reading event."

PURPOSE 1: READ FOR UNDERSTANDING. In college, studying involves reading for the purpose of comprehending the material. The two main components of comprehension are *general ideas* and *specific facts or examples*. These components depend on each other. Facts and examples help to explain or support ideas, and ideas provide a framework that helps the reader to remember facts and examples.

- *General Ideas.* General-idea reading is rapid reading that seeks an overview of the material. You search for general ideas by focusing on headings, subheadings, and summary statements.
- *Specific Facts or Examples.* At times, readers may focus on locating specific pieces of information—for example, the stages of intellectual development in young children. Often, a reader may search for examples that support or explain more general ideas—for example, the causes of economic recession. Because you know exactly what you are looking for, you can skim the material quickly.

PURPOSE 2: READ TO EVALUATE CRITICALLY. Critical evaluation involves understanding. It means approaching the material with an open mind, examining causes and effects, evaluating ideas, and asking questions that test the writer's argument and search for assumptions. Critical reading brings an understanding of material that goes beyond basic information recall (see p. 158 for more on critical reading). A student evaluating a fellow student's essay, or an employee reading a draft of a press release, will read critically.

PURPOSE 3: READ FOR PRACTICAL APPLICATION. A third purpose for reading is to gather usable information that you can apply toward a specific goal. When you read a textbook preface or an instruction booklet for a new software package, your goal is to learn how to do something. Reading and action usually go hand in hand. Remembering the specifics requires a certain degree of general comprehension.

PURPOSE 4: READ FOR PLEASURE. Some materials you read for entertainment, such as *Sports Illustrated* magazine or the latest John Grisham courtroom thriller. Entertaining reading may also go beyond materials that seem obviously designed to entertain. Whereas some people may read a Jane Austen novel for a class assignment, others may read her books for pleasure.

As Yale professor Harold Bloom points out, reading for pleasure gives you the opportunity to enlarge your life and to enter into "alternate realities." "Why read?" he asks. "Because you can know, intimately, only a very few people, and perhaps you never know them at all. After reading [the Thomas Mann masterpiece] *The Magic Mountain* you know Hans Castorp thoroughly, and he is greatly worth knowing."[2]

Purpose Determines Pace

George M. Usova, senior education specialist and graduate professor at Johns Hopkins University, explains: "Good readers are flexible readers. They read at a variety of rates and adapt them to the reading purpose at hand, the difficulty of the material, and their familiarity with the subject area."[3] For example, you may need to read academic or unfamiliar materials more slowly, whereas you will increase your reading speed for journalism, magazines, and online publications. As Table 5.1 shows, good readers link the pace of reading to their reading purpose.

No barrier of the senses shuts me out from the sweet, gracious discourse of my book friends. They talk to me without embarrassment or awkwardness.

HELEN KELLER

A strong vocabulary increases reading speed and comprehension—when you understand words you are reading, you don't have to stop to think about what they mean. The next section will help you learn strategies to expand your vocabulary.

HOW DO YOU BUILD A BETTER VOCABULARY?

As your reading materials at school and at work become more complex, how much you comprehend—and how readily you do it—will depend on your vocabulary. Is your word power minimal, general, and static? Or is it large, specialized, and ever-expanding?

The best way to build your vocabulary is to commit yourself to learning new and unfamiliar words as you encounter them. Building your vocabulary in the context of a work is at the heart of the meaning-making process you learned about earlier. This involves the following steps.

Analyze Word Parts

Often, if you understand part of a word, you will be able to figure out what the entire word means. This is true because many English words are made up of a combination of Greek and Latin prefixes, roots, and suffixes. *Prefixes* are word parts that are added to the beginning of a **root**. *Suffixes* are added to the end of the root. Table 5.2 contains just a few of the prefixes, roots, and suffixes you will encounter as you read. There are literally thousands more. Taking the time to memorize these verbal building blocks will dramatically increase your vocabulary because you will encounter them over and over again in different words.

Figure 5.2 shows how one root can be the stem of many different words.

> **ROOT**
>
> The central part or basis of a word, around which prefixes and suffixes can be added to produce different words.

TABLE 5.1   Linking purpose to pace.

TYPE OF MATERIAL	READING PURPOSE	PACE
Academic readings • Textbooks • Original sources • Articles from scholarly journals • Online publications for academic readers • Lab reports • Required fiction	• Critical analysis • Overall mastery • Preparation for tests	Slow, especially if the material is new and unfamiliar
Manuals • Instructions • Recipes	Practical application	Slow to medium
Journalism and nonfiction for the general reader • Nonfiction books • Newspapers • Magazines • Online publications for the general public	Understanding of general ideas, key concepts, and specific facts for personal understanding and/or practical application	Medium to fast
Nonrequired fiction	Understanding of general ideas, key concepts, and specific facts for enjoyment	Variable, but tending toward the faster speeds

Source: Adapted from Nicholas Reid Schaffzin, *The Princeton Review Reading Smart.* New York: Random House, 1996, p. 15.

Using prefixes, roots, and suffixes, you can piece together the meaning of many of the new words you encounter. To use a simple example, the word *prologue* is made up of the prefix *pro* (before) and the root *logue* (to speak). Thus, *prologue* refers to words spoken or written before the main text.

Use a Dictionary

When reading a textbook, the first "dictionary" to search is the glossary. Textbooks often include an end-of-book glossary that explains technical words and concepts. The definitions there are usually limited to the meaning of the term as it is used in the text.

Common prefixes, roots, and suffixes.

PREFIX	PRIMARY MEANING	EXAMPLE
a, ab	from	abstain, avert
ad, af, at	to	adhere, affix, attain
con, cor, com	with, together	convene, correlate, compare
di	apart	divert, divorce
il	not	illegal, illegible
ir	not	irresponsible
post	after	postpone, postpartum
sub, sup	under	subordinate, suppose

ROOT	PRIMARY MEANING	EXAMPLE
-com	fill	incomplete
-strict	bind	restriction
-cept	take	receptacle
-chron	time	synchronize
-ann	year	biannual
-sper	hope	desperate
-clam	cry out	proclamation
-voc	speak, talk	convocation

SUFFIX	PRIMARY MEANING	EXAMPLE
-able	able	recyclable
-arium	place for	aquarium, solarium
-cule	very small	molecule
-ist	one who	pianist
-meter	measure	thermometer
-ness	state of	carelessness
-sis	condition of	hypnosis
-y	inclined to	sleepy

Standard dictionaries provide broader information such as word origin, pronunciation, part of speech, synonyms (words that are similar), antonyms (words with opposite meanings), and multiple meanings. Using a dictionary whenever you read will increase your comprehension. Buy a standard dictionary, keep it nearby, and consult it for help in understanding passages that contain unfamiliar words. Although electronic dictionaries offer fewer definitions, with less extensive explanations, they are a handy tool because of their speed in accessing words.

FIGURE

5.2

Building words from a single root.

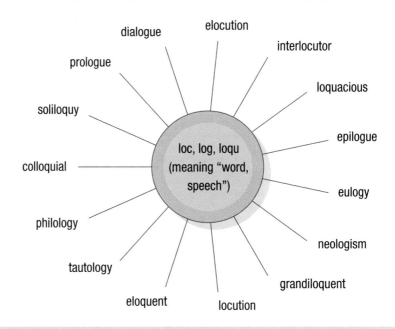

You may not always have time for the following suggestions, but when you can use them, they will help you make the most of your dictionary.

READ EVERY MEANING OF A WORD, NOT JUST THE FIRST. Think critically about which meaning suits the context of the word in question, and choose the one that makes the most sense to you.

SAY THE WORD OUT LOUD—THEN WRITE IT DOWN TO MAKE SURE YOU CAN SPELL IT. Check your pronunciation against the dictionary symbols as you say each word. Speaking and writing new words as you use them will boost your recall.

SUBSTITUTE A WORD OR PHRASE FROM THE DEFINITION FOR THE WORD. Use the definition you have chosen. Imagine, for example, that you encounter the following sentence and do not know what the word *indoctrinated* means: The cult indoctrinated its members to reject society's values.

In the dictionary, you find several definitions, including *brainwashed* and *instructed*. You decide that the one closest to the correct meaning is *brainwashed*. With this term, the sentence reads as follows: The cult brainwashed its members to reject society's values.

RESTATE THE DEFINITION IN YOUR OWN WORDS. To make sure you really know what a word means, define it again in your own words. When you can do this with ease, you know that you understand the meaning and are not merely parroting a dictionary definition.

KEEP A JOURNAL OF EVERY NEW WORD YOU LEARN, INCLUDING DEFINITIONS. Review the journal on a regular basis and watch your vocabulary grow.

Use Memory Aids To Ensure Recall

Your next task is to memorize your new vocabulary—to learn new words permanently so that you can use them at will in writing and speaking and understand them when you hear or read them.

You'll need tools to help you memorize, including mnemonic devices and flash cards. These are discussed in detail in Chapter 6. Most students find that their most important vocabulary-building tool is the flash card. Your efforts will be painless if you study several cards a day and push yourself to use your new words in conversation and writing. You may also want to work together with another student to review the cards both of you have made. A buddy system may give you the motivation to master your new vocabulary as it exposes you to the vocabulary your partner has identified.

Learn Specialized Vocabulary

When you focus on one academic subject by working toward a major, or when you begin working, you may encounter a very specialized vocabulary that few outsiders know. Most of these words, phrases, and initials may be unfamiliar to you even if you were born and raised in the United States. To learn them, take the same approach you used to improving your basic vocabulary. Even if you feel like you are diving into a foreign language, you can take comfort in knowing that you will quickly learn this new language because you are being exposed to it every day.

For example, if you are studying or working in banking and finance, here are just a few of the new terms you will encounter:

bear market	prime rate
bull market	warrant
book value	yield
common stocks	IPO
compound interest	leveraged buy-out
price/earnings ratio	

Similarly, if you are pursuing work in the medical field, you may encounter the following terms:

HMO	preferred provider organization (PPO)
Medicare	ER
Medicaid	resident
CAT Scan	intern
stress test	specialist
EKG	co-payment

Much of acquiring the vocabulary specific to any discipline or career field involves learning as you go. Don't rush through materials that have unfamiliar words or concepts—look them up, ask other students or coworkers about them, and relate them to concepts you already know. Only on a solid knowledge base can you build additional learning; give yourself that base by taking the time to understand the vocabulary of what you study and what you do.

If you are not a native English speaker, you may find that particular words and phrases in American English are as unfamiliar to you as the vocabulary specific to your field. You can approach this problem much as you would any new vocabulary.

Become Comfortable Reading American English

You may be one of the millions of students in the United States who speak English as a second language or who are unfamiliar with American English because you came from an English-speaking country other than the United States, such as Jamaica, Ireland, or South Africa. Although you are comfortable enough with the basics of American English to pursue a college degree, you may have trouble understanding the idiosyncrasies of American English—the slang and initials that are often used in written materials and in speech.

These can be learned in the same way as you learn new vocabulary. Try to define them in the context of the sentence. Look them up in a dictionary or in a specialized reference book. (An excellent volume is Robert L. Chapman, *American Slang: The Abridged Edition of the Dictionary of American Slang,* New York: HarperPerennial, 1998.) Fix them in your memory with mnemonics and flash cards.

Understanding American Slang

Slang is nonstandard English that has accepted usage among all or part of the population and that expresses thoughts in an informal way. Often, the words and phrases of slang seem to have little direct relation to their meaning, yet our culture accepts the meaning. Word experts, known as lexicographers, have successfully traced the meanings of many slang expressions back to their origin. For example, the phrase, *to toe the mark* means *to behave properly* and derives from runners placing their toes at the mark that indicates the starting point of a race. Table 5.3 includes a number of common slang expressions you may encounter as you read.

Understanding Commonly Used Initials

As a nonnative speaker, you may also encounter commonly used initials that you are expected to recognize. Table 5.4 includes just a few initials that you may encounter as you read.

With so much to read now and in your future career, it is important to set a goal to improve your reading speed along with your comprehension. You will learn techniques to become a faster reader next.

HOW CAN YOU INCREASE YOUR READING SPEED?

Most students lead busy lives, carrying heavy academic loads while perhaps working or even caring for a family. It's difficult to make time to study at all, let alone handle the reading assignments for your different

Common slang you may encounter in writing and speech.

EXPRESSION PART OF SPEECH	MEANING	DERIVATION
also-ran (noun)	A loser, a person, product etc. that does not succeed.	From the term for a racehorse who runs fourth or worse.
bite the bullet (verb)	To do something painful but necessary; to accept the cost of a course of action.	From the early surgical practice of having the patient bite hard on a bullet to divert the mind from pain and prevent screaming.
catch-22 (noun)	A condition or requirement very hard to fulfill, especially one that flatly contradicts others.	From the title of a 1961 satirical war novel by Joseph Heller.
dot com (noun)	A virtual business with a presence on the Internet.	From the .com suffix for commercial enterprises on the World Wide Web.
ego trip (noun)	Something done primarily to build one's self-esteem or display superior qualities.	Based on drug-induced psychedelic narcotic experiences, or trips.
freewheeling (noun)	Independence of action.	From the feature of certain 1930s cars permitting them to coast freely without being slowed by the engine.
go for the gold	To strive for the highest reward.	From the gold medal awarded to the first place finisher in Olympic competitions.
hit pay dirt (verb)	To find what one is looking for or needs; to earn a profit.	From the efforts of workers to drill through dirt until they hit oil, a saleable commodity.
in the red (noun)	In debt, losing money.	From the color of the ink traditionally used by bookkeepers to record financial losses.
off the charts (adjective phrase)	Too large to be measured.	From the published charts that show top-selling musical albums.

Source: Examples from Robert L. Chapman and Barbara Ann Kipfer, *American Slang,* 2nd ed., New York: HarperPerennial, 1998.

classes. In the workplace, many jobs have such a fast pace and so many tasks to be done that very little time is available for the reading that needs to be done. When physicians need to read medical journals to keep up with the latest research, teachers need to read updated curriculum guides, or public servants need to read the latest news reports, they often have to do so on their own time outside of the workplace. Increasing your reading comprehension and speed will save you valuable time and effort.

Initials that convey meaning.

INITIAL	MEANING
ASAP	as soon as possible
AWOL	absent without leave
FBI	Federal Bureau of Investigation
FYI	for your information
IRA	Individual Retirement Account
MVP	most valuable player
SRO	standing room only
VCR	video cassette recorder
VIP	very important person

Rapid reading won't do you any good if you can't remember the material or answer questions about it. However, reading too slowly can eat up valuable time and give your mind space to wander. Your goal is to read for maximum speed *and* comprehension. Because greater comprehension is the primary goal and actually promotes faster reading, make comprehension your priority over speed.

Test Your Speed and Comprehension

To make your own reading-speed assessment, time how rapidly you read the following 500-word selection from start to finish without stopping. This excerpt, entitled "Back to School at Middle Age," is adapted from the seventh edition of Grace J. Craig's college text *Human Development:*[4]

> Although today's college campuses are filled with 18- to 22-year-olds, they are also filled with older, nontraditional students who are returning to school. Nearly 1.5 million women and more than 700,000 men over the age of 35 are attending college—as 4-year students, in 2-year degree programs, and as graduate students. While there has been a dramatic increase in this segment of the college population, the percentage of typical college students—men and women between the ages of 18 and 22—has actually declined since 1980.
>
> This dramatic demographic shift coincides with the recognition that humans are lifelong learners with cognitive abilities that adapt to life demands. Despite societal stereotypes that the primary period for learning is over after adolescence, we now know that it is during middle age that adults acquire the information and skills they need to meet the changing demands

of their jobs. This is as true for bankers as it is for computer scientists, both of whom work in fields that have changed radically in recent years as a result of an explosion in technology.

In large part, middle-aged students are returning to school because they have to. Many are unemployed—the victims of corporate downsizing. Others are moving into the job market after spending time at home as full-time parents. A financial planner who stopped working for 5 years to raise her daughter may need recertification before any firm will hire her. Even adults who worked part-time during their child-rearing years may have to return to school to acquire the knowledge they need to qualify for a full-time job. This is especially true in fields with a high degree of professional obsolescence.

Whatever the reason for their return, studies show that the majority of middle-aged students are conscientious about their work. They attend classes regularly and get better grades, on average, than other segments of the student population.

The decision to return to school involves personal introspection and assessment of one's skills and abilities. The student role is generally different from the other roles middle-aged adults assume, and it requires considerable adaptation. A student is in a subordinate position as a learner. Also, mature adults may find themselves among a large number of students who are considerably younger than they are, and the faculty may also be younger. Initially, the age difference may be a source of discomfort.

Family members must often take on new responsibilities when a middle-aged member assumes the role of college student. A husband may have to do more household chores, while a wife may have to return to work to supplement the family income. In addition, the student may need emotional support. Sometimes this involves awkward role reversals and the disruption of familiar interaction patterns.

With the realization that middle-aged students are here to stay, community colleges and universities are making substantial adjustments to meet their needs. In addition many students receive the training they need at work. Many large corporations run training departments designed to maintain a competent work force.

Source: Human Development, 7/E by Craig, © 1994. Adapted by permission of Prentice-Hall, Inc., Upper Saddle River, NJ.

Use the following formula to calculate how quickly you read this material:

- Note the time it took you in minutes to read the passage. Use decimals for fractions of a minute. That is, if it took you 1 minute and 45 seconds, then write 1.75 minutes.
- Divide the number of words in the passage by your reading time.

The number you come up with is your reading speed in words per minute. If you spent 1.75 minutes reading this 500-word selection, you would divide 500 by 1.75 to come up with a reading speed of approximately 286 words per minute.

Now answer the following questions without looking back at the text:

1. How many men and women over the age of 35 are now enrolled in various college programs?

   A. approximately 1.5 million women and 700,000 men

B. 5 million men and women

C. approximately 1.5 million men and 700,000 women

2. How has the enrollment of 18- to 22-year-old college students changed since 1980 in relation to the total college population?

A. The percentage of students in this age group has increased.

B. The percentage of students in this age group has remained the same.

C. The percentage of students in this age group has decreased.

3. According to the passage, which one of the following reasons does not describe why older adults return to school?

A. Unemployed adults return to school to acquire new work-related skills.

B. After spending time at home raising children, many adults are moving onto another stage of life, which involves returning to work.

C. Adults with discretionary income are choosing to invest money in themselves.

4. According to the text, why is the student role different from the other roles middle-aged adults assume?

A. As learners, students are in a subordinate position, which can be uncomfortable for mature adults.

B. Adults are not used to studying.

C. Middle-aged adults often find it difficult to talk to young adults.

Here are the correct answers: 1A, 2C, 3C, 4A. You should have gotten at least three of the four questions correct. In general, your comprehension percentage, as judged by the number of questions like these that you answer correctly, should be above 70 percent. Lower scores mean that you are missing or forgetting important information.

Problems and Solutions for Slower Readers

The average American adult reads between 150 and 350 words per minute. Slow readers fall below this range while faster readers are capable of speeds of 500 to 1,000 words per minute and sometimes faster.[5] Researchers point to a number of specific causes for slow reading. Identifying these patterns in your own reading style is your first step to correcting them. You are then ready to apply proven solutions.[6]

WORD-BY-WORD READING. When you first learned to read, as a young child, your teachers may have told you to read one word at a time as you moved systematically from one line to the next. This technique limits your reading speed. As a speed reader, you must train your eyes to "capture" and read groups of words at a time. Try swinging your eyes from side to side as you read a passage instead of stopping at various points to read individual words. When reading narrow columns, focus your eyes in the middle of the column and read down the page. With practice, you'll be able to read the entire column width.

LACK OF CONCENTRATION. Word-by-word reading inevitably leads to poor concentration. That is, you may be reading too slowly to keep your mind occupied, and soon your thoughts begin to wander. As a result, you may find reading boring, and even find it a sure-fire method to put yourself to sleep. Reading groups of words, instead of single words, will help counteract this effect as you provide your mind with the stimulation it needs to remain engaged.

VOCALIZATION AND SUBVOCALIZATION. Both **vocalization** and **subvocalization** will slow your reading speed. Your first step to changing this behavior is awareness. Monitor your reading; if you notice either habit cropping up, make a conscious effort to stop what you're doing. A self-adhesive note in the margin with the reminder DON'T VOCALIZE may help your efforts in the early stages.

LIMITED VOCABULARY. If your vocabulary is small, you may be continually puzzled by the meanings of words. As you try to figure out meaning from context or consult a dictionary, your reading speed will slow. Follow the suggestions from the vocabulary-building section earlier in the chapter to build your vocabulary. Try to learn as many prefixes, roots, and suffixes as you can with the help of memory aids and flash cards.

UNCONSCIOUS REGRESSION. This involves rereading words that you've already read because your eyes stay on the same line instead of moving ahead. If you find yourself doing this, use your index finger as a visual guide. Reading expert Steve Moidel explains the technique:

> When you finish a line, bring your index finger to the beginning of the next line with a motion as fast and smooth as you can make it. It is important that the return be fluid. If you jerk your finger back, it may become a distraction and ultimately hurt your comprehension. Pretend that your finger is gliding, skiing, or ice skating back to the beginning of the next line: fast yet smooth.[7]

SLOW RECOVERY TIME. The time it takes your eye to move from the end of one line to the beginning of the next is known as *recovery time*. Slow readers spend far too long searching for the next line. Using your finger as a guide will also help speed your recovery time.

The key to building reading speed is practice and more practice, says reading expert Steve Moidel. To achieve your goal of reading between 500 and 1,000 words per minute, Moidel suggests that you start practicing at three times the rate you want to achieve, a rate that is much faster than you can comprehend. For example, if your goal is 500 words per minute, speed up to 1,500 words per minute. Reading at such an accelerated rate will push your eyes and mind to adjust to the faster pace. When you slow down to 500 words per minute—the pace at which you can read and comprehend—your reading rate will feel comfortable even though it is much faster than your original speed.

Now that you have set the stage for reading success, you are ready to hone your reading strategies so that you can master any kind of content as you study. As you will see next, a key to mastery is found in the technique SQ3R.

VOCALIZATION

The practice of speaking words or moving your lips while reading.

SUBVOCALIZATION

The practice of inwardly pronouncing every word while reading.

Using a separate sheet of paper, complete the following.

Thinking Back

1. List four purposes for reading and describe the relation between pace and purpose.

2. Explain how an understanding of word parts can help you grow your vocabulary.

3. Explain how using a dictionary can help improve reading comprehension.

4. List six problems that cause slow reading and ways to solve each problem.

Thinking Ahead

1. Explain the reading strategies that help you retain information most effectively.

2. If you were to design a study method for yourself, what might that method involve?

3. List what you think are the three most important skills required to be a critical reader.

4. How do you help make study groups productive?

HOW CAN SQ3R HELP YOU OWN WHAT YOU READ?

When you study, you take ownership of the material you read. "Owning" what you read means that you learn it well enough to apply it to what you do. For example, by the time students studying to be computer-hardware technicians complete their course work, they should be able to analyze hardware problems that lead to malfunctions. On-the-job computer technicians use the same study technique to keep up with changing technology. Studying to understand and learn also gives you mastery over concepts. For example, a dental hygiene student learns the causes of gum disease, and a journalism student learns about reporting and rhetoric.

SQ3R is a technique that will help you grasp ideas quickly, remember more, and review effectively for tests. The symbols S-Q-3-R stand for *survey, question, read, recite,* and *review*—all steps in the studying process. Developed more than 55 years ago by Francis Robinson, the technique is still being used today because it works.[8] It is particularly helpful for studying all kinds of textbooks.

Moving through the stages of SQ3R requires that you know how to skim and scan. **Skimming** involves rapid reading of chapter elements, including introductions, conclusions, and summaries; the first and last lines of paragraphs; boldface or italicized terms; pictures, charts, and diagrams. In

SKIMMING

Rapid, superficial reading of material to determine central ideas and main elements.

contrast, **scanning** involves the careful search for specific facts and examples. You might use scanning during the review phase of SQ3R, when you need to locate particular information (such as a chemistry formula).

As you explore the steps of SQ3R, approach the system as a framework on which you build your particular house, not as a tower of stone. In other words, instead of following each step by rote, bring your personal learning styles and study preferences to SQ3R. For example, you and another classmate may focus on elements in a different order when you survey, write different types of questions, read at a different pace, prefer different ways of reciting, and favor different sets of review strategies. Take in all of the information about the system, explore the strategies, evaluate what works and what doesn't, and then use the system in a way that makes it your own.

> **SCANNING**
>
> Reading material in an investigative way, searching for specific information.

Survey

When reading textbooks, surveying can help you learn and is encouraged. *Surveying* refers to the process of previewing, or pre-reading, a book before you study it. Compare it to looking at a map before you drive somewhere—those few minutes taking a look at your surroundings and where you intend to go will save you a lot of time and trouble once you are on the road.

Most textbooks include devices that give students an overview of the whole text as well as of the contents of individual chapters. When you survey, pay attention to the following elements.

THE FRONT MATTER. Before you even get to page 1, most textbooks have a table of contents, a preface, and other materials. The table of contents gives you an important overview. Seeing what the book covers, which topics are emphasized, in what order the topics are placed, and the special features each chapter contains can give you valuable preliminary clues about a book. The preface, in particular, can point out the book's unique approach. For example, the preface for the American history text *Out of Many* states that it "offers a distinctive and timely approach to American history, highlighting the experiences of diverse communities of Americans in the unfolding story of our country."[9] This tells you right away that the text looks at American history through the eyes of the different peoples who settled the North American continent, and informs you that cultural diversity will be a central theme.

THE CHAPTER ELEMENTS. Generally, each chapter has numerous devices that help you make meaning out of the bulk of its text. Among these are:

- The chapter title, which establishes the topic and often the author's perspective toward the topic
- The chapter introduction, outline, list of objectives, or list of key topics, designed to give you a helpful overview
- Within the chapter, headings large and small, tables and figures, quotes, marginal notes, and photographs and captions that help you perceive the structure of the material, isolate main ideas, and pull out important concepts
- Special chapter features, often presented in boxes set off from the main text, that point you to ideas connected to themes that run through the text

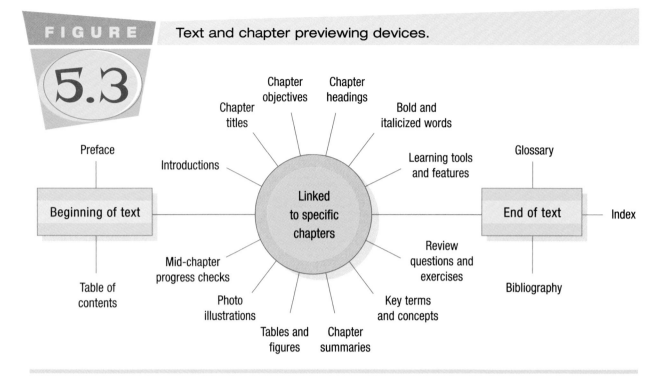

FIGURE 5.3 Text and chapter previewing devices.

- Particular styles or arrangements of type (**boldface,** *italics,* <u>underline,</u> larger fonts, bulletpoints, text with adjusted margins, boxed text) that call your attention to new words, words that are defined in the glossary, or important concepts

At the end of a chapter, a summary may help you tie concepts together. Review questions and exercises help you review and think critically about the material.

THE BACK MATTER. Many textbooks have a text-specific "dictionary" called a glossary that defines terms found in the text. You will also find an index to help you locate individual topics and a bibliography that lists additional reading on particular topics covered in the text.

Figure 5.3 shows the many devices that books employ. Think about how many of these devices you already use, and which you can start using now to boost your comprehension.

Question

Your next step is to examine the chapter headings and, on your own paper, write *questions* linked to them. If your reading material has no headings, develop questions as you read. These questions focus your attention and increase your interest, helping you build comprehension and relate new ideas to what you already know. You can take questions from the textbook or from your lecture notes, or come up with them on your own when you survey, based on what ideas you think are most important.

The table below indicates how this technique works. The column on the left contains primary- and secondary-level headings from a section of *Out of Many.* The column on the right rephrases these headings in question form.

The Meaning of Freedom	What did freedom mean for both slaves and citizens in the United States?
Moving About	Where did African Americans go after they were freed from slavery?
The African American Family	How did freedom change the structure of the African American family?
African American Churches and Schools	What effect did freedom have on the formation of African American churches and schools?
Land and Labor After Slavery	How was land farmed and maintained after slaves were freed?
The Origins of African American Politics	How did the end of slavery bring about the beginning of African American political life?

There is no "correct" set of questions. Given the same headings, you could create your own particular set of questions. The more useful kinds of questions engage the critical-thinking mind actions and processes found in Chapter 4.

Read

Your questions give you a starting point for *reading,* the first R in SQ3R. Learning from textbooks requires that you read *actively. Passive* reading—reading the material without interacting with it by questioning, writing, noting, or highlighting—is a trap many students fall into out of fatigue, boredom, or simply not knowing how else to approach a text. When you read passively, you receive very little learning and retention for your efforts.

Active reading means engaging with the material through questioning, writing, note taking, and other activities. If you spend your time and energy wisely, engaged in active reading, you will receive enormous benefits. As you can see in Figure 5.4, the activities of SQ3R promote active reading. Following are some specific strategies that will keep you active when you read.

FOCUS ON YOUR Q STAGE QUESTIONS. Read the material with the purpose of answering each question you raised. As you come on ideas and examples that relate to your question, write them down or note them in the text.

LOOK FOR CENTRAL IDEAS. Pay special attention to the first and last lines of every paragraph, which should tell you what the paragraph is about. As you read, record key words, phrases, and concepts in your notebook. Some students divide the notebook into two columns, writing questions on the left and answers on the right. This method is called the Cornell note-taking system (see Chapter 7).

MARK UP YOUR TEXTBOOK. Being able to make notations will help you to make sense of the material—for this reason, owning your textbooks is an enormous

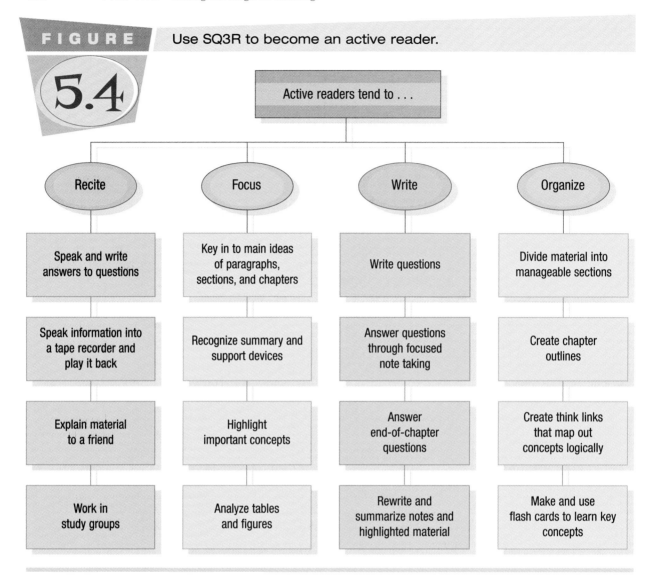

FIGURE 5.4 Use SQ3R to become an active reader.

Active readers tend to . . .

Recite	Focus	Write	Organize
Speak and write answers to questions	Key in to main ideas of paragraphs, sections, and chapters	Write questions	Divide material into manageable sections
Speak information into a tape recorder and play it back	Recognize summary and support devices	Answer questions through focused note taking	Create chapter outlines
Explain material to a friend	Highlight important concepts	Answer end-of-chapter questions	Create think links that map out concepts logically
Work in study groups	Analyze tables and figures	Rewrite and summarize notes and highlighted material	Make and use flash cards to learn key concepts

advantage. You may want to write notes in the margins, circle key ideas, or highlight key points. Some people prefer to underline, although underlining adds more ink to the lines of text and may overwhelm your eyes. Bracketing an entire key passage is a good alternative to underlining. Selective highlighting may help you pinpoint material to review before an exam, although excessive highlighting may actually interfere with comprehension.

Here are some tips on how to strike a balance.

- Mark the text after you read the material once through. If you do it on the first reading, you may mark less important passages.
- Highlight key terms and concepts. Mark the examples that explain and support important ideas.
- Avoid overmarking. A phrase or two in any paragraph is usually enough. Set off long passages with brackets rather than marking every line.
- Don't mistake highlighting for learning. You will not learn what you highlight unless you interact with it through careful review—questioning, writing, and reciting.

One critical step in this phase is to divide your reading into digestible segments. Pace your reading so that you understand as you go. If you find you are losing the thread of the ideas you are reading, you may want to try smaller segments, or you may need to take a break and come back to it later. Try to avoid reading in mere sets of time—such as, "I'll read for 30 minutes and then quit"—or you may destroy the meaning by stopping in the middle of a key explanation.

Recite

Once you finish reading a topic, stop and answer the questions you raised in the Q stage of SQ3R. You may decide to *recite* each answer aloud, silently speak the answers to yourself, tell the answers to another person as though you were teaching her, or write your ideas and answers in brief notes. Writing is often the most effective way to solidify what you have read because writing from memory checks your understanding.

Don't discount the value of reciting aloud from the text. Although it may seem silly or embarrassing, speaking greatly increases your chance of remembering and learning because it engages three body processes at the same time: One, your eyes take in the information as you read it. Two, speaking the information engages your physical muscle memory. Three, hearing yourself speak engages your ears to further solidify the memory of the information.

Keep your learning styles (Chapter 3) in mind when you explore different strategies. For example, an intrapersonal learner may prefer writing, while an interpersonal learner might want to recite answers aloud to a classmate. A logical–mathematical learner may benefit from organizing material into detailed outlines, while a musical learner might want to chant information aloud to a rhythm.

After you finish one section, read the next. Repeat the question-read-recite cycle until you complete the entire chapter. If during this process you find yourself fumbling for thoughts, you may not yet "own" the ideas. Reread the section that's giving you trouble until you master its contents. Understanding each section as you go is crucial because the material in one section often forms a foundation for the next.

Review

Review soon after you finish a chapter. Reviewing, both immediately and periodically in the days and weeks after you read, is a crucial step of the process. Chances are good that if you close the book after you read, much of your focused reading work will slip away from memory. See review as an opportunity to clarify the main ideas, solidify your understanding, and enable you to move into a more critical evaluation of the material. Reviewing makes learning possible. Here are some techniques for reviewing—try many, and use what seems to work best for you.

> *The best effect of any book is that it excites the reader to self-activity.*
>
> **THOMAS CARLYLE**

- Skim and reread your notes. Then, try summarizing them from memory.
- Answer the text's end-of-chapter review, discussion, and application questions.

- Quiz yourself, using the questions you raised in the Q stage. If you can't answer one of your own or one of the text's questions, go back and scan the material for answers.
- Review and summarize in writing the material you have highlighted or bracketed.
- Create a chapter outline in standard outline form or think-link form.
- Reread the preface, headings, tables, and summary.
- Recite important concepts to yourself, or record important information on a cassette tape and play it on your car's tape deck or your portable cassette player.
- Make flash cards that have an idea or word on one side and examples, a definition, or other related information on the other. Test yourself.
- Think critically: Break ideas down into examples, consider similar or different concepts, recall important terms, evaluate ideas, and explore causes and effects (see the next section, "How Can You Respond Critically to What You Read?")
- Discuss the concepts with a classmate or in a study group. Trying to teach study partners what you learned will pinpoint the material you know and what still needs work.
- Make think links that show how important concepts relate to one another.

If you need help clarifying your reading material, ask your instructor. Pinpoint the material you want to discuss, schedule a meeting during office hours, and bring a list of questions.

Speaking of review, see Table 5.5 for a review of the steps of SQ3R.

Refreshing your knowledge is easier and faster than learning it the first time. Set up regular review sessions, for example, once a week. Reviewing in as many different ways as possible increases the likelihood of retention. Critical reading may be the most important of these ways.

H OW CAN YOU RESPOND CRITICALLY TO WHAT YOU READ?

You've surveyed, questioned, read, recited, and reviewed. You've taken in new information and developed a solid basic understanding of what you've read. Now comes the real learning, the work that takes your understanding to a deeper and more productive level.

Critical reading is both making meaning of the original text and adding your personal response to it. It goes beyond rote memorization (taking in and regurgitating material) because it involves analyzing the material in light of what you already know. Critical reading enables you to develop a thorough understanding of reading material through evaluation and analysis.

Think of critical reading as an extension of the Q stage, one that comes after you have completed the initial steps of SQ3R. In Q, you raise questions based on chapter headers—when you read critically, you develop new questions and relate answers to other information. Your answers to Q questions help you identify key ideas—when you read critically, you can explore

The steps of SQ3R.

STAGE OF THE PROCESS	DESCRIPTION
Survey	Pre-reading a book before studying it involves skimming, scanning, and examining book elements such as the table of contents, chapter objectives, headers within the text, and study questions.
Question	Involves developing questions linked to chapter headings or to ideas that popped out during the S stage. Questions can be inspired by lecture notes as well, and help to engage critical thinking while reading.
Read	Involves reading the material with the purpose of answering the questions formulated in the Q stage. May also involve taking notes on the reading and marking the text to identify key ideas and information.
Recite	Involves answering the questions from the Q stage, either recited aloud, spoken silently to yourself, told to a study partner, or written down in brief notes.
Review	Involves using various techniques—skimming and summarizing notes, answering study questions, writing outlines or think links, reciting concepts, using flash cards, thinking critically, and so on—to renew and solidify your knowledge.

whether those ideas are true or accurate, and you can also synthesize those ideas to come up with the central idea of the material. A critical reader can also compare one piece of information or material to another and evaluate which makes more sense, which proves its thesis more successfully, or which is more useful for the reader's purposes.

Engage your critical-thinking processes by using the following suggestions.

Use SQ3R to "Taste" Reading Material

Sylvan Barnet and Hugo Bedau, authors of *Critical Thinking, Reading, and Writing—A Brief Guide to Argument*, suggest that the active reading of SQ3R will help you form an initial idea of what a piece of reading material is all about. Through surveying, skimming for ideas and examples, highlighting and writing comments and questions in the margins, and reviewing, you can develop a basic understanding of its central ideas and contents.[10] This understanding is the "raw material" that you then begin to examine critically.

Summarizing, part of the SQ3R review process, is one of the best ways to develop an understanding of a piece of reading material. To construct a **summary**, focus on the central ideas of the piece and the main examples that support them. A summary does not contain any of your own ideas or your evaluation of the material. It simply condenses the material, making it easi-

SUMMARY

A concise restatement of the material, in your own words, that covers the main points.

er to focus on the structure and central ideas of the piece when you go back to read more critically. At that point, you can begin to ask questions, evaluating the piece and introducing your own ideas. Using the mind actions will help you.

Ask Questions Based on the Mind Actions

Instead of simply accepting what you read, seek a more thorough understanding by questioning the material as you go along. Using the mind actions to formulate your questions will help you understand the material.

What parts of the material you focus on will depend on your purpose for reading. For example, if you are writing a paper on the causes of World War II, you might look at how certain causes fit your thesis. If you are comparing two pieces of writing that contain opposing arguments, you may focus on picking out their central ideas and evaluating how well the writers use examples to support them. You can question components such as the following:

- The central idea of the entire piece
- A particular idea, statement, or supposed fact
- The examples that support an idea, statement, or fact

Following are some ways to critically question reading material, based on the mind actions. Apply them to any component you want to question by substituting the component for the words *it* and *this*.

 Similarity: What does this remind me of or how is it similar to something else I know?

 Difference: What different conclusions are possible?

How is this different from my experience?

 Cause and Effect: Why did this happen or what caused this?

What are the effects or consequences of this?

What effect does the author intend or what is the purpose of this material?

What effects support a stated cause?

 **Example to Idea:**   How would I classify this or what is the best idea to fit this example?

How would I summarize this or what are the key ideas?

What is the thesis or central idea?

 Idea to Example: What evidence supports this or what examples fit this idea?

 Evaluation: How would I evaluate this? Is it useful or well constructed?

Does this example support my thesis or central idea?

Is this information or point of view important to my work? If so, why?

Engage Critical-Thinking Processes

Certain thinking processes, introduced in Chapter 4, can help to deepen your analysis and evaluation of what you read. These processes are establishing truth and constructing an argument. Within these processes you will ask questions that use the mind actions.

Thinking Logically

With what you know about logical thinking, you can evaluate any statement in your reading material, identifying it as fact, opinion, or assumption and challenging how it is supported. Evaluate statements, ideas, or entire pieces of material using questions such as the following:

- Is this fact? Is the factual statement true? How does the writer know?
- Is this opinion? How could I test its validity?
- What assumptions underlie this?
- What else do I know that is similar to or different from this?
- What information that I already know supports or disproves this?
- What examples disprove this as fact or do not fit this assumption?

For example, imagine that a piece of writing states, "The dissolving of the family unit is the main cause of society's ills." You may question this statement by looking at what facts and examples support it or by comparing it to other materials. You may question the writer's sources of information. You could find hidden assumptions underneath this statement, such as an assumed definition of what a family is or of what constitutes "society's ills." You could also find examples that do not fit this assumption, such as successful families that don't fit the traditional definition of "family" used by the writer.

Evaluating an Argument

As you read in Chapter 4, an argument is a persuasive case that seeks to prove or disprove a point. When reading material contains one or more arguments, use what you know about arguments to evaluate whether the writer has constructed his argument effectively. Ask questions like the following:

- Do I believe this argument? How is the writer trying to persuade me?
- If the author uses cause-and-effect reasoning, does it seem logical?
- Do the examples adequately support the central idea of the argument?
- Is the evidence fact or opinion? Is it true or verifiable?
- What different and perhaps opposing arguments seem just as valid?
- If I'm not sure whether I believe this, how could I construct an opposing argument?

For example, say you are reading an article in support of one flat income tax rate for all citizens. You might start by examining whether you believe the argument right off the bat. Then, look at the examples that the writer uses to support this position. First of all, are they fact or opinion, and how do you know? Secondly, do they support the idea effectively? Then, consider what other arguments may be valid, and why—you could consider arguments favoring the current tax system. This may involve additional research if you are uncertain of other points of view or if your information is out of date. Finally, if you are not convinced, you might devise an argument against the flat tax, supporting it with adequate examples.

Don't rule out the possibility that you may agree completely with an argument. However, use critical thinking to make an informed decision, rather than accepting the argument outright.

Be Media Literate

Even seemingly objective textbooks are written by a person or persons who have particular points of view that may influence the information they include or how they include it. For instance, the growing awareness of the multicultural heritage of the United States has prompted revisions of history texts that previously ignored or shortchanged topics such as Native American history; *Out of Many* is a prime example. In all your reading, remember the following:

- Authors may use particular wording or tone to create an effect on a reader.
- Different readers may have different interpretations of a piece of reading material, depending on individual perspective and experience.
- Any written material carries the values of the people who created it and is influenced, to varying degrees, by the perspectives and intents of the authors.

To analyze perspective as you read, seek to unearth the ideas that influence the material by questioning its perspective. Consider what the author or authors want you to believe, and why. Evaluate how they support their perspective, and decide if you think the examples they use are valid. As a media-literate reader, you have the ability to stay aware of these realities and to sift through your materials critically so that you gain from them what is most useful to you. (See Chapter 4 for more on media literacy.)

Seek Understanding

The fundamental purpose of all college reading is comprehension. Reading critically allows you to reach the highest possible level of understanding. Think of your reading process as an archaeological dig. The first step is to excavate a site and uncover the artifacts, which corresponds to your initial survey and reading of the material. As important as the excavation is, the process would be incomplete if you took home a bunch of dirt-covered items and stopped there. The second half of the process is to investigate each item, evaluate what each one means, and derive new knowledge and ideas from what you discover. Critical reading allows you to complete that crucial second half of the process.

Critical reading is the process of making order and meaning out of what might often be seemingly chaotic materials. Finding order within chaos is an important skill, not just in the mastery of reading, but also in life. This skill can give you power by helping you "read" (think through) work dilemmas, personal problems, and educational situations.

Windows on the World

How can I cope with my reading disabilities?

Darrin Estepp, *Ohio State University, Columbus, Ohio, Undeclared*

In elementary school I needed extra help with reading. By high school, I was having a hard time keeping up, and I felt stupid. A test I took showed I had dyslexia. Study assistance helped, but I attended high school for an extra year to improve my record. Then, I enrolled in community college and worked part-time as a nursing home cook. I transferred to Ohio State after two years.

I wanted to major in Special Education so I could help people with learning disabilities, but the classes were too much of a struggle. I still

want to help others—I can see myself being on the lookout for the early signs of people with disabilities like mine. Recently, I was diagnosed with another learning disability. I have always had trouble sitting for

long periods of time. About 45 minutes into a 2 1/2 hour history class I found I couldn't remain seated. I kept standing up. Later, I took a test that showed that I have ADHD (Attention Deficit Hyperactivity Disorder).

I have trouble with spelling too. In class, by the time I figure out how to spell a word for my notes, I'm far behind. I learn best by hearing, seeing, and doing all at once. If I just hear something it doesn't sink in very well. Not long ago I went to see my learning disability counselor because it seems no matter how hard I try it's never enough. I keep hanging in there though because I want to prove that I can graduate from a major university. What suggestions do you have for how I can cope with my disabilities?

Morgan Paar, *Graduate Student, Academy of Art College, San Francisco, California*

I remember dreading reading out loud to my fourth-grade class. Other students would laugh. Fortunately, this is when my disability was discovered. One thing I learned in college was that there is more than one way to succeed. First, I attended every single class without exception. Second, if I got behind in my note taking (and I often did), I would borrow a friend's notes and rewrite mine, combining them with my friend's. Third, I made friends with my teachers, and they would help me during their office hours.

One incident showed me anything was possible. A friend worked for a newspaper and asked me to write a story. I laughed—I said I could barely spell my name, never mind write an article. He said, "Come on, computers have spell check." I labored through it, my friend loved it (though he did say that I had some very creative

grammar), and it appeared in the travel section. I have since had 17 articles published.

It never gets easy—but one route to success is to do something you love. I write travel stories because I love

traveling and sharing stories. I am now a filmmaker, and I am studying film in graduate school so I can someday teach it. Darrin, you already know the skills you need to achieve your goals, though maybe they are deep in your subconscious mind. I was 27 years old before I knew what I really wanted to do. Keep following your passions, never give up; figure out what you need to do to achieve your goals, and know that there is more than one path to your destination. If you truly love what you do, nothing can stop you.

Remember that critical reading takes time and focus. Give yourself a chance to be a successful critical reader by finding a time, place, and purpose for your reading. Take advantage of the opportunity to learn from others by working in pairs or groups whenever you can.

HOW AND WHY SHOULD YOU STUDY WITH OTHERS?

So much of what you know and will learn comes from the interactions you have with others. This is why study groups can help you succeed in school. You learn from listening to group members, reading their class notes and essays, and jointly working through difficult problems.

Benefits of Working With Others

When you study with a partner or in a group, you will benefit from shared knowledge, solidified knowledge, increased motivation, and increased teamwork ability.

SHARED KNOWLEDGE. Each student has a unique body of knowledge and individual strengths. Students can learn from one another. To have individual students pass on their knowledge to each other in a study group requires less time and energy than for each of those students to learn all of the material alone.

The wise person learns from everyone.

ETHICS OF THE FATHERS

SOLIDIFIED KNOWLEDGE. Study group members don't just help each other gather knowledge, they also help each other solidify and retain it. When you discuss concepts or teach them to others, you reinforce what you know and strengthen your critical thinking. Part of the benefit comes from simply repeating information aloud and rewriting it on paper, and part comes from how you think through information in your mind before you pass it on to someone else.

INCREASED MOTIVATION. When you study by yourself, you are accountable to yourself alone. In a study group, however, others will see your level of work and preparation, which may increase your motivation. It is natural for all of us to want to perform well in front of others.

INCREASED TEAMWORK ABILITY. The more you understand the dynamics of working with a group and the more experience you have at it, the more you will build your ability to work well with others. This is an invaluable skill for the workplace, and it will contribute to your personal marketability.

Strategies for Study Group Success

Not all study groups work the same way. The way you operate your group may depend on the group's personalities, the subject you study, the location of the group, and the size of the group. No matter what your particular group's situation, though, certain general strategies will help.

CHOOSE A LEADER FOR EACH MEETING. Rotating the leadership helps all members take ownership of the group. Be flexible. If a leader has to miss class for any reason, choose another leader for that meeting.

SET MEETING GOALS. At the start of each meeting, compile a list of questions you want to address.

ADJUST TO DIFFERENT PERSONALITIES. Respect and communicate with members whom you would not necessarily choose as friends. The art of getting along will serve you well in the workplace, where you don't often choose your coworkers.

SHARE THE WORKLOAD. The most important factor is a willingness to work, not a particular level of knowledge.

SET GENERAL GOALS. Determine what the group wants to accomplish over the course of a semester.

SET A REGULAR MEETING SCHEDULE. Try every week, every two weeks, or whatever the group can manage.

CREATE STUDY MATERIALS FOR ONE ANOTHER. Give each group member the task of finding a piece of information to compile, photocopy, and review for the other group members.

HELP EACH OTHER LEARN. One of the best ways to solidify your knowledge of something is to teach it to someone else. Have group members teach certain pieces of information; make up quizzes for each other; go through flash cards together.

POOL YOUR NOTE-TAKING RESOURCES. Compare notes with your group members and fill in any information you don't have. Try other note-taking styles: If you generally use outlines, rewrite your notes in a think link. If you tend to map out ideas in a think link, try recompiling your notes using the Cornell method (see Chapter 7 for more on note taking).

читать

This word may look completely unfamiliar to you, but anyone who can read the Russian language and alphabet will know that it means "read." People who read languages that use different kinds of characters, such as Russian, Japanese, or Greek, learn to process those characters as easily as you process the letters of your native alphabet. Your mind learns to process individually each letter or character you see. This ability enables you to move to the next level of understanding—making sense of those letters or characters when they are grouped to form words, phrases, and sentences.

Think of this concept when you read. Remember that your mind processes immeasurable amounts of information so that you can understand the concepts on the page. Give it the best opportunity to succeed by reading often and by focusing on all of the elements that help you read to the best of your ability.

IMPORTANT POINTS *to remember*

1. What will help you understand what you read?

Your life experiences, prior knowledge, family background, and other factors affect reading comprehension. You can boost your comprehension by making reading part of your daily routine, thinking positively about your ability to understand, thinking critically to capture meaning, and making extra efforts to build a better vocabulary.

2. How can you set the stage for reading?

You can help prepare yourself to read by taking an active, positive approach to every reading assignment and by choosing a setting that will minimize distractions. It is also important to define your purpose for reading. Having a purpose helps you structure your approach toward reading assignments because different purposes require different levels of time and effort. The four main purposes are comprehension (both general ideas and specific examples), critical evaluation, practical application, and pleasure.

3. How can you build a better vocabulary?

Vocabulary building techniques include analyzing word parts—prefixes, roots, and suffixes—using a dictionary to learn the meanings of new words, learning the specialized vocabulary of your field, mastering commonly used initials, and, if English is your second language, becoming comfortable reading American English, including slang.

4. How can you increase your reading speed?

Becoming a faster reader is an important goal because your reading requirements in college have increased so much. To increase your reading speed, it is important to identify habits that are slowing you down and practice methods to become a faster reader. Common problems include word-by-word reading, lack of concentration, vocalization and subvocalization, limited vocabulary, unconscious regression, and slow recovery time.

5. How can SQ3R help you own what you read?

SQ3R, the process of surveying, questioning, reading, reciting, and reviewing, encourages active studying. Surveying refers to previewing a book before studying it. During the questioning phase, you write questions linked to chapter headings. During the reading stage, you read the material in order to answer these questions and take notes. During the reciting stage, you answer the questions you raised by reciting aloud or silently to yourself, telling another person, or writing them in a notebook. The review stage involves skimming and rereading your notes.

6. How can you respond critically to what you read?

Critical-reading skills help you select important ideas, identify supporting examples, and ask questions about any text, developing an understanding of the material through evaluation and analysis. Critical reading involves the use of SQ3R to "taste" the material, asking questions based on the mind actions, and engaging critical-thinking processes (establishing the truth of what you read, evaluating its arguments, and analyzing its perspective). It also means remembering that reading material, like all media, is affected by the perspective and intentions of its authors.

7. How and why should you study with others?

Studying with one or more people can enhance your learning and improve teamwork skills that will serve you well in the workplace. Benefits include shared and solidified knowledge, increased motivation, and an increased ability to work with others. Strategies for effective group study include setting goals, sharing the workload, setting a meeting schedule, and respecting one another.

NAME   DATE

CRITICAL THINKING
APPLYING LEARNING TO LIFE

SQ3R READING AND GROUP DISCUSSION. Take a few minutes to individually preview an article or other short section of reading material assigned to you for this class (other than your textbook). Write here the title, author, and source of the material you are reading.

As you preview, skim the material with the intention of developing questions to answer during more focused reading. In the lines below, write down two or three questions that came up during your preview.

Then, divide into small groups of three or four. Share your questions with one another, and have each person select one question to focus on while reading (no two people should have the same question). Group members should then read the material on their own, using critical-thinking skills to explore their particular questions as they read, and finally they should write down answers to their questions. Write your question here:

When you answer your question, focus on finding ideas that help to answer the question and examples that support them. Consider other information you know, relevant to your question, that may be similar to or different from the material in the passage. If your question looks for causes or effects, scan for them in the passage. Be sure to make notes as you read. Write your answer below. (Continue on a separate page, if necessary.)

_____

_____

_____

_____

_____

When you have finished reading critically, gather as a group. Each person should take a turn presenting the question, the response or answer that was derived through critical reading, and any other ideas that came up while reading. The group then has an opportunity to present any other ideas to add to the discussion. Continue until each person has had a chance to present what he or she worked on. If it is helpful to you, make photocopies of each person's work to distribute to all group members.

How was this group reading exercise helpful to you? In the following space, describe the positive effects the experience had for you.

_____

_____

_____

_____

TEAMWORK

COMBINING FORCES

ORGANIZING A STUDY GROUP. Organize a study group with three or four members of your class. At the group's first meeting:

- Using the techniques you learned in Chapter 2, write a mission statement for the group and create a weekly schedule.
- Talk about the specific ways you will work together. Discuss which of the following methods you want to try in the group: pooling your notes, acting as tutors and students to teach each other difficult concepts; making up, administering, and grading quizzes for each other; creating study flash cards; using SQ3R to review required readings.

Try the group study methods you have chosen over several weeks. Then, individually, evaluate the methods. Decide on those that worked best for you—that helped you master the course material—and those with little value. Come together as a group to share your evaluations, and revise the group's methods based on a consensus of what worked best.

WRITING
DISCOVERY THROUGH JOURNALING

To record your thoughts, use a separate journal or the lined page at the end of the chapter.

READING CHALLENGES. What is your most difficult college reading challenge? A challenge might be a particular kind of reading material, a reading situation, or the achievement of a reading goal. Considering the tools that this chapter presents, make a plan that addresses this challenge. What techniques might be able to help, and how will you test them? What positive effects do you anticipate they may have?

CAREER PORTFOLIO
CHARTING YOUR COURSE

READING SKILLS ON THE JOB. No matter your occupation, you will continue to read and to learn on the job as the demands of the workplace change. Realizing this, companies seek employees who are literate and who understand the necessity of lifelong learning. As a recent *Condition of Education* report states, "In recent years, literacy has been viewed as one of the fundamental tools necessary for successful economic performance in industrialized societies. Literacy is no longer defined merely as a basic threshold of reading ability, but rather as the ability to understand and use printed information in daily activities, at home, at work, and in the community."[11]

On a separate sheet of paper, do the following: For each of the reading-related skill areas below, list the different ways you currently use that skill on the job or will probably use it in your future career. Then, also for each skill, rate your ability on a scale from 1 to 10, with 10 being highest. Finally, on the same sheet of paper, circle the two skills that you think will be most important for your career.

- ability to define and focus on your reading purpose
- ability to read rapidly, when necessary
- ability to understand what you read
- ability to continue to grow your vocabulary
- ability to use SQ3R to study and learn new material
- ability to respond critically to what you read

For the two skill areas in which you rated yourself lowest, think through how you can improve your abilities. Make a problem-solving plan for each, using an outline or a think link as on pages 217 and 219.

UGGESTED READINGS

Armstrong, William H. and M. Willard Lampe II. *Barron's Pocket Guide to Study Tips: How to Study Effectively and Get Better Grades.* New York: Barron's Educational Series (1990).

Chesla, Elizabeth. *Reading Comprehension Success: In 20 Minutes a Day,* 2nd ed. Garden Grove, CA: Learning Express (1998).

Frank, Steven. *The Everything Study Book.* Holbrook, MA: Adams Media (1996).

Luckie, William R., Wood Smethurst, and Sarah Beth Huntley. *Study Power Workbook: Exercises in Study Skills to Improve Your Learning and Your Grades.* Cambridge, MA: Brookline Books (1999).

Silver, Theodore. *The Princeton Review Study Smart: Hands-on, Nuts and Bolts Techniques for Earning Higher Grades.* New York: Villard Books (1996).

NTERNET RESOURCES

SQ3R Method: www.u.arizona.edu/ic/wrightr/other/sq3r.html

Study Web: www.studyweb.com

NDNOTES

1. Sherwood Harris. *The New York Public Library Book of How and Where to Look It Up.* Upper Saddle River, NJ: Prentice Hall (1991), p. 13.

2. Harold Bloom. *How To Read and Why.* New York: Scribner (2000).

3. George M. Usova. *Efficient Study Strategies: Skills for Successful Learning.* Pacific Grove, CA: Brooks/Cole (1989), p. 45.

4. Grace J. Craig. *Human Development,* 7th ed. Upper Saddle River, NJ: Prentice Hall (1996), pp. 568–569.

5. Steve Moidel. *Speed Reading.* Hauppauge, NY: Barron's Educational Series (1994), p. 18.

6. Ibid., pp. 18–25.

7. Ibid., p. 32.

8. Francis P. Robinson. *Effective Behavior.* New York: Harper & Row (1941).

9. John Mack Faragher, et al. *Out of Many,* 3rd ed. Upper Saddle River, NJ: Prentice Hall, p. xxxvii.

10. Sylvan Barnet and Hugo Bedau. *Critical Thinking, Reading, and Writing: A Brief Guide to Argument,* 2nd ed. Boston: Bedford Books of St. Martin's Press (1996), pp. 15–21.

11. U.S. Department of Education, National Center for Education Statistics, The Condition of Education 1996, NCES 96-304, by Thomas M. Smith. Washington, DC: U.S. Government Printing Office (1996), p. 84.

Journal

NAME

DATE

Thinking It Through

Check those statements that apply to you right now:

- Although I listen to my instructors, I often do not remember what they say.

- When I hear something I don't agree with, I argue with the instructor in my head.

- I spend a lot of time memorizing facts for a test, but I forget a lot of material after the test is over.

- I use memory games to help me remember important information.

- I know that mnemonic devices are supposed to help memory, but I rarely use them.

IN THIS CHAPTER,

you will explore answers to the following questions:

- How can you become a better listener?
- How does memory work?
- How can you improve your memory?
- How can you use mnemonic devices to boost memory power?

Listening and Memory

L istening is a vital skill that will help you to know and understand the world around you. You take in countless bits of information as you listen to instructors, students, study partners, coworkers, and others. With so much time spent listening, learning how to focus your listening is crucial to your success. Compare your listening ability to a camera. Even when you see an image through the viewfinder, you may not be able to tell what it is until you carefully focus the lens. Similarly, careful listening will allow you to clarify what you have heard.

Once you've listened to the facts, opinions, and ideas to which college exposes you daily, you need to be able to remember them and build knowledge that you can use throughout your life. Imagine that you're a nursing student: What good is an A on an anatomy exam if you can't remember the location of a particular gland or bone when you meet your first patient? This chapter will explore specific techniques to boost your ability to take in and remember what you learn.

CHAPTER

6

TAKING IN AND REMEMBERING INFORMATION

HOW CAN YOU BECOME A BETTER LISTENER?

LISTENING

A process that involves sensing, interpreting, evaluating, and reacting to spoken messages.

The act of hearing isn't quite the same as the act of **listening**. Whereas *hearing* refers to sensing spoken messages from their source, *listening* involves a complex process of communication. Successful listening results in the speaker's intended message reaching the listener. In school and at home, poor listening may cause communication breakdowns and mistakes. Skilled listening, however, promotes progress and success. Listening is a teachable—and learnable—skill.

Listening is also one of the most important skills in the workplace. The way in which employees and managers listen to customers and to one another affects their efficiency and effectiveness. If you don't accurately hear what others tell you, the quality of your work can be undermined, no matter how many hours you have spent completing an assignment. For example, if you fail to act on a coworker's request for immediate action on an important project and the project falls apart because of your failure, claiming that you never heard the request will get little sympathy and may even cost you your job. Accurate listening is an important key to your personal career success and the success of your organization.

To see how complex listening can be, look at Figure 6.1. The left-hand column contains an excerpt from a typical classroom lecture on peer-group influence during adolescence, and the right-hand column records some examples of what an 18- or 19-year-old student might be thinking while the instructor is speaking. In many ways, the column on the right is more interesting than the one on the left because it reveals the complexity of listening, as well as some of the barriers that block communication.

During the act of listening to a typical classroom lecture, this student doesn't focus consistently on the information presented. Instead, she reacts to specific parts of the message and gets caught up in evaluating and judging what she hears. Internal and external distractions, in the form of hunger and whispering, also affect her concentration.

The example in Figure 6.1 represents the kinds of thoughts that can interfere with effective listening. Understanding the listening process and why people may have trouble listening well can help you overcome these barriers.

Know the Stages of Listening

Listening is made up of four stages that build on one another: sensing, interpreting, evaluating, and reacting. These stages take the message from the speaker to the listener and back to the speaker (see Figure 6.2).

During the *sensation* stage (also known as hearing), your ears pick up sound waves and transmit them to the brain. For example, you are sitting in class and hear your instructor say, "The only opportunity to make up last week's test is Tuesday at 5:00 P.M."

In the *interpretation* stage, listeners attach meaning to a message. This involves understanding what is being said and relating it to what you already know. You relate this message to your knowledge of the test, whether you need to make it up, and what you are doing on Tuesday at 5:00 P.M.

The complexity of listening.

FIGURE

6.1

A peer group is a social group made up of members with a lot in common. During adolescence, common interests often center on dating, popular music, clothing, and sports.

The appeal of the group often comes from the fact that adults would not approve of what group members are doing. As a result, illicit activities—such as car racing, alcohol abuse, and drugs—are often the most popular.

Peer groups exert such a strong influence during adolescence because they give students the opportunity to form social relationships that are separate and apart from the one they have with their families. This is a time of rebellion and breaking away: a rough time for both adolescents and their parents.

The good news for parents is that peer group pressure is generally strongest during adolescence. Teens achieve a greater balance between the influence of family and friends as the years pass. This doesn't make it any easier for parents trying to persuade their sons and daughters not to dye their hair green or pierce their eyebrows, but at least it tells them that the rebellion is temporary.

"Peer groups!" I've heard that term before. I'd better take notes; it'll probably be on the test.

What's this guy saying? That my friends and I do things just because our parents would object? Yeah, I guess I want to be different, but gimme a break! I don't drink and drive. I don't do drugs. I don't ignore my school work. Anyway, I'd better remember the connection between peer group popularity and adult disapproval. What were his exact words? I wish I remembered . . . on second thought maybe he has a point. I know kids who do things just to get a rise out of their parents.

Is it lunchtime yet? I'm really hungry! Stop thinking of food and start listening . . . back to work! Yeah, he's right, social relationships that have nothing to do with my family are important to me. I'd better write this down.

Why is he talking down to us? Why is he reassuring parents instead of focusing on how hard it is for teens to deal with life? He must be a parent himself . . . I wish those guys behind me would stop talking! I can't hear the lecture . . . there's a generation gap coming from the front of the room that's the size of the Grand Canyon! What's wrong with green hair and pierced eyebrows? He sounds like he knows all the answers and that we'll eventually see the light. I'm going to ask him how teens are supposed to act when they believe that their parents' values are wrong. Now, how should I word my question . . .

In the *evaluation* stage of listening, you decide how you feel about the message—whether, for example, you like it or agree with it. This involves evaluating the message as it relates to your needs and values. If the message goes against your values or does not fulfill your needs, you may reject it, stop listening, or argue in your mind with the speaker. In this example, if you do need to make up the test but have to work Tuesday at 5:00 P.M., you may evaluate the message as less than satisfactory. As you saw in Figure 6.1, what happens during the evaluation phase can interfere with listening.

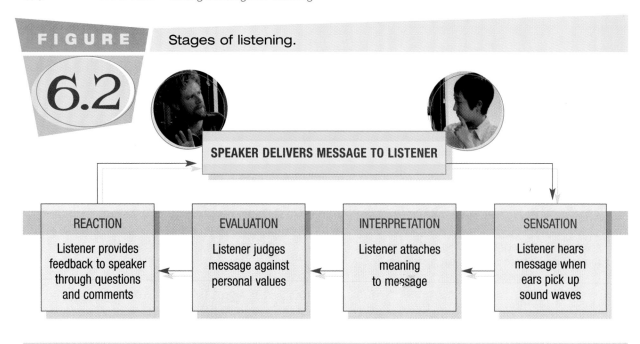

FIGURE 6.2 Stages of listening.

SPEAKER DELIVERS MESSAGE TO LISTENER			
REACTION	**EVALUATION**	**INTERPRETATION**	**SENSATION**
Listener provides feedback to speaker through questions and comments	Listener judges message against personal values	Listener attaches meaning to message	Listener hears message when ears pick up sound waves

The final stage of listening is a *reaction* to the message in the form of direct feedback. In a classroom, direct feedback often comes in the form of questions and comments. Your reaction, in this case, may be to ask the instructor if she can schedule another test time. If the student in Figure 6.1 actually asks a question, she will give the instructor the opportunity to clarify the lecture or, perhaps, to add information.

Improving your learning skills involves two primary actions: managing listening challenges and becoming an active listener. Although becoming a better listener will help in every class, it is especially important in subjects that are challenging for you. For example, if your natural strength is in English, your ability to listen in physics class may affect how much you learn and whether you pass the course. According to psychologist Beatrice Harris, "People can be trained to listen to content and tone. But learning takes persistence and motivation."[1]

Manage Listening Challenges

Communication barriers can interfere with listening at every stage. In fact, classic studies have shown that immediately after listening, students are likely to recall only half of what was said. This is partly due to particular listening challenges, such as divided attention and distractions, the tendency to shut out the message, the inclination to rush to judgment, and partial hearing loss or learning disabilities.[2]

To help create a positive listening environment in both your mind and your surroundings, explore how to manage these challenges.

Divided Attention and Distractions

Imagine yourself at a noisy end-of-year party, talking with a friend about plans for the summer, when you hear your name mentioned across the room.

Your name was not shouted, and you weren't consciously listening to any-thing outside your own conversation. However, once you hear your name, you strain to hear more as you now listen with only half an ear to what your friend is saying. Chances are you hear neither person very well.

Situations like this happen all the time and demonstrate the consequences of divided attention. Although you are capable of listening to more than one message at the same time, you may not completely hear or understand any of them. Learning to focus your attention—even as it is being pulled in dif-ferent directions—is one of your most important listening challenges.

Internal and external distractions often divide your attention. *Internal distractions* include anything from hunger to headache to personal worries. Something the speaker says may also trigger a recollection that may cause your mind to drift. In contrast, *external distractions* include noises (e.g., whispering, police sirens) and excessive heat or cold. It can be hard to listen in an overheated room that is putting you to sleep.

Your goal is to reduce distractions so that you can focus on what you're hearing. Sitting where you can clearly see and hear will help. You may even be more willing to listen because knowing that instructors can see you may encourage you to receive their messages more actively. To avoid distracting activity, you may want to avoid sitting near or with people who might chat or make noise.

Make sure you are as relaxed and alert as possible. Work to concentrate on class when you're in class and save worrying about personal problems for later. Try to avoid being hungry or thirsty. Dress comfortably. Bring a sweater or sweatshirt if you anticipate that the classroom will be too cold. If there's a chance it will be overheated, wear a removable layer of clothing.

Shutting Out the Message

Instead of paying attention to everything the speaker says, many students fall into the trap of focusing on specific points and shutting out the rest of the message. If you perceive that a subject is too difficult or uninteresting, you may tune out. Shutting out the message makes it tough to listen well from that point on because the information you miss may be the foundation for what goes on in future classes.

Creating a positive listening environment includes accepting responsibil-ity for listening. Although the instructor is responsible for communicating information to you, he cannot force you to listen. You are responsible for taking in the information that comes your way during class.

One important motivation is believing that what your instructors say is valuable. For example, some students might assume that anything not cov-ered in the textbook isn't really important. During class, however, instructors often cover material from outside the textbook and then test on that materi-al. If you work to take in the whole message in class, you will be able to read over your notes later and think critically about what is most important.

The Rush to Judgment

As the student's thoughts in Figure 6.1 show, people may tend to stop lis-tening during the evaluation stage when they hear something they don't like. If you rush to judge what you've heard, your focus turns to your personal reaction rather than the content of the speaker's message. Students who disagree during a lecture often spend a lot of their thinking time figuring out exactly how they want to word a question or comment in response.

Judgments also involve reactions to the speakers themselves. If you do not like your instructors or if you have preconceived notions about their ideas or cultural background, you may decide that their words have little value. Anyone whose words have ever been ignored because of race, ethnic background, gender, or disability understands how prejudice can interfere with listening. (See Chapter 11 for more about how prejudice can stifle communication.)

> *No one cares to speak to an unwilling listener. An arrow never lodges in a stone; often it recoils upon the sender of it.*
>
> **ST. JEROME**

Understanding how your emotions and opinions can interfere with listening will help you recognize and control your judgments. Being aware of what you tend to judge will help you avoid putting up a barrier against messages that clash with your opinions or feelings. Consider education as a continuing search for evidence, regardless of whether that evidence supports or negates your point of view.

Partial Hearing Loss and Learning Disabilities

Good listening techniques don't solve every listening problem. Students who have a partial hearing loss have a physical explanation for why listening is difficult. If you have some level of hearing loss, seek out special services that can help you listen in class. You may require special equipment or you might benefit from tutoring. You may be able to arrange to meet with your instructor outside class to clarify your notes.

Other disabilities, such as attention deficit disorder (ADD) or a problem with processing spoken language, can add to listening difficulties. People with these problems may have trouble paying attention or understanding what they hear. Although some may find ways to compensate for their listening problems, others may continue to struggle. If you have a disability that creates a listening challenge, don't blame yourself. Instead, seek help through your counseling or student health center, an advisor, or an instructor.

Become an Active Listener

On the surface, listening seems like a passive activity; you sit back and listen as someone else speaks. Effective listening, however, is really an active process that involves setting a purpose for listening, asking questions, putting listening "spaces" to good use, paying attention to **verbal signposts**, and knowing what helps and hinders listening.

> **VERBAL SIGNPOSTS**
>
> Spoken words or phrases that call your attention to the information that follows.

Set Purposes for Listening

Active listening is only possible if you know (and care) why you are listening. In any situation, establish what you want to achieve through listening, such as greater understanding of the material, staying awake in class, or better note taking. Having a purpose gives you a goal that motivates you to listen.

Ask Questions

Asking questions is not a sign of a lack of intelligence. In fact, a willingness to ask questions shows a desire to learn and is the mark of an active listener and critical thinker. Some questions are informational—seeking information—such as any question beginning with the phrase, "I don't understand. . . ." *Clarifying* questions state your understanding of what you have just heard and ask if that understanding is correct. Whereas some clarifying questions focus on a key concept or theme (e.g., "So, some learning disorders can be improved with treatment?"), others highlight specific facts (e.g., "Is it true that dyslexia can cause people to reverse letters and words?"). (For the role questions play in critical thinking, see Chapter 4.)

Although your questions and comments make you an active participant in the listening process, you might spend so much time thinking about what to ask that you miss some of the message. One way to avoid this is to quickly jot down your questions and come back to them during a discussion period or when you can talk to the instructor alone. When you know that your question is on paper, you may be more able to relax and listen.

Pay Attention to Verbal Signposts

You can identify important facts and ideas and predict test questions by paying attention to the speaker's specific choice of words. For example, an idea described as "new and exciting" or "classic" is more likely to be on a test than one described as "interesting." Verbal signposts often involve transition words and phrases that help organize information, connect ideas, and indicate what is important and what is not. Let phrases like those in Table 6.1 direct your attention to the material that follows them.

Paying attention to verbal signposts.

SIGNALS POINTING TO KEY CONCEPTS	SIGNALS OF SUPPORT
There are two reasons for this. . .	For example, . . .
A critical point in the process involves. . .	Specifically, . . .
Most importantly, . . .	For instance, . . .
The result is. . .	Similarly, . . .

SIGNALS POINTING TO DIFFERENCES	SIGNALS THAT SUMMARIZE
On the contrary, . . .	Finally, . . .
On the other hand, . . .	Recapping this idea, . . .
In contrast, . . .	In conclusion, . . .
However, . . .	As a result, . . .

TABLE 6.2   What helps and hinders listening.

LISTENING IS HELPED BY . . .	LISTENING IS HINDERED BY . . .
. . . making a conscious decision to work at listening; viewing difficult material as a listening challenge.	. . . caring little about the listening process; tuning out difficult material.
. . . fighting distractions through concentration.	. . . refusing to listen at the first distraction.
. . . continuing to listen when a subject is difficult or dry, in the hope that one might learn something interesting.	. . . giving up as soon as one loses interest.
. . . withholding judgment until hearing everything.	. . . becoming preoccupied with a response as soon as a speaker makes a controversial statement.
. . . focusing on the speaker's theme by recognizing organizational patterns, transitional language, and summary statements.	. . . getting sidetracked by unimportant details.
. . . adapting a note-taking style to the unique style and organization of the speaker.	. . . always taking notes in outline form, even when a speaker is poorly organized, leading to frustration.
. . . pushing past negative emotional responses and forcing oneself to continue to listen.	. . . letting an initial emotional response shut off continued listening.
. . . using excess thinking time to evaluate, summarize, and question what one just heard and anticipating what will come next.	. . . thinking about other things and, as a result, missing much of the message.

Know What Helps and Hinders Listening

Ralph G. Nichols, a pioneer in listening research, wanted to define the characteristics of successful and unsuccessful listeners. To do so, he studied 200 students in the freshman class at the University of Minnesota over a nine-month period. His findings, summarized in Table 6.2, demonstrate that effective listening depends as much on a positive attitude as on specific skills.[3]

Make Strategic Use of Tape Recorders

The selective use of a tape recorder can provide helpful backup to your listening skills. If you want to use a tape recorder, here are some guidelines:

- Use a tape recorder in class only when permitted by the instructor. Ask your instructor whether you may use one.

- Participate actively in class. Don't let the tape recorder act as a substitute for your participation. Take notes just as you would if the tape recorder were not there.

- Use the tapes effectively when studying. Listen to important sections of the lecture again, or clarify sections that confused you.

Although effective listening will enable you to acquire knowledge, retaining that knowledge demands that you remember what you've heard. A good memory is made up of skills that improve with practice.

Using a separate sheet of paper, complete the following.

Thinking Back

1. List and briefly describe the four stages of listening.

2. Name two internal and two external distractions that may interfere with listening.

3. List four methods for becoming an active listener.

4. Look again at Table 6.2. Which habits, helpful or not so helpful, are part of your listening pattern?

Thinking Ahead

1. How do you rate your memory? Describe its strengths and weaknesses.

2. List two techniques that you have used to improve your ability to remember.

3. Do you find that it is easier to remember certain types of information than others? Which types are easier for you? If you can think of a reason why, name it.

4. Do you aim to remember information long after your exams are over, or is doing well on tests your primary memory goal? Explain.

OW DOES MEMORY WORK?

Human memory works like a computer. Both have essentially the same purpose: to encode, store, and retrieve information.

During the *encoding* stage, information is changed into usable form. On a computer, this occurs when keyboard entries are transformed into electronic symbols and stored on a disk. In the brain, sensory information becomes impulses that the central nervous system reads and codes. You are encoding, for example, when you study a list of chemistry formulas.

During the *storage* stage, information is held in memory (the mind's version of a computer hard drive) so it can be used later. In this example, after you complete your studying of the formulas, your mind stores them until you need to use them.

During the *retrieval* stage, memories are recovered from storage by recall, just as a saved computer program is called up by name and used again. In this example, your mind would retrieve the chemistry formulas when you had to take a test or solve a problem.

Memories are stored in three different storage banks. The first, called *sensory memory,* is an exact copy of what you see and hear and lasts for a second or less. Certain information is then selected from sensory memory and moves into *short-term memory,* a temporary information storehouse that lasts no more than 10 to 20 seconds. You are consciously aware of material in your short-term memory. Whereas unimportant information is quickly dumped, important information is transferred to *long-term memory*—the mind's more permanent information storehouse.

Suppose your history instructor lists five major causes of the Civil War. As you listen to the causes, the incoming information immediately becomes part of sensory memory, and because you are paying attention, it is quickly transferred to short-term memory. Nearby whispering may never get past the stage of sensory memory because your mind selectively pays attention to some things while ignoring others. Realizing that you will probably be tested on this information, you consciously decide that it is important enough to remember. It then becomes part of long-term memory.

Having information in long-term memory does not necessarily mean that you will be able to recall it when needed. Particular techniques can help you improve your recall.

HOW CAN YOU IMPROVE YOUR MEMORY?

Your accounting instructor is giving a test tomorrow on bookkeeping programs. You feel confident because you spent hours last week memorizing the material. Unfortunately, by the time you take the test, you may remember very little—most forgetting occurs within minutes after memorization.

In a classic study conducted in 1885, researcher Herman Ebbinghaus memorized a list of meaningless three-letter words such as CEF and LAZ. He then examined how quickly he forgot them. It happened in a surprisingly short time: Within one hour he had forgotten more than 50 percent of what he had learned; after two days, he knew fewer than 30 percent of the memorized words. Although Ebbinghaus's recall of the nonsense syllables remained fairly stable after that, his experiment shows how fragile memory can be—even when you take the time and expend the energy to memorize information.[4]

If forgetting is so common, why do some people have better memories than others? Some may have an inborn talent for remembering. More often, though, they succeed because they have practiced and mastered techniques for improving recall. Remember that techniques aren't a cure-all for memory difficulties, especially for those with learning disabilities. If you have a disability, the following strategies may help but might not be enough. Seek specific assistance if you consistently have trouble remembering.

Use Specific Memory Strategies

As a student, your job is to understand, learn, and remember information—everything from general concepts to specific details. Remembering involves two kinds of memory processes: general remembering and verbatim memorization.

General remembering, the most common type of memory task, involves remembering ideas but not the exact words in which the ideas are expressed.

Verbatim memorization involves learning a mathematical formula, an unfamiliar language, the sequence of operating a machine, and so on.

The following suggestions will help improve your recall in both memory processes.

Have Purpose and Intention

Why can you remember the lyrics to dozens of popular songs but not the functions of the pancreas? Perhaps this is because you want to remember the lyrics, you connect them to a visual image, or you have an emotional tie to them. To achieve the same results at school or on the job, make sure you have a purpose for what you are trying to remember. When you know why it is important, you will be able to strengthen your intention to remember it.

> *The true art of memory is the art of attention.*   SAMUEL JOHNSON

One particular experiment demonstrates what developing the will to remember can do for you. Think for a moment about the common, ordinary U.S. penny. Although it is easy to remember that Abraham Lincoln's picture is engraved on the penny's head, it is hard to recall anything else. Try it yourself. What are the phrases on the coin? Where are they located? What image is on the reverse side?

Most people have trouble describing a penny accurately because it was never important for them to focus on the details of the coin's design. Thus, they "forget" because they never created the memory in the first place.[5]

Understand What You Memorize

Make sure that everything you want to remember makes sense to you. Something that has meaning is easier to recall than something that is gibberish. This basic principle applies to everything you study—from biology and astronomy to history and English literature. If something you need to memorize makes no sense, consult textbooks, fellow students, or an instructor for an explanation.

Determine logical connections in the information you are trying to remember, and use them. For example, in a plant biology course, memorize plants by grouping them according to family or a particular trait; in a history course, memorize events by linking them chronologically or in a cause-and-effect chain.

Finally, use organizational tools such as a formal or informal outline or a think link to record the material you want to recall and the logical connections between the elements. These tools will expose gaps in your understanding as they help you study and learn.

Recite, Rehearse, and Write

When you *recite* material, you repeat key concepts aloud, in your own words, to remember them. *Rehearsing* is similar to reciting but is done silently. It is the process of mentally repeating, summarizing, and associating information with other information. *Writing* is reciting on paper.

All three processes actively involve you in learning and memorizing the material. When you recite, using your voice to speak concepts and using your ears to hear what you say helps solidly plant the concepts in memory. Rehearsing encourages you to think about concepts and relate them to other information as you read. Writing further imprints concepts through the experience of physically writing them and visually seeing them again as you write.

You will get the greatest benefit if you separate your learning into the following steps:

- Focus as you read on the key points you want to remember. These are usually found in the topic sentences of paragraphs. Then recite, rehearse, or write the ideas down.

- Convert each main idea into a key word or phrase—something that is easy to recall and that will set off a chain of memories that will bring you back to the original information. Write each key word or phrase on an index card.

- One by one, look at the key words on your cards and recite, rehearse, or write all the associated information you can recall. Check your recall against your original material.

Reciting, rehearsing, and writing involve much more than simply rereading material—parroting words out loud, in your head, or on paper. You can reread without thinking or learning because there is no involvement. You cannot help but think and learn as you convert text concepts into key points, key points into key words and phrases, and judge your learning by assessing and evaluating what you know and what you still need to learn.

Separate Main Points From Unimportant Details

As you just learned, one of your most important tasks is to use your critical-thinking skills to select and focus on the most important information so that you can avoid overloading your memory with extra clutter. To focus on key points, highlight only the most important information in your texts and write notes in the margins about central ideas. When you review notes, highlight or rewrite the most important information to remember. Figure 6.3 shows how this is done on a marketing textbook section that introduces the concept of markets.[6]

Study During Short but Frequent Sessions

Research has shown that you can improve your chances of remembering material if you learn it more than once. To get the most out of your study sessions, spread them over time. A pattern of short sessions followed by brief periods of rest is more effective than continual studying with little or no rest. Even though you may feel as though you accomplish a lot by studying for an hour without a break, you'll probably remember more from three 20-minute sessions. With this in mind, try studying during breaks in your schedule. Although studying between classes isn't for everyone, you may find that it can help you remember more of what you study.

Sleep can actually aid memory because it reduces the interference that new memories can create. Because you can't always go to sleep immediately after studying for an exam, try postponing the study of other subjects until your exam is over. When studying for several tests at a time, avoid studying two similar subjects back to back. You'll be less confused when you study history right after biology rather than, for example, chemistry after biology.

Effective highlighting and marginal notes aid memory.

FIGURE 6.3

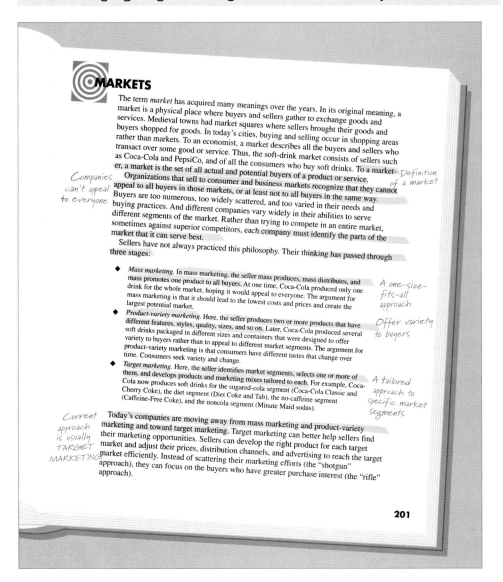

Source: Excerpt from *Marketing: An introduction,* 4th ed., Philip Kotler and Gary Armstrong, © 1997, p. 201. Reprinted with permission of Prentice-Hall, Inc., Upper Saddle River, NJ.

Separate Material into Manageable Sections

Generally, when material is short and easy to understand, studying it from start to finish improves recall. With longer material, however, you may benefit from dividing it into logical sections, mastering each section, putting all the sections together, and then testing your memory of all the material. Actors take this approach when learning the lines of a play, and it can work just as well for students trying to learn new concepts.

Practice the Middle

When you are trying to learn something, you usually study some material first, attack other material in the middle of the session, and approach still other topics at the end. The weak link in your recall is likely to be the material you study midway. It pays to give this material special attention in the form of extra practice.

Create Groupings

GROUPING

Forming digestible information segments that are easy to remember.

When items do not have to be remembered in any particular order, the act of **grouping** can help you recall them better. Say, for example, that you have to memorize these five 10-digit numbers:

    9806875087   9876535703   7636983561   6724472879   3122895312

It may look impossible. If you group the numbers to form telephone numbers, however, the job may become more manageable:

    (980) 687-5087   (987) 653-5703   (763) 698-3561   (672) 447-2879   (312) 289-5312

In general, try to keep groups to around ten items or fewer. It's hard to memorize more at one time.

Use Visual Aids

Any kind of visual representation of study material can help you remember. Try converting material into a think link or outline. Use any visual that helps you recall it and link it to other information.

Flash cards are a great memory tool. They give you short, repeated review sessions that provide immediate feedback. Make your cards from 3-by-5-inch index cards. Use the front of the card to write a word, idea, or phrase you want to remember. Use the back side for a definition, explanation, and other key facts. Figure 6.4 shows two flash cards used to study for a psychology exam.

Here are some suggestions for making the most of your flash cards:

- *Use the cards as a self-test.* Divide them into two piles—the material you know and the material you are learning. You may want to use rubber bands to separate the piles.
- *Carry the cards with you and review them frequently.* You'll learn the most if you start using cards early in the course, well ahead of exam time.
- *Shuffle the cards and learn the information in various orders.* This will help avoid putting too much focus on some information and not enough on others.

Flash cards help you memorize important facts.

FIGURE

6.4

Card 1 THEORY	• Definition: Explanation for a phenomenon based on careful and precise observations • Part of the scientific method • Leads to hypotheses
FRONT	BACK

Card 2 HYPOTHESIS	• Prediction about future behavior that is derived from observations and theories • Methods for testing hypotheses: case studies, naturalistic observations, and experiments
FRONT	BACK

- *Test yourself in both directions.* First, look at the terms and provide the definitions or explanations. Then, turn the cards over and reverse the process.

Use Tape Recorded Material

Questions on tape can work like audio flash cards. One way to do it is to record short-answer study questions, leaving 10 to 15 seconds between questions for you to answer out loud. Recording the correct answer after the pause will give you immediate feedback. For example, part of a recording for a writing class might say, "The three elements of effective writing are. . . . (10–15 seconds). . . . topic, audience, and purpose."

Use Critical Thinking

Your knowledge of the critical-thinking mind actions can help you remember information. Many of the mind actions use the principle of association—considering new information in relation to information you already know. The more you can associate a piece of new information with your current knowledge, the more likely you are to remember it.

Imagine that you have to remember information about a specific historical event—for example, the signing of the Treaty of Versailles, the agreement that ended World War II. You might put the mind actions to work in the following ways:

- *Recall* everything that you know about the topic.

- Think about how this event is *similar* to other events in history, recent or long ago.

- Consider what is *different* and unique about this treaty in comparison to other treaties.

- Explore the *causes* that led up to this event, and look at the event's *effects*.

- From the general *idea* of treaties that ended wars, explore other *examples* of such treaties.

- Think about *examples* of what happened during the treaty signing, and from those examples come up with *ideas* about the tone of the event.

- Looking at the facts of the event, *evaluate* how successful you think the treaty was.

Working through every mind action might take time; you don't always have to use every one in every memory situation. Choose the ones that will help you most. The more information and ideas you can associate with the new item you're trying to remember, the more successful you will be.

HOW CAN YOU USE MNEMONIC DEVICES TO BOOST MEMORY POWER?

Certain performers entertain their audiences by remembering the names of 100 strangers or flawlessly repeating 30 ten-digit phone numbers. These performers probably have superior memories, but genetics alone can't produce these results. They also rely on memory techniques, known as **mnemonic devices** (pronounced neh MAHN ick), for assistance.

Mnemonic devices depend on associations (relating new information to other information). Instead of learning new facts by rote (repetitive practice), associations give you a hook on which to hang these facts and to retrieve them. Mnemonic devices make information familiar and meaningful through unusual, unforgettable mental associations and visual pictures.

There are different kinds of mnemonic devices, including visual images and associations and acronyms. Study how these devices work; then apply them to your own memory challenges.

> **MNEMONIC DEVICES**
>
> Memory techniques that involve associating new information with simpler information or information you already know.

Create Visual Images and Associations

Visual images are easier to remember than images that rely on words alone. In fact, communication through visual images goes back to the prehistoric era, when people made drawings that still exist on cave walls. It is no accident that the phrase "a picture is worth a thousand words" is so familiar. The best mental images often involve bright colors, three dimensions, action scenes, inanimate objects with human traits, ridiculousness, and humor.

Turning information into mental pictures helps improve memory, especially for visual learners. To remember that the Spanish artist Picasso painted *The Three Women*, you might imagine the women in a circle dancing to a Spanish song with a pig and a donkey (pig-asso). Don't reject

Windows on the World

How can I improve my memory?

Shyama Parikh, *Depaul University, Chicago, Illinois, Psychology/Pre-Law Major*

Recently I took a memory test in one of my psychology classes. I discovered that I'm better at remembering a full definition to a word rather than reading the definition and remembering the word. Most of my classmates had the same results. This surprised all of us; it seems like it would be easier to recall a word than an entire definition, but that was not the case.

Sometimes I find memorization work difficult, even though I know I have the ability. For instance, I know I have the material written down in my notes, down to the exact page, but then on the test, I sometimes can't remember the answers. I find biology especially hard for that reason; there's a lot more memorization because of all the diagrams and classification systems.

I'm aware of mnemonic devices and I try to incorporate those into my study time, but that doesn't always work. I know rereading and repetition probably reinforce what I've studied, but I don't always have enough time. I am involved in so many other activities on campus that it's hard to find the time to devote to retaining information for five classes. I think memorization for me is the first step in learning, so I need to learn more effective ways to memorize.

I've just been accepted to law school, and I'm concerned because it seems that law requires learning a lot of technical terms. Can you suggest ways for me to improve my memory?

Stephen Beck, *Director, Learn-to-Learn Company, Winston-Salem, North Carolina*

A combination of organization, reading comprehension and reinforcement will help with your memory concerns. First, an important point: The definitions exercise you took in your psychology class illustrates how meaning enhances memory. The reason you are more likely to remember a sentence of 30 words than a list of 15 random words is because the sentence is organized in such a way that it has meaning to you. Keep this point in mind.

When you study, understand how the material is organized. For example, if a chapter outline makes sense to you, then the material is more likely to make sense. Organization improves recall (that's

why mnemonics help when memorizing unrelated items). Because understanding is just as important, though, you need to both organize *and* understand. For instance, if a system of categorizing biology terms makes sense to you, then you are more likely to understand and recall the terms. Mentally placing information in logical categories enhances memory.

Reading comprehension is similar. To enhance your reading comprehension, preview the entire textbook or chapter before reading it. Read the table of contents, chapter titles, sections, and subsections. By understanding the organization of the textbook you can more actively make meaningful connections and, therefore, learn the details more efficiently.

The final technique is reinforcement. As you read a text, continually ask yourself whether the information makes sense. If not, try to figure out why you're stuck. How do you know if you have memorized a list? Write it down to find out exactly what you do and do not know. For reinforcement of reading comprehension, pause at good stopping points and try taking notes from memory. Your notes are proof that you can recall and understand the material. This pause and reflect technique is critical for learning new material. Good luck!

TABLE 6.3   Visual images aid recall.

SPANISH VOCABULARY	DEFINITION	MENTAL IMAGE
carta	letter	A person pushing a shopping cart filled with letters into a post office.
río	river	A school of sharks rioting in the river. One of the sharks is pulling a banner inscribed with the word *riot*. A killer shark bites off the *t* in riot as he takes charge of the group. "I'm the king of this river," he says.
dinero	money	A man is eating lasagna at a diner. The lasagna is made of layers of money.

outlandish images—as long as they help you. Often the strongest, oddest, most vivid images are the most effective.

Here is another example. Say you are trying to learn some basic Spanish vocabulary, including the words *carta, río,* and *dinero.* Instead of trying to learn these words by rote, you might come up with mental images such as those in Table 6.3.

Using Visual Images to Remember Items in a List

Two mental imagery techniques will help you remember items in a list: taking a mental walk in a familiar place and forming an idea chain.

A *mental walk* is a memory strategy in which you imagine that you store new ideas in familiar locations. Think, for example, of the route you take to and from the library. You pass the college theater, the science center, the bookstore, the cafeteria, the athletic center, and the social science building before reaching the library. At each spot along the route, you "place" an idea or concept you want to learn. Say, for example, that in biology you have been assigned the task of remembering the major endocrine glands, starting in the brain and working downward through the body. Using the mental walk technique, here is how you would do this (see Figure 6.5 for a visual representation of this technique):

> *Memory is the stepping-stone to thinking, because without remembering facts, you cannot think, conceptualize, reason, make decisions, create, or contribute.*
>
>
> HARRY LORAYNE

At the campus theater, you would place the pituitary gland; at the science center, the thyroid gland; at the campus bookstore, the thymus gland; at the cafeteria, the adrenal gland; at the athletic center, the pancreas; at the social science building the ovaries (female); and at the library, the testes (male).

An *idea chain* is a memory strategy that involves forming exaggerated mental images of 20 or more items. The first image is connected to the second image, which is connected to the third image, and so on. Imagine, for

A mental walk.

FIGURE

6.5

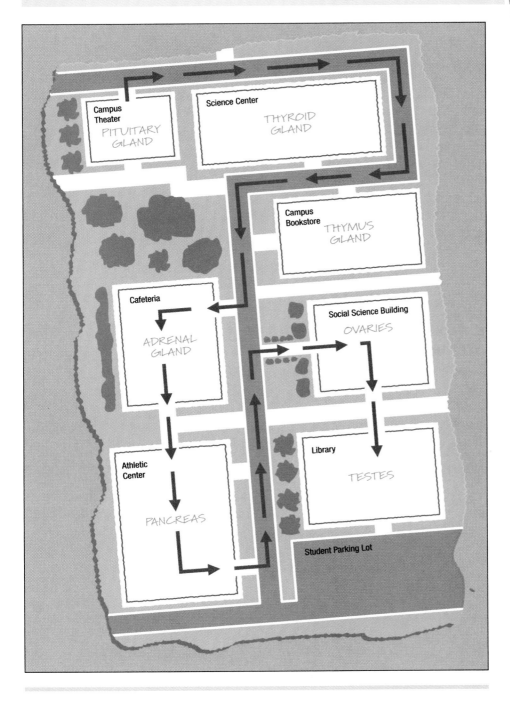

example, that you want to remember the seven mind actions that appear in the critical-thinking chapter: recall, similarity, difference, cause and effect, example to idea, idea to example, and evaluation. You can use the visual icons to form an idea chain that goes like this:

The letter R rolls down a hill (*recall*) and bumps into two similar intersecting circles (*similarity*) that start rolling and bump into two different intersecting circles (*difference*). Everything rolls past a sign with two circling arrows on it telling them to keep rolling (*cause and effect*), and then it bumps into an "EX" at the bottom of the hill that turns on a light bulb (*example to idea*). That light bulb shines on another "EX" (*idea to example*). The two "EX"s are sitting on either side of a set of scales (*evaluation*).

Create Acronyms

ACRONYM

A word formed from the first letters of a series of words, created to help you remember the series.

Another helpful association method involves the use of the **acronym**. In history, you can remember the Allies during World War II—Britain, America, and Russia—with the acronym BAR. This is referred to as a *word acronym* because the first letters of the items you want to remember spell a word. The word (or words) spelled don't necessarily have to be real words; see Figure 6.6 for a word acronym that often helps students remember the colors of the spectrum.

Other acronyms take the form of an entire sentence in which the first letter of each word in each sentence stands for the first letter of the memorized term. This is also called a *list order acronym*. For example, when science students want to remember the list of planets in order of their distance from the sun (Mercury, Venus, Earth, Mars, Jupiter, Saturn, Uranus, Neptune, and Pluto), they learn the sentence:

My very elegant mother just served us nine pickles.

Here's another example from music. Use this phrase to remember the notes that correspond to the lines on the treble clef (E, G, B, D, and F):

Every Good Boy Does Fine.

You can create your own acronyms. Suppose you want to remember the names of the first six presidents of the United States. You notice that the first letters of their last names—Washington, Adams, Jefferson, Madison, Monroe, and Adams—together read W A J M M A. To remember them, first you might add an *e* after the *J* and create a short nonsense word: *wajemma*. Then, to make sure you don't forget the nonsense word, you might picture the six presidents sitting in a row and wearing pajamas.

FIGURE 6.6   Spectrum acronym.

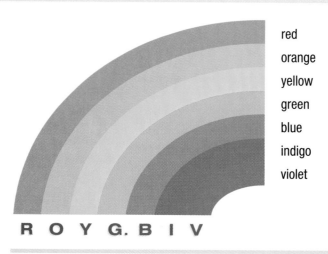

red
orange
yellow
green
blue
indigo
violet

R O Y G. B I V

Use Songs or Rhymes

Some of the most classic mnemonic devices are rhyming poems that tend to stick in your mind effectively. One you may have heard is the rule about the order of "i" and "e" in spelling:

> I before E, except after C, or when sounded like "A" as in "neighbor" and "weigh."
>
> Four exceptions if you please: either, neither, seizure, seize.

Make up your own poems or songs, linking tunes or rhymes that are familiar to you with information you want to remember. Thinking back to the "wajemma" example from the previous section, imagine that you want to remember the presidents' first names as well. You might set those first names—George, John, Thomas, James, James, and John—to the tune of "Happy Birthday." Or, to extend the history theme, you might use the first musical phrase of the National Anthem.

Improving your memory requires energy, time, and work. In school, it also helps to master SQ3R, the textbook study technique that was introduced in Chapter 5. By going through the steps in SQ3R and using the specific memory techniques described in this chapter, you will be able to learn more in less time—and remember what you learn long after exams are over.

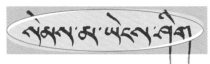

In Sanskrit, the written language of India and other Hindu countries, the characters above read *sem ma yeng chik,* meaning "do not be distracted." This advice can refer to the focus for a task or job at hand, the concentration required to critically think and talk through a problem, the mental discipline of meditation, or many other situations.

Think of this concept as you strive to improve your listening and memory techniques. Focus on the task, the person, or the idea at hand. Try not to be distracted by other thoughts, other people's notions of what you should be doing, or any negative messages. Be present in the moment to truly hear and remember what is happening around you. Do not be distracted.

IMPORTANT POINTS *to remember*

1. How can you become a better listener?

Listening has four progressive stages: sensing, interpreting, evaluating, and reacting. Listening involves managing listening challenges, including divided attention and distractions, the tendency to shut out all or part of the speaker's message, and the tendency to judge what you hear. Create a more positive listening environment by working to eliminate distractions, taking responsibility for listening, believing that what your instructors say is valuable, making sure your emotions and opinions don't interfere with listening, and making strategic use of tape recorders when permitted.

Effective listening is also active listening. You will become more involved with what you hear if you set a purpose for listening, ask questions, put "extra" listening time to good use, pay attention to verbal signposts, and know what helps and hinders listening.

2. How does memory work?

Like a computer, the human memory is a system that encodes, stores, and retrieves information. Memories stored in the human brain are placed in three different storage banks: sensory memory (an exact copy of what you see and hear, lasting for a second or less), short-term memory (a 10–20 second temporary memory storehouse), and long-term memory (the more permanent storehouse).

3. How can you improve your memory?

Use specific memory strategies such as having purpose and intention; understanding what you memorize; reciting, rehearsing, and writing; focusing on important points while ignoring unimportant details; scheduling short and frequent study sessions; separating material into manageable sections; practicing the material you learn in the middle of a study session; grouping material into easy-to-learn segments; using visual aids; and using tape-recorded material. Using critical thinking can also boost your memory power—mind actions like cause and effect and example to idea help you connect new information to what you already know.

4. How can you use mnemonic devices to boost memory power?

Mnemonic devices are memory techniques that associate new information with information you already know. The most effective mnemonics are linked to visual images. You can use visual images to remember items in a list by creating a memory walk or an idea chain. Acronyms, another mnemonic, are words formed from the first letters of words in a series. Songs or poems may help information stick in your mind through their use of music, rhythm, and rhyme.

CRITICAL THINKING

APPLYING LEARNING TO LIFE

OPTIMUM LISTENING CONDITIONS. Think of a recent situation (this semester or last semester) in which you have been able to understand and retain most of what you heard in the classroom.

Describe the environment (course title, type of classroom setting, etc.):

_____

_____

Describe the instructor's style (lecture, group discussion, Q&A, etc.):

_____

_____

Describe your level of preparation for the class:

_____

_____

Describe your attitude toward the course:

_____

_____

Describe any barriers to listening that you had to overcome in this situation:

_____

_____

Now describe a classroom situation you recently experienced where you feel you *didn't* retain information well.

Describe the environment (course title, type of classroom setting, etc.):

_____

_____

Describe the instructor's style (lecture, group discussion, Q&A, etc.):

_____

_____

Describe your level of preparation for the class:

_____

_____

Describe your attitude toward the course:

_____

_____

Describe any barriers to listening that were present in this situation:

_____

_____

Examine the two situations. Based on your descriptions, name two conditions that seem crucial for you to listen effectively and retain information.

1. _____

2. _____

Now name two conditions that seem to create the biggest listening challenges for you.

1. _____

2. _____

Finally, using what you learned about mnemonic devices, create a mnemonic that allows you to remember what you consider the most important principles of listening. Write your mnemonic here.

TEAMWORK

COMBINING FORCES

BOOST YOUR MEMORY. Gather as a class if your class is under 15 people, or divide into two groups if it is larger. Each person in your group should contribute one item to lay on a table (make sure you have as few repeats as possible). When all the items are laid out, allow one minute for everyone to look at them (use a watch with a second hand to time yourselves). Then, cover the items, and allow five minutes for each person to individually attempt to list all of the items. Compare lists to see how you did.

If you have time, go through the same process again, but have each group member choose a specific memory technique to try—for example, two people could use reciting and rehearsing, three could try to make an acronym, two people could try to link images in an idea chain, and the other three could try visual associations. After you evaluate your success, talk about the different techniques and what worked well (or not so well) for whom.

WRITING
DISCOVERY THROUGH JOURNALING

To record your thoughts, use a separate journal or the lined page at the end of the chapter.

MANAGING YOUR EMOTIONS AND OPINIONS. Describe your feelings about having to listen to an instructor, supervisor, or other authority with whom you do not agree. How do you react? Do you stop listening? Do you get caught up in an internal argument? Do you try to figure out how you will comment? Write about what happened when you had to listen to someone with different views than yours. Brainstorm ideas about what you can do when this kind of situation comes up.

CAREER PORTFOLIO
CHARTING YOUR COURSE

LISTENING AND MEMORY ON THE JOB. Any career that you pursue will make use of your listening and memory skills. Whereas memorizing facts for an anatomy test might not seem particularly crucial, for example, a doctor will find that being able to remember where a particular artery is can make the difference in a life-or-death situation.

On a separate sheet of paper, make a list of all of the various listening and memory skills that you can recall from this chapter. Try to write down 12 or more different skills.

Then, show your list to three different people who are currently in the work force either part-time or full time. Ask them to indicate for you the five skills from your list that they consider to be the most important for workplace success.

When you have completed your three interviews, tally the votes and write your three top skills on another sheet of paper (if you have any tie votes, make the choice yourself of which skill you feel is most important). For each skill, write a brief story about a time when this skill was important to you at work or, if you have not yet been employed, in the classroom.

UGGESTED READINGS

Robbins, Harvey A. *How to Speak and Listen Effectively.* New York: AMACOM (1992).

Higbee, Kenneth L. *Your Memory: How it Works and How to Improve It.* Marlowe & Co. (2001).

Lorayne, Harry. *Super Memory—Super Student: How to Raise Your Grades in 30 Days.* Boston: Little, Brown & Co. (1990).

Lorayne, Harry. *The Memory Book: The Classic Guide to Improving Your Memory at Work, at School, and at Play.* New York: Ballantine Books (1996).

Roberts, Billy. *Educate Your Memory: Improvement Techniques for Students of All Ages.* London: Allison & Busby (2000).

Roberts, Billy. *Working Memory: Improving Your Memory for the Workplace.* London Bridge Trade (1999).

 ## INTERNET RESOURCES

ForgetKnot: A Source for Mnemonic Devices:
http://members.tripod.com/~ForgetKnot/

 ## ENDNOTES

1. Harris quoted in Louis E. Boone and David L. Kurtz. *Contemporary Business Communication.* Upper Saddle River, NJ: Prentice Hall (1994), p. 39.

2. Ralph G. Nichols. "Do We Know How to Listen? Practical Helps in a Modern Age." *Speech Teacher* (March 1961), pp. 118–124.

3. Ibid.

4. Herman Ebbinghaus. *Memory: A Contribution to Experimental Psychology,* transl. H. A. Ruger and C. E. Bussenius New York: Teachers' College, Columbia University (1885).

5. Based on an experiment by R. S. Nickerson and M. J. Adams. "Long-Term Memory for a Common Object," *Cognitive Psychology,* 1979 (11), pp. 287–307.

6. Philip Kotler and Gary Armstrong. *Marketing: An Introduction,* 4th ed. Upper Saddle River, NJ: Prentice Hall (1997), p. 201.

KEYS TO EFFECTIVE LEARNING KEYS TO EFFECTIVE LEARNING KEYS TO EFFECTIVE LEARNING KEYS TO EFFECTIVE LEARNING KEYS

DATE

NAME

C hoose two chapters to read from a textbook you are using for one of your current classes. Read one chapter the way you normally do. Then, go to www.prenhall.com/success and click on the Reading link in the Study Skills section. Explore each of the steps outlined there— the parts in a "well-planned reading episode." Before your read the second chapter, survey it (the first of the steps) and answer the following questions on a separate sheet of paper.

1. How many pages is the chapter? How much time do you estimate it will take you to read?
2. How is the chapter organized?
3. What note-taking system will work best for this chapter?
4. What questions do you want to be able to answer by the time you finish reading the chapter? Write down three to five questions that you think are important.

Next, read the chapter keeping the steps in mind. Finally, answer the following questions after you have finished reading.

1. Describe your usual method for reading. How does this strategy compare?
2. Which steps in the Reading link had the most positive effect for you?
3. Answer the questions you raised while surveying the chapter.
4. Click on the word "Article" and read Mary Bixby's article about reading. Write down what you consider your biggest "problem on the page" and "problem off the page" and describe some ideas you have to solve these problems.
5. Using a search engine, locate and list three sites that have helpful information on reading. For each site, write down one helpful hint that you would like to try when reading your texts.

Targeting Success in School

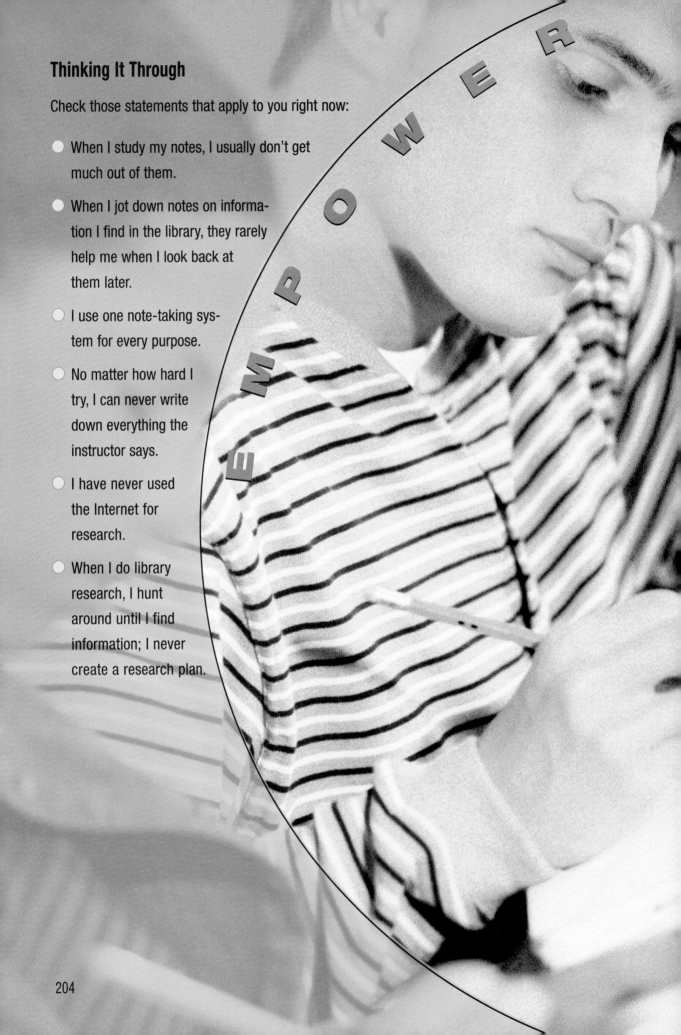

Thinking It Through

Check those statements that apply to you right now:

- When I study my notes, I usually don't get much out of them.

- When I jot down notes on information I find in the library, they rarely help me when I look back at them later.

- I use one note-taking system for every purpose.

- No matter how hard I try, I can never write down everything the instructor says.

- I have never used the Internet for research.

- When I do library research, I hunt around until I find information; I never create a research plan.

IN THIS CHAPTER,

you will explore answers to the

following questions:

- How does taking notes help you?
- How can you make the most of class notes?
- What note-taking system should you use?
- What are research notes and how can you use them?
- How can you write faster when taking notes?
- How can you make the most of your library?
- How do you use a search strategy to conduct research?
- How can you do research on the Internet?

Note Taking and Research

B oth in school and out, you spend much of your time like a detective in search of knowledge. When you listen to your instructors during class lectures, do independent research, or learn on the job, you are uncovering and gathering information that you may put to use, now or in the future. Note taking and library research can empower you to create new ideas from what you learn. The more knowledge you gather in your "detective work," the more resources you have at your disposal when you soar ahead into new realms of thinking and discovery.

The search for knowledge requires varied skills. First, you need an effective note-taking system to record what you hear or read. Second, you need the skill to harness the vast resources of your college library and the Internet. This chapter will introduce you to note-taking and research techniques that can help you make your searches for information successful.

LEARNING FROM OTHERS

HOW DOES TAKING NOTES HELP YOU?

Note taking can be a challenge. You might feel that it prevents you from watching your instructor or that you can't write fast enough to get everything down. You may also be convinced that you can remember all that you need to know even when you don't take notes. The truth is that the act of note taking involves you in the learning process in many important ways. Weigh whatever you feel are the negative effects of note taking against its potential for good. You may see why the simple act of taking clear notes that you can use to prepare for tests and as study tools can influence—and improve—your academic success (see Figure 7.1).

Because it is virtually impossible to take notes on everything you hear or read, the act of note taking encourages you to think critically and evaluate what is worth remembering. Asking yourself questions like the following will help you judge what is important enough to write down:

- Do I need this information?
- Is the information important to the lecture or reading or is it just an interesting comment?
- Is the information fact or opinion? If it is opinion, is it worth remembering? (To explore this question, see "Distinguishing Fact from Opinion" in Chapter 4.)

Your responses will guide your note taking in class and help you decide what to study before an exam. Similarly, the notes you take while doing research will affect your research efforts. Learn what class notes and research notes are and how to use each to your advantage.

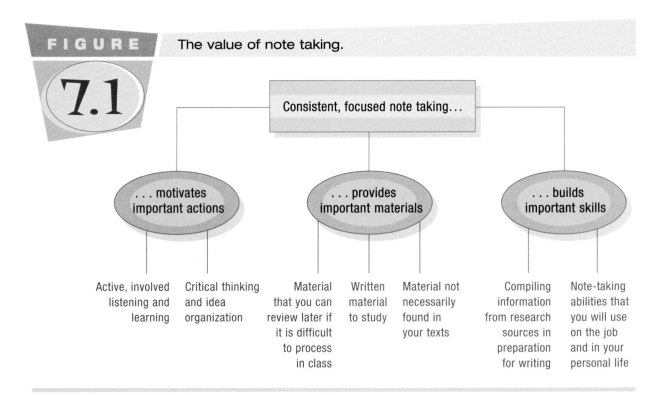

FIGURE 7.1   The value of note taking.

Consistent, focused note taking...

...motivates important actions
...provides important materials
...builds important skills

| Active, involved listening and learning | Critical thinking and idea organization | Material that you can review later if it is difficult to process in class | Written material to study | Material not necessarily found in your texts | Compiling information from research sources in preparation for writing | Note-taking abilities that you will use on the job and in your personal life |

OW CAN YOU MAKE THE MOST OF CLASS NOTES?

Class notes—the notes you take while listening to an instructor—may contain key terms and definitions (e.g., Marketing research is . . .), explanations of concepts and processes (e.g., what happens during photosynthesis), or narratives of who did what to whom and when (e.g., The events that led to the contested presidential election between Al Gore and George W. Bush are . . .). If lectures include material that is not in your text or if your instructor talks about specific test questions, your class notes become even more important as a study tool.

Prepare for Note Taking

Your class notes have two purposes: First, they should reflect what you heard in class, and second, they should be a resource for studying, writing, or comparing with your text material. Taking good class notes depends on good preparation.

PREVIEW YOUR READING MATERIAL. Survey the text (or any other assigned reading material) to become familiar with the topic and any new concepts that it introduces. Visual familiarity helps note taking during lectures.

GATHER YOUR SUPPLIES. Use separate pieces of 8 1/2-by-11-inch paper for each class. If you use a three-ring binder, punch holes in handouts and insert them immediately following your notes for that day. Make sure your pencils are sharp and your pens aren't about to run out.

LOCATION, LOCATION, LOCATION. Find a comfortable seat where you can easily see and hear—sitting near the front, where you minimize distraction and maximize access to the lecture or discussion, might be your best bet. Be ready to write as soon as the instructor begins speaking.

CHOOSE THE BEST NOTE-TAKING SYSTEM. Select a system that is most appropriate for the situation. Later in the chapter, you will learn about different note-taking systems. Take the following factors into account when choosing one to use in any class:

- *The instructor's style.* (You'll be able to determine this style after a few classes). Whereas one instructor may deliver organized lectures at a normal speaking rate, another may jump from topic to topic or talk very quickly.
- *The course material.* You may decide that an informal outline works best for a highly structured philosophy course, but that a think link is the right choice for a looser sociology course. Try the note-taking system you choose for a few classes, then make whatever adjustments are necessary.
- *Your learning style.* Choose strategies that make the most of your strong points and help boost weaker areas. A visual–spatial learner might prefer think links or the Cornell system; a Thinker type might stick to outlines; an interpersonal learner might use the Cornell system and fill in the cue column in a study group setting (see Chapter 3 for a

complete discussion of learning styles). You might even find that one system is best in class and another works best for review sessions.

GATHER SUPPORT. For each class, set up a support system with two students. That way, when you are absent, you can get the notes you missed from one or the other.

Record Information Effectively During Class

Because no one has time to write down everything she hears, the following strategies will help you choose and record what you feel is important in a format that you can read and understand later. This is not a list of "musts." Rather, it is a source list of ideas to try as you work to find the note-taking system that works best for you. Keep an open mind and experiment with these strategies until you feel that you have found a successful combination.

Remember that the first step in note taking is to listen actively; you can't write down something that you don't hear. Use the listening strategies in Chapter 6 to make sure you are prepared to take in the information that comes your way during class.

- Date and identify each page. When you take several pages of notes during a lecture, add an identifying letter or number to the date on each page: 11/27A, 11/27B, 11/27C, for example, or 11/27—1 of 3, 11/27—2 of 3, 11/27—3 of 3. This will help you keep track of page order.

- Add the specific topic of the lecture at the top of the page. For example:

  11/27A—*U. S. Immigration Policy After World War II*

  Because an instructor may revisit a topic days or even weeks after introducing it, this suggestion will help you gather all your notes on the same topic when it is time to study.

- If your instructor jumps from topic to topic during a single class, it may help to start a new page for each new topic.

- Some students prefer to use only one side of the notepaper because this can make notes easier to read. Others prefer to use both sides, which can be a more economical paper-saving option. Choose what works best for you.

- Record whatever your instructor emphasizes. See Figure 7.2 for more details about how an instructor might call attention to particular information.

- Write down all key terms and definitions, especially those your instructor emphasizes. If, for example, your instructor is discussing the stages of mental development in children, as defined by psychologist Jean Piaget, your notes would probably mention such terms as *sensorimotor* and *preoperational development.*

- Avoid writing out every word your instructor says. If you use short phrases instead of full sentences, you will save yourself a lot of time and trouble. For example, write "German—nouns capitalized" instead of "In the German language, all nouns are capitalized;" "Abraham Lincoln was elected president in the year 1860" becomes "Lincoln—elec. Pres. 1860."

- Continue to take notes during class discussions and question-and-answer periods. What your fellow students ask about may help you as well.

How to pick up on instructor cues.

FIGURE
7.2

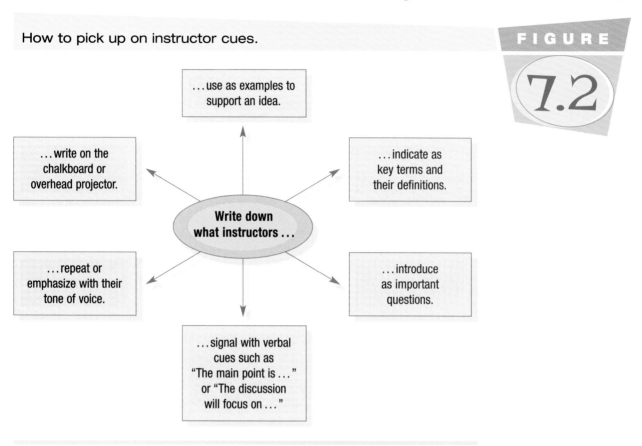

...use as examples to support an idea.

...write on the chalkboard or overhead projector.

...indicate as key terms and their definitions.

Write down what instructors ...

...repeat or emphasize with their tone of voice.

...introduce as important questions.

...signal with verbal cues such as "The main point is ..." or "The discussion will focus on ..."

- Write down all questions raised by the instructor; the same questions may appear on a test.

- Leave one or more blank spaces between points. This white space will help you review your notes because information will be in self-contained segments. (This suggestion does not apply if you are using a think link.)

- Draw pictures and diagrams that help illustrate ideas.

- Write quickly but legibly, perhaps using a form of personal shorthand. (See the section on short-hand on p. 219 of this chapter.)

- Indicate material that is especially important with a star, underlining, a highlighter pen, a different color pen, or capital letters.

- If you don't understand something, leave space and place a question mark in the margin. Then take advantage of your resources—ask the instructor to explain it after class, discuss it with a classmate, or consult your textbook—and fill in the blank when the idea is clear.

- Take notes until the instructor stops speaking. If you stop writing a few minutes before the class is over, you might miss critical information.

- Make your notes as legible and organized as possible—you can't learn from notes that you can't read or understand. Don't be so fussy, howev-

er, that you miss information while you are dotting every *i* and crossing every *t*. Remember that you can always rewrite and improve your notes.

- Consider that your notes are part, but not all, of what you need to learn. Using your text to add to your notes after class makes a superior, "deeper and wider" set of information to study.

Review and Revise Your Notes

Even the most comprehensive notes in the world won't do you any good unless you review them. The crucial act of reviewing helps you solidify the information in your memory so that you can recall it and use it. It also helps you link new information to information you already know, which is a key step in building new ideas. The review and revision stage of note taking should include time for planning, critical thinking, adding information from other sources, summarizing, and working with a study group.

Consistency is important. If you use the same system of indicating importance, such as indenting, spacing, or underlining on each page of your notes, your mind will perceive the key information with a minimum of effort.

WILLIAM H. ARMSTRONG
M. WILLARD LAMPE II

Plan a Review Schedule

As you learned in Chapter 6, when you review your notes affects how much you are likely to remember. Reviewing right after the lecture but not again until the test, reviewing here and there without a plan, or cramming it all into one crazy night will not allow you to make the most of your abilities. Do yourself a favor by trying to plan your time as strategically as possible.

REVIEW WITHIN A DAY OF THE LECTURE. If you can, plan your first review for the day following the lecture. Reviewing while the material is still fresh in your mind will help you to remember it more effectively. You don't have to sit down for two hours and focus on every word. Just set some time aside to reread your notes and perhaps write questions and comments on them. If you know you have an hour between classes, for example, that would be an ideal time to work in a quick review.

REVIEW REGULARLY. Try to schedule times during the week for reviewing notes from that week's class meetings. For example, if you know you always have from 2 P.M. to 5 P.M. free every Tuesday and Thursday afternoon, you can plan to review notes from two courses on Tuesday and from two others on Thursday. Having a routine helps assure that you will look at material regularly.

REVIEW WITH AN EYE TOWARD TESTS. When you have a test coming up, step up your efforts. Schedule longer review sessions, call a study group meeting, and review more frequently. As you may recall from the memory chapter, shorter sessions of intense review work interspersed with breaks may be more effective than long hours of continuous studying. Some students find that recopying their notes before an exam or at an earlier stage helps cement key concepts in memory.

Read and Rework Using Critical Thinking

The critical-thinking mind actions will help you make the most of your notes.

RECALL. Read your notes to learn the information, clarify points, write out abbreviations, and fill in missing information.

SIMILARITY. Consider what similar facts or ideas the information brings to mind. Write them in the margins or white space on the page if they are helpful to you.

DIFFERENCE. Consider how the information differs from what you already know. Is there a discrepancy you should examine? If something seems way off base, could you have written it down inaccurately?

CAUSE AND EFFECT. Look at how ideas, facts, and statements relate to one another. See if any of them have cause-and-effect connections. You might even want to use another color pen to draw a line linking related ideas or facts on the page.

EXAMPLE TO IDEA. Think about what new ideas you can form from the information in your notes. If any come to mind, write them in your notes or on a separate page. If particular information seems to fit together more specifically than your notes initially indicate, you may want to add headings and subheadings, and insert clarifying phrases or sentences.

IDEA TO EXAMPLE. Think carefully about the ideas in your notes. What do they mean? See if the examples in your notes support or negate them. If you have no examples in your notes as written, add them as you review.

EVALUATION. Use your evaluation skills to select and underline or highlight the most important ideas and information. Think about why they are important and make sure you understand them as completely as possible.

Revise Using Other Sources

Revising and adding to your notes using material from your texts, other required course readings, and the Internet is one of the best ways to build your understanding and link new information to information you already know. Try using the following critical-thinking actions when you add to your notes:

- Brainstorm and write down examples from other sources that illustrate central ideas in your notes.
- Pay attention to similarities between your text materials and class notes (ideas that appear in both are probably important to remember).
- Think of facts or ideas from the reading that can support and clarify ideas from your notes.
- Consider what in your class notes differs from your reading, and why.
- Write down any new ideas that come up when reviewing your notes.

- Look at cause-and-effect connections between material from your notes and reading material. Note how ideas, facts, and examples relate to one another.

Summarize

Writing a summary of your notes is another important review technique. Summarizing involves critically evaluating which ideas and examples are most important and then rewriting the material in a shortened form, focusing on those important ideas and examples.

You may prefer to summarize as you review, with the notes in front of you. If you are using the Cornell system (see p. 216), you would summarize in the space saved at the bottom of the page. Other ideas include summarizing on a separate page that you insert in your loose-leaf binder, or summarizing on the back of the previous page (this is possible if you only take notes on one side of the paper).

Another helpful review technique is to summarize your notes from memory after you review them. This will give you an idea of how well you have retained the information. You may even want to summarize as you read, then summarize from memory, and compare the two summaries.

Work With Study Groups

When you work with a study group, you have the opportunity to review both your personal notes and those of other members of the class. This can be an enormous help if, for example, you lost concentration during part of a lecture and your notes don't make much sense. You and another student may even have notes that contradict each other or have radically different information. When this happens, try to reconstruct what the instructor said and, if necessary, bring in a third group member to clear up the confusion. See Chapter 5 for more on effective studying in groups.

WHAT ARE RESEARCH NOTES AND HOW CAN YOU USE THEM?

Research notes are the notes you take while gathering information to answer a research question. Research notes take two forms: source notes and content notes.

Source notes are the preliminary notes you take as you review available research. They include vital bibliographic information, as well as a short summary and critical evaluation of the work. Write these notes when you consider a book or article interesting enough to look at again. They do not signal that you have actually read something all the way through, only that you plan to review it later on.

Each source note should include the author's full name; the title of the work; the edition (if any); the publisher, year, and city of publication; issue and/or volume number when applicable (such as for a magazine); and the page numbers you consulted. Many students find that index cards work best for source notes. See Figure 7.3 for an example of how you can write source notes on index cards.

Sample source note.

FIGURE 7.3

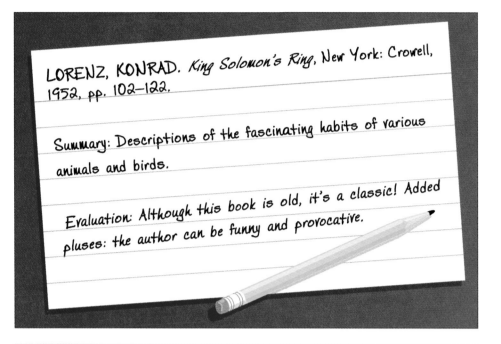

LORENZ, KONRAD. *King Solomon's Ring.* New York: Crowell, 1952, pp. 102–122.

Summary: Descriptions of the fascinating habits of various animals and birds.

Evaluation: Although this book is old, it's a classic! Added pluses: the author can be funny and provocative.

The second type of research notes is *content notes*. Unlike brief informational source notes, content notes provide an in-depth look at the source, taken during a thorough reading. Use them to record the information you need to write your draft. Here are some suggestions for taking effective content notes:

- When a source looks promising, begin reading it and summarizing what you read. Use standard notebook paper that fits into a three-ring binder. This gives you space to write, as well as the flexibility to rearrange the pages into any order that makes sense. (If you prefer using large index cards for content notes, choose 5-by-6-inch or 5-by-8-inch sizes.)
- Include bibliographic information and page numbers for every source.
- Limit each page to a single source.
- If you take notes on more than one subject from a single source, create a separate page for each subject.
- If the notes on a source require more than one page, label the pages and number them sequentially. For example, if the source is *Business Week* magazine, your pages might be labeled BW1, BW2, and so on.
- Identify the type of note that appears on each page. Evaluate whether it is a summary in your own words, a quotation, or a **paraphrase**.
- Write your summary notes in any of the note-taking systems described later in the chapter.

Notations that you make directly on photocopies of sources—marginal notes, highlighting, and underlining—can supplement your content notes. Say, for example, that you are writing a paper on the psychological development of adolescent girls. During your research, you photocopy an article

PARAPHRASE

A restatement of a written text or passage in another form or other words; often to clarify meaning.

by Dr. Carol Gilligan, an expert in the field. On the photocopy, you high-light important information and make marginal notes that detail your immediate reactions to some key points. Then, you take content notes on the article. When it is time to write your paper, you have two different and helpful resources to consult.

Try to divide your time as equally as possible between photocopy notes and content notes. If you use photocopies as your primary reference without making any of your own content notes, you may have more work to do when you begin writing because you will need to spend time putting the source material in your own words. Writing paraphrases and sum-maries in content notes ahead of time will save you some work later in the process.

Whether you are taking notes in class or while doing research, there are different note-taking systems from which you can choose.

WHAT NOTE-TAKING SYSTEM SHOULD YOU USE?

You will benefit most from the system that feels most comfortable to you and makes the most sense for the type of content covered in any given course. For example, you might take notes in a different style for a his-tory class than for a foreign language class, or use a different system during a work-related planning meeting than for a professional conference. As you consider each system, remember your learning style from Chapter 3. Everyone has a different learning and working style, so don't wedge your-self into a system that doesn't work for you. The most common note-taking systems include outlines, the Cornell system, and think links.

Taking Notes in Outline Form

When a reading assignment or lecture seems well organized, you may choose to take notes in outline form. Outlining means constructing a line-by-line representation, with certain phrases set off by varying indentations, showing how ideas relate to one another and are supported by facts and examples.

Formal versus Informal Outlines

Formal outlines indicate ideas and examples with Roman numerals, capi-tal and lowercase letters, and numbers. The rules of formal outlines require at least two headings on the same level. That is, if you have a IIA, you must also have a IIB. Similarly, if you have a IIIA1, you must also have a IIIA2. In contrast, informal outlines show the same associations but replace the formality with a system of consistent indenting and dashes. Figure 7.4 shows the difference between the two outline forms. Because making a for-mal outline can take time, many students find that using informal outlines is better for in-class note taking. Figure 7.5 shows how a student has used the structure of a formal outline to write notes on the topic of civil-rights legislation.

The structure of an outline.

FIGURE

7.4

FORMAL OUTLINE	INFORMAL OUTLINE
TOPIC	TOPIC
I. First Main Idea	First Main Idea
A. Major supporting fact	—Major supporting fact
B. Major supporting fact	—Major supporting fact
1. First reason or example	—First reason or example
2. Second reason or example	—Second reason or example
a. First supporting fact	—First supporting fact
b. Second supporting fact	—Second supporting fact
II. Second Main Idea	Second Main Idea
A. Major supporting fact	—Major supporting fact
1. First reason or example	—First reason or example
2. Second reason or example	—Second reason or example
B. Major supporting fact	—Major supporting fact

When you use an outline to write class notes, you may have trouble when an instructor rambles or jumps from point to point. The best advice in this case is to abandon the outline structure for the time being. Focus instead on taking down whatever information you can and on drawing connections between key topics. After class, try to restructure your notes and, if possible, rewrite them in outline form.

Guided Notes

From time to time, an instructor may give you a guide, usually in the form of an outline, to help you take notes in class. This outline may be on the board, on an overhead projector, or on a page that you receive at the beginning of the class.

Although guided notes help you follow the lecture and organize your thoughts during class, they do not replace your own notes. Because they are more of a basic outline of topics than a comprehensive coverage of information, they require that you fill in what they do not cover in detail. If your mind wanders because you think that the guided notes are all you need, you may miss important information.

When you receive guided notes on paper, write directly on the paper if there is room. If not, use a separate sheet and write on it the outline

FIGURE

7.5

Sample formal outline.

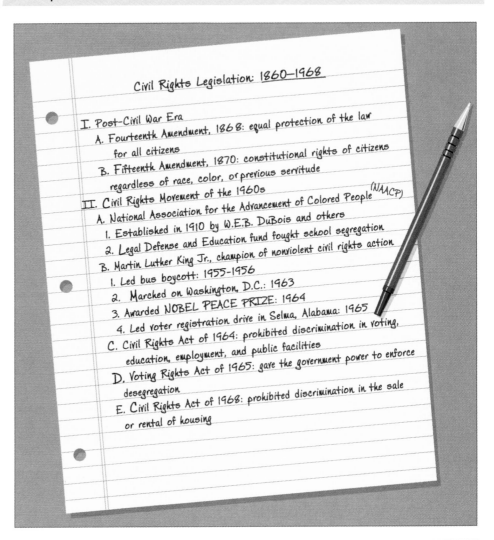

Civil Rights Legislation: 1860–1968

I. Post-Civil War Era
   A. Fourteenth Amendment, 1868: equal protection of the law
     for all citizens
   B. Fifteenth Amendment, 1870: constitutional rights of citizens
     regardless of race, color, or previous servitude
II. Civil Rights Movement of the 1960s
   A. National Association for the Advancement of Colored People (NAACP)
     1. Established in 1910 by W.E.B. DuBois and others
     2. Legal Defense and Education fund fought school segregation
   B. Martin Luther King Jr., champion of nonviolent civil rights action
     1. Led bus boycott: 1955–1956
     2. Marched on Washington, D.C.: 1963
     3. Awarded NOBEL PEACE PRIZE: 1964
     4. Led voter registration drive in Selma, Alabama: 1965
   C. Civil Rights Act of 1964: prohibited discrimination in voting,
     education, employment, and public facilities
   D. Voting Rights Act of 1965: gave the government power to enforce
     desegregation
   E. Civil Rights Act of 1968: prohibited discrimination in the sale
   or rental of housing

categories that the guided notes suggest. If the guided notes are on the board or overhead, copy them, leaving plenty of space in between for your own notes.

Using the Cornell Note-Taking System

The Cornell note-taking system, also known as the T-note system, was developed more than 45 years ago by Walter Pauk at Cornell University and is now in use throughout the world.[1] The system is successful because it is simple—and because it works. It consists of three sections on ordinary notepaper.

- *Section 1*, the largest section, is on the right. Record your notes here in informal outline form, or in whatever form is most comfortable for you.
- *Section 2*, to the left of your notes, is the *cue column*. Leave it blank while you read or listen; then fill it in later as you review. You might

fill it with comments that highlight main ideas, clarify meaning, suggest examples, or link ideas and examples. You can even draw diagrams. Many students use this column to raise questions that they will ask themselves when they study. By placing specific questions in the cue column, you can help yourself focus on critical details and understand their meaning.

- *Section 3,* at the bottom of the page, is known as the *summary area.* Here you use a sentence or two to summarize the notes on the page. Use this section during the review process to reinforce concepts and provide an overview of what the notes say.

When you use the Cornell system, create the note-taking structure before class begins. Picture an upside-down letter *T* as you follow these directions and use Figure 7.6 as your guide.

- Start with a sheet of standard loose-leaf paper. Label it with the date and title of the lecture.
- To create the *cue column,* draw a vertical line about 2.5 inches from the left side of the paper. End the line about 2 inches from the bottom of the sheet.
- To create the *summary area,* start at the point where the vertical line ends (about 2 inches from the bottom of the page) and draw a horizontal line that spans the entire paper.

Figure 7.6 shows how a student used the Cornell system to take notes in a business course.

Creating a Think Link

A *think link,* also known as a mind map, is a visual form of note taking. When you draw a think link, you diagram ideas by using shapes and lines that link ideas and supporting details and examples. The visual design makes the connections easy to see, and the use of shapes and pictures extends the material beyond just words. Many learners respond well to the power of **visualization.** You can use think links to brainstorm ideas for paper topics as well.

One way to create a think link is to start by circling your topic in the middle of a sheet of paper. Next, draw a line from the circled topic and write the name of one major idea at the end of the line. Circle that idea also. Then, jot down specific facts related to the idea, linking them to the idea with lines. Continue the process, connecting thoughts to one another by using circles, lines, and words. Figure 7.7 shows a think link on social stratification (a sociology concept) that follows this particular structure.

You can design any kind of think link that feels comfortable to you. Different examples include stair steps showing connected ideas that build toward a conclusion, or a tree shape with roots as causes and branches as effects. Look back to Figure 7.1 on p. 206 for a type of think link sometimes referred to as a "jellyfish."

A think link may be difficult to construct in class, especially if your instructor talks quickly. In this case, use another note-taking system during class. Then, make a think link as part of the review process.

VISUALIZATION

The interpretation of verbal ideas through the use of mental visual images.

FIGURE

7.6

Notes taken with the Cornell system.

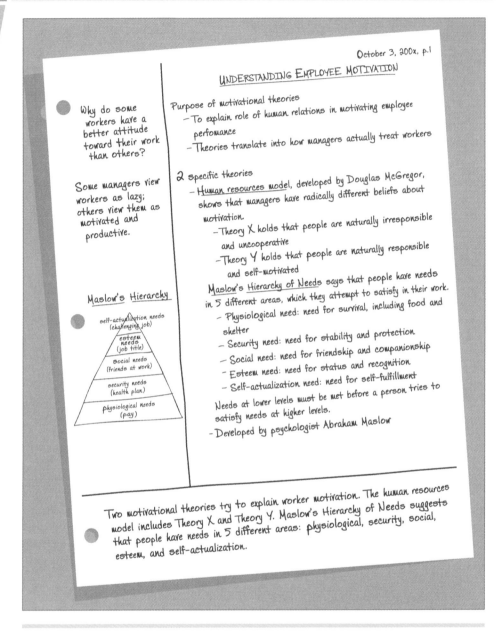

October 3, 200x, p.1

UNDERSTANDING EMPLOYEE MOTIVATION

Purpose of motivational theories
 — To explain role of human relations in motivating employee performance
 — Theories translate into how managers actually treat workers

2 specific theories
 — Human resources model, developed by Douglas McGregor, shows that managers have radically different beliefs about motivation
  — Theory X holds that people are naturally irresponsible and uncooperative
  — Theory Y holds that people are naturally responsible and self-motivated
 Maslow's Hierarchy of Needs says that people have needs in 5 different areas, which they attempt to satisfy in their work.
  — Physiological need: need for survival, including food and shelter
  — Security need: need for stability and protection
  — Social need: need for friendship and companionship
  — Esteem need: need for status and recognition
  — Self-actualization need: need for self-fulfillment
 Needs at lower levels must be met before a person tries to satisfy needs at higher levels.
 — Developed by psychologist Abraham Maslow

Why do some workers have a better attitude toward their work than others?

Some managers view workers as lazy; others view them as motivated and productive.

Maslow's Hierarchy

self-actualization needs (challenging job)
esteem needs (job title)
social needs (friends at work)
security needs (health plan)
physiological needs (pay)

Two motivational theories try to explain worker motivation. The human resources model includes Theory X and Theory Y. Maslow's Hierarchy of Needs suggests that people have needs in 5 different areas: physiological, security, social, esteem, and self-actualization.

Other Visual Note-Taking Strategies

Several other note-taking strategies will help you organize your information and are especially useful to visual learners. These strategies may be too involved to complete quickly during class, so you may want to use them when taking notes on a text chapter or when rewriting your notes for review.

TIME LINES. A time line can help you organize information—such as dates of French Revolution events or eras of different psychology practices—into chronological order. Draw a vertical or horizontal line on the page and connect each item to the line, in order, noting the dates.

Sample think link.

FIGURE

7.7

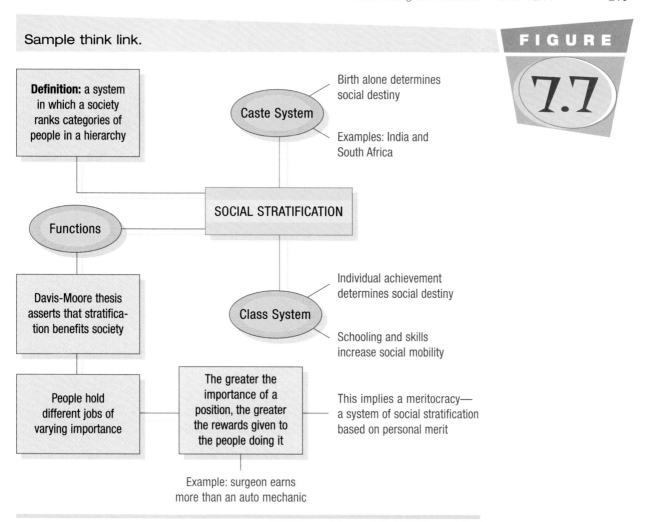

Definition: a system in which a society ranks categories of people in a hierarchy

Caste System

Birth alone determines social destiny

Examples: India and South Africa

SOCIAL STRATIFICATION

Functions

Davis-Moore thesis asserts that stratification benefits society

Class System

Individual achievement determines social destiny

Schooling and skills increase social mobility

People hold different jobs of varying importance

The greater the importance of a position, the greater the rewards given to the people doing it

This implies a meritocracy—a system of social stratification based on personal merit

Example: surgeon earns more than an auto mechanic

TABLES. You will notice tables throughout this text that show information through vertical or horizontal columns. Use tables to arrange information according to particular categories.

HIERARCHY CHARTS. Charts showing the **hierarchy** of information can help you understand that information in terms of how each piece fits into the hierarchy. A hierarchy chart could show levels of government, for example, or levels of scientific classification of animals and plants.

Once you choose a note-taking system, your success will depend on how well you use it. Personal shorthand will help you make the most of whatever system you choose.

OW CAN YOU WRITE FASTER WHEN TAKING NOTES?

When taking notes, many students feel that they can't keep up with the speaker. Using some personal **shorthand** (not standard secretarial shorthand) can help you push your pen faster. Because you are the only intended reader, you can misspell and abbreviate words in ways that only you understand.

HIERARCHY

A graded or ranked series.

SHORTHAND

A system of rapid handwriting that employs symbols, abbreviations, and shortened words to represent words, phrases, and letters.

The only danger with shorthand is that you might forget what your writing means. To avoid this problem, review your shorthand notes while your abbreviations and symbols are fresh in your mind. If there is any confusion, spell out words as you review.

Here are some suggestions that will help you master this important skill:

1. Use standard abbreviations in place of complete words.

w/	with	cf	compare, in comparison to
w/o	without	ff	following
→	means; resulting in	Q	question
←	as a result of	p.	page
↑	increasing	*	most importantly
↓	decreasing	<	less than
∴	therefore	>	more than
∵	because	=	equals
≈	approximately	%	percent
+ or &	and	△	change
−	minus; negative	2	to; two; too
NO. or #	number	vs	versus; against
i.e.	that is	e.g.	for example
etc.	and so forth	c/o	care of
ng	no good	lb	pound

2. Shorten words by removing vowels from the middle of words.

prps	=	purpose
lwyr	=	lawyer
cmptr	=	computer

3. Substitute word beginnings for entire words.

assoc	=	associate; association
info	=	information
subj	=	subject

4. Form plurals by adding *s* to shortened words.

prblms	=	problems
drctrys	=	directories
prntrs	=	printers

5. Make up your own symbols and use them consistently.

b/4	=	before
4tn	=	fortune
2thake	=	toothache

6. Use standard or informal abbreviations for proper nouns such as places, people, companies, scientific substances, events, and so on.

DC	=	Washington, D.C.
H_2O	=	water
Moz.	=	Wolfgang Amadeus Mozart

7. If you know you are going to repeat a particular word or phrase often throughout the course of a class period, write it out once at the beginning of the class and then establish an abbreviation that you will use through the rest of your notes. For example, if you are taking notes on the rise and fall of Argentina's former first lady Eva Peron, you might start out by writing "Eva Peron (EP)" and then use "EP" throughout the rest of the class period.

Finally, throughout your note taking, remember that the primary goal is for you to generate materials that help you learn and remember information. No matter how sensible any note-taking strategy, abbreviation, or system might be, it won't do you any good if it doesn't help you reach that goal. Keep a close eye on what works for you and stick to it.

If you find that your notes aren't comprehensive, legible, or focused enough, think critically about how you might improve them. Can't read your notes? You might just have been too sleepy, or you might have a hand-writing issue. Lots of confusing gaps in the information? You might be distracted in class, have an instructor who jumps around in the lecture, or have a deeper lack of understanding of the course material. Put your problem-solving skills to work and address your note-taking issues, brain-storming solutions from the variety of strategies in this chapter. With a little time and effort, your notes will truly become a helpful learning tool in school and beyond.

As you saw earlier in this chapter, you'll need note-taking skills to record the information and sources you uncover in your research. These skills will be invaluable to you in your college library and on the Internet.

Using a separate sheet of paper, complete the following.

Thinking Back

1. List three ways in which note taking will help you succeed in college.

2. Identify two steps you should take during each stage of class note taking (preparation stage, during class, and after class).

3. Explain the differences between source notes and content notes.

4. Look back at the different note-taking systems discussed in this chapter. Consider one particular course you are currently taking. Which system are you likely to use in that class and why?

5. Rewrite and shorten the following paragraph, using shorthand symbols.

   "When you start a new writing project, you face many decisions even before you sit at a keyboard or pick up a pen. What is the most efficient way to sort out all you need to think about? Start by focusing separately on groups of decisions about topic, purpose, audience, and the specific writing situation. Then try to fit the groups together, adjusting them to create a whole."[2]

Thinking Ahead

1. How do you think you will use library and Internet research in the career you plan to enter? If you currently work, how do you use research on the job right now?

2. What specific search tools do you expect to find in your school's main library?

3. How have you used computers to explore the resources of your library? Why do you think library computers have changed the research process?

4. Based on your experience doing Internet research, are you always sure that the information you find is accurate?

HOW CAN YOU MAKE THE MOST OF YOUR LIBRARY?

A library is a home for information; consider it the "brain" of your college. Libraries contain a world of information—from every novel Toni Morrison ever wrote to scholarship and financial aid directories to online job listings to medical journal articles on breast cancer research. It's all there waiting for you; your job is to find what you need as quickly and efficiently as you can.

Start with a Road Map

Most college libraries are bigger than high school and community libraries. You may feel lost on your first visit, or even a few visits after that. Make your life easier right away by learning how your library is organized. Although every library has a different layout, all libraries have certain areas in common.

REFERENCE AREA. Here you'll find reference books, including encyclopedias, public- and private-sector directories, dictionaries, almanacs, and atlases. You'll also find librarians and other library employees who can help direct you. Computer terminals, containing the library's catalog of holdings, as well as online bibliographic and full-text databases, are usually part of the reference area.

BOOK AREA. Books—and, in many libraries, magazines and journals in bound or boxed volumes—are stored in the *stacks*. A library with "open stacks" will allow you to search for materials on your own. In a "closed-stack" system, a staff member will retrieve materials for you.

PERIODICALS

Magazines, journals, and newspapers that are published on a regular basis throughout the year.

PERIODICALS AREA. Here you'll find recent issues of popular and scholarly magazines, journals, and newspapers. Most college libraries collect **periodicals** ranging from *Time* to *Advertising Age* to the *New England Journal of Medicine*. Because you usually cannot check out unbound periodicals, you may find photocopy machines nearby, where you can copy the pages that you need.

AUDIO/VISUAL MATERIALS AREAS. Many libraries have specialized areas for video, art and photography, and recorded music collections.

COMPUTER AREAS. Computer terminals, linked to databases and the Internet, are increasingly found in libraries and may be scattered throughout the building or set off in special areas. You may be able to access these databases and the Internet from the college's computer labs and writing centers, or even from your own computer if you have one. Many dorm rooms also have access to Internet service.

MICROFORM AREAS. Most libraries have microform reading areas or rooms. Microforms are materials printed in reduced size on film, either *microfilm* (a reel of film) or *microfiche* (a sheet or card of film), that is read through special viewing machines. Many microform reading machines can print hard copies of stored images and text.

To learn about your college library, take a library tour or a training session. You might also ask for a pamphlet that describes the layout, and then take some time for a self-tour. Almost all college libraries offer some kind of orientation on how to use their books, periodicals, databases, and Internet hookups. If your school has a network of libraries, including one or more central libraries and other smaller, specialized libraries, explore each one you intend to use.

Learn How to Conduct an Information Search

The most successful and time-saving library research involves following a specific *search strategy*—a step-by-step method for finding information that takes you from general to specific sources. Starting with general sources usually works best because they provide an overview of your research topic and can lead you to more specific information and sources. For example, an encyclopedia article on the archaeological discovery of the Dead Sea Scrolls—manuscripts written between 250 B.C. and A.D. 68 that trace the roots of Judaism and Christianity—may mention that one of the most important books on the subject is *Understanding the Dead Sea Scrolls,* edited by Hershel Shanks (New York: Random House, 1992). This book, in turn, will lead you to 13 experts who wrote specialized text chapters.

Defining your exact topic is critical to the success of your search. Although "the Dead Sea Scrolls" may be too broad for your research paper, possibilities of narrower topics may include the following:

- how the Dead Sea Scrolls were discovered by Bedouin shepherds in 1947
- the historical origins of the scrolls
- the process archaeologists used to reconstruct scroll fragments

Conducting a Keyword Search

A *keyword search*—a search for information through the use of specific words and phrases related to the information—will help you narrow your topic. Use your library's computer database for keyword searches. For example, instead of searching through the broad category *art*, you can use a keyword search to narrow your focus to *French art* or more specifically to *French art in the nineteenth century.*

Keyword searches are relatively easy because they use natural language, rather than specialized classification vocabulary. Table 7.2 includes some keyword search tips. The last three entries, describing how to use "or," "and," and "not" to narrow searches, describe what is called Boolean logic.

As you search, keep in mind that:

Seeing research as a quest for an answer makes clear that you cannot know whether you have found something unless you know what it is you are looking for.

LYNN QUITMAN TROYKA

- Double quotes around a word or phrase will locate the term exactly as entered ("financial aid").
- Using upper or lower case will not affect the search (*Scholarships* will find *scholarships*).
- Singular terms will find the plural (*scholarship* will find *scholarships*).

TABLE 7.2 How to perform an effective keyword search.

IF YOU ARE SEARCHING FOR. . .	DO THIS	EXAMPLE
A word	Type the word normally	Aid
A phrase	Type the phrase in its normal word order (use regular word spacing) or surround the phrase with double quotation marks	financial aid or "financial aid"
Two or more keywords without regard to word order	Type the words in any order, surrounding the words with quotation marks (use "and" to separate the words)	"financial aid" and "scholarships"
Topic A or topic B	Type the words in any order (use "or" to separate the words)	"financial aid" or "scholarships"
Topic A but not topic B	Type topic A first and then topic B (use "not" to separate the words)	"financial aid" not "scholarships"

Library search strategy.

FIGURE 7.8

Check general and specific reference works	Check the book catalog for authors and book titles	Check periodical indexes for author and article titles	Check the Internet, online services, and CD-ROM databases for complete articles and other data
↓	↓	↓	↓
Read appropriate sections	Read books	Read articles	Read computer screen and print information

HOW DO YOU USE A SEARCH STRATEGY TO CONDUCT RESEARCH?

Knowing where to look during each phase of your search will help you find information quickly and efficiently. A successful search strategy often starts with general reference works and then moves to more specific reference works, books, and periodicals (see Figure 7.8). Your search may also involve the use of electronic sources such as the Internet (more about Internet research later in this chapter).

Use General Reference Works

Begin your research with *general reference works.* These works cover hundreds—and sometimes thousands—of different topics in a broad, nondetailed way. General reference guides are often available online or on **CD-ROM.** Among the works that fall into the general reference category are these:

- Encyclopedias such as the multivolume *Encyclopedia Americana* and the single-volume *New Columbia Encyclopedia*
- Almanacs such as the *World Almanac and Book of Facts*
- Yearbooks such as the *McGraw-Hill Yearbook of Science and Technology* and the *Statistical Abstract of the United States*
- Dictionaries such as *Webster's New World College Dictionary*
- Biographical reference works such as *American Writers,* the *New York Times Biographical Service,* and *Webster's Biographical Dictionary,* and *Who's Who* (There are various *Who's Who* editions for different regions and fields, including art and music, law, literature, and medicine.)
- Bibliographies such as *Books in Print* (especially the *Subject Guide to Books in Print*)

Scan these sources for an overview of your topic. Bibliographies at the end of encyclopedia articles may also lead to other important sources.

> **CD-ROM**
>
> A compact disk containing millions of words and images that can be read by a computer (CD-ROM stands for "compact disk read-only memory).

Search Specialized Reference Works

After you have an overview of your topic, *specialized reference works* will help you find more specific facts. Specialized reference works include encyclopedias and dictionaries that focus on a narrow field. Although the entries you find in these volumes are short summaries, they focus on critical ideas and on the key words you will need to conduct additional research. Bibliographies that accompany the articles point to the names and works of recognized experts. Examples of specialized reference works, organized by subject, include the following:

Fine Arts (including music, art, film, television, and theatre)
- *International Cyclopedia of Music and Musicians*
- *Oxford Companion to Art*
- *The McGraw-Hill Encyclopedia of World Drama*

History
- *Dictionary of American Biography*
- *Encyclopedia of American History*
- *New Cambridge Modern History*

Science and Technology
- *Encyclopedia of Computer Science and Technology*
- *The Encyclopedia of Biological Sciences*
- *Grzimek's Animal Life Encyclopedia*

Social Sciences
- *Dictionary of Education*
- *Encyclopedia of Psychology*
- *International Encyclopedia of the Social Sciences*

Current Affairs
- *Social Issues Resources Series (SIRS)*
- *Great Contemporary Issues Series*
- *Facts on File*

Browse Through Books on Your Subject

Use the *library catalog* to find books and other materials on your topic. The catalog tells you which publications the library owns and where they can be found. Before computers, most library catalogs consisted of endless cards filed in tiny drawers. Today most of these "card catalogs" have been replaced by online computer catalogs. When general and specialized reference works lead to a dead end, the catalog may provide a good topic overview.

Many school libraries now offer students the ability to search the card catalog and other databases from personal computers, enabling them to pull up full-text articles, abstracts, and other information from the comfort of their rooms. You can also reserve books via your personal computer and find them waiting for you at the library.

The library catalog contains a list of every library holding, searchable by author, title, and subject. For example, a library that owns *The Artist's Way: A Spiritual Path to Higher Creativity* by Julia Cameron may list the book in the author catalog under Cameron, Julia, (last name first); in the title catalog, under *Artist's Way* (articles such as *the, a,* and *an* are dropped from the beginnings of titles and subjects); in the subject catalog under "Creative Ability—problems, exercises, etc.," "Self-actualization—psychology," and "Creation—literary, artistic, etc." If you are using a keyword search, you may be able to find this book using "Art" and "Creativity" or "Art" and "Spirituality."

Library Classification Systems

Each catalog listing refers to the library's classification system, which tells you exactly where the publication can be found. Getting to know your library's system will help save time and trouble in your research because you will more quickly know where to go to find what you need. The Dewey Decimal System (which classifies materials into 10 major subject categories each with a specific call number) and the Library of Congress System (which uses a letter-based classification system to divide library holdings according to subject categories) are among the most common classification systems. Ask your librarian which system is in use at your library and how that particular system works.

Use Periodical Indexes to Search for Periodicals

Because of their frequent publication, periodicals are a valuable source of current information. *Journals* are periodicals written for readers with special knowledge and expertise. Whereas *Newsweek* magazine may run a general-interest article on AIDS research, the *Journal of the American Medical Association* may print the original scientific study and direct the article to physicians and scientists. Many libraries display periodicals that are up to a year or two old and convert older copies to microfilm or microfiche. Some libraries also bind recent issues into volumes.

Periodical indexes will lead you to specific articles. There are many different indexes; only a few are mentioned here. One of the most widely used for general information is the *Reader's Guide to Periodical Literature,* available on CD-ROM and in book form. The *Reader's Guide* indexes articles in more than 240 general-interest magazines and newspapers. Many libraries also carry the *Reader's Guide Abstracts,* which include article summaries.

You'll discover other general periodical indexes within the *Infotrac* family of databases (available online or on CD-ROM), including:

- *Magazine Index Plus*—an index, summaries, and full text of recent general-interest periodicals
- *Health Reference Center*—an index, summaries, and full text of journal articles, reference books, and pamphlets on health and medicine
- *General Business File*—an index, summaries, and full text of recent business and trade journals with company information and investment analysts' reports.

Another periodical database family—Ebsco Host—catalogs general and health-related periodicals.

Indexing information is listed in the *Standard Periodical Directory, Ulrich's International Periodicals Directory,* and in *Magazines for Libraries,* edited by Bill Katz. In addition, each database lists the magazines and periodicals it indexes. Because there is no all-inclusive index for technical, medical, and scholarly journal articles, you'll have to search indexes that specialize in such narrow subject areas as history, art, and psychology. Such indexes also include *abstracts* (article summaries), and can be found in electronic or book form. Here are just a few of the indexes you may find in your research:

ABI/Inform	Applied Science and Technology
Art Index	Business Periodicals Index
BIOSIS Previews	Child Development Abstracts and Bibliography
Education Index	ERIC (Educational Resources Information Center)
Film Literature Index	General Science Index
Historical Index	Hispanic American Periodicals Index
Humanities Index	Index to Legal Periodicals
Index Medicus	Index to United States Government Periodicals
Music Index	Modern Language Association Bibliography
Psychological Abstracts	Public Affairs Information Index
PsycINFO	Social Science Citation Index
Social Science Index	Women Studies Abstracts

You'll also find separate newspaper indexes at your library in print, microform, CD-ROM, or online. Some include many different newspapers, whereas others index a single publication:

Chicago Tribune Index	Christian Science Monitor Index
Dow Jones Index	National Newspaper Index
Index To Black Newspapers	Newspaper Abstracts OnDisc
Newsbank	New York Times Index
Wall Street Journal Index	Washington Post Index

Almost no library owns all the publications listed in these and other specialized indexes. However, journals that are not part of your library's collection or that are not available in full-text form online may be available through an interlibrary loan. *Interlibrary loan* is a process by which you can have your library request materials from another library. You can then use the materials at your library, but must return them by a specified date. Interlibrary loans can be helpful, but the amount of time you will have to wait for the materials can be unpredictable and may stretch out for weeks.

Ask the Librarian

Librarians are information experts who can provide valuable assistance in solving research problems. They can help you locate unfamiliar or hard-to-find sources, navigate computer catalogs and databases, and uncover shortcuts in your research.

Say, for example, you are researching a gun-control bill that is currently before Congress, and you want to contact organizations on both sides of the issue. The librarian may lead you to the *Encyclopedia of Associations,* which lists the National Rifle Association, a pro-gun lobbying organization, and Handgun Control Inc., a gun-control group. By calling or e-mailing these groups or visiting their websites, you will get their information on current legislation.

Note that librarians are not the only helpful people in the library. For simplicity's sake, this book will use the word *librarian* to refer to both librarians and other staff members who are trained to help.

Among the specific services librarians provide are the following.

SEARCH SERVICES. Here are some tips on getting the best advice:

Be prepared. Know what you're looking for so that you can make a specific request. Instead of asking for information on the American presidency, focus on the topic you expect to write about in your American history paper—for example, how President Franklin D. Roosevelt's physical disability may have affected his leadership during World War II.

Be willing to reach out. Don't feel you have to do it all yourself. Librarians will help you, whether with basic sources or more difficult problems. Asking questions is a sign of willingness to learn, not weakness.

Ask for help when you can't find a specific source—for example, when a specific book is not on the shelf. The librarian may direct you to another source that will work just as well.

INFORMATION SERVICES. Most libraries answer phone inquiries that can be quickly researched. For example, if you forget to write down the publisher and date of publication of a particular book, call a staff member with the title and author.

INTERLIBRARY LOANS. If a publication is not available in your library, the librarian can arrange for an interlibrary loan.

Use Critical Thinking to Evaluate Every Source

If all information were equal, you could trust the accuracy of every source, no matter who wrote it or where it appeared. Because that isn't the case, use critical-thinking skills to evaluate research sources. Here are some critical-thinking questions to ask about every source:

Is the author a recognized expert? A journalist who writes his first article on child development may not have the same credibility as an author of three child-development texts.

Does the author write from a particular perspective? An article evaluating liberal democratic policies written by a Republican conservative would almost certainly have a bias.

Is the source recent enough for your purposes? Whereas a history text published in 1990 on the U.S. Civil War will probably be accurate in the year 2001, a 1990 analysis of current computer technology will be hopelessly out of date.

Are the author's sources reliable? Where did the author get the information? Check the bibliography and footnotes not only for the number of

How can I take more complete notes?

Jose L. Ivarez, Jr., *Wright College, Chicago, Illinois, Computer Engineering Major*

When I started college two semesters ago, I didn't know how important note taking was going to be. I now know that it's one of the main ways to learn in class. At the end of my very first college class, I had only one sheet of notes. The other students had filled up several sheets. I felt frustrated that they were flipping through pages while I had only a few sentences written down. I realized then that I didn't know the first thing about how to do this.

I have a couple of note-taking problems. First, I tend to daydream. My mind wanders—then, all of a sudden, I realize I've missed some important information. A couple of my friends said they do this too. I think students get distracted by thinking about personal problems. I know that's what happens to me sometimes. Also, my attention span drops off after about 15 or 20 minutes, so staying focused for an entire lecture period can be a problem. Finally, I can't keep up with how fast the professor talks. I try to concentrate on what's being said, and I may jot down the first point, but then I miss the next three sentences. I seem to have trouble picking out key ideas. But I keep trying. I figure writing down something is better than nothing.

I'm sure my note-taking skills have improved a little since I first started college, but I still have a long way to go. I have a pretty good memory, so that even if I haven't written something down, I still might recall it just from having heard it, but I know my grades would be better if my notes weren't so poor. Can you give me suggestions about how I can take more complete notes?

Angela D. Kvasnica, *University of Michigan, Ann Arbor, Michigan, Industrial & Operations Engineering Major*

Note taking can get very frustrating, but I've found several ways to help me keep my focus and gather all the information, too. First, I always try to sit in front of the class. This helps eliminate distractions such as staring at the clock, other student's conversations, and people walking into class late. Also, sitting in front will allow you to hear the lecturer more clearly, and you can make eye contact, which keeps you more involved in what's being said.

A second way to focus is to prepare yourself ahead of time. Skim the text readings before the lecture so you will become familiar with the topic and main ideas. While taking notes, focus on writing down as much information as possible. However, it's not necessary to write down everything word for word. You don't need complete sentences. To keep up, use abbreviations and paraphrases, and don't worry about spelling, form, or organization. You can always  recopy your notes later, and rewriting your notes will help reinforce your learning.

Third, put question marks next to the topics or ideas you didn't understand or left incomplete. Then, ask your professor for clarification after class or during office hours. To help you gather more complete information, you might want to try using a hand-held, mini-cassette recorder. Then, you can review the lectures and listen for information you may have missed. One note of caution: Ask your instructor for permission to use a recorder.

Finally, compare notes with another student in class. This way you can help each other fill in the gaps. Maybe you and this person can even study together. Most importantly: Don't give up. If you keep at it, you will become better and better at taking notes, and eventually you'll develop a system that works for you.

sources listed but also for their quality. Find out whether they are reputable, established publications. If the work is based on *primary evidence,* the author's original work or direct observation, does solid proof support the conclusions? If it is based on *secondary evidence,* an analysis of the works of others, are the conclusions supported by evidence?

Have content experts reviewed articles submitted to academic and scientific journals before they were published? Recognized journals have panels of experts who analyze the merits of every article's academic research before accepting the material for publication. For example, the editorial board of the *New England Journal of Medicine,* one of the country's leading medical journals, is made up of physicians who analyze every article's scientific merits and publish only those that meet the highest standards.

As you will see later in the chapter, critical-thinking skills are especially important when using the Internet. Accepting information you find there on face value—no matter the source—is often a mistake and may lead to incorrect conclusions.

The library is one of your college's most valuable resources, so take advantage of it. Your library research and critical-thinking skills will give you the ability to collect information, weigh alternatives, and make decisions. These skills will last a lifetime and may serve you well if you choose one of the many careers that require research ability. You may need to find a particular article that reviewed your pharmaceutical company's latest drug, for example, or you may need to locate materials on depression for your counseling center.

The library is not your only research resource. Whether for school or work, the Internet is becoming a primary research tool because access is so widespread and because the Internet portal is only as far as your computer.

HOW CAN YOU DO RESEARCH ON THE INTERNET?

The *Internet* is a worldwide computer network that links businesses, universities, governments, and people. A miracle of technology, it can connect you to endless sources of information instantaneously—all while you sit in front of your computer terminal.

The Internet is becoming a frequently used research tool on college campuses. According to a survey of 1,200 students by *Student Monitor,* college students are spending an average of 8.1 hours online each week, and more than 44 percent of these students reported that researching was their highest-priority online activity.[3] With its speed and accessibility, the Web appeals to today's technology-oriented, time-crunched college students.

Education is a matter of building bridges.

RALPH ELLISON

Because of its widespread reach through the ever-increasing sea of information, the Internet can be a helpful research tool—if used wisely. Like any tool, it has its advantages and disadvantages. The information in this section will help you to make the most of its good points and avoid the pitfalls.

The Basics

With a basic knowledge of the Internet, you can access facts and figures, read articles and other written materials, download files, software, and images, send typed messages electronically to others, and even "talk" to people in real time by typing messages that pop up on the screen as soon as you send them. Following is some information that you should know.

ACCESS. Users access the Internet through Internet Service Providers (ISPs). Some ISPs are commercial, such as America Online or Earthlink. Others are linked to companies, colleges, and other organizations. When you sign up with an ISP, you are given (or can choose) a *screen name,* which is the "address" that others can use to send you mail or files.

INFORMATION LOCATIONS. Much of the information on the Internet is displayed on "Web pages" or "websites," individual locations in cyberspace developed by companies, government agencies, organizations, or individuals. Together, these sites are referred to as the *World Wide Web.* By visiting particular websites, you can do extensive research on any topic as well as buy, sell, and market products on the Internet. Other "locations" where information resides include newsgroups (collections of messages from people interested in a particular topic), FTP sites (FTP stands for File Transfer Protocol—such sites provide the means for you to download files), and other non-websites that give you access to databases or library holdings (often stored by universities and government agencies using a system called "Gopher").

FINDING LOCATIONS. Another kind of online address is the string of text and numbers that identifies a site on the Internet. These strings are called *URLs* (Universal Resource Locators). You can type in a URL to access a specific site. On any given website you might also find a *hyperlink*—a URL that appears underlined and in a highlighted color—that you can click on to go directly to the location it lists.

One of the problems of the Internet is that it is an immense, constantly growing sea of information, from sources of every level of reliability, not easily navigated by even the savviest researcher. Now that you have some basic knowledge, explore how to search for information.

Search Directories and Search Engines

You will almost always need to use a system, or "tool," to find and select websites and other information locations likely to have the information you need. Usually, you will use either a *search directory* or a *search engine* to locate information or websites. Following are some details about the systems you will use and how to use them.

Search Directories

A search directory is an index of websites that allows you to search for topics using keywords. Its searching capabilities are limited to websites only. Search directories are basically large collections of websites sorted by category, much in the way that the Yellow Pages organizes business telephone numbers.

When searching, you might want to start with a search directory first because the results may be more manageable than with a search engine (search engines can produce a large number of "hits"—occurrences of your keyword). Some of the most popular and effective search directories include the following (names and URLs):

- Yahoo: www.yahoo.com
- Galaxy: http://galaxy.einet.net/galaxy.html
- Snap: www.snap.com
- Excite: www.excite.com
- Magellan: http://mckinley.com

Each search directory has its own particular features. Some have different search options (simple search, advanced search); some are known for having strong lists of sites for particular topics; some have links that connect you to lists of sites that fall under particular categories. The search directory's website will help you learn how to best use the directory.

Search Engines

Slightly different than search directories, a *search engine* searches for keywords through the entire Internet—newsgroups, websites, and other resources—instead of just websites. This gives you wider access but may yield an enormous list of hits unless you know how to limit your search effectively.

Some useful search engines include:

- AltaVista: http://altavista.com
- HotBot: www.hotbot.com
- Lycos: www.lycos.com
- GoTo: www.goto.com
- Ask Jeeves: www.askjeeves.com

As with search directories, each search engine has its own set of resources and its own particular helpful search tools and guides.

Search Strategy

Although any search may take you in a unique direction, start with this basic search strategy when researching online.

1. *Think carefully about what you want to locate.* Professor Eliot Soloway of the University of Michigan School of Education recommends that you first phrase your search in the form of a question; for example, What vaccines are given to children before the age of 5? Then, he advises you to consider what the important words in that question are (*vaccines, children, before the age of 5*). Write them down; then, write down other words you can think of that may be related to those words (*chicken pox, tetanus, polio, shot, pediatrics,*

and so on). This will give you a useful collection of words to use in different combinations as you search.[4]

2. *Use a search directory to isolate a list of sites under your desired topic or category.* Save the sites that look as though they might have information useful to you (most ISPs have a way for you to save or "bookmark" sites that you want to be able to easily find again).

3. *Explore these sites to get a general idea of what's out there.* If by chance your search is fairly general and the directory takes you where you need to go, you're in luck. More often in academic research situations, though, you will need to dig deeper and range farther. Use what you have found in the search directory to notice useful keywords and information locations.

4. *Move on to a search engine to narrow your search.* Use your keywords in a variety of ways to come up with as many possibilities as you can.

   - Vary their order if you are using more than one (e.g., search under *education, college, statistics* and *statistics, education, college.*)
   - Use *Boolean operators*—the words "and," "not," and "or"—in ways that limit your search specifically (you will recall some of these techniques from Table 7.2 on using keywords for library searches).
   - Put quotation marks around a word or phrase that you want to find *exactly as it appears* (for this reason, be sure your spelling is correct).

5. *Evaluate the list of links that pop up.* If there are too many, narrow your search by using more keywords or by being more specific with your keywords (*Broadway* could become *Broadway musical theatre* or *Broadway* AND *"fall season"* AND *2001*). If there are too few or none that seem useful, broaden your search by using fewer or different keywords.

6. *Bookmark the links that you think you will be able to use.* This will enable you to go right back to them without having to go through the search process again.

7. *When you think you are done, choose another search directory or search engine and perform your search again—just to be sure.* Because different systems have access to different information, you never know what may appear.

Non-Web Resources

The Web is not your only source of information. Newsgroups and Gopher can also help you achieve your research goals.

Newsgroups

Usenet, the system of *newsgroups,* is a series of "bulletin boards" where users can type in messages and "post" them on the newsgroup. Then, other users can read posts and respond to them. Posts are grouped in "threads" (a thread is a series of posts that follow, and are in response to, one particular topic or post). Like chat rooms, newsgroups focus on individual topics—and there are thousands, from silent film stars to modern architecture to text fonts.

When you search newsgroups, you may want to post a question to the newsgroup and start a new thread, or look at the titles of existing threads to see if your question has already been discussed there. Chances are, the more specific your question, the better your chances of getting a coherent answer. Looking through threads may ultimately reward you with information; on the down side, however, it often takes a good deal of time and patience because you can only search post by post within a thread that may be as long as a few hundred posts.

Be careful to choose your newsgroups carefully when researching. Many newsgroups are more recreational than information-focused. For example, if you are looking for information on plants, *sci.bio.botany* will probably be more of a pertinent scientific resource ("Second European Symposium on Aerobiology" reads one thread) than *rec.gardens.edible,* with threads like "couple of green tomatoes." Every newsgroup has a helpful FAQ (Frequently Asked Questions list) that you should read before you post. You may also want to "lurk" a while (read posts without posting yourself) to get a better sense of what the newsgroup is all about.

Gopher Searches

There are over 5,500 known Gopher servers, or sites, mostly located on campuses or at government agencies (the name comes from the mascot of the University of Minnesota, where the Gopher system was developed). These servers contain data and archived writings available to the public for searching and retrieval. The data is arranged much like in a library, with keywords that refer to sections, divided repeatedly into subsections, eventually arriving at the smallest segments of information. Gopher is not as flashy as the World Wide Web, and many former users of Gopher have transferred their material to websites. However, quite a few institutions only offer their information through Gopher.

Particular tools are useful for searching Gopher sites. One is called *Veronica,* which helps to match your keywords to long and detailed Gopher entries. Veronica does for your Gopher search what a search engine does for your website search—it helps you sort through the vast amounts of information. You can access Veronica through your ISP. Look for "Gopher Worldwide" to find a list of the servers, organized by continent, country, and organization.

Be a Critical Researcher

The Internet has millions of Web pages and sites, containing information from a huge variety of sources—everything from the federal government to random individuals creating sites from their home computers. It is up to you to evaluate the truth and usefulness of the information you find. As you saw earlier in the chapter, as a researcher it is up to you to determine the value of all your sources, including those you find on the Internet. Because the Internet is largely an uncensored platform for free-flowing information, you must decide which sources have value and which should be ignored and discarded.

If you are informed about the potential pitfalls of Internet research and do your best to avoid them, you will get the most from your time and effort. Critical thinking is the key to making sure you get valid information.

Consider discovering how valuable each source is to be a challenge that you have the power to meet. Address this challenge using the following strategies[5]:

BE PREPARED FOR INTERNET-SPECIFIC PROBLEMS. The nature of the Internet causes particular problems for researchers, such as the following:

- changing information (new information arrives daily; old information may not be removed or updated)
- technology problems (Internet access might be slow or unavailable; websites may have moved, been deleted, or have tech trouble that results in users being denied access)

You may want to budget extra time to anticipate tech problems or to investigate whether the information you find is current.

EVALUATE THE SOURCE. Note the website name and the organization that creates and maintains the site where you have located the information. Is the organization reputable? Is it known as an authority on the topic you are researching? If you are not sure of the source, the URL will usually give you a clue. For example, URLs ending in *.edu* originate at an educational institution, and *.gov* sites originate at government agencies.

EVALUATE THE AUTHOR. Look carefully to find out who exactly wrote the article or gathered and compiled the data. Again, think about whether this author is reliable and reputable in the field (refer back to the material on evaluating library sources on p. 229). What are the author's credentials? If you cannot find any indication of credentials or affiliation, that may be a warning in and of itself.

EVALUATE THE MATERIAL. Can you tell if the material is valid and accurate? Evaluate it the way you would evaluate any other material you read (see Chapters 4 and 5 for more detail on how to critically evaluate reading material). See if sources are noted and if you trust them. Is the source a published document (e.g., newspaper article, professional journal article), or is it simply one person's point of view? Can you verify the data by comparing it to any other material? Pay attention, also, to the general quality of the material. Text that has errors in grammar or spelling, is poorly organized, or contains mistaken names or dates is likely to be unreliable.

Perhaps your best bet is to combine library and Internet resources. Remember that the library is laid out using an established system and may be more navigable than the tangle of Internet sites. Plus, library employees are there to help you in person, and sometimes that kind of one-on-one assistance can be more valuable than any hyperlink or Boolean operator. You might want to seek out library materials to help you verify the authenticity of what you discover on the Internet.

Take advantage of the wealth of material the Internet offers you—but take your time and be picky. Always remember that your mind is your greatest asset when researching the Internet and that your work will only be as strong as your critical thinking demands. If you work hard to ensure that your research is valid and comprehensive, the products of your efforts will speak for themselves.

Testa dura

An Italian parent might use this phrase, literally meaning "hard head," to describe the attitude of a stubborn child. People who are single-mindedly determined to have something or do something and won't give up until they have reached the goal might be seen as hardheaded. Even though the phrase is often used in a somewhat negative way, there are some positive aspects to being a *testa dura*. The accompanying determination, strength, and patience can make hardheadedness a useful trait.

Think of the concept of *testa dura* as you take notes and pursue your research goals. When you take notes, be sure you to listen for critical information and to record what you hear in a useful way. If your notes need revision, become a *testa dura* and spend all the time you need to transform your notes into valuable study tools.

Research can take you down paths that lead to dead ends and information that is useless to you. Libraries can be overwhelming; the Internet can connect you with sources that are neither accurate nor reputable. When you are tempted to give up, or to use information that is substandard, make the decision to be hardheaded. Stay the course; take the time to press on and exhaust every resource until you have found what will truly make your work the best it can be. The determination of *testa dura* will take you far.

IMPORTANT POINTS *to remember*

1. How does note taking help you?

Notes help you learn when you are in class, doing research, or studying. The positive effects of taking notes include having written study material, becoming an active and involved listener, and improving a skill that you will use on the job and in your personal life. Note taking also encourages you to think critically and to evaluate what is worth remembering. The notes you take during library research record what you learn from the sources you consult.

2. How can you make the most of class notes?

Class notes may contain critical definitions, explanations of difficult concepts, and narratives of events. Taking comprehensive class notes requires preclass preparation, the skill to report accurately what you hear during class, and a commitment to review the notes after class using critical thinking.

3. What are research notes and how can you use them?

Research notes, the notes you take while gathering information to answer a research question, consist of source notes and content notes. Source notes are preliminary notes that you take as you briefly review available research. Content notes are an in-depth critical look at each source. Index cards work well for either source notes or content notes. Marginal notes and highlighting on photocopied research materials are also helpful.

4. What note-taking system should you use?

You can choose among several note-taking systems for class and research. These include formal or informal outlining, the Cornell system, and think links. Your goal is to find a system you are comfortable using, one that fits the special needs of the situation. For example, the Cornell system or informal outlining may work best during class, whereas think links and formal outlining may be most useful for rewriting your notes during review sessions.

5. How can you write faster when taking notes?

Note taking often requires rapid writing, especially in class. Using a version of personal shorthand, which replaces words with shorter words or symbols, will help you accurately record what the instructor says. To avoid the problem of forgetting what your shorthand means, review your notes while the abbreviations and symbols are fresh in your mind, and spell out words as you review.

6. How can you make the most of your library?

The first step in getting to know this "home for information" is to participate in an orientation or tour. Most libraries will contain one or more reference areas, book areas, a periodicals area, audio-visual materials areas, computer areas, and a microform area. Begin a search strategy by conducting a keyword search, using your library's computer database.

7. How do you use a search strategy to conduct research?

A library search strategy is a step-by-step method, moving from general to specific sources, for finding information. The strategy starts with general reference works and then moves to specialized reference works, the library's book catalog, periodical indexes, and electronic sources including the Internet and CD-ROMs. Conducting a successful search involves being familiar with library classification systems, taking advantage of help from library employees, and using critical thinking to evaluate sources.

8. How can you do research on the Internet?

Doing research on the Internet requires technical knowledge of what the Internet is comprised of and how to navigate it. Your access to the World Wide Web, for example, is through such search directories as Yahoo and Galaxy and search engines as AltaVista and HotBot. A step-by-step search strategy will help you locate information and gather reliable sources. Because the Internet lacks safeguards to keep out false or misleading information, it is important to be a critical, skeptical researcher.

CRITICAL THINKING
APPLYING LEARNING TO LIFE

LIBRARY RESEARCH. Think of a time you recently spent researching a topic in the library—or, if you have research to do for an upcoming project, spend an afternoon in the library doing it. Then, using a separate sheet of paper, answer the following questions:

- What parts of the library search strategy did you use?

- What role did the Internet play in your research?

- How did you use your critical-thinking skills to evaluate sources? Did your media literacy help in this evaluation?

- Were your research notes effective? How could you improve them for your next library visit?

- Did you ask the librarian for help? What were the circumstances? What kinds of questions did you ask the librarian to get the information you needed?

- What steps can you take to improve the efficiency and reliability of your research?

- How do you think acquiring solid research skills will impact the work you do in your chosen career?

TEAMWORK
COMBINING FORCES

STUDY GROUP NOTES EVALUATION. Choose one particular meeting of this class from the last two weeks. Join with two or three other classmates, all of whom were in class that day, and make a temporary study group. Each of you should make enough photocopies of your own notes to pass around to each of the other group members.

First, look over the sets of notes on your own. Within the context of the other note sets, think about:

- Readability of handwriting: Can you read what you have written? Indicate specific letters, words, or phrases that are difficult to read.

- Information covered: Did you cover everything adequately—the big picture and the details? If you missed important information, why do you think it got by you?

- Note-taking systems used: Which did you choose and why?

- Clarity of the ideas and examples: Does everything make sense to you?

Then, gather again and talk through the four note sets together, one by one. Approach the notes as though you were in a study group session.

- Can you read each other's handwriting? If not, the information won't be of much use to you.
- Did you cover the same information? If someone missed a topic, someone else can help him fill in the blanks.
- Did you use the same or different note-taking systems? You might gather insight from the way others structure their notes.
- Could you understand what the notes were saying? If you are confused about something in your own notes, someone else might have a helpful perspective. If you don't understand someone else's notes, together you can figure out what information is confusing or missing.

Finally, write one or more changes you plan to make in your note-taking based on what you learned in this exercise.

Which notes can you understand better? Why do you think that's true?

WRITING

DISCOVERY THROUGH JOURNALING

To record your thoughts, use a separate journal or the lined page at the end of the chapter.

RESEARCH THOUGHTS. Which of the following statements more closely reflects your attitude toward library research?

- "When I use a library search strategy, I feel like an investigative reporter in search of the facts I need to write a successful story. The more useful sources I find, the better."

- "When I use a library search strategy, I feel like I'm overdoing it. I can usually find everything I need in one source, and looking for more information seems like a waste of time."

Describe in more detail how you feel about research. How do you think you might use research skills both in school and on the job? How did reading this chapter affect your attitude toward the usefulness of library research skills?

CAREER PORTFOLIO

CHARTING YOUR COURSE

RESEARCH A CAREER. Activate your research skills by doing research on one career that interests you. Put together an informal "research paper" that catalogs all of the basics that you think you would need to know to make a decision on whether to pursue this career in the future.

Use these sources in your research:

- general and specific reference works that describe the career on which you are focusing

- periodicals (especially current newspapers, where you can find up-dated information on the status of your particular career)

- reliable Internet sites, including government sites (look for the suffix ".gov") and corporate sites (look for the suffix ".com") as well as Internet career sites

- relevant sources from your school's career center

Focus your research on the following topics (as well as any others that seem pertinent to you):

- recent growth status of your career (whether opportunities are increasing or decreasing)

- strength of this career in the geographic area where you live or want to live

- educational requirements (degrees, certificates, and certification exams)

- different industries that hire people in this career area

- starting salary range

- typical benefits (this may vary from industry to industry)
- general duties and skills for an entry-level position
- opportunities for advancement
- time and location flexibility, if any

Keep this information on hand when you are ready to start pursuing your career in earnest.

 ## SUGGESTED READINGS

Branscomb, H. Eric. *Casting Your Net: A Student's Guide to Research on the Internet.* Boston, MA: Allyn & Bacon (2000).

DePorter, Bobbi and Mike Hernacki. *Quantum Notes: Whole-Brain Approaches to Note-Taking.* Chicago, IL: Learning Forum (2000).

Dunkel, Patricia A., Frank Pialorsi, and Joane Kozyrez. *Advanced Listening Comprehension: Developing Aural & Note-Taking Skills.* Boston, MA: Heinle & Heinle (1996).

Klein, Brock and Matthew Hunt. *The Essential Workbook for Library and Internet Research Skills.* NY: McGraw-Hill (1999).

Lebauer, R. Susan. *Learn to Listen, Listen to Learn: Academic Listening and Note-Taking.* Upper Saddle River, NJ: Prentice Hall (2000).

Levin, Leonard. *Easy Script Express: Unique Speed Writing Methods to Take Fast Notes and Dictation.* Chicago, IL: Legend Publishing (2000).

 ## INTERNET RESOURCES

Internet Search FAQ: www.purefiction.com/pages/res1.htm

Writer's Toolbox—Internet Resources for Writers:
www.writerstoolbox.com/

 ## ENDNOTES

1. Walter Pauk. *How to Study in College,* 7th ed. Boston: Houghton Mifflin (2001), pp. 236–241.

2. Lynn Quitman Troyka. *Quick Access Reference for Writers.* Upper Saddle River, NJ: Simon & Schuster (1995), p. 1.

3. Lisa Guernsey. "For the New College B.M.O.C., 'M' Is for 'Machine,'" *The New York Times,* August 10, 2000, p. G7.

4. Lori Leibovich. "Choosing Quick Hits Over the Card Catalog," *The New York Times,* August 10, 2000, p. 1.

5. Floyd H. Johnson (May 1996). "The Internet and Research: Proceed With Caution" (online). Available:
www.lanl.gov/SFC/96/posters.html#johnson (August 2000).

Journal

NAME

DATE

Thinking It Through

Check those statements that apply to you right now:

- I'm not sure it matters if I'm not a good writer.

- I try to consider the specifics of the assignment before I sit down and write.

- When I write, I don't think much about the people who will read my work.

- My goal is to be able to write a perfect paper the first time around.

- I don't necessarily consider what I already know about a subject before I start my research and writing.

- When I revise and edit a paper, I focus mostly on getting my words right.

8

IN THIS CHAPTER,

you will explore answers to the following questions:

- Why does good writing matter?
- What are the elements of effective writing?
- What is the writing process?

Words, joined to form ideas, have enormous power. Far more than a skill needed just for schoolwork, writing is as important today as it has ever been. Instead of disappearing in an age that celebrates computer technology, writing has become the communication tool of choice for people using the Internet, as well as for workers in a wide variety of fields.

People have sought ways to record written forms of communication since ancient times. For the Egyptians, for example, that communication took the form of hieroglyphics. Written communication preserves concepts so that they can reach far beyond one person's circle of acquaintances. Writing allows you to take your ideas out of the realm of thought and give them a form that other people can read and consider.

Effective Writing

Whether you are zapping electronic mail across the globe or using a pencil and pad to write a research paper for your history professor, your level of successful communication depends on your ability to express your written ideas completely and well. In this chapter, you will explore the many aspects of learning to be a good writer. Writing is a key to success in school, at work, and in your personal life.

WHY DOES GOOD WRITING MATTER?

In school, almost any course you take will require you to communicate your knowledge and thought processes by writing essays or papers. To express yourself successfully, you need good writing skills. Knowing how to write and communicate ideas is essential outside of school as well, as the following example demonstrates. Imagine that you run a summer internship program at a major TV network. You have two qualified student candidates vying for one internship position. Each student sends you a letter, trying to convince you that she is the better person for the job. Parts of each student's response are shown in Figures 8.1 and 8.2.

Which candidate would you choose? The second student's letter is well written, persuasive, logical, and error-free. In contrast, the first student's letter is not thought through clearly and has technical errors. Good writing quality gives the edge to the second student.

As this hypothetical example demonstrates, the ability to write clearly and well can make a huge difference both in school and after graduation because instructors, supervisors, and others judge your thinking ability according to what you write and how you write it. Over the next few years you may write papers, essays, answers to essay test questions, job application letters, résumés, business proposals and reports, memos to coworkers, and letters to customers and suppliers. Good writing skills will help you achieve the goals you set out to accomplish with each writing task.

FIGURE 8.1   First student's writing sample.

I am a capable student whose interests are many. I like the news business so much so that I want you to offer me the internship with your company.

My experience will impress you, as I'm sure you will agree I am a reporter for a college news station, and I can be a reporter for you as well. If you let me try. Instructors who know my work like my style. I prefer to think of myself as an individual with a unique style that nothing can match.

I want the summer internship because it will pit me at the center of the action. At this point in my education, I deserve the chance to learn from the masters of the business.

I look forward to hearing from you and to the news that I got the internship.

Second student's writing sample.

FIGURE
8.2

From the time I was 8 years old, I was hooked on the news. Instead of watching cartoons on television, I watched Tom Brokaw, Dan Rather, and Peter Jennings. I celebrated the day that CNN started a 24-hour all-news network.

It seemed like a natural step to go into the news business. I started in high school as a reporter, and then I became editor-in-chief of the school paper. As a college freshman, I am majoring in broadcast journalism, and I am also working at the school TV station. Even though I am starting at the bottom, I believe that there's a learning opportunity around every corner. By the time I take on my first reporting assignment next year, I feel that my knowledge and experience will have grown. I hope it will be enough to make me a competent journalist.

Your internship program will help me learn the news business in an environment I never dreamed of experiencing until later in my career. I look forward to hearing from you and to the possibility of working for your station this summer.

Right now, you may consider writing to be more of a final product of your study efforts than a study skill itself. However, it is most emphatically a study skill, and a very important one. Writing is an essential ingredient in how you take in information, how you retain it, and how you express it. When you write well, your notes are comprehensive and understandable. When you write well, you fulfill expectations on essay tests (as you will see in Chapter 10). When you write well, you solidify knowledge as you rewrite notes, write summaries, and compile study sheets in preparation for tests.

Writing well is linked to reading and critical thinking. Through reading, you learn new words and expressions as you are exposed to new ideas. The more you read, the more you will appreciate that there is no "right" or "wrong" way to express ideas (as long as they are well written, of course). On the contrary, you will see that what you write—and how you write it— are as unique as you are.

To keep things simple, this chapter focuses primarily on the writing of an essay. However, the skills involved can apply to nearly any writing situation you encounter in your studies or your career. As you read, ask critical-thinking questions about how you would apply what you are learning: "How might I use freewriting for an essay test? How might brainstorming help me in a study group session? How will knowing my audience help me write a grant proposal for my organization?"

WHAT ARE THE ELEMENTS OF EFFECTIVE WRITING?

Every writing situation is different, depending on three elements. Your goal is to understand each element before you begin to write:

- *Your purpose:* What do you want to accomplish with this particular piece of writing?
- *Your topic:* What is the subject about which you will write?
- *Your audience:* Who will read your writing?

Figure 8.3 shows how these elements depend on one another. As a triangle needs three points to be complete, a piece of writing needs these three elements. Consider purpose and **audience** even before you begin to plan. Topic will come into play during the planning stage (the first stage of the writing process).

AUDIENCE

The reader or readers of any piece of written material.

Writing Purpose

Writing without having a clear purpose is like driving without deciding where you want to go. You'll get somewhere, but chances are it won't be the right place. Therefore, when you write, always decide what you want to accomplish before you start. Although there are many different writing purposes, the two you will most commonly use for school and on the job are to inform and to persuade.

The purpose of *informative writing* is to present and explain ideas. A research paper on how hospitals use donated blood to save lives informs readers without trying to mold opinions. The writer presents facts in an unbiased way, without introducing a particular point of view. Most newspaper articles, except on the opinion and editorial pages, are examples of informative writing.

Persuasive writing has the purpose of convincing readers to adopt your point of view. For example, as the health editor of a magazine, you write a column attempting to persuade readers to give blood. Examples of persuasive writing include newspaper editorials, business proposals, and books and magazine articles with a point of view.

FIGURE 8.3   The three elements of writing.

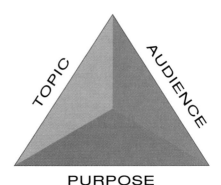

Knowing Your Audience

In almost every case, a writer creates written material so that others can read it. The writer and audience are partners in this process. Knowing who your audience is will help you communicate successfully.

Key Questions About Your Audience

In school, your primary audience is your instructors. For many assignments, instructors will want you to assume that they are typical readers. Writing for "typical readers" usually means that you should be as complete as possible in your explanations. You may also write for "informed readers" who know a great deal about your topic. At work, your audience may be coworkers, supervisors, customers or clients, students, or others. In every case, ask yourself some or all of the following questions to help you define your readers' needs:

- What are my readers' ages, cultural backgrounds, interests, and experiences?
- What are their roles? Are they instructors, students, employers, or customers?
- How much do they know about my topic? Are they experts in the field or beginners?
- Are they interested, or do I have to convince them to read what I write?
- Can I expect my audience to have open or closed minds?

After you answer the questions about your audience, take what you have discovered into consideration as you write.

Your Commitment to Your Audience

Your goal is to communicate—to organize your ideas so that readers can follow them. Suppose, for example, you are writing an informative research paper for a nonexpert audience on using Internet job banks to get a job. One way to accomplish your goal is to first explain what these employment services are and the kinds of help they offer, then describe each service in detail, and finally conclude with how these services will change job hunting in the twenty-first century.

Using a separate sheet of paper, complete the following.

Thinking Back

1. Describe the three primary elements that affect every writing situation.

2. List three questions you might ask yourself as you try to picture your readers.

3. As the primary audience for your written work in school, what do instructors expect?

Thinking Ahead

1. What process do you prefer to follow in the course of writing a paper?

2. What planning do you go through before you begin to write?

3. After you finish planning a paper, what do you prefer to do to go from generating ideas to actual writing?

4. List four activities that come to mind when you think about revising and editing.

WHAT IS THE WRITING PROCESS?

The writing process provides an opportunity for you to state and refine your thoughts until you have expressed yourself as clearly as possible. Critical thinking plays an important role every step of the way. The four main parts of the process are planning, drafting, revising, and editing.

Planning

Planning gives you a chance to think about what to write and how to write it. Planning involves brainstorming for ideas, defining and narrowing your topic by using **prewriting strategies,** conducting research if necessary, writing a thesis statement, and writing a working outline. Although these steps are listed in sequence, in real life the steps overlap one another as you plan your document.

Open Your Mind Through Brainstorming

Whether your instructor assigns a specific topic (e.g., the unfolding relationship between mothers and daughters in Amy Tan's novel, *The Joy Luck Club*), a partially defined topic (e.g., novelist Amy Tan) or a general category within which you make your own choice (e.g., Asian-American authors), you should brainstorm to develop ideas about what you want to write. Brainstorming is a creative technique that involves generating ideas about a subject without making judgments (see pp. 119).

First, let your mind wander. Write down anything on the assigned subject that comes to mind, in no particular order. Then, organize that list into an outline or think link that helps you see the possibilities more clearly. To make the outline or think link, separate list items into general ideas or categories and sub-ideas or examples. Then, associate the sub-ideas or examples with the ideas they support or fit. Figure 8.4 shows a portion of an outline that student Michael B. Jackson constructed from his brainstorming list. The assignment is a five-paragraph essay on a life-changing event. Here Michael chose to brainstorm the topic of "boot camp" as he organized his ideas into categories.

PREWRITING STRATEGIES

Techniques for generating ideas about a topic and finding out how much you already know before you start your research and writing.

Part of a brainstorming outline.

FIGURE 8.4

> Boot camp
> — physical conditioning
>   • swim tests
>   • intensive training
>   • ENDLESS push-ups!
> — Chief who was our commander
> — mental discipline
>   • military lifestyle
>   • perfecting our appearance
> — self-confidence
>   • walk like you're in control
>   • don't blindly accept anything

Narrow Your Topic Through Prewriting Strategies

When your brainstorming has generated some possibilities, narrow your topic. Focus on the sub-ideas and examples from your brainstorming session. Because they are relatively specific, they will be more likely to point you toward possible topics. Choose one or more sub-ideas or examples that you like and explore them by using prewriting strategies such as brainstorming, freewriting, and asking journalists' questions.[1]

Prewriting strategies will help you decide which of your possible topics you would most like to pursue.

BRAINSTORMING. The same process you used to generate ideas will also help you narrow your topic further. Generate thoughts about the possibility you have chosen and write them down. Then, organize them into categories, noticing any patterns that appear. See if any of the sub-ideas or examples seem as if they might make good topics.

FREEWRITING. Another technique that encourages you to put ideas on paper as they occur to you is called *freewriting*. When you freewrite, you write whatever comes to mind without censoring ideas or worrying about grammar, spelling, punctuation, or organization. Freewriting helps you think creatively and gives you an opportunity to begin weaving in information you know. Freewrite on the sub-ideas or examples you have created to see if you want to pursue any of them. Here is a sample of freewriting:

> Boot camp for the Coast Guard really changed my life. First of all, I really got in shape. We had to get up every morning at 5 A.M., eat breakfast, and go right into training. We had to do endless military-style push-ups but we later found out that these have a purpose, to prepare us to hit the deck in the event of enemy fire. We had a lot of aquatic tests, once we were awakened at 3 A.M. to do one in full uniform! Boot camp also helped me to feel confident about myself and be disciplined. Chief Marzloff was the main person who made that happen. He was tough but there was always a reason. He got angry when I used to nod my head whenever he would speak to me, he said that made it seem like I was blindly accepting whatever he said, which was a weakness. From him I have learned to keep an eye on my body's movements when I communicate. I learned a lot more from him too.

ASKING JOURNALISTS' QUESTIONS. When journalists begin work on a story, they ask themselves, Who? What? Where? When? Why? and How? You can use these *journalists' questions* to focus your thinking. Ask these questions about any sub-idea or example to discover what you may want to discuss.

Who?	Who was at boot camp? Who influenced me the most?
What?	What about boot camp changed my life? What did we do?
When?	When in my life did I go to boot camp, and for how long? When did we fulfill our duties?
Where?	Where was camp located? Where did we spend our day-to-day time?
Why?	Why did I decide to go there? Why was it such an important experience?
How?	How did we train in the camp? How were we treated? How did we achieve success?

As you prewrite, keep an eye on paper length, assignment due date, and any other requirements (such as topic area or purpose). These requirements influence your choice of a final topic. For example, if you have a month to write an informative 20-page paper on a learning disability, you might discuss the symptoms, effects, and treatment of attention deficit disorder (ADD). If you have a week to write a five-page persuasive essay, you might write about how elementary students with ADD need special training. If you are writing about ADD for a professional journal, you may also have a limit of a particular number of words and a due date that gets your work in before the publishing deadline.

Prewriting will help you develop a topic broad enough to give you something with which to work but narrow enough to be manageable. See Table 8.1 for an overview of how two different topics can be narrowed from broad ideas to possible topics. Prewriting also helps you see what you know and what you don't know. If your assignment requires more than you already know, you may need to do research.

TABLE 8.1 How to define and narrow your writing topic.

FOCUS ON	EXAMPLE 1	EXAMPLE 2
Broad Topic	Computers	Families
Writing Context	Business communication course	Sociology course
Purpose	Informative	Informative
Audience	Instructor and classmates	Instructor
Length	1,500 words	1,000 words
Deadline	2 weeks	1 week
Possible Topics	Using online services to find work. Using online services to conduct business research.	Major changes in the American family since 1970. How shifts in government welfare policies during the early 1990s affected families in poverty.

Conduct Research

Some college writing, such as an opinion essay or exam essay, will rely on what you already know about a subject. In these cases, prewriting strategies may generate all the ideas and information you need. In other writing situations, outside sources are necessary. Try doing your research in stages. In the first stage, look for a basic overview that can lead to a thesis statement. In the second stage, go into more depth, tracking down information that will help you fill in gaps and complete your thoughts. Chapter 7 goes into detail about how to research effectively.

> *Clear a space for the writing voice . . . you cannot will this to happen. It is a matter of persistence and faith and hard work. So you might as well just go ahead and get started.*
>
> ANNE LAMOTT

Write a Thesis Statement

Your work up until this point has prepared you to write a thesis statement, the central message you want to communicate. The thesis statement states your subject and point of view, reflects your writing purpose and audience, and acts as the organizing principle of your paper. It tells your readers what they should expect to read. On the following page is an example from Michael's paper.

A thesis statement is just as important in a short document, such as a letter, as it is in a long paper. For example, when you write a job application letter, a clear thesis statement will help you tell the recruiter why you deserve the job.

> Topic   Coast Guard boot camp
>
> Purpose   To inform
>
> Audience   Instructor who probably knows little
>   about the topic
>
> Thesis statement
>
> Chief Marzloff, our Basic Training Company
> Commander at the U.S. Coast Guard Basic
> Training Facility, shaped my life through physical
> conditioning, developing our self-confidence, and
> instilling strong mental discipline.

Write a Working Outline

The final step in the preparation process is writing a working outline. Use this outline as a loose guide instead of a final structure. As you draft your paper, your ideas and structure may change many times. Only by allowing changes and refinements to occur can you get closer and closer to what you really want to say. Some students prefer a more formal outline structure, while others like to use a think link. Choose whatever form suits you best.

Create a Checklist

Use the checklist in Table 8.2 to make sure your preparation is complete. Under Date Due, create your own writing schedule, giving each task an intended completion date. Work backward from the date the assignment is due and estimate how long it will take to complete each step. Refer to Chapter 2 for time-management skills that will help you schedule your writing process.

As you develop your schedule, remember that you'll probably move back and forth between tasks. You might find yourself doing two and even three things on the same day. Stick to the schedule as best you can, while balancing the other demands of your busy life, and check off your accomplishments on the list as you complete them.

Drafting

Some people aim for perfection when they write a first draft. They want to get everything right—from word choice to tone to sentence structure to paragraph organization to spelling, punctuation, and grammar. Try to resist

TABLE 8.2 Preparation checklist.

DATE DUE	TASK	IS IT COMPLETE?
	Brainstorm	
	Define and narrow	
	Use prewriting strategies	
	Conduct research if necessary	
	Write thesis statement	
	Write working outline	
	Complete research	

this tendency because it may lead you to shut the door on ideas before you even know they are there.

A *first draft* involves putting ideas down on paper for the first time—but not the last. You may write many different versions of the assignment until you do one you like. Each version moves you closer to communicating exactly what you want to say in the way you want to say it. It is as if you started with a muddy pond and gradually cleared the mud away until your last version became a clear body of water, showing the rocks and the fish beneath the surface. Think of your first draft as a way of establishing the pond before you start clearing it up.

The process of writing a first draft includes freewriting, crafting an introduction, organizing the ideas in the body of the paper, formulating a conclusion, citing sources, and soliciting feedback. When you think of drafting, it might help you to imagine that you are creating a kind of "writing sandwich." The bottom slice of bread is the introduction, the top slice is the conclusion, and the sandwich stuffing is made of central ideas and supporting examples (see Figure 8.5).

Freewriting Your Draft

If the introduction, body, and conclusion are the three parts of the sandwich, freewriting is the process of searching the refrigerator for the ingredients and laying them all on the table. Take everything that you have developed in the planning stages and freewrite a very rough draft. Don't censor yourself. For now, don't consciously think about your introduction, conclusion, or structure within the paper's body. Focus on getting your ideas out of the realm of thought and onto the paper, in whatever form they prefer to be at the moment.

The "writing sandwich."

When you have the beginnings of a paper in your hands, you can start to shape it into something with a more definite form. First, work on how you want to begin.

Writing an Introduction

The introduction tells your readers what the rest of the paper will contain. A thesis statement is an essential ingredient. Here, for example, is a draft of an introduction for Michael's paper about the Coast Guard. The thesis statement is underlined at the end of the paragraph:

> Chief Marzloff took on the task of shaping the lives and careers of the youngest, newest members of the U.S. Coast Guard. During my eight weeks in training, he was my father, my instructor, my leader, and my worst enemy. He took his job very seriously and demanded that we do the same. <u>The Chief was instrumental in conditioning our bodies, developing our self-confidence, and instilling mental discipline within us.</u>

HOOKS

Elements—including facts, quotes, statistics, questions, stories, or statements—that catch the reader's attention and encourage him to want to continue to read.

When you write an introduction, you might try to draw the reader in with an anecdote—a story that is related to the thesis. You can try other **hooks**, including a relevant quotation, dramatic statistics, a pertinent story, and questions that encourage critical thinking. Whatever strategy you choose, link it to your thesis statement.

After you have an introduction that seems to set up the purpose of your paper, make sure the body fulfills that purpose.

Creating the Body of a Paper

The body of the paper contains your central ideas and supporting **evidence.** Look at the array of ideas and evidences in your draft in its current state. Think about how you might group certain items of evidence with the particular ideas they support. Then, try to find a structure that helps you to organize such evidence groups into a clear pattern. Here are some strategies to consider.

EVIDENCE

Proof that informs or persuades, consisting of facts, statistics, examples, and expert opinion.

- *Arrange ideas by time.* Describe events in order or in reverse order.
- *Arrange ideas according to importance.* You can choose to start with the idea that carries the most weight and move to ideas with less value or influence. You can also move from the least important to the most important idea.
- *Arrange ideas by problem and solution.* Start with a specific problem; then discuss one or more solutions.

Writing the Conclusion

Your conclusion is a statement or paragraph that communicates that your paper is complete. Summarize the information that is in the body of your paper and critically evaluate what is important about it. Try one of the following strategies:

- summarize main points (if material is longer than three pages)
- relate a story, statistic, quote, or question that makes the reader think
- call the reader to action
- look to the future

As you work on your conclusion, try not to introduce new facts or restate what you feel you have proved (e.g., "I have successfully proven that violent cartoons are related to increased violence in children."). Let your ideas as they are presented in the body of the paper speak for themselves. Readers should feel that they have reached a natural point of completion.

PLAGIARISM

The act of using someone else's exact words, figures, unique approach, or specific reasoning without giving appropriate credit.

Crediting Authors and Sources

When you write a paper using any materials other than your own thoughts and recollections, the ideas you gathered in your research become part of your own writing. This does not mean that you can claim these ideas as your own or fail to attribute them to someone. To avoid **plagiarism**, you need to credit authors for their ideas and words.

Writers own their writings just as a computer programmer owns a program that she designed or a photographer owns an image that he created. A piece of writing and its ideas are the writer's products, or "intellectual property." Using an idea, phrase, or word-for-word paragraph without crediting its author is the same as using a computer program without buying it or printing a photograph without paying the photographer. It is just as serious as any other theft and may have unfavorable consequences. Most colleges have stiff penalties for plagiarism, as well as for any other cheating offense.

To avoid plagiarism, learn the difference between a quotation and a paraphrase. A *quotation* refers to a source's exact words, which are set off from the rest of the text by quotation marks. A *paraphrase* is a restatement of the quotation in your own words, using your own sentence structure. Restatement requires that you completely rewrite the idea, not just remove or replace a few words. A paraphrase may not be acceptable if it is too close to the original. Figure 8.6 demonstrates these differences.

Avoid plagiarism by learning how to paraphrase.

FIGURE

8.6

QUOTATION*

"The most common assumption that is made by persons who are communicating with one another is . . . that the other perceives, judges, thinks, and reasons the way he does. Identical twins communicate with ease. Persons from the same culture but with a different education, age, background, and experience often find communication difficult. American managers communicating with managers from other cultures experience greater difficulties in communication than with managers from their own culture."

UNACCEPTABLE PARAPHRASE *(The underlined words are taken directly from the quoted source.)*

When we communicate, we assume that the person to whom we are speaking <u>perceives, judges, thinks, and reasons the way</u> we do. This is not always the case. Although <u>identical twins communicate with ease, persons from the same culture but with a different education, age, background, and experience often</u> encounter communication problems. Communication problems are common among American managers as they attempt to <u>communicate with managers from other cultures.</u> They experience greater communication problems than when they communicate <u>with managers from their own culture.</u>

ACCEPTABLE PARAPHRASE

Many people fall into the trap of believing that everyone sees the world exactly as they do and that all people communicate according to the same assumptions. This belief is difficult to support even within our own culture as African-Americans, Hispanic-Americans, Asian-Americans, and others often attempt unsuccessfully to find common ground. When intercultural differences are thrown into the mix, such as when American managers working abroad attempt to communicate with managers from other cultures, clear communication becomes even harder.

---

*Philip R. Harris and Robert T. Moran, *Managing Cultural Differences*, 3d ed. (Houston, TX: Gulf Publishing Company, 1991), p. 59.

Plagiarism often begins by accident during research. You may forget to include quotation marks around a word-for-word quotation from the source, or you may intend to cite it or paraphrase but never find the time to do so. To avoid forgetting, try writing something like "Quotation from original; rewrite later" next to quoted material, and note at that time the specifics of the original document (title, author, source, page number, etc.), so you don't spend hours trying to locate it later.

Even an acceptable paraphrase requires a citation of the source of the ideas within it. Take care to credit any source that you quote, paraphrase, or use as evidence. To credit a source, write a footnote or endnote that describes it. Use the format preferred by your instructor. Writing handbooks such as the *Modern Language Association* (MLA) *Handbook* contain acceptable formats.

Solicit Feedback

Having one or more pairs of eyes look over your work is one of the most valuable steps you can take when writing any kind of paper. It is difficult to have perspective on your writing when you are in the midst of a project—another person, however, will have more of a chance to be objective. Make an appointment with your instructor and show your draft to her. Ask a classmate, a friend, or a coworker if he would take a look. Perhaps you can look over a draft of your readers in return.

> *Omit needless words . . . This requires not that the writer make all his sentences short, or that he avoid all detail and treat his subjects only in outline, but that every word tell.*
>
>
> **WILLIAM STRUNK, JR.**

If you have ideas about the issues you find particularly difficult or confusing when you write, ask your readers to look for specific things. Ask them if there are any sections that they cannot understand, and have them explain why. Ask if any sections don't seem linked to the rest of the paper, if any information seems unimportant, or if any information is missing that should be included. Be open-minded about the comments you receive from your readers—consider each one carefully and then make a decision about what changes you intend to make.

Continue Your Checklist

Create a checklist for your first draft (see Table 8.3). The elements of a first draft do not have to be written in order. In fact, many writers prefer to write the introduction after they complete the body of the paper, so the introduction will reflect the paper's content and tone. Whatever order you choose, make sure your schedule allows you to get everything done—with enough time left over for revisions.

Revising

When you revise, you critically evaluate the word choice, paragraph structure, and style of your first draft. Any draft, no matter how good, can always be improved. Be thorough as you add, delete, replace, and reorganize words, sentences, and paragraphs. You may want to print out your draft and then

First draft checklist.

DATE DUE	TASK	IS IT COMPLETE?
	Freewrite a draft	
	Plan and write introduction	
	Organize the body of the paper	
	Include research evidence in the body	
	Plan and write the conclusion	
	Check for plagiarism and rewrite passages to avoid it	
	Credit sources	
	Solicit feedback	

make notes and corrections on the hard copy before you make changes on a typewritten or computer printed version. Figure 8.7 shows a paragraph from Michael's first draft, with revision comments added.

In addition to revising on your own, some classes may include peer review (having students read one another's work and offer suggestions). A peer reviewer can tell you what comes across well and what seems confusing. Having a different perspective on your writing is extremely valuable. Even if you don't have an organized peer-review system, you may want to ask a classmate to review your work as a favor.

The elements of revision include being a critical writer, evaluating paragraph structure, and checking for clarity and conciseness.

Being a Critical Writer

Critical thinking is as important in writing as it is in reading. Thinking critically when writing will help you move beyond restating what you have researched and learned. Of course, your knowledge is an important part of your writing. What will make your writing even more important and unique, however, is how you use critical thinking to construct your own new ideas and knowledge from what you have learned.

One key to critical writing is asking the question, "So what?" For example, if you were writing a piece on nutrition, you might discuss a variety of good eating habits. Asking "So what?" could lead into a discussion of why these habits are helpful, or, what positive effects they have. If you were writing a paper on egg imagery in the novel *All the King's Men* by Robert Penn Warren, you might list all the examples of it that you noticed. Then, asking "So what?" could lead you to evaluate why that imagery is so strong and what idea you think those examples convey.

FIGURE

8.7

Sample revision comments.

> Of the changes that ~~happened to us,~~ the physical
> *military recruits undergo*
>
> transformation is the ~~biggest. When we arrived at the~~
> *most evident*
>
> ~~training facility, it was January, cold and cloudy. At the~~
> *Too much ↗*
>
> ~~time,~~ I was a little thin, but I had been working out and
> *Maybe— upon my January arrival at the*
>
> thought that I could physically do anything. Oh boy, was
> *training facility,*
>
> I wrong! The Chief said to us right away: "Get down,
>
> maggots!" Upon this command, we all to drop to the
> *↙ his trademark phrase   were*
>
> ground and do military-style push-ups. Water survival
> *endless*
>
> tactics were also part of the training ~~that we had to~~
>
> ~~complete.~~ Occasionally, my dreams of home were
> *unnecessary*
>
> interrupted at 3 a.m. when we had a surprise aquatic
>
> test. Although we ~~didn't feel too happy about~~ this
> *resented   mention how chief was involved*
>
> sub-human treatment at the time, we learned to
>
> appreciate how the conditioning was turning our bodies
>
> into fine-tuned machines.
> *say more about this (swimming in uniform incident?)*

Another key, if your paper contains an argument, is to make sure that argument is well constructed and convincing. Using what you know about arguments from the discussion in Chapter 4, think through your ideas and provide solid support for them with facts and examples.

Use the mind actions to guide your revision. As you revise, ask yourself questions that can help you think through ideas and examples, come up with your own original insights about the material, and be as complete and clear as possible. Here are some examples of questions you may ask:

Are these examples clearly connected to the idea?

Are there any similar concepts or facts I know of that can add to how I support this?

What else can I recall that can help to support this idea?

Windows on the World

How can I become more confident about my writing?

Beverly Andre, *Triton College, River Grove, Illinois, Continuing Education*

The best thing I ever wrote was in the sixth grade. My teacher let us pick a topic, and I chose to write about riding horses because I loved to do it and knew a lot about it. In high school, writing was okay because my English teacher was helpful. On the other hand, writing college papers has been a real challenge. For one thing, I don't think I'm very original when it comes to topic ideas. I also feel like I have to come up with college-level vocabulary and mine is not that advanced. If a professor assigns a topic that I know nothing about, I usually don't have as much interest as I do when I'm writing on something I already know about.

One of the reasons I don't like to write is because I don't like looking up information. Knowing how to begin the research gets confusing because  there's so much to choose from. Once I do manage to pull the information together, I can't seem to expand on an idea without being redundant. I also have trouble sticking to the point so I go off on all sorts of tangents.

Occasionally I come up with something a professor thinks is interesting. I'm always a little surprised when that happens. The bottom line is that I find it difficult to put my thoughts to paper. Can you help me become a better writer?

Raymond Montolvo, Jr., *Writer's Program, University of Southern California, Los Angeles, California*

No matter what your writing goal, in most cases the person you are writing for, your instructor, wants you to improve. Keeping this in mind may help you concentrate on trying to improve your skills instead of worrying about getting a good grade.

I suggest a two-pronged approach to better writing. The first step is to read. Read novels, the newspaper, and nonfiction articles. Reading will help you learn to organize your thoughts, and it increases your vocabulary. If you want to study a specific area, such as what you plan to major in, read publications in that area on your own. Create  file folders for pieces of writing that you like. For example, make a copy of a business letter that you think is well-written, and refer to it when you need to write similar correspondence.

Second, bridge the gap between what you should know and what an instructor can tell you. Ask your instructor what he thinks you need to work on. Focus your energy on understanding the assignment and strengthening technical skills such as sentence structure and grammar. Another tip is to read what you've written, sentence by sentence, and think about how you could say it better.

If you don't know where to begin your research, start with what feels comfortable. If you are at ease with computers, use the Internet. If you prefer libraries, start by asking the reference librarian for assistance. The main point with research is to jump right in. Once you read something that relates to your topic it will refer you to something else.

Finally, don't get frustrated by setbacks. Writing is a process. Set goals you can attain. Instead of sitting down and trying to write a ten-page paper, write a three-page one. Finishing something builds confidence.

In evaluating any event or situation, have I clearly indicated the causes and effects?

What new idea comes to mind when I think about these examples or facts?

How do I evaluate any effect, fact, or situation? Is it good or bad, useful or not?

What different arguments might a reader think of that I should address here?

Finally, critical thinking can help you evaluate the content and form of your paper. As you start your revision, ask yourself the following questions.

- Will my audience understand my thesis and how I've supported it?
- Does the introduction prepare the reader and capture attention?
- Is the body of the paper organized effectively?
- Is each idea fully developed, explained, and supported by examples?
- Are my ideas connected to one another through logical **transitions**?
- Do I have a clear, concise, simple writing style?
- Does the paper fulfill the requirements of the assignment?
- Does the conclusion provide a natural ending to the paper?

TRANSITIONS

Words and phrases that build bridges between ideas, leading the reader from one idea to the next.

Evaluating Paragraph Structure

Think of your paragraphs as mini-versions of your paper, each with an introduction, a body, and a conclusion. Make sure that each paragraph has a *topic sentence* that states the paragraph's main idea (a topic sentence does for a paragraph what a thesis statement does for an entire paper). The rest of the paragraph should support the idea with examples and other evidence. Although some topic sentences may occur just after the first sentence of a paragraph, or even at the end, most occur at the beginning. An example follows in the box on the next page.

Examine how your paragraphs flow into one another by evaluating your use of transitions. For example, words like *also, in addition,* and *next* indicate that another idea is coming. Similarly, *finally, as a result,* and *in conclusion* tell readers a summary is on its way.

See revision as 'envisioning again.' If there are areas in your work where there is a blur or vagueness, you can simply see the picture again and add the details that will bring your work closer to your mind's picture.

NATALIE GOLDBERG

Checking for Clarity and Conciseness

Aim to say what you want to say as clearly and concisely as you can. Try to eliminate extra words and phrases. Rewrite wordy phrases in a more straightforward, conversational way. For example, you can write "if" instead of "in the event that," or "now" instead of "at this point in time."

Chief Marzloff played an integral role in the development of our self-confidence. He taught us that anything less than direct eye contact was disrespectful to both him and ourselves. He encouraged us to be confident about our own beliefs and to think about what was said to us before we decided whether to accept it. Furthermore, the Chief reinforced self-confidence through his own example. He walked with his chin up and chest out, like the proud parent of a newborn baby. He always gave the appearance that he had something to do and that he was in complete control.

Editing

In contrast to the critical thinking of revising, *editing* involves correcting technical mistakes in spelling, grammar, and punctuation, as well as checking style consistency for such elements as abbreviations and capitalizations. Editing comes last, after you are satisfied with your ideas, organization, and style of writing. If you use a computer, you might want to use the grammar check and spell check functions to find mistakes. A spell checker helps, but you still need to check your work on your own. Although a spell checker won't pick up the mistake in the following sentence, someone who is reading for sense will: They are not hear on Tuesdays.

Look also for *sexist language,* which characterizes people according to their gender. Sexist language often involves the male pronoun *he* or *his*. For example, "An executive often spends hours each day going through his electronic mail" implies that executives are always men. A simple change will eliminate the sexist language: "Executives often spend hours each day going through their electronic mail," or "An executive often spends hours each day going through his or her electronic mail." Try to be sensitive to words that leave out or slight women. *Mail carrier* is preferable to *mailman; student* to *coed*.

Proofreading is the last editing stage and happens after your paper is in its final form. Proofreading means reading every word and sentence to make sure they are accurate. Look for technical mistakes, run-on sentences, and sentence fragments. Look for incorrect word usage and unclear references.

Teamwork can be a big help as you edit and proofread because another pair of eyes may see errors that you didn't notice on your own. If possible, have someone look over your work. Ask for feedback on what is clear and what is confusing. Then, ask the reader to edit and proofread for errors.

A Final Checklist

You are now ready to complete your revising and editing checklist. All the tasks listed in Table 8.4 should be complete when you submit your final paper. Figure 8.8 shows the final version of Michael's paper.

Your final paper reflects all the hard work you put in during the writing process. Ideally, when you are finished, you have a piece of work that is in a clearly readable format, shows your writing ability, and most importantly, communicates interesting and important ideas. Writing is speaking using the written word—take the time and effort to make your ideas known.

TABLE 8.4   Revising and editing checklist.

DATE DUE	TASK	IS IT COMPLETE?
	Check the body of the paper for clear thinking and adequate support of ideas	
	Finalize introduction and conclusion	
	Check word spelling, usage, and grammar	
	Check paragraph structure	
	Make sure language is familiar and concise	
	Check punctuation and capitalization	
	Check transitions	
	Eliminate sexist language	
	Get feedback from peers and/or instructor	

FIGURE 8.8

Sample final version of paper.

March 19, 2001   Michael B. Jackson

BOYS TO MEN

His stature was one of confidence, often misinterpreted by others as cockiness. His small frame was lean and agile, yet stiff and upright, as though every move was a calculated formula. For the longest eight weeks of my life, he was my father, my instructor, my leader, and my worst enemy. His name is Chief Marzloff, and he had the task of shaping the lives and careers of the youngest, newest members of the U.S. Coast Guard. As our Basic Training Company Commander, he took his job very seriously and demanded that we do the same. Within a limited time span, he conditioned our bodies, developed our self-confidence, and instilled within us a strong mental discipline.

Of the changes that recruits in military basic training undergo, the physical transformation is the most immediately evident. Upon my January arrival at the training facility, I was a little thin, but I had been working out and thought that I could physically do anything. Oh boy, was I wrong! The Chief wasted no time in introducing me to one of his trademark phrases: "Get down, maggots!" Upon this command, we were all to drop to the ground and produce endless counts of military-style push-ups. Later, we found out that exercise prepared us for hitting the deck in the event of enemy fire. Water survival tactics were also part of the training. Occasionally, my dreams of home were interrupted at about 3 a.m. when our company was selected for a surprise aquatic test. I recall one such test that required us to swim laps around the perimeter of a pool while in full uniform. I felt like a salmon swimming upstream, fueled only by natural instinct. Although we resented this sub-human treatment at the time, we learned to appreciate how the strict guidance of the Chief was turning our bodies into fine-tuned machines.

Beyond physical ability, Chief Marzloff also played an integral role in the development of our self-confidence. He would often declare in his raspy voice, "Look me in the eyes when you speak to me! Show me that you believe what you're saying!" He taught us that anything less was an expression of disrespect. Furthermore, he appeared to attack a personal habit of my own. It seemed that whenever he would speak to me individually, I would nervously nod

FIGURE

8.8   Continued.

my head in response. I was trying to demonstrate that I understood, but to him, I was blindly accepting anything that he said. He would roar, "That is a sign of weakness!" Needless to say, I am now conscious of all bodily motions when communicating with others. The Chief also reinforced self-confidence through his own example. He walked with his square chin up and chest out, like the proud parent of a newborn baby. He always gave the appearance that he had something to do, and that he was in complete control. Collectively, all of the methods that the Chief used were successful in developing our self-confidence.

Perhaps the Chief's greatest contribution was the mental discipline that he instilled in his recruits. He taught us that physical ability and self-confidence were nothing without the mental discipline required to obtain any worthwhile goal. For us, this discipline began with adapting to the military lifestyle. Our day began promptly at 0500 hours, early enough to awaken the oversleeping roosters. By 0515 hours, we had to have showered, shaved, and perfectly donned our uniforms. At that point, we were marched to the galley for chow, where we learned to take only what is necessary, rather than indulging. Before each meal, the Chief would warn, "Get what you want, but you will eat all that you get!" After making good on his threat a few times, we all got the point. Throughout our stay, the Chief repeatedly stressed the significance of self-discipline. He would calmly utter, "Give a little now, get a lot later." I guess that meant different things to all of us. For me, it was a simple phrase that would later become my personal philosophy on life. The Chief went to great lengths to ensure that everyone under his direction possessed the mental discipline required to be successful in boot camp or in any of life's challenges.

Chief Marzloff was a remarkable role model and a positive influence on many lives. I never saw him smile, but it was evident that he genuinely cared a great deal about his job and all the lives that he touched. This man single-handedly conditioned our bodies, developed our self-confidence, and instilled a strong mental discipline that remains in me to this day. I have not seen the Chief since March 28, 1992, graduation day. Over the years, however, I have incorporated many of his ideals into my life. Above all, he taught us the true meaning of the U.S. Coast Guard slogan, "Semper Peratus" (Always Ready).

Suá is a Shoshone Indian word, derived from the Uto-Aztecna language, meaning "think." Whereas much of the Native-American tradition in the Americas focuses on oral communication, written languages have allowed Native-American perspectives and ideas to be understood by readers outside the Native-American culture. The writings of Leslie Marmon Silko, J. Scott Momaday, and Sherman Alexis have expressed important insights that all readers can consider.

Think of *suá*—and how thinking can be communicated to others through writing—every time you begin to write. The power of writing allows you to express your own insights so that others can read them and perhaps benefit from knowing them. Explore your thoughts, sharpen your ideas, and remember the incredible power of the written word.

IMPORTANT POINTS *to remember*

1. Why does good writing matter?

You will often need to write essays or papers for your courses. Good writing skills are necessary to communicate your knowledge and thought process clearly. Clear, effective writing is also important for your career and in your personal life because others will judge your thinking ability according to what you write and how your write it. A well-written job application letter, for example, can make the difference between getting a job and being turned away.

2. What are the elements of effective writing?

The three primary elements are your purpose, your topic, and your audience. Start by defining your purpose for writing: to inform or persuade. Then, decide who your readers are and what they know about the topic, so that you can determine how you should write to best suit that audience. Your goal is to write in a complete and organized manner so that your audience can follow your ideas easily. Successful writing communicates your message in a way your readers can understand.

3. What is the writing process?

The writing process includes four stages: planning, drafting, revising, and editing. During the planning stage, you brainstorm, establish guidelines, define and narrow your topic by using prewriting strategies, conduct research, write a thesis statement, create a working outline, and complete your research. During the drafting stage, you create a first draft, which will almost certainly change before you finish the paper. Drafting involves freewriting, writing an introduction, organizing the ideas in the body of the paper, formulating a conclusion, and citing sources. During the revision stage, you evaluate and improve your first draft by asking critical-thinking questions, evaluating paragraph structure, and aiming for clear and concise language. Finally, you correct errors in spelling, grammar, punctuation, and consistency of usage during the editing stage. Editing involves careful proofreading to make sure the paper is error free.

NAME   DATE

CRITICAL THINKING

APPLYING LEARNING TO LIFE

GETTING READY TO WRITE. As a reporter for your college newspaper, you have been assigned the job of writing a story about some part of campus life. You submit the following suggestions to your editor-in-chief:

- The campus parking lot squeeze: Too many cars and too few spaces.
- Diversity: How students accept differences and live and work together.
- Drinking on campus: Is the problem getting better or worse?

Your editor-in-chief asks you the following questions about reader response. Consider that your different "audiences" include students, faculty and administrators, and community members.

1. Which subject would most likely appeal to all audiences at your school, and why?

_____

_____

_____

2. How would you adjust your writing according to how much readers know about the subject?

_____

_____

_____

3. For each topic, name the audience (or audiences) that you think would be most interested. If you think one audience would be equally interested in more than one topic, you can name an audience more than once.

Campus parking lot _____

Student diversity _____

Drinking on campus _____

271

Now choose a topic you are interested in and know something about—for example, college sports or handling stress. Narrow your topic, then use the following prewriting strategies to discover what you already know about the topic and what you would need to learn if you had to write an essay about the subject for one of your classes. (If necessary, continue this prewriting exercise on a separate sheet of paper.)

Brainstorm your ideas:

_____

_____

_____

_____

_____

Freewrite:

_____

_____

_____

_____

_____

Ask journalists' questions:

_____

_____

_____

_____

Finally, write two thesis statements for your topic. The first statement should inform the reader, and the second should persuade. In each case, use the thesis statement to narrow the topic.

Write your topic here: _____

Thesis with an informative purpose:

_____

_____

Thesis with a persuasive purpose:

_____

_____

TEAMWORK
COMBINING FORCES

COLLABORATIVE WRITING. In many jobs, you may be asked to work with other employees to produce written documents, including reports, proposals, procedure manuals, and even important letters and memos. Writing in groups, also known as collaborative writing, involves planning, drafting, revising, and editing.

To see what collaborative writing is like, join three classmates and choose a general topic you are all interested in—for example, "What Colleges Can Do to Help Students Juggle School, Work, and Family" or "Teaching Safe Sex in an Age When Sex Isn't Safe." Now imagine that you and other group members have to write a persuasive paper on some aspect of this topic. Writing the paper involves the following steps:

- Each group member should spend an hour in the library to get an overview of the topic so that everyone is able to write about it in general terms.

- The group should come together to brainstorm the topic, narrow its focus, and come up with a thesis. Use your research and thesis to write a working outline that specifies what the paper will say and the approach it will take. Divide the writing assignment into parts and assign a part to each group member.

- Each group member should draft his or her portion of the paper. Each section should be about two or three paragraphs long.

- Photocopy each draft and give a copy to each group member. Working independently, each person should use the suggestions in this chapter to evaluate and revise each section. After the independent revision work is done, come together as a group to hammer out differences and prepare a final, unedited version.

- Photocopy this version and distribute it to group members. Have everyone edit the material, looking for mistakes in spelling, grammar, punctuation, and usage. Incorporate the group's changes into a final version you all agree on, and ask every group member to read it. The group's goal is to produce a finished paper that satisfies the thesis and also looks good.

- Working alone, each group member should answer the following questions. Finally, compare your responses with those of other group members.

On a separate sheet of paper, answer the following questions:

1. What do you see as the advantages and disadvantages of collaborative writing? Is it difficult or easy to write as a team member?

2. What part of the collaborative writing project worked best? Where did you encounter problems?

3. What did you learn from this experience that will make you a more effective collaborative writer on the next project?

WRITING

DISCOVERY THROUGH JOURNALING

To record your thoughts, use a separate journal or the lined page at the end of the chapter.

AFFECTING WORDS. What piece of powerful writing have you read most recently? Did it make you feel something, think something, or do something? If so, why did it affect you in the way it did? What can you learn from this piece that you can use in your own writing?

CAREER PORTFOLIO

CHARTING YOUR COURSE

WRITING SAMPLE: A JOB INTERVIEW LETTER. To secure a job interview, you may have to write a letter describing your background and value to the company. To include in your portfolio, write a one-page, three-paragraph cover letter to a prospective employer. (The letter will accompany your résumé.) Be creative—you may use fictitious names, but select a career and industry that interest you. Use the format shown in Figure 8.9.

Introductory paragraph: Start with an attention getter—a statement that convinces the employer to read on. For example, name a person the employer knows who told you to write, or refer to something positive about the company that you read in the paper. Identify the position for which you are applying and tell the employer that you are interested in working for the company.

Middle paragraph: Sell your value. Try to convince the employer that hiring you will help the company in some way. Center your "sales effort" on your experience in school and the workplace. If possible, tie your qualifications to the needs of the company. Refer indirectly to your enclosed résumé.

Final paragraph: Close with a call to action. Ask the employer to call you, or tell the employer to expect your call to arrange an interview.

Exchange first drafts with a classmate. Read each other's letters and make notes in the margins. Discuss each letter, and make whatever corrections are necessary to produce a well-written, persuasive letter. Create a final draft for your portfolio.

Sample cover letter.

First name Last name
1234 Your Street
City, ST 12345

January 1, 2002
Ms. Prospective Employer
Prospective Company
5432 Their Street
City, ST 54321

Dear Ms. Employer:

On the advice of Mr. X, career center advisor at Y College, I am writing to inquire about the open position of production assistant at KKKK Radio. I read the description of the job and the company as it was listed on the career center board, and I wish to offer myself as a candidate for the position.

I am a senior at Y College and will graduate this spring with a degree in communications. Since my junior year when I declared my major, I have wanted to pursue a career in radio. For the last year, I have worked as a production intern at KCOL Radio, the college's station, and have occasionally filled in as a disc jockey on the evening news show. I enjoyed being on the air, but my primary interest is production and programming. My enclosed résumé will tell you more about my background and experience.

I would be pleased to talk with you in person about the position. You can reach me anytime at 555/555-5555 or by e-mail at xxxx@xx.com. Thank you for your consideration, and I look forward to meeting you.

Sincerely,

(*sign your name here*)

First name Last name

Enclosure(s) (*use this notation if you have included a résumé or other item with your letter*)

SUGGESTED READINGS

Cameron, Julia. *The Right to Write: An Invitation Into the Writing Life.* New York: Putnam (1999).

Gibaldi, Joseph and Phyllis Franklin. *MLA Handbook for Writers of Research Papers,* 5th ed. New York: Modern Language Association of America (1999).

LaRocque, Paula. *Championship Writing: 50 Ways to Improve Your Writing.* Oak Park, IL: Marion Street Press (2000).

Markman, Peter T. and Roberta H. Markman. *10 Steps in Writing the Research Paper,* 5th ed. New York: Barron's Educational Series (1994).

Strunk, William, Jr. and E. B. White. *The Elements of Style,* 3d ed. New York: Macmillan (1995).

Troyka, Lynn Quitman. *Simon & Schuster Handbook for Writers,* 5th ed. Upper Saddle River, NJ: Prentice Hall (1999).

Walsch, Bill. *Lapsing into a Comma: A Curmudgeon's Guide to the Many Things That Can Go Wrong in Print—and How to Avoid Them.* New York: Contemporary Books (2000).

INTERNET RESOURCES

Online Writing Lab—Purdue University: http://owl.english.purdue.edu
Researchpaper.com: http://researchpaper.com

ENDNOTES

1. Analysis based on Lynn Quitman Troyka. *Simon & Schuster Handbook for Writers.* Upper Saddle River, NJ: Prentice Hall (1996), pp. 22–23.

DATE

NAME

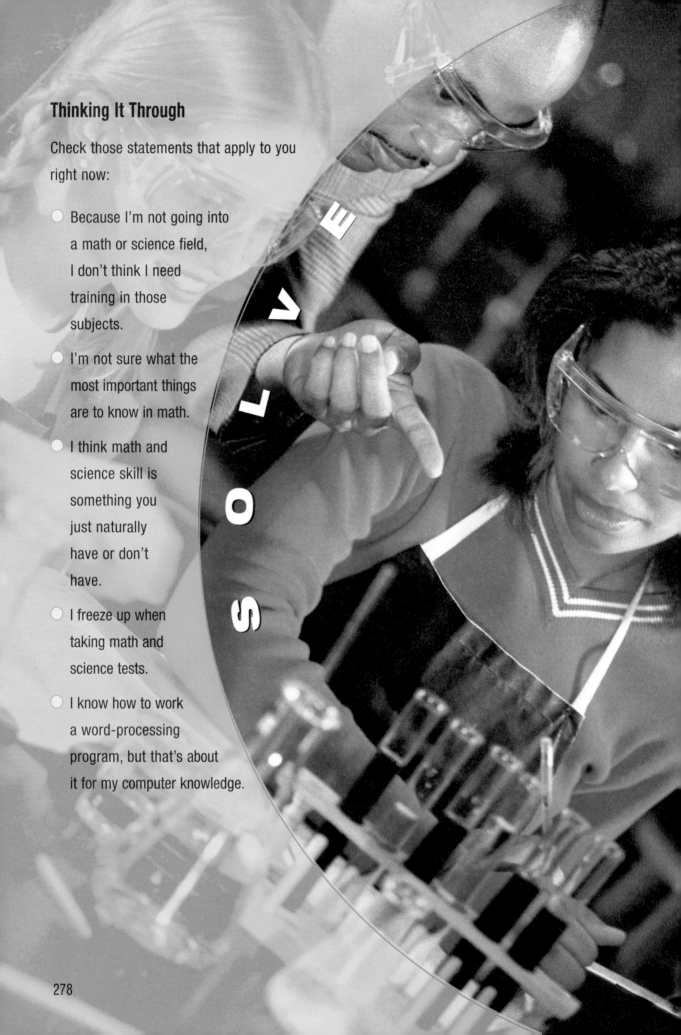

Thinking It Through

Check those statements that apply to you right now:

- Because I'm not going into a math or science field, I don't think I need training in those subjects.

- I'm not sure what the most important things are to know in math.

- I think math and science skill is something you just naturally have or don't have.

- I freeze up when taking math and science tests.

- I know how to work a word-processing program, but that's about it for my computer knowledge.

IN THIS CHAPTER,

you will explore answers to the
following questions:

- Why do you need to be able to think
  quantitatively?
- How can you master math and science basics?
- How can you overcome math anxiety?
- What techniques will improve your performance on math
  and science tests?
- What basics should you know about computers?
- How can you "read" visual aids?

Quantitative Learning

When asked about math or science, many students reply by saying, "I hate math" or "I was never any good at math and science." In today's world, however, a basic knowledge of *quantitative thinking*—thinking in terms of measurable quantities, including math, science, and computer technology—is as necessary as the ability to read and write. You will need to think quantitatively for school courses and at work, as well as in your personal life—for example, to manage your personal finances and computer software applications. Along with communication and leadership skills, employers look for quantitative thinking in the people they hire. Even if you are not a math or science major, you will benefit by learning more about these subjects. This chapter will help you become more adept at quantitative thinking and understand its importance.

WHY DO YOU NEED TO BE ABLE TO THINK QUANTITATIVELY?

Math is, at heart, a problem-solving discipline that moves you from questions to solutions as it reinforces critical thinking. Consider the following practical examples of problems requiring quantitative thinking:

- You make $2,000 per month in your job. How do you determine how you allocate your money to pay your bills?
- You want to carpet your house. However, many of the rooms and hallways are not regularly shaped. How do you determine how much carpet you need to buy?
- You are trying to schedule your classes for next semester. Each of your classes is only offered at certain times. How do you go about making the best possible schedule?

As these examples demonstrate, everyone needs a certain comfort and competence in math. These skills can be broken down into the following broad areas.

ARITHMETIC. Many everyday tasks require arithmetic (numerical computations such as addition, subtraction, multiplication, and division, plus fractions and other ratios). You are using arithmetic when you calculate how much tuition you can cover in a semester or figure out what to tip in a restaurant.

ALGEBRA

A generalization of arithmetic in which letters representing unknown quantities are combined, often with other numbers, into equations according to the rules of arithmetic.

ALGEBRA. A knowledge of **algebra** is needed almost as frequently as arithmetic. You use algebra when you figure out the interest on a loan or compute your GPA. Algebra involves determining an unknown value using known values.

GEOMETRY. The most important uses of geometry occur in determining areas and volumes. However, geometric ideas occur in many other forms. Examples of geometry in everyday life include determining how closely you can pass a car and packing a suitcase so that it can close.

PROBABILITY

The study of the chance that a given event will occur.

PROBABILITY AND STATISTICS. A knowledge of basic **probability** and **statistics** is needed for understanding the relevance and importance of the overwhelming amount of statistical information you encounter. For example, if a woman reads breast cancer statistics, her statistical and probability knowledge can help her determine her risk of getting the disease. Careers such as actuarial or genetic science demand a strong background in these subjects, and some areas of business, economics, and engineering require strong skills as well.

STATISTICS

Collection, analysis, and interpretation of numerical data.

CALCULUS AND DIFFERENTIAL EQUATIONS. Calculus and differential equations are needed for most engineering fields, business and economics, physics, and astronomy. Any problem in which a rate of change is needed involves calculus and differential equations. Many problems that involve work, water pressure, areas, and volumes also use calculus.

SCIENCES. Biology, anatomy, and other sciences directly related to the human body can help you to better manage your health through a greater understanding of how your body works. Chemistry can help you figure out how to substitute ingredients in a recipe and understand the chemical makeup of any medications you are taking and the interactions that are possible. A knowledge of physics can help you appreciate how airplanes fly and automobiles stop.

Ultimately, both math and science are relevant to your other subjects because of their involvement with problem solving and critical thinking. When you put your brain through the paces of mathematical and scientific problem solving, you are building the kind of critical-thinking ability that you can apply to problem solving in any subject. You'll be using the same analytical process when you write an essay on the causes of an historical event or reconcile different perspectives in a philosophy course.

OW CAN YOU MASTER MATH AND SCIENCE BASICS?

Certain thinking strategies will help improve your ability to think quantitatively. Mastering math and science basics involves a critical approach to the classroom, the textbook, studying and homework, and word problems.

Classroom Strategies

When taking a math or science class, as with any other class, the two most important factors are being in class and being prepared. If you build your base of knowledge before class by reading about the topic being covered that day, you will have a context in which to ask questions about the material. Asking questions will allow you to think critically about the important aspects of the material and help you retain and apply it. When you take notes, focus on the central ideas and connect supporting examples to those ideas. Try keeping a highlighter handy and highlight items or examples that confuse you so that you can go back and focus on them later.

You might also find that college math and science are quite different from high school courses—and that the differences require you to be more focused and diligent about attending class and keeping up with homework. Among the differences you may notice are the following:

- courses are faster-paced
- assignments are crucial (although they may not always be collected)
- class time may be more focused on theories and ideas than on problem solving
- class size might be considerably larger, with smaller lab sections
- technological proficiency may be important (using graphing calculators or software specific to the course)

How to Approach Your Textbook

Math textbooks move sequentially (later chapters build on concepts and information introduced in previous chapters) and are problem-and-solution based. Instead of just reading through math material, interact with it critically as you go. Keep a pad of paper nearby and take notes of the examples as you read. If steps are left out, as they often are, work them out on your pad. Draw sketches as you read to help visualize the material. Try not to move on until you understand the example and how it relates to the central ideas. Write down questions you want to ask your instructor or fellow students.

Also, note what **formulas** are given. Evaluate whether these formulas are important and recall whether the instructor emphasized them. Be aware that in some classes you are responsible for gathering all formulas through your reading, while in others, the instructors will provide them to you. Read the assigned material to prepare you for any assigned homework.

Science textbooks, like math textbooks, generally move in a sequence—your command of later material depends on how well you learned material in earlier chapters. Science textbooks are often packed with vocabulary specific to that particular science (e.g., a chapter in a psychobiology course may give medical names for the parts of the brain). Put your memory skills to use when reading science texts—use mnemonic devices, test yourself using flash cards, and rehearse aloud or silently (see Chapter 6). Selective highlighting and writing summaries of your readings, in table format for example, will also help.

Because many sciences rely on a base of mathematical knowledge, your math reading strategies will help you understand and remember the formulas that may appear in your science reading. As with math, make sure you understand the principle behind the formula, and do as many problems as you can to solidify your knowledge.

> **FORMULA**
>
> A general fact, rule, or principle usually expressed in mathematical symbols.

> *The proper and immediate object of science is the acquirement, or communication, of truth.*
>
> SAMUEL TAYLOR COLERIDGE

Studying and Homework

Following class, it is crucial to review your notes as soon as possible. Fill in missing steps in the instructor's examples before you forget them. When reviewing notes, have the book alongside and look for similarities and differences between the lecture information and the book. Then, work on the homework.

Doing a lot of problems is critical for math courses as well as many science courses (chemistry, physics, and astronomy are quite often problem-solving focused). Do not expect to complete every problem without effort. To fight frustration, stay flexible. If you are stuck on a problem, go on to another one. Sometimes you need to take a break to clear your head.

If you have done the assigned homework but still aren't sure about the method, do some other problems. Doing a lot of problems will give you a base of examples that will help to clarify ideas (concepts and formulas) for you. Plus, doing a group of problems similar to one another will help you apply the ideas to similar problems on other assignments and on tests.

Study groups can facilitate quantitative thinking. Other peoples' perspectives can often help you break through a mental block. Even if your math and science classes have smaller lab sessions, try to set up study groups outside of class. Do as much of your homework as you can and then meet to discuss the homework and work through additional problems. Be open to other perspectives, and don't hesitate to ask other students to explain their thought processes in detail.

Word Problems

Because word problems are the most common way you will encounter quantitative thinking throughout your life, the ability to solve them is a necessary skill. Word problems can be tough, however, because they force you to translate between two languages—English and mathematics. Although math is a precise language, English and other living languages are not so precise. This difference in precision makes the process of translating more difficult.

Steps to Solving Word Problems

Translating English or any other language into math takes a lot of practice. George Polya, in his 1945 classic, *How To Solve It,* devised a four-step method for attacking word problems.[1] The basic steps reflect the general problem-solving process you explored in Chapter 4, and will work for any word problem, whether in a math or science course.

1. *Understand the individual elements of the problem.* Read the problem carefully. Understand what it is asking. Know what information you have. Know what information is missing. Draw a picture, if possible. Take the given information and translate it from words into mathematical language (e.g., numbers, symbols, formulas).

2. *Name and explore potential solution paths.* Think about similar problems that you understand and how those were solved. Consider whether this problem is an example of a mathematical idea that you know. In your head, try out different ways to solve the problem to see which may work best.

3. *Carry out your plan.* Choose a solution path and solve the problem. Check each of your steps.

4. *Review your result.* Check your answer, if possible. Make sure you've answered the question the problem is asking. Does your result seem logical in the context of the problem? Are there other ways to do the problem?

Different problem-solving strategies will be useful to you when solving word problems. You use your critical-thinking skills both by evaluating which strategy will work best on a given problem and by applying the strategy itself. The following section lays out several problem-solving strategies by working through different types of word problem examples.[2]

Problem-Solving Strategies

STRATEGY 1. LOOK FOR A PATTERN. G. H. Hardy (1877–1947), an eminent British mathematician, described mathematicians as makers of patterns and ideas. The search for patterns is one of the best strategies in problem solving. When you look for a pattern, you think inductively, observing a series of examples and determining the general idea that links the examples together.

Example: Find the next three entries in the following:

a. 1, 2, 4, ___, ___, ___

b. O, T, T, F, F, S, S, ___, ___, ___

Solutions to Example:

a. When trying to identify patterns, you may find a different pattern than someone else. This doesn't mean yours is wrong. Example *a* actually has several possible answers. Here are two:

1. Each succeeding term of the sequence is twice the previous term. In that case, the next three values would be 8, 16, 32.

2. The second term is 1 more than the first term and the third term is 2 more than the second. This might lead you to guess the fourth term is 3 more than the third term, the fifth term is 4 more than the fourth term, and so on. In that case, the next three terms are 7, 11, 16.

b. Example *b* is a famous pattern that often appears in puzzle magazines. The key to it is that "O" is the first letter of *o*ne, "T" is the first letter of *t*wo, and so on. Therefore, the next three terms would be E, N, and T for *e*ight, *n*ine, and *t*en.

STRATEGY 2. MAKE A TABLE. A table can be used to help organize and summarize information. This may enable you to see how examples form a pattern that leads you to an idea and a solution.

Example: How many ways can you make change for a half dollar using only quarters, dimes, nickels, and pennies?

Solutions to Example: You might construct several tables and go through every possible case. You could start by seeing how many ways you can make change for a half dollar without using a quarter, which would produce the following tables:

Quarters	0	0	0	0	0	0	0	0	0	0	0	0	0	0	0	0	0	0
Dimes	0	0	0	0	0	0	0	0	0	0	0	1	1	1	1	1	1	1
Nickels	0	1	2	3	4	5	6	7	8	9	10	0	1	2	3	4	5	6
Pennies	50	45	40	35	30	25	20	15	10	5	0	40	35	30	25	20	15	10

Quarters	0	0	0	0	0	0	0	0	0	0	0	0	0	0	0	0	0	0
Dimes	1	1	2	2	2	2	2	2	2	3	3	3	3	3	4	4	4	5
Nickels	7	8	0	1	2	3	4	5	6	0	1	2	3	4	0	1	2	0
Pennies	5	0	30	25	20	15	10	5	0	20	15	10	5	0	10	5	0	0

There are 36 ways to make change for a half dollar without using a quarter. Using one quarter results in this table:

Quarters	1	1	1	1	1	1	1	1	1	1	1	1
Dimes	0	0	0	0	0	0	1	1	1	1	2	2
Nickels	0	1	2	3	4	5	0	1	2	3	0	1
Pennies	25	20	15	10	5	0	15	10	5	0	5	0

Using 1 quarter, you get 12 different ways to make change for a half dollar. Lastly, using two quarters, there's only one way to make change for a half dollar. Therefore, the solution to the problem is that there are 36+12+1=49 ways to make change for a half dollar using only quarters, dimes, nickels, and pennies.

STRATEGY 3. IDENTIFY A SUBGOAL. Breaking the original problem into smaller and possibly easier problems may lead to a solution to the original problem. This is often the case in writing a computer program.

Example: Arrange the nine numbers 1, 2, 3, ..., 9 into a square subdivided into nine sections in such a way that the sum of every row, column, and main diagonals is the same. This is what is called a magic square.

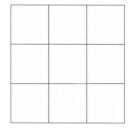

Solution to Example: Because each number will go into one of the squares, the sum of all the numbers will end up being three times the sum of any given row, column, or main diagonal. The sum of 1+2+3+4+5+6+7+8+9=45. Therefore, each row, column, and main diagonal needs to sum to 45/3=15. Now, you need to see how many ways you can add three of the numbers from 1 to 9 and get 15. In doing this, you should get:

9 + 1 + 5 = 15	8 + 3 + 4 = 15
9 + 2 + 4 = 15	7 + 2 + 6 = 15
8 + 1 + 6 = 15	7 + 3 + 5 = 15
8 + 2 + 5 = 15	6 + 4 + 5 = 15

Now, looking at your magic square, notice that the center position will be part of four sums (a row, a column, and the two main diagonals). Looking back at your sums, you see that 5 appears in four different sums, therefore 5 is in the center square.

	5	

Now, in each corner, the number there appears in 3 sums (row, column, and a diagonal). Looking through your sums, you find that 2, 4, 6, and 8 each appear in three sums. Now, you need to place them in the corners in such a way that your diagonals add up to 15.

2		6
	5	
4		8

Then, to finish, all you need to do is fill in the remaining squares to get the needed sum of 15 for each row, column, and main diagonal. The completed square is as follows:

2	7	6
9	5	1
4	3	8

STRATEGY 4. EXAMINE A SIMILAR PROBLEM. Sometimes a problem you are working on has similarities to a problem you've already read about or solved. In that case, it is often possible to use a similar approach to solve the new problem.

Example: Find a magic square using the numbers 3, 5, 7, 9, 11, 13, 15, 17, and 19.

Solution to Example: This problem is very similar to the example for Strategy 3. Approaching it in the same fashion, you find that the needed row, column, and main diagonal sum is 33. Writing down all the possible sums of three numbers to get 33, you find that 11 is the number that appears 4 times, so it is in the center.

	11	

The numbers that appear three times in the sums and will go in the corners are 5, 9, 13, and 17. This now gives you:

13		17
	11	
5		9

Finally, completing the magic square gives you:

13	3	17
15	11	7
5	19	9

The word impossible is not in my dictionary. NAPOLEON

STRATEGY 5. WORK BACKWARDS. With some problems, you may find it easier to start with the perceived final result and work backwards.

Example: In the game of "Life," Carol had to pay $1,500 when she was married. Then, she lost half the money she had left. Next, she paid half the money she had for a house. Then, the game was stopped, and she had $3,000 left. With how much money did she start?

Solution to Example: Carol ended up with $3,000. Right before that she paid half her money to buy a house. Because her $3,000 was half of what she had before her purchase, she had 2($3,000)=$6,000 before buying the house. Prior to buying the house, Carol lost half her money. This means that the $6,000 is the half she didn't lose. So, before losing half her money, Carol had 2($6,000)=$12,000. Prior to losing half her money, Carol had to pay $1,500 to get married. This means she had $12,000+$1,500=$13,500 before getting married. Because this was the start of the game, Carol began with $13,500.

STRATEGY 6. DRAW A DIAGRAM. Drawing a picture is often an aid to solving problems, especially for visual learners. Although pictures are especially useful for geometrical problems, they can be helpful for other types as well.

Example: There were 20 people at a round table for dinner. Each person shook hands with the person to her immediate right and left. At the end of the dinner, each person got up and shook hands with everybody except the people who sat on her immediate right and left. How many handshakes took place after dinner?

Solution to Example: To solve this with a diagram, it might be a good idea to examine several simpler cases to see if you can determine a pattern of any kind that might help. Starting with 2 or 3 people, you can see there are no handshakes after dinner because everyone is adjacent to everyone else.

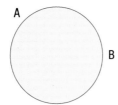
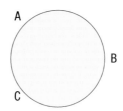

Now, in the case of 4 people, we get the following diagram, connecting those people who shake hands after dinner:

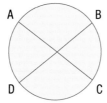

In this situation, you see there are two handshakes after dinner, AC and BD. In the case of five people, you get this picture:

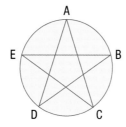

In this case, you have five after dinner handshakes, AC, AD, BD, BE, and CE. Looking at one further case of six people seated around a circle gives the following diagram:

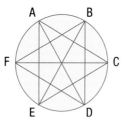

In this diagram, there are now a total of 9 after dinner handshakes, AC, AD, AE, BD, BE, BF, CE, CF, and DF. In noticing from the diagrams what is happening, you realize that if there are N people, each person would shake N-3 people's hands after dinner. (They don't shake their own hands or the hands of the two people adjacent to them.) Because there are N people that would lead to N(N-3) after dinner handshakes. However, this would double count every handshake because AD would also be counted as DA. Therefore, this is twice as many actual handshakes. So, the correct number of handshakes is [N(N-3)]/2. So finally, if there are 20 people, there would be 20(17)/2=170 after dinner handshakes.

STRATEGY 7. TRANSLATE WORDS INTO AN EQUATION. This is often used in algebra.

Example: A farmer needs to fence a rectangular piece of land. He wants the length of the field to be 80 feet longer than the width. If he has 1,080 feet of fencing available, what should the length and width of the field be?

Solution to Example: The best way to start this problem is to draw a picture of the situation and label the sides.

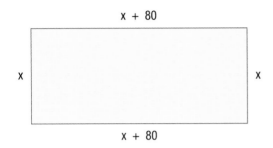

Let x represent the width of the field and $x+80$ represent the length of the field. The farmer has 1,080 feet of fencing and he will need $2x+2(x+80)$ feet of fencing to fence his field. This gives you the equation:

$$2x + 2(x + 80) = 1080$$

Multiplying out: $\qquad\qquad\qquad 2x + 2x + 160 = 1080$

Simplifying and subtracting 160: $\qquad\qquad 4x = 920$

Dividing by 4: $\qquad\qquad\qquad\qquad\qquad x = 230$

Therefore, $\qquad\qquad\qquad\qquad x + 80 = 310$

As a check, you find that $\qquad 2(230) + 2(310) = 1080$

These sample problems are designed to boost your ability to think critically through some basic math strategies. If they have made you feel anxious, however, you will benefit from some information about math anxiety.

Using a separate sheet of paper, complete the following.

Thinking Back

1. Name the six broad areas of math and science skills.

2. How do you use quantitative knowledge in your everyday life?

3. Name the steps in the four-step method to solving problems.

4. Name five word problem solving strategies.

Thinking Ahead

1. Do you consider yourself to have math anxiety? If so, when in your life do you remember it starting?

2. What strategies or attitudes, if any, help you handle your quantitative learning assignments?

3. How do you approach math and science tests? How do they make you feel?

4. Describe your relationship with computer technology—what you know, what you use, and your comfort level.

OW CAN YOU OVERCOME MATH ANXIETY?

MATH ANXIETY

Any of several uncomfortable, high-stress feelings that appear in relation to quantitative thinking.

Math anxiety is often a result of common misconceptions about math, such as the notion that people are born with or without an ability to think quantitatively, or the idea that real quantitative thinkers solve problems quickly in their heads. Some students feel that they can't do any math at all and, as a result, may give up without asking for help. Use the questionnaire in Figure 9.1 to get an idea of your math anxiety level.

Math anxiety most commonly occurs right before or during an exam. As a student gets ready to take a test or reads a particular problem on a test, he experiences rising anxiety or even what can be described as "blanking out." This can happen on exams for other subjects, but seems to occur espe-

FIGURE 9.1 Explore your math anxiety.

Answer the following statements by marking a number from 1 (Disagree) to 5 (Agree).

1. ____ I don't like math classes, and haven't since high school.

2. ____ I do okay at the beginning of a math class, but I always feel it will get to the point where it is impossible to understand.

3. ____ I can't seem to concentrate in math classes. I try, but I get nervous and distracted and think about other things.

4. ____ I don't like asking questions in math class. I'm afraid that the teachers or the other students will think I'm stupid.

5. ____ I stress out when I'm called on in math class. I seem to forget even the easiest answers.

6. ____ Math exams scare me far more than any of my other exams.

7. ____ I can't wait to finish my math requirement so that I'll never have to do any math again.

Scoring Key: 28–35: You suffer from full-blown math anxiety.
                       21–27: You are coping, but you're not happy about mathematics.
                       14–20: You're doing okay.
                         7–13: So what's the big deal about math? You have very little problem with anxiety.

Source: Freedman, Ellen (March 1997). *Test Your Math Anxiety* [online]. Available: http://fc.whyy.org/CCC/algl/anxtest.htm (March 1998).

Ten ways to reduce math anxiety.

1. Overcome your negative self-image about math.

2. Ask questions of your teachers, your friends, and seek outside assistance.

3. Math is a foreign language—practice it often.

4. Don't study mathematics by trying to memorize information and formulas.

5. READ your math textbook.

6. Study math according to your personal learning style.

7. Get help the same day you don't understand something.

8. Be relaxed and comfortable while studying math.

9. "TALK" mathematics. Discuss it with people in your class. Form a study group.

10. Develop a sense of responsibility for your own successes and failures.

Source: Freedman, Ellen (March 1997). *Ten Ways to Reduce Math Anxiety* [online]. Available: http://fc.whyy.org/CCC/algl/reduce.htm (March 1998).

cially often in tests involving quantitative thinking. Your best strategies include practice, using your resources, taking responsibility for your quantitative learning, and knowing your rights as a quantitative learner.

PRACTICE. The best way to overcome test-time anxiety is to practice quantitative thinking to increase your confidence. Keeping up with your homework, attending class, preparing well for tests, and doing extra problems will help you feel confident because they increase your familiarity with the material. Figure 9.2 shows additional ways to reduce math anxiety.

USE RESOURCES. Your school can help with math and science courses. Most schools have math or science learning labs, tutors, or computer programs that can help you practice difficult quantitative processes. You can visit your instructor during office hours or present a lab assistant or TA with your questions. Sometimes you will even have an extra review session set up by an instructor or TA so that students can ask questions before a major test. Don't hesitate to make the most of these helpful resources.

TAKE RESPONSIBILITY. Even though math anxiety is a real problem, students must take some responsibility for their responses to quantitative thinking. You can't change the math experiences you have had in the past, but you can make choices about how to respond to quantitative material from here on out. Some of your responsibilities as a quantitative thinker include:[3]

- to attend all classes and do homework
- to seek extra help when necessary, from an instructor, tutor, or fellow student

- to speak up in class when you have questions
- to be realistic about your abilities and to work to improve them
- to approach quantitative thinking with an open mind, not assuming the worst

KNOW YOUR RIGHTS. Finally, along with being a responsible student, you also have rights regarding your mathematical learning. These include:[4]

- the right to learn at your own pace
- the right to ask questions
- the right not to understand
- the right to be treated as a competent person
- the right to believe you are capable of thinking quantitatively

Beyond working to control your math anxiety, several other techniques will help you do your very best when you are tested on your math skills.

WHAT TECHNIQUES WILL IMPROVE YOUR PERFORMANCE ON MATH AND SCIENCE TESTS?

In addition to the general strategies for test taking that you have explored, here are several other techniques that can help you achieve better results on math and science exams.

READ THROUGH THE EXAM FIRST. When you first get an exam, read through every problem quickly. Make notes on how you might attempt to solve the problem, if something occurs to you immediately.

> **THEOREM**
>
> A formula or statement, often mathematical, proposed or accepted as a demonstrable truth.

ANALYZE PROBLEMS CAREFULLY. Categorize problems according to what type they are. Take all the "givens" into account, and write down any formulas, theorems, or definitions that apply before you begin your calculations. Focus on what you want to find or prove, and take your time—precision demands concentration. If some problems seem easier than others, do them first in order to boost your confidence.

ESTIMATE BEFORE YOU BEGIN TO COME UP WITH AN APPROXIMATE SOLUTION. Then, work the problem and check the solution against your guess. The two answers should be close. If they're not, recheck your calculations. You may have made a simple calculation error.

> **ESTIMATE**
>
> To calculate the approximate amount of; to make a rough or preliminary calculation.

BREAK THE CALCULATION INTO THE SMALLEST POSSIBLE PIECES. Go step-by-step and don't move on to the next step until you are clear about what you've done so far.

RECALL HOW YOU SOLVED SIMILAR PROBLEMS. Past experience can give you valuable clues to how a particular problem should be handled.

DRAW A PICTURE TO HELP YOU SEE THE PROBLEM. This can be a diagram, a chart, a probability tree, a geometric figure, or any other visual image that relates to the problem at hand.

BE NEAT. When it comes to numbers, mistaken identity can mean the difference between a right and a wrong answer. A 4 that looks like a 9, for example, can mean trouble.

USE THE OPPOSITE OPERATION TO CHECK YOUR WORK. When you come up with an answer, work backward to see if you are right. Use subtraction to check your addition; use division to check multiplication; and so on.

LOOK BACK AT THE QUESTIONS TO BE SURE YOU DID EVERYTHING THAT WAS ASKED. Did you answer every part of the question? Did you show all the required work? Be as complete as you possibly can.

All the strategies you are learning aren't just useful in your math and science classes. Many technology classes have a mathematical element that will require you to use your math knowledge. Beyond math strategy, you may want to have a few technology basics under your belt as you encounter an increasingly technological world.

WHAT BASICS SHOULD YOU KNOW ABOUT COMPUTERS?

The role of computers is becoming increasingly prevalent as time goes by. In almost every job, knowledge of basic computer use is a necessity. On campus, computer use is more and more widespread—and more and more crucial for academic success. "The computer has . . . become the portal through which students do everything they need to do on campus," says Lisa Guernsey in *The New York Times.* "Using the Internet they register for classes, turn in assignments, order books, browse the library catalog, listen to music, talk to friends, read the news, write papers, play games, pay bills, watch movies and carry on heated political discussions."[5]

The *Student Monitor* reports that, on average, students spend more than eight hours a week using their computers for school.[6] Although much of this time is spent writing, Internet usage comprises a large percentage of computer time. Instructors report that most courses require students to use the Internet in some way, whether to access a Web page where they can read the syllabus, research online for assignments, take interactive quizzes, or communicate with instructors and fellow students on topics pertinent to the course.[7]

These statistics demonstrate to you how important your command of basic computer use is now and will be in the future. Computer basics fall into four general categories: word processing, databases and spreadsheets, the Internet, and e-mail.

Word Processing

The ability to use a computer to write letters, papers, briefs, and so on is now a requirement at most institutes of higher learning. Many businesses also require the use of these skills. There are many word-processing soft-

Windows on the World
REAL LIFE STUDENT ISSUES

How can I improve my performance in the sciences?

Julie Wheeler, *University of Colorado at Denver, English Major*

Even though writing term papers is like second nature to me, I am not predisposed to doing well in the sciences. I remember having to struggle through high school chemistry class, where I sat every day watching other students taking down notes and nodding their heads in the receipt of newfound knowledge. I never quite understood the information that the professor scribbled on the board. The book was a little better, as I could read over it several times, but when tests came, it was obvious to me that I was missing the point. Unfortunately, my grades reflected my level of understanding, and I feel like the experience forever tainted my ability to comprehend science.

The university I attend requires me to take science classes to fulfill my general requirements, and I am dreading having to tackle these classes. When I look at my choices, I can only imagine what I will have to endure in each one. Biology and chemistry definitely seem over my head, and I don't know much about the others. The list spans from physics to geology, but I don't know how to decide which of these classes would be the lesser of the evils. How do I choose which science classes to take, and then make it through them so that I can graduate?

Jason Schierkolk, *Arapahoe Community College, Emergency Medical Science Major*

Doing well in the sciences can sometimes be difficult. Because my major is heavily weighted

on science, I have become very adept in the area. However, for students who are not in scientific majors, most universities and colleges offer classes that will fulfill your requirements without forcing you into something that you feel destined to fail. Some of these courses include geology, environmental science, and astronomy. They are still "scientific" in terms of concrete knowledge and even some formulas, but are not as technical as courses such as physics, chemistry, and biology. Also, there are sometimes courses that are offered specifically for non-scientific majors. They might be listed as "biology for non-majors," and so on.

In the event that you must take a science class without the slightest idea of how you will pass, one key to doing well in these courses is organization. Most professors will give you several formulas and processes to solve most of the problems you will face. Be sure to keep them organized and clearly marked for quick reference. Also, keeping a tape recorder with you in class will help if you need to go back to something you don't understand. Professors are almost always willing to help students who are having a hard time, especially if you show that you are willing to learn and are staying caught up in the reading. Come to them with specific problems or questions that they can help you to work through.

If you keep an open mind, you can likely do well in whatever you set your mind to, be it chemistry, physics, or any other wall you come up against. You will have to work hard—harder than you may have ever worked before—but you will find that the most helpful secret to these classes is giving it all you've got.

294

ware programs, and each has its own quirks. Two of the most commonly used are Microsoft Word and Word Perfect. Besides composing documents, features such as a spell check and a grammar checker are extremely useful.

Databases and Spreadsheets

The ability to organize and store large volumes of information and data has always been important in most businesses. The easiest way to do this is through the use of some type of computer software for managing databases and spreadsheets. Again, there are many software programs specifically designed to handle, organize, and analyze large volumes of information. Some of the more common programs are Lotus, Symphony, and Microsoft Excel. A knowledge of one or more of these is becoming increasingly beneficial for most careers in business and science, as well as for maintaining personal finance records on a home computer.

The Internet

The Internet, a large worldwide network of connected businesses, universities, governments, and people, is expanding continually. The ability to use the Internet allows you to access the world and communicate with others almost instantaneously. You can now do extensive research on any topic as well as buy, sell, and market products on the Internet. It will be hard to be well prepared for the workforce if you have no Internet experience. Refer to Chapter 7 for more information on researching on the Internet.

E-mail

The ability to send mail electronically is revolutionizing the way people communicate. The major advantage is the speed that electronic mail (e-mail) can be sent, received, and responded to. If your college has an e-mail system in place, you may be required to communicate with your instructor via e-mail, submit homework via e-mail, and even take exams via e-mail. To learn about e-mail, many schools offer some type of orientation. Every student who has access to e-mail should spend time becoming proficient in electronic communication.

The use of computers in composing letters, desktop publishing, maintaining databases, keeping spreadsheets, working on the Internet, communicating by e-mail, and numerous other tasks will make computer literacy a requirement in the job market. The more capable you are of learning and using various computer systems, the more employable you will be.

HOW CAN YOU "READ" VISUAL AIDS?

Whether they appear on a website, in a magazine article that your instructor photocopied for use in a course, or in the pages of a textbook, visual aids help to clarify quantitative concepts. Visual aids, including tables and charts, present statistical information in a visual format and thereby clarify the information for the reader. Often what doesn't "click" when read in text form will make sense when viewed in a table or chart. Because they usually involve quantitative information, tables and charts are commonly used to present mathematical and scientific concepts.

Visual aids highlight statistical comparisons that show the following:

- trends over time (e.g., the number of televisions per household in 1997 as compared to the number in 1957)
- relative rankings (e.g., the size of the advertising budgets of four major consumer products companies)
- distributions (e.g., students' performance on standardized tests by geographic area)
- cycles (e.g., the regular upward and downward movement of the nation's economy as defined by periods of prosperity and recession)

Tables and charts also summarize concepts that are presented in paragraph form. Knowing what to look for in visual aids will help you learn to "read" the information they present. The visuals in the following section are from actual textbooks published by Prentice Hall and others.

People seldom see the halting and painful steps by which the most insignificant success is achieved.

ANNIE SULLIVAN

Understanding Tables

The two basic types of tables are data tables and word tables. Data tables present numerical information—for example, the number of students taking a standardized test in 50 states. Word tables summarize and consolidate complex information, making it easier to study and evaluate. Look back at Table 6.1 on page 181 for an example of a word table. Table 9.2 is a model of a typical table, including the individual parts and their arrangement on the page.

TABLE 9.2 The parts and arrangements of a table.

TABLE NUMBER   TITLE OF TABLE

STUB HEAD	CAPTION		CAPTION		CAPTION	
	SUBCAPTION	SUBCAPTION	SUBCAPTION	SUBCAPTION	SUBCAPTION	SUBCAPTION
Stub	XXXX	XXXX	XXXX	XXXX	XXXX	XXXX
Stub	XXXX	XXXX[a]	XXXX	XXXX	XXXX	XXXX
Stub	XXXX	XXXX	XXXX	XXXX	XXXX	XXXX
Total	XXXX	XXXX	XXXX[b]	XXXX	XXXX	XXXX

[a]Footnote   [b]Footnote
Source:

Source: "The Parts and Arrangements of a Table" from *Business writing,* 2e by J. Harold Janis and Howard R. Dresner. Copyright © 1956, 1972 by J. Harold Janis. Reprinted by permission of HarperCollins Publishers, Inc.

- The table number identifies the table and is usually referred to in the text.
- The table title helps readers focus on the table's message.
- Captions, also known as column titles, identify the material that falls below them.
- Subcaptions divide the columns into smaller sections.
- The stubs refer to the captions running along the horizontal rows. The nature of the stubs is identified by the stub head.
- Footnotes are used to explain specific details in the table.
- The source acknowledges where the information comes from.

Understanding Charts

Charts, also known as graphs, present numerical data in visual form to show associations between the data. Types of charts include pie charts, bar charts, and line charts.

The pie chart is the most common and easy-to-understand visual aid. It presents data as wedge-shaped sections of a circle to show the relative size of each item as a percentage of the whole. For example, the pie chart in Figure 9.3 shows a projected breakdown of U.S. population in 2050.

Bar charts consist of horizontal bars of varying lengths and show the relative rankings of each bar. Whereas pie charts focus on the size of individual components as compared to the whole, bar charts demonstrate how items compare with one another. The bar chart in Figure 9.4 shows the number of multinational clients of five major advertising agencies. The information

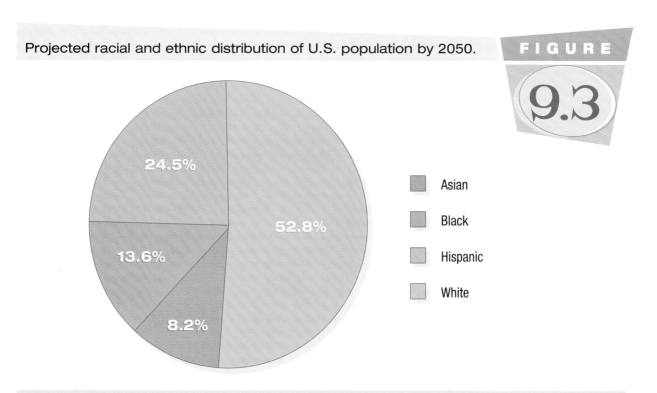

Projected racial and ethnic distribution of U.S. population by 2050.

FIGURE 9.3

- 24.5%
- 52.8%
- 13.6%
- 8.2%

Asian
Black
Hispanic
White

Source: U.S. Bureau of the Census.

9.4

Number of multinational clients of major advertising agencies.

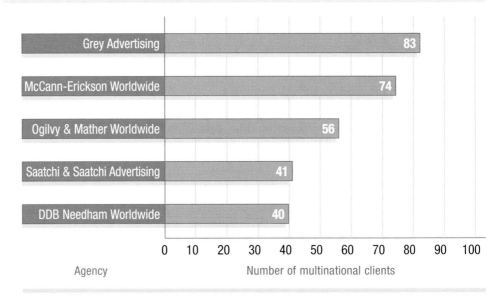

Source: Information courtesy of DDB Needham Worldwide.

presented from left to right is on the horizontal axis. The information presented from the top to the bottom is on the vertical axis. Here the horizontal axis shows the number of clients, and the vertical shows the agencies' names. Because the values of the horizontal bars are clear, no scale is needed (scales are used to clarify values).

Finally, the lines in line charts show continuous trends over time. The horizontal axis shows a span of time, and the vertical axis represents a specific measurement such as dollars or units of various kinds. The line chart in Figure 9.5 shows how the number of men and women earning bachelor's degrees has increased in the past 50 years.

9.5

Number of men and women earning bachelor's degrees.

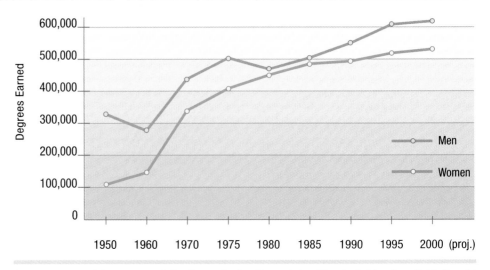

Source: Psychology, 2/e by Davis and Palladino © 1997. Reprinted by permission of Prentice Hall, Inc., Upper Saddle River, NJ.

Tables and charts help to make quantitative information comprehensible and appealing to the reader. They are valuable study aids that can add to your understanding of what you read.

al-Khowârizmî

Mohammed ibn Musa al-Khowârizmî was an Arabic astronomer who lived around 825. An 1857 Latin translation of a book no longer existing in the original begins "Spoken has Algoritmi. . ." Hence, his name had become Algoritmi, from which was derived the present word *algorithm*. An algorithm is a series of steps used to solve a particular problem in mathematics or the sciences. Many computer software programs are simply strings of algorithms used to do certain functions.

For those of you who don't know Arabic, this word may seem completely out of your realm of knowledge. Just as if you were to study Arabic or any other language, however, success in math boils down to steady work and focus. When you put your mind to it, you can become as fluent in math, science, and technology as you are in your native language.

IMPORTANT POINTS *to remember*

1. Why do you need to be able to think quantitatively?

Practical problems that come up from time to time, such as in personal finances or scheduling, require quantitative thinking. Many everyday tasks require skills such as arithmetic, algebra, geometry, and statistics. Most importantly, math is a problem-solving discipline; when you perform mathematical and scientific problem solving, you build critical-thinking skills that you can apply to any problem in school, work, or life.

2. How can you master math and science basics?

Mastering the basics involves classroom focus (being prepared and asking questions), textbook focus (taking careful notes, noting formulas, working problems), and studying and homework focus (doing as many problems as you can, even outside of assigned homework). Solve word problems (the most common problems) by following the four-step method: Understand the problem, name and explore potential solution paths, carry out your solution plan, and review your result. Other helpful word-problem strategies include looking for a pattern, making a table, drawing a diagram, working backwards, and examining a similar problem.

3. How can you overcome math anxiety?

Math anxiety is a high-stress feeling appearing in relation to quantitative thinking. It is often a result of common misconceptions such as the notion that you are born with or without an ability to do math. Strategies to overcome math anxiety include extensive practice, using human and text resources, taking responsibility for your quantitative learning, and knowing your rights as a quantitative learner.

4. What techniques will improve your performance on math and science tests?

General test-taking strategies certainly apply. In addition, you may want to analyze problems carefully, estimate before beginning a problem, break a calculation into the smallest possible pieces, recall how you solved similar problems, draw a picture to help you see a problem, use an opposite operation to check your work, write neatly, and make sure you did everything a question asks.

5. What basics should you know about computers?

Almost every student and employee needs some basic computer knowledge in today's technology-driven world. You will benefit from knowledge in word processing (creating documents on the computer), databases and spreadsheets (storing and organizing large volumes of information and data), the Internet (navigating this worldwide network of businesses, universities, governments, and people), and e-mail (communicating to others through typed notes transmitted electronically).

6. How can you "read" visual aids?

Visual aids, including tables and charts, highlight statistical comparisons (including trends over time, relative rankings, distributions, and cycles) and summarize information. Learning to read visual aids depends on understanding their value as learning tools and on learning how tables and charts are constructed and the messages they convey.

CRITICAL THINKING

APPLYING LEARNING TO LIFE

PROBLEM STRATEGIES AND REACTIONS. Using a math or science book, copy down two questions from the text. For each question, name a problem-solving strategy or strategies from this chapter that will help you solve the problem. Solve the problem on a separate piece of paper. Afterwards, state here why you chose the strategies you did. Are there other ways to solve the same problem?

Problem 1:

_____

_____

Strategies:

_____

_____

_____

Problem 2:

_____

_____

Strategies:

_____

_____

_____

  Think about how doing these problems, and working on other math and science problems, makes you feel. Evaluate your level of math anxiety by responding to the following statements as accurately as possible.

1. When I make an error on a math problem, I

2. When I'm unable to solve a particular problem, I

3. If I were able to do mathematics, I would

4. When I'm able to solve a problem that was difficult, I feel

5. One thing I enjoy about doing math is

6. Working on mathematics makes me feel

TEAMWORK
COMBINING FORCES

THE STUDY GROUP APPROACH TO QUANTITATIVE LEARNING. Choose one or two people from one of your math or science classes—fellow students with whom you feel comfortable working. Use problems from your assigned text.

1. *Choose one problem.* Each of you work on the same problem separately. After finishing the problem, come together to share your methods of solution. Discuss how each of you approached the problem. What steps did you each take in solving the problem? What strategies did you use? How did you check to see if your procedures were correct?

2. *Now pick a different problem on which to work together.* After solving this problem, discuss how you went through the problem-solving process. Did you learn more or less by working together as compared to working separately? Were you able to solve the problem faster by working together than you did when you worked alone? Did you gain a better understanding of the problem by working together?

3. *Generalize your experiences to discuss attitudes about math and science.* What do each of you do to overcome challenges? What positive steps do you each take in problem solving?

WRITING

DISCOVERY THROUGH JOURNALING

To record your thoughts, use a separate journal or the lined page at the end of the chapter.

PAST EXPERIENCES. Reflect on your experiences as a high school student in math or science. What attitudes toward quantitative learning did you form at that time and why? Have these attitudes helped or hurt you? If your experiences have produced problematic attitudes and perspectives, describe what you plan to do to counteract them.

CAREER PORTFOLIO

CHARTING YOUR COURSE

QUANTITATIVE LEARNING IN THE WORKING WORLD. Consider your possible choice of a major or career. What mathematics or science will you need to achieve your goals? Did your feelings and experiences in math or science affect your choice of major or career? If so, in what ways?

Interview several people, including an instructor, about your choice of major or career. Ask them these questions (and any others you may think of):

- How much math and science are needed, and why, for this major or career?
- Did you choose it based on the level of math or science necessary?
- Now that you are in this field, is the amount of math or science and problem-solving skills more or less than you expected?
- What types of problem-solving skills are needed?

In addition, investigate this major or career by looking at the course catalog to see what math and science are needed, and, if you have access, search out information about your major or career choice on the Internet.

After completing your investigation, write a short essay reflecting on the roles math, science, and problem solving have in your choice of a major or career.

 # UGGESTED READINGS

Gralla, Preston, Sarah Ishida (Illustrator), Mina Reimer (Illustrator), and Steph Adams. *How the Internet Works: Millennium Edition.* Indianapolis, IN: Que (1999).

Hart, Lynn and Deborah Najee-Ullich. *Studying for Mathematics.* New York: HarperCollins College Publishers (1997).

Lerner, Marcia. *Math Smart: Essential Math for These Numeric Times.* New York: Villard Books (1995).

Levine, John R., Carol Baroudi, and Margaret Levine Young. *The Internet for Dummies.* New York: Hungry Minds, Inc. (2000).

Maran, Ruth. *Teach Yourself Computers and the Internet Visually.* New York: Hungry Minds, Inc. (1998).

Polya, George. *How to Solve It.* London: Penguin (1990).

White, Ron, Timothy Downs (Illustrator), and Stephen Adams (Illustrator). *How Computers Work,* 5th ed. Indianapolis, IN: Que (1999).

 INTERNET RESOURCES

Algebra Online: www.algebra-online.com

Professor Freedman's Math Help: www.mathpower.com

Math.com—The World of Math Online: www.math.com

Math Homework Help: http://erols.com/bram/column2.html

 ENDNOTES

1. George Polya. *How to Solve It.* London: Penguin (1990).

2. Rick Billstein, Shlomo Libeskind, and Johnny W. Lott. *A Problem Solving Approach to Mathematics for Elementary School Teachers.* Reading MA: Addison-Wesley Longman (1993), pp. 5–36.

3. Adapted from Acker, Kathy (March 1997). *Math Anxiety Code of Responsibilities* [online]. Available: http://fc.whyy.org/CCC/alg1/code.htm (March 1998).

4. Sheila Tobias. *Overcoming Math Anxiety.* New York: W.W. Norton & Company (1993), pp. 226–227.

5. Lisa Guernsey. "For the New College B.M.O.C., 'M' Is for 'Machine,'" *New York Times,* August 10, 2000, p. G7.

6. Ibid.

7. Ibid.

Journal

NAME

DATE

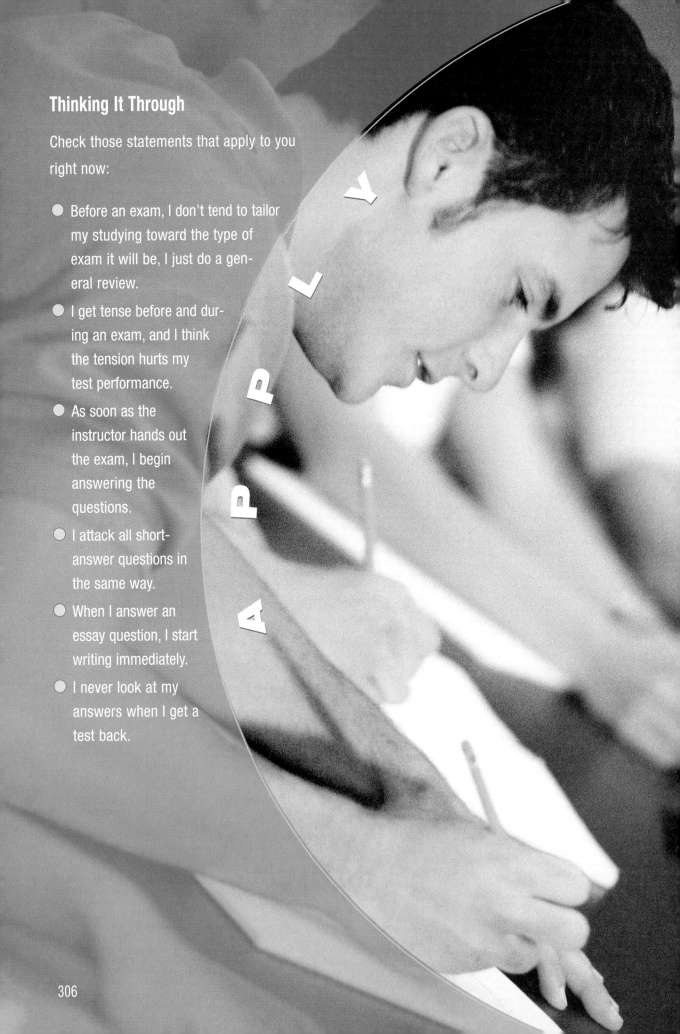

Thinking It Through

Check those statements that apply to you right now:

- Before an exam, I don't tend to tailor my studying toward the type of exam it will be, I just do a general review.

- I get tense before and during an exam, and I think the tension hurts my test performance.

- As soon as the instructor hands out the exam, I begin answering the questions.

- I attack all short-answer questions in the same way.

- When I answer an essay question, I start writing immediately.

- I never look at my answers when I get a test back.

10

you will explore answers to the following
questions:

- How can preparation help improve test scores?
- How can you work through test anxiety?
- What general strategies can help you succeed on tests?
- How can you master different types of test questions?
- How can you learn from test mistakes?

Test Taking

For a runner, a race is the equivalent of a test because it measures ability at a given moment. Doing well in a race requires training, which is similar to the studying you do to master material for exams. The best runners—and test takers—understand that they train not just for the race—or test—but to achieve a level of competence that will stay with them for as long as they need it. Runners are trying to condition their bodies so that exercise can be part of their daily routine. Similarly, test takers are trying to master material they may use in their college and graduate courses, in their careers, and to enrich their lives.

Knowing that you will continue to use the skills on which you are being tested will give you the perspective that *owning* these skills is more important than achieving a perfect score. This is the beginning of the positive attitude that you need to do well on exams and to retain what you learn.

Testing is part of education, even though few students look forward to it. See your exams as preparation for life. When you get a job, act as a volunteer, or even work through your family budget, you'll have to apply what you know and put your skills into action—exactly what you do when you take a test.

SHOWING WHAT YOU KNOW

HOW CAN PREPARATION HELP IMPROVE TEST SCORES?

Test taking involves more than showing up on time with a pencil in hand. It's about preparation, endurance, and strategy. It's also about conquering fears, paying attention to details, and learning from mistakes. Like a runner who prepares for a marathon by exercising, eating right, taking practice runs, and getting enough sleep, you can take steps to master your exams. The primary step, occupying much of your preparation time, is to listen when material is presented, read carefully, and study until you know the material that will be on the test (Chapter 5 examines the art of effective studying). In this sense, staying on top of your class meetings, readings, and assignments over the course of the semester is one of the best ways to prepare yourself for tests. Other important steps are the preparation strategies that follow.

Identify Test Type and Material Covered

Before you begin studying, find out as much as you can about the type of test you will be taking and what it will cover. Try to identify:

- The type of questions on the test—objective (multiple choice, true/false, sentence completion), subjective (essay), or a combination.
- What topics the test will cover. (Will it cover everything since the semester began, or will it be limited to a narrower topic?)
- What material you will be tested on. (Will the test cover only what you learned in class and in the text, or will it also cover outside readings?)

Your instructors may answer these questions for you. Even though they may not reveal specific test questions, they might let you know the question format or information covered. Some instructors may even drop hints throughout the semester about possible test questions, either directly ("I might ask a question on this subject on your next exam") or more subtly ("One of my favorite theories is. . .").

Here are a few other strategies for predicting what may be on a test.

USE SQ3R TO IDENTIFY IMPORTANT IDEAS AND FACTS. Often, the questions you write and ask yourself when you read assigned materials may be part of the test. Textbook study questions are also good candidates.

TALK TO PEOPLE WHO TOOK THE COURSE OR TEST BEFORE. Try to find out how difficult the tests are, whether they focus more on assigned readings or notes, what materials are usually covered, and what types of questions are used. Ask also about instructors' preferences. If you learn that the instructor pays close attention to factual accuracy, for example, make up flash cards and drill yourself on major and minor facts. If she especially appreciates neatness, writing carefully and cleanly will make an impression.

EXAMINE OLD TESTS IF INSTRUCTORS MAKE THEM AVAILABLE IN CLASS OR ON RESERVE IN THE LIBRARY. Old tests help to answer the following questions:

- Does the instructor focus on examples and details, general ideas and themes, or a combination?

- Can you do well through straight memorization or does the material require critical thinking?
- Are the questions straightforward or confusing and sometimes tricky?
- Do the tests require the integration of facts from different areas to draw conclusions?

If you can't get copies of old tests and your instructor doesn't give too many details about the test, use clues from the class to predict test questions. After taking the first exam in the course, you will have more information about what to expect in the future.

Choose Study Materials

Once you have identified as much as you can about the subject matter of the test, choose the materials that contain the information you need to study. Save time by making sure that you aren't studying anything you don't need to. Go through your notes, your texts, related primary source materials, and any handouts; then, set aside any materials you don't need.

> *The secret of a leader lies in the tests he has faced over the whole course of his life and the habit of action he develops in meeting those tests.*
>
> **GAIL SHEEHY**

Create an Organized Study Plan and Schedule

Use your time-management skills to set a schedule that will help you feel as prepared as you can be. Consider all the relevant factors—the materials you need to study, how many days or weeks until the test date, and how much time you can study each day. If you establish your schedule ahead of time and write it in your date book, you will be much more likely to follow it.

Schedules vary widely according to situation. For example, if you have three days before the test and no other obligations during that time, you might set two 2-hour study sessions during each day. On the other hand, if you have two weeks before a test, classes during the day, and work three nights a week, you might spread out your study sessions over the nights you have off during those two weeks.

A checklist, like the one in Figure 10.1, will help you get organized and stay on track as you prepare for each test. Use a checklist like this to assign specific tasks to particular study times and sessions. That way, not only will you know when you have time to study, but you will also have defined your goals for that study session.

Prepare Through Careful Review

Thorough review of your materials will give you the best shot at remembering their contents. Use the following strategies when you study.

USE SQ3R. The reading method you studied in Chapter 5 provides an excellent structure for reviewing your reading materials.

- *Surveying* will give you an overview of topics.

10.1 Pretest checklist.

Course: _____   Teacher: _____

Date, time, and place of test: _____

Type of test (e.g., Is it a midterm or a minor quiz?): _____

What the instructor has told you about the test, including the types of test questions, the length of the test, and how much the test counts toward your final grade: _____

_____

_____

_____

Topics to be covered on the test in order of importance:

1. _____
2. _____
3. _____
4. _____
5. _____

Study schedule, including materials you plan to study (e.g., texts and class notes) and dates you plan to complete each:

MATERIAL   DATE OF COMPLETION

1. _____
2. _____
3. _____
4. _____
5. _____

Materials you are expected to bring to the test (e.g., your textbook, a sourcebook, a calculator): _____

_____

Special study arrangements (e.g., plan study group meetings, ask the instructor for special help, get outside tutoring): _____

_____

_____

Life-management issues (e.g., make child-care arrangements, rearrange work hours): _____

_____

_____

Source: Adapted from *Ace Any Test,* 3rd ed., Ron Fry, (Franklin Lakes, NJ: Career Press), pp. 123–124.

- *Questioning* will help you focus on important ideas and determine what the material is trying to communicate.
- *Reading* (or, in this case, rereading) will remind you of the ideas and supporting information.
- *Reciting* will help to anchor the concepts in your head.
- *Review* tasks such as quizzing yourself on the Q stage questions, summarizing sections you have highlighted, making flash cards for important concepts, and constructing a chapter outline will help you solidify your learning so that you will be able to use it at test time and beyond.

REVIEW YOUR NOTES. Recall the section in Chapter 7 on note taking for making your notes a valuable after-class reference. Use the following techniques to effectively review notes:

- *Time your reviews carefully.* Review notes for the first time within a day of the lecture, if you can, and then review again closer to the test day.
- *Mark up your notes.* Reread them, filling in missing information, clarifying points, writing out abbreviations, and highlighting key ideas.
- *Organize your notes.* Consider adding headings and subheadings to your notes to clarify the structure of the information. Rewrite them using a different organizing structure—a think link if you have originally written them in longhand, for example, or an outline if you originally used a think link.
- *Summarize your notes.* Evaluate which ideas and examples are most crucial, and then rewrite your notes in shortened form, focusing on those ideas and examples. Summarize your notes in writing or with a summary think link. Try summarizing from memory as a self-test.

THINK CRITICALLY. Using the techniques from Chapter 4, approach your test preparation as an active, critical thinker, working to understand material rather than just to repeat facts. As you study, try to connect ideas to examples, analyze causes and effects, establish truths, and look at issues from different perspectives.

Those who grade your tests often look for evidence that you can link seemingly unrelated ideas into logical patterns. As you study, try to explore concepts from different perspectives and connect ideas and examples that, on the surface, appear to be unrelated. Although you'll probably find answers to these questions in your text or class notes, you may have to work at putting different ideas together. Critical thinking takes work but may promote a greater understanding of the subject and probably a higher grade on the exam.

Critical thinking is especially important for essay tests that ask you to develop and support a thesis. Prepare by identifying three or four potential essay questions and write out your responses.

Take a Pretest

Use questions from your textbook to create your own pretest. Most textbooks, although not all, will include such questions at the end of the chapters. If your course doesn't have an assigned text, develop questions from your notes and from assigned outside readings. Choose questions that are likely to be covered on the test, then answer them under test-like conditions—in quiet, with no books or notes to help you (unless your exam is open book), and with a clock telling you when to quit. Try to come as close as you can to duplicating the actual test situation.

Prepare Physically

When taking a test, you often need to work efficiently under time pressure. If your body is tired or under stress, you might not think as clearly or perform as well as you usually do. If you can, avoid staying up all night. Get some sleep so that you can wake up rested and alert. Remember that adequate sleep can help cement your memories by reducing interference from new memories (see Chapter 6). If you tend to press the snooze button in your sleep, try setting two alarm clocks and placing them across the room from your bed.

Eating right is also important. Sugar-laden snacks will bring up your energy, only to send you crashing back down much too soon. Also, too much caffeine can add to your tension and make it difficult to focus. Eating nothing will leave you drained, but too much food can make you sleepy. The best advice is to eat a light, well-balanced meal before a test. When time is short, grab a quick-energy snack such as a banana, orange juice, or a granola bar.

Make the Most of Last-Minute Studying

CRAMMING

Hasty, last-minute preparing for an examination.

Cramming often results in information going into your head and popping right back out shortly after. Study conditions, however, aren't always ideal. Sometimes a busy week may leave you only a few hours to prepare for a big exam. Nearly every student crams sometime during college. If you have a tight schedule, use these hints to make the most of your study time:

- *Go through your flash cards,* if you have them, one last time.
- *Focus on crucial concepts;* don't worry about the rest. Resist going through your notes or textbook page by page.
- *Create a last-minute study sheet.* On a single sheet of paper, write down key facts, definitions, formulas, and so on. Try to keep the material short and simple. If you prefer visual notes, use think links to map out ideas and their supporting examples.
- *Arrive early.* Study the sheet or your flash cards until you are asked to clear your desk.
- *While it is still fresh in your mind, record any helpful information on a piece of scrap paper.* Do this before looking at any test questions. Review this information as needed during the test.

After your exam, evaluate the effects cramming had on your learning. Even if you passed, you might remember very little of the material. This low level of retention won't do you much good in the real world where you have to actually make use of information instead of just recalling it for a test. Think about how you can plan strategically to start earlier and improve the situation next time.

Whether you have to cram or not, you may experience anxiety on test day. Following are some ideas for how to handle test anxiety when it strikes.

OW CAN YOU WORK THROUGH TEST ANXIETY?

A certain amount of stress can be a good thing. Your body is alert, and your energy motivates you to do your best. For some students, however, the time before and during an exam can be miserable. Many students have experienced some level of **test anxiety** at some time during their studies. Test anxiety can also cause physical symptoms such as sweating, nausea, dizziness, headaches, and extreme fatigue. Work through test anxiety by dealing with its two primary aspects: preparation and attitude.

> **TEST ANXIETY**
>
> A bad case of nerves that makes it hard to think or remember during an exam.

Preparation

Preparation is the basic defense against anxiety. The more confident you feel about your knowledge of the material, the more you'll feel able to perform on test day. In this way, you can consider all of the preparation and study information in this chapter as test anxiety assistance. Also, finding out what to expect on the exam will help you feel more in control. Seek out information about what material will be covered, the question format, the length of the exam, and the points assigned to each question.

Making and following a detailed study plan will help you build the kind of knowledge that can help you fight off anxiety. Divide the plan into a series of small tasks. As you finish each one, you will build your sense of accomplishment, confidence, and control.

Preparation is all about action. Instead of sitting and worrying about the test, put your energy toward concrete, active steps that will help you succeed.

Attitude

Although good preparation will help build your confidence, maintaining a positive *attitude* toward testing is as important as studying. Here are some key ways to maintain an attitude that will help you.

SEE THE TEST AS AN OPPORTUNITY TO LEARN. Sometimes students see a test as an opportunity to fail. Turn this around by focusing on learning. Begin to think of a test as an opportunity to show what you have learned, as well as to learn something new about the material and about test taking itself.

SEE THE TEST AS A SIGNPOST. It's easy to see a test as a contest to be won or lost. If you pass, or "win" the contest, you might feel no need to retain what you've learned. If you fail, or "lose" the contest, you might feel no need to try again. However, if you see the test as a signpost along the way to a greater goal, you may be more likely to try your best, learn from the experience, and move on. A test is only a small part of your life, and your grade does not reflect your ability to succeed.

GIVE YOUR INSTRUCTOR A POSITIVE ROLE. Your instructors don't want to make you miserable. They test you to give you an opportunity to grow and to demonstrate what you have accomplished. They test you so that, in rising to this challenge, you will become better prepared for the challenges outside of school. Don't hesitate to engage your instructors in your quest to learn and succeed—go to their office hours and take the time to clarify material and issues with them before tests.

SEEK STUDY PARTNERS WHO CHALLENGE YOU. Your anxiety may get worse if you study with someone who feels just as anxious and unprepared as you do. Find someone who can inspire you to do your best. For more on how to study effectively with others in study groups, see Chapter 5.

SET YOURSELF UP FOR SUCCESS. Try not to expect failure before you even start. Expect progress of yourself. Take responsibility for creating a setting for success through your preparation and attitude. Know that you are ultimately responsible for the outcome.

PRACTICE RELAXATION. When you feel test anxiety coming on, take some deep breaths, close your eyes, and visualize positive mental images related to the test, such as getting a good grade and finishing confidently, with time to spare. Do whatever you have to do to ease muscle tension—stretch your neck; tighten and then release your muscles; even take a trip to the rest room to do a couple of forward bends.

These strategies will help in most every test anxiety situation. Students returning to college later in life, however, may have issues surrounding test taking that require particular attention.

Test Anxiety and the Returning Student

If you're returning to school after 5, 10, or even 20 years, you may wonder if you can compete with younger students or if your mind is still able to learn new material. To counteract these feelings of inadequacy, focus on how your life experiences have given you useful skills. For example, managing work and a family requires strong time-management, planning, and communication skills that can help you plan your study time, juggle school responsibilities, and interact with students and instructors.

Fear is nature's warning sign to get busy.

HENRY C. LINK

In addition, life experiences give you examples through which you can understand ideas in your courses. For example, your relationship experiences may help you understand psychology concepts, managing your finances may help you understand economics or accounting practices, and work may give you a context for what you learn in a business management course. If you let yourself feel positive about your knowledge and skills, you may improve your ability to achieve your goals.

Parents who have to juggle child care with study time can find the challenge especially difficult before a test. Here are some suggestions that might help:

TELL YOUR CHILDREN WHY THIS TEST IS IMPORTANT. Discuss the situation in concrete terms that they can understand. For example, a better education and job for you might mean for them a better home, more money to plan outings and vacations, more time to spend as a family, and a happier parent (you).

EXPLAIN THE TIME FRAME. Tell them your study schedule and when the test will occur. Plan a reward after your test—going for ice cream, seeing a movie, or having a picnic.

KEEP CHILDREN ACTIVE WHILE YOU STUDY. Stock up on games, books, and videos. If a child is old enough, have him invite a friend to play.

FIND HELP. Ask a relative or friend to watch the children during study time, or arrange for your child to visit a friend. Consider trading baby-sitting hours with another parent, hiring a baby-sitter who will come to your home, or enrolling your child in a day-care center.

When you have prepared by using the strategies that work for you, you are ready to take your exam. Now you can focus on methods to help you succeed when the test begins.

WHAT GENERAL STRATEGIES CAN HELP YOU SUCCEED ON TESTS?

Even though every test is different, there are general strategies that will help you handle almost all tests, including short-answer and essay exams.

Write Down Key Facts

Before you even look at the test, write down any key information—including formulas, rules, and definitions—that you studied recently or even just before you entered the test room. Use the back of the question sheet or a piece of scrap paper for your notes (be sure it is clear to your instructor that this scrap paper didn't come into the test room already filled in). Recording this information right at the start will make forgetting less likely.

Begin with an Overview of the Exam

Although exam time is precious, spend a few minutes at the start of the test to get a sense of the kinds of questions you'll be answering, what type of thinking they require, the number of questions in each section, and their point values. Use this information to schedule your time. For example, if a two-hour test is divided into two sections of equal point value—an essay section with four questions and a short-answer section with 60 questions—you can spend an hour on the essays (15 minutes per question) and an hour on the short-answer section (one minute per question).

As you make your calculations, think about the level of difficulty of each section. If you think you can handle the short-answer questions in less than an hour and that you'll need more time for the essays, rebudget your time in that way.

Read Test Directions

Although it seems obvious, reading test directions carefully can save you trouble. For example, although a history test of 100 true-or-false questions and one essay may look straightforward, the directions may tell you to answer 80 of the 100 questions or that the essay is an optional bonus. If the directions indicate that you are penalized for incorrect answers—meaning that you will lose points instead of simply not gaining points—avoid guessing unless you're fairly certain. These questions may do damage, for example, if you earn two points for every correct answer and lose one point for every incorrect answer.

When you read directions, you may learn that some questions or sections are **weighted** more heavily than others. For example, the short-answer questions on a test may be worth 30 points, whereas the essays are worth 70. In this case, it's smart to spend more time on the essays than on the short answers. To stay aware of the specifics of the directions, circle or underline key words and numbers.

> **WEIGHTED**
>
> Given a higher or lower point value.

Work from Easy to Hard

Begin with the parts or questions that seem easiest to you. One advantage of this strategy is that you will tend to take less time to answer the questions you know well, leaving more time to spend on the questions that may require increased effort and thinking. If you like to work through questions in order, mark difficult questions as you reach them and return to them after you answer the questions you know.

Another advantage of answering easier questions first is that knowing the answers can boost your confidence, helping you to continue to believe in yourself when you work on more difficult sections.

Watch the Clock

Keep track of how much time is left and how you are progressing. You may want to plan your time on a piece of scrap paper, especially if you have one or more essays to write. Wear a watch or bring a small clock with you to the test room. A wall clock may be broken, or there may be no clock at all.

Some students are so concerned about time that they rush through the test and have time left over. In such situations, it's easy to leave early. The best move, however, is to take your time. Stay until the end so that you can refine and check your work; it couldn't hurt, and it might help.

Master the Art of Intelligent Guessing

When you are unsure of an answer on a short-answer test, you can leave it blank or you can guess. In most cases, provided that you are not penalized for incorrect answers, guessing will help you. "Intelligent guessing," writes Steven Frank, an authority on student studying and test taking, "means taking advantage of what you do know in order to try to figure out what you don't. If you guess intelligently, you have a decent shot at getting the answer right."[1]

First, eliminate all the answers you know—or believe—are wrong. Try to narrow your choices to two possible answers; then choose the one you think is more likely to be correct. Strategies for guessing the correct answer in a multiple-choice test will be discussed later in the chapter.

When you check your work at the end of the test, ask yourself whether you would make the same guesses again. Chances are that you will leave your answers alone, but you may notice something that will make you change your mind—a qualifier that affects meaning, a remembered fact that will enable you to answer the question without guessing, or a miscalculated step in a math problem.

Follow Directions on Machine-Scored Tests

Machine-scored tests require that you use a special pencil to fill in a small box on a computerized answer sheet. When the computer scans the sheet, it can tell whether you answered the questions correctly.

Taking these tests requires special care. Use the right pencil (usually a number 2) and mark your answer in the correct space. Periodically, check the answer number against the question number to make sure they match. If you mark the answer to question 4 in the space for question 5, not only will you get question 4 wrong, but also your responses for every question that follows will be off by a line. One way to avoid getting off track is to put a small dot next to any number you skip and plan to return to later on.

Neatness counts on these tests because the computer can misread stray pencil marks or partially erased answers. If you mark two answers to a question and only partially erase one, the computer will read both responses and charge you with a wrong answer. Completely fill each answer space and avoid any other pencil marks that could be misinterpreted by the computer.

Use Critical Thinking to Avoid Errors

Critical thinking can help you work through each question thoroughly and avoid errors. Following are some critical-thinking strategies to use during a test.

RECALL FACTS, PROCEDURES, RULES, AND FORMULAS. Base your answers on the information you recall. Think carefully to make sure you recall it accurately.

THINK ABOUT SIMILARITIES. If you don't know how to attack a question or problem, consider any similar questions or problems that you have worked on in class or while studying.

NOTICE DIFFERENCES. Especially with objective questions, items that seem different from that material you have studied may indicate answers you can eliminate.

THINK THROUGH CAUSES AND EFFECTS. For a numerical problem, think about how you plan to solve it and see if the answer—the effect of your plan—

makes sense. For an essay question that asks you to analyze a condition or situation, consider both what caused it and what effects it has.

 FIND THE BEST IDEA TO MATCH TO THE EXAMPLE OR EXAMPLES GIVEN. For a numerical problem, decide what formula (idea) best applies to the example or examples (the data of the problem). For an essay question, decide what idea applies to, or links, the examples given.

 SUPPORT IDEAS WITH EXAMPLES. When you put forth an idea in an answer to an essay question, be sure to back up your idea with an adequate number of examples that fit.

Evaluate each test question. In your initial approach to any question, decide what kinds of thinking will best help you solve it. For example, essay questions often require cause-and-effect and idea-to-example thinking, whereas objective questions often benefit from thinking about similarities and differences.

The general strategies you have explored also can help you to address specific types of test questions.

Using a separate sheet of paper, complete the following.

Thinking Back

1. List three questions you can ask that will help predict test content.

2. Describe two strategies that can help you identify the material covered on a test.

3. Explain the two primary factors in combating text anxiety.

4. List the steps to take to get an overview of an exam before you begin answering questions.

5. Name three ways you can use critical thinking to avoid common test errors.

Thinking Ahead

1. Consider how you do on short-answer tests that include multiple-choice, true-or-false, matching, or fill-in-the-blank questions. What are your favorite kinds of short-answer questions? Which kinds do you tend to make mistakes on, and why do you think this happens?

2. Describe how you generally handle essay questions. Do you plan your answers by using an outline or think link, or do you write the first thing that comes to your mind?

3. Would you ever consider retaking a test if an improved grade would not count? Why or why not?

HOW CAN YOU MASTER DIFFERENT TYPES OF TEST QUESTIONS?

Although the goal of all test questions is to discover how much you know about a subject, every type of question has a different way of doing so. Answering different types of questions is part science and part art. The strategy changes according to whether the question is objective or subjective.

For **objective questions**, you choose or write a short answer you believe is correct, often making a selection from a limited number of choices. Multiple-choice, fill-in-the-blank, and true-or-false questions fall into this category. **Subjective questions** demand the same information recall as objective questions, but they also require you to plan, organize, draft, and refine a written response. They may also require more extensive critical thinking and evaluation. All essay questions are subjective. Although some guidelines will help you choose the right answers to both types of questions, part of the skill is learning to "feel" your way to an answer that works.

OBJECTIVE QUESTIONS

Short-answer questions that test your ability to recall, compare, and contrast information and link ideas to examples.

SUBJECTIVE QUESTIONS

Essay questions that require you to express your answer in terms of your own personal knowledge and perspective.

Multiple-Choice Questions

Multiple-choice questions are the most popular type of question on standardized tests. The following strategies can help you answer them.

CAREFULLY READ THE DIRECTIONS. In the rush to get to work on a question it is easy to read directions too quickly or to skip them. Directions, however, can be tricky. For example, whereas most test items ask for a single correct answer, some give you the option of marking several choices that are correct. For some tests, you might be required to answer only a certain number of the questions.

READ EACH QUESTION THOROUGHLY BEFORE LOOKING AT THE CHOICES. Then, try to answer the question. This strategy will reduce the possibility that the choices will confuse you.

UNDERLINE KEY WORDS AND PHRASES IN THE QUESTION. If the question is complicated, try to break it down into small sections that are easy to understand.

PAY SPECIAL ATTENTION TO WORDS THAT COULD THROW YOU OFF. For example, it is easy to overlook negatives in a question ("Which of the following is *not...*").

IF YOU DON'T KNOW THE ANSWER, ELIMINATE THOSE ANSWERS THAT YOU KNOW OR SUSPECT ARE WRONG. Your goal is to leave yourself with two possible answers, which would give you a 50–50 chance of making the right choice. The following are questions you can ask as you eliminate choices:

- Is the choice accurate in its own terms? If there's an error in the choice—for example, a term that is incorrectly defined—the answer is wrong.
- Is the choice relevant? An answer may be accurate, but it may not relate to the essence of the question.

- Are there any qualifiers? Absolute qualifiers like *always, never, all, none,* or *every* often signal an exception that makes a choice incorrect. For example, the statement that "normal children always begin talking before the age of two" is an untrue statement (most normal children begin talking before age two, but some start later). Analysis has shown that choices containing conservative qualifiers (*often, most, rarely,* or *may sometimes be*) are often correct.

- Do the choices give clues? Does a puzzling word remind you of a word you know? If you don't know a word, does any part of the word—its prefix, suffix, or root—seem familiar? (See Chapter 5 for information on the meanings of common prefixes, suffixes, and roots.)

LOOK FOR PATTERNS THAT MAY LEAD TO THE RIGHT ANSWER; THEN MAKE AN EDUCATED GUESS. The ideal is to know the material so well that you don't have to guess, but that isn't always possible. Test-taking experts have found patterns in multiple-choice questions that may help you. Here is their advice:

- Consider the possibility that a choice that is *more general* than the others is the right answer.

- Consider the possibility that a choice that is *longer* than the others is the right answer.

- Look for a choice that has a middle value in a range (the range can be from small to large or from old to recent). It is likely to be the right answer.

- Look for two choices that have similar meanings. One of these answers is probably correct.

- Look for answers that agree grammatically with the question. For example, a fill-in-the-blank question that has an *a* or *an* before the blank gives you a clue to the correct answer.

MAKE SURE YOU READ EVERY WORD OF EVERY ANSWER. Instructors have been known to include answers that are almost right, except for a single word. Focus especially on qualifying words such as *always, never, tend to, most often,* and *frequently.*

WHEN QUESTIONS ARE KEYED TO A LONG READING PASSAGE, READ THE QUESTIONS FIRST. This will help you, when you read the passage, to focus on the information you need to answer the questions.

On the following page are some examples of the kinds of multiple-choice questions you might encounter in an Introduction to Psychology course[2] (the correct answer follows each question).

True-or-False Questions

True-or-false questions test your knowledge of facts and concepts. Read them carefully to evaluate what they truly say. If you're stumped, guess (unless you're penalized for wrong answers).

Look for qualifiers in true-or-false questions—such as *all, only,* and *always* (the absolutes that often make a statement false) and *generally, often, usually,* and *sometimes* (the conservatives that often make a statement

1. Arnold is at the company party and has had too much to drink. He releases all of his pent-up aggression by yelling at his boss, who promptly fires him. Arnold normally would not have yelled at his boss, but after drinking heavily he yelled because _____.

   A. parties are places where employees are supposed to be able to "loosen up"

   B. alcohol is a stimulant

   C. alcohol makes people less concerned with the negative consequences of their behavior

   D. alcohol inhibits brain centers that control the perception of loudness

(The correct answer is C)

2. Which of the following has not been shown to be a probable cause of or influence in the development of alcoholism in our society?

   A. intelligence   C. personality

   B. culture   D. genetic vulnerability

(The correct answer is A)

3. Geraldine is a heavy coffee drinker who has become addicted to caffeine. If she completely ceases her intake of caffeine over the next few days, she is likely to experience each of the following EXCEPT _____.

   A. depression   C. insomnia

   B. lethargy   D. headaches

(The correct answer is C)

true)—that can turn a statement that would otherwise be true into one that is false or vice versa. For example, "The grammar rule 'I before E except after C' is always true" is false, whereas "The grammar rule 'I before E except after C' is usually true" is true. The qualifier makes the difference.

Here are some examples of the kinds of true-or-false questions you might encounter in an Introduction to Psychology course. The correct answer follows each question:

Are the following questions true or false?	
1. Alcohol use is clearly related to increases in hostility, aggression, violence, and abusive behavior.	(True)
2. Marijuana is harmless.	(False)
3. Simply expecting a drug to produce an effect is often enough to produce the effect.	(True)
4. Alcohol is a stimulant.	(False)

Matching Questions

Matching questions ask you to match the terms in one list with the terms in another list, according to directions. For example, the directions may tell you to match the names of different countries with the explorers who discovered them. Or you may be asked to match a communicable disease with the pathogen that usually causes it. The following strategies will help you handle these questions.

MAKE SURE YOU UNDERSTAND THE DIRECTIONS. The directions will tell you whether each answer can be used only once or any number of times.

WORK FROM THE COLUMN THAT HAS THE LONGEST ENTRIES. Working from the column with the longest phrases will save precious moments because you won't have to continually reread the longer items as you attempt to find the right matches. You'll be looking at each long phrase only once as you scan the column with the shorter phrases for the match.

> *A little knowledge that acts is worth infinitely more than much knowledge that is idle.*
>
> KAHLIL GIBRAN

START WITH THE MATCHES YOU KNOW. On your first run-through, mark these matches immediately with a penciled line, waiting to make your final choices until you've completed all the items. Keep in mind that if you can use an answer only once, you may have to change many answers if you reconsider any of your original choices.

FINALLY, TACKLE THE MATCHES YOU'RE NOT SURE OF. On your next run-through, focus on the more difficult matches. Look for clues and connections you might not have thought of at first. Think back to your class lectures, notes, and study sessions and try to visualize the correct response.

Consider the possibility that one of your sure-thing answers is wrong. If one or more phrases seem to have no correct answer, look back at your easy matches to be sure that you did not jump too quickly. See if another other phrase can be used instead, thus freeing up an answer for use in another match.

Fill-in-the-Blank Questions

Fill-in-the-blank questions, also known as sentence completion questions, ask you to supply one or more words or phrases with missing information that will complete the sentence. Here are some strategies that will help you make the right choices.

BE LOGICAL. Make sure the answer you choose completes the sentence in a logical way. Reread the sentence from beginning to end to be sure you're satisfied that it is factually and grammatically correct and that it makes sense. Few instructors will intentionally mislead you by manipulating the sentence's grammatical structure.

NOTE THE LENGTH AND NUMBER OF THE BLANKS. Use length and number of blanks as important clues, but not as absolute guideposts. If two blanks appear right after one another, the instructor is probably looking for a two-word answer. If a blank is longer than usual, the correct response may require this additional space. However, if you are certain of a one-word answer for a multiple-blank space, go with that answer. Trust your knowledge and instincts.

PAY ATTENTION TO HOW BLANKS ARE SEPARATED. If there is more than one blank in a sentence and the blanks are widely separated, treat each one separately. Answering each as if it were a separate sentence-completion question will minimize your stress as it increases the likelihood that you will get at least one of the answers correct. Here is an example:

When Toni Morrison was awarded the _____ Prize for Literature, she was a professor at _____ University.

(Answer: Morrison received the Nobel Prize and is a professor at Princeton University.)

In this case and in many other cases, your knowledge of one answer has little impact on your knowledge of the other answer.

THINK OUT OF THE BOX. If you can think of more than one correct answer, put them both down. Your instructor may never have thought of one of your responses and may be impressed with your assertiveness and creativity.

MAKE A GUESS. If you are uncertain of an answer, make an educated guess. Use qualifiers like may, sometimes, and often to increase the chance that your answer is at least partially correct. Have faith that after hours of studying, the correct answer is somewhere in your subconscious mind and that your guess is not completely random.

Essay Questions

An essay question allows you to express your knowledge and views on a topic in a much more extensive manner than any short-answer question can provide. With the freedom to express your views, though, comes the challenge to both exhibit knowledge and show you have command of how to organize and express that knowledge clearly.

Strategies for Answering Essay Questions

Using the following steps will help you make the most of your time and resources when answering essay questions. Many of these essay-test guidelines reflect the methods you should use when you approach any writing assignment—you will go through an abbreviated version of the writing process as you plan, draft, revise, and edit (see Chapter 8). The primary difference here is that you are writing under time pressure and that you are working from memory.

1. *Start by reading the questions.* Decide which to tackle (if there's a choice). Then, focus on what each question is asking and the mind actions you will need to use. Read directions carefully and do everything that you are asked to do. Some essay questions may contain more than one part. Knowing what you need to accomplish, budget

your time accordingly. For example, if you have one hour to answer three questions, you might budget 20 minutes for each question and break that down into stages (3 minutes for planning, 15 minutes for drafting, 2 minutes for revising and editing).

2. *Watch for action verbs.* Certain verbs can help you figure out how to think. Figure 10.2 explains some words commonly used in essay questions. Underline these words as you read the question, clarify what they mean, and use them to guide your writing.

3. *Plan your essay.* Brainstorm ideas and examples. Create an informal outline or think link to map your ideas and indicate the examples you plan to cite in support. (See Chapter 7 for a discussion of these organizational devices.)

4. *Draft your essay.* Start with a thesis statement or idea that states in a straightforward way what your essay will say. (See Chapter 8 for a dis-

FIGURE 10.2 Common action verbs on essay tests.

Analyze—Break into parts and discuss each part separately.

Compare—Explain similarities and differences.

Contrast—Distinguish between items being compared by focusing on differences.

Criticize—Evaluate the positive and negative effects of what is being discussed.

Define—State the essential quality or meaning. Give the common idea.

Describe—Visualize and give information that paints a complete picture.

Discuss—Examine in a complete and detailed way, usually by connecting ideas to examples.

Enumerate/List/Identify—Recall and specify items in the form of a list.

Evaluate—Give your opinion about the value or worth of something, usually by weighing positive and negative effects, and justify your conclusion.

Explain—Make the meaning of something clear, often by making analogies or giving examples.

Illustrate—Supply examples.

Interpret—Explain your personal view of facts and ideas and how they relate to one another.

Outline—Organize and present the main examples of an idea or sub-ideas.

Prove—Use evidence and argument to show that something is true, usually by showing cause and effect or giving examples that fit the idea to be proven.

Review—Provide an overview of ideas and establish their merits and features.

State—Explain clearly, simply, and concisely, being sure that each word gives the image you want.

Summarize—Give the important ideas in brief.

Trace—Present a history of the way something developed, often by showing cause and effect.

cussion of thesis statements.) Then, devote one or more paragraphs to the main points in your outline. Back up the general statement that starts each paragraph with evidence in the form of logical connections, examples, statistics, and so on. Use simple, clear language, and look back at your outline to make sure you are covering everything. Wrap it up with a conclusion that is short and to the point. This step differs from the drafting stage of the writing process in that you most likely won't have time to do any further drafts. Therefore, you will need to be more complete and organized than you might be when drafting a paper that you don't have to turn in right away.

5. *Revise your essay.* Make sure you have answered the question completely and that you used the points you came up with in the planning stage. Look for ideas you left out, ideas you didn't support with enough examples, paragraphs with faulty structure, and sentences that might confuse the reader. Make cuts or changes or add sentences in the margins, indicating with an arrow where they should fit into the paragraph, if you need to. Marking up your paper can be worth it—just be as neat as possible when making last-minute changes.

6. *Edit your essay.* Check for mistakes in grammar, spelling, punctuation, and usage. No matter what you are writing about, having a command of these factors will make your work more complete and impressive.

Neatness is a crucial factor in your essay writing. Try to write legibly; if your instructor can't read your ideas, it doesn't matter how good they are. You might consider printing and skipping every other line if you know your handwriting is problematic. Avoid writing on both sides of the paper because it will make your handwriting even harder to read. You may even want to discuss the problem with the instructor. If your handwriting is so poor that it will be a hardship for the instructor to read, ask about the possibility of taking the test on a laptop computer.

Here are three examples of essay questions you might encounter in an Interpersonal Communication course. In each case, notice the action verbs from Figure 10.2. Figure 10.3 shows an effective response to the third question.

1. Summarize the role of the self-concept as a key to interpersonal relationships and communication.
2. Explain how internal and external noise affects the ability to listen effectively.
3. Describe three ways that body language affects interpersonal communication.

Oral Exams

In an oral exam, your instructor asks you to present verbally your responses to exam questions or to discuss a preassigned topic. Exam questions may be similar to the essay questions on written exams. They may be broad and general, or they may focus on a narrow topic, which you are expected to explore it in depth.

You may have never had an oral exam; depending on your course of study and particular needs, you may never have one in school. However, the

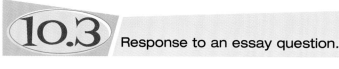

FIGURE 10.3   **Response to an essay question.**

QUESTION: Describe three ways that body language affects interpersonal communication.

Body language plays an important role in interpersonal communication and helps shape the impression you make, especially when you are making a first impression. Two of the most important functions of body language are to contradict and reinforce verbal statements. When body language contradicts verbal language, the message conveyed by the body is dominant. For example, if a friend tells you that she is feeling "fine," but her posture is slumped, her eye contact minimal, and her facial expression troubled, you have every reason to wonder whether she is telling the truth. If the same friend tells you she is feeling fine and she is smiling, walking with a bounce in her step, and has direct eye contact, her body language is accurately reflecting and reinforcing her words.

The nonverbal cues that make up body language also have the power to add shades of meaning. Consider this statement: "This is the best idea I've heard all day." If you were to say this three different ways—in a loud voice while standing up, quietly while sitting with arms and legs crossed and looking away, and while maintaining eye contact and taking the receiver's hand—you might send three different messages.

Finally, the impact of nonverbal cues can be greatest when you meet someone for the first time. Although first impressions emerge from a combination of nonverbal cues, tone of voice, and choice of words, nonverbal elements (cues and tone) usually come across first and strongest. When you meet someone, you tend to make assumptions based on nonverbal behavior such as posture, eye contact, gestures, and speed and style of movement.

In summary, nonverbal communication plays a crucial role in interpersonal relationships. It has the power to send an accurate message that may belie the speaker's words, offer shades of meaning, and set the tone of a first meeting.

skills involved in taking an oral examination are useful in public speaking in classroom settings and when speaking in front of others at work meetings. Furthermore, students with learning disabilities that affect their writing may need to take all of their exams orally. If you have a disability that fits into this category, speak with your advisor and your instructors to set up a system of taking exams that works for you.

Here are a few strategies to remember when taking an oral exam. Refer also to the section in Chapter 11 on oral presentations for other ideas that will help.

PLAN YOUR PRESENTATION. Brainstorm your topic if it is pre-assigned, narrow it with the prewriting strategies you learned in Chapter 8, determine your central idea or argument, and write an outline that will be the basis of your talk. Draft an outline of your thoughts using "trigger" words or phrases that will remind you of what you want to say.

PRACTICE YOUR PRESENTATION. Use index cards or notes to keep yourself on target. Pay attention to body positioning and voice. Do a test run with friends or alone—you might also want to audiotape or videotape yourself. Time yourself if you will have a time limit. If you can, try it out in the actual setting where you will be speaking. Know where your instructor will be sitting and what you may have around you to use, such as a podium, table, chair, or white board.

BE PREPARED FOR QUESTIONS. Anticipate some questions that may come up, and plan how you would respond to them.

BE PHYSICALLY AND MENTALLY READY. Get a good night's sleep before the exam so you'll speak with energy. Avoid drinking too much coffee or any alcohol. Take deep breaths and have some water handy. Visualize your own success—see yourself speaking with knowledge, confidence, and poise.

No matter what kind of test you take, you may be tempted to drop the experience from your mind the minute you leave the test room. If you take the time to examine your test after the results come in, however, you can often learn a great deal from any mistakes that you have made.

OW CAN YOU LEARN FROM TEST MISTAKES?

The purpose of a test is to see how much you know, not merely to achieve a grade. Making mistakes, or even failing a test, is human. Rather than ignoring mistakes, examine them and learn from them as you learn from mistakes on the job and in your relationships. Working through your mistakes will help you avoid repeating them again on another test—or outside of school life. The following strategies will help.

TRY TO IDENTIFY PATTERNS IN YOUR MISTAKES. Look for the following:

Windows on the World

REAL LIFE STUDENT ISSUES

How can I combat test anxiety?

Peter Changsak, *Sheldon-Jackson College, Sitka, Alaska*

I am a Yu'pik Eskimo from a village on the Yukon River. Before attending college, I worked for six years as a clerk at the Native Corporation, a gas station and general store. When the manager passed away, the business offered to make me a manager. Even though I knew how to do much of the work, I didn't feel I was ready, so I decided to go to school for more training.

College life is different from what I am accustomed to. The hardest part has been taking tests. I study hard for the exams, but then when I get in class and the test begins, I forget everything. My mind goes blank. Then, in class, I have a hard time listening. I might be in my math class, but I'm thinking about the 10-page paper that is due in my social studies class. When I read, I understand what I'm reading, but as soon as I close

the book I can't remember what I just read. My favorite class is biology lab, probably because we can walk around.

I love mechanics and construction. When I worked at the Native Corporation, we made a new building. I felt like I was a success at work, but I don't feel successful as a student. Sometimes I feel like quitting school altogether, but I also think it can help me have more choices if I stick with it. I'm learning how to be a serious student, but it isn't easy. Can you give suggestions about how I can get over my test anxiety?

Tim Nordberg, *Executive Director, Chicago Youth Ministries*

In many ways my experience in college was similar to yours. I was raised in a car industry town. I was the first person in my family to go to college, which was intimidating. My first year was hard—I discovered that I read at an 8th grade level. I hated studying and tak-

ing tests. During the spring, the college began a building project. Local Amish people came and laid blocks. I wanted to be outside doing manual work too. I constantly felt a battle going on within me.

Two factors gave me the endurance to go on. One was seeing my old high school buddies who seemed stuck in the past. A second factor was my desire to fulfill my goals. I thought, "If I fail it won't be because I haven't given it my best. I'm not going to fail because I refuse to try."

That summer I took a reading class. School was still not easy that fall, but I was not studying

as much out of fear or duty; rather I was studying to do my best. Classes began to take on a different meaning. I was beginning to learn because I enjoyed the challenge. I took tests to see how well I knew the

subject. Today I still love sports and carpentry, but I also love to learn.

Don't fear failure. Just try to do your best. Concentrate on the task at hand. Study to learn, not to take a test. Good test scores will reflect your passion to know what you have studied rather than how good you are at test taking. You are being challenged to survive in new ways, and you are not alone. Ask the student services office to help you through this adjustment process. Ask your advisor if they offer a class that teaches study and test-taking tips.

My advice to you is try to remember why you came to college in the first place—to better equip yourself. As you prepare for classes and tests, spend time reminding yourself what this experience will do for you someday when it is all behind you. Growing in any area of life isn't always fun, and may not seem within reach. But if we give up, we may miss out on a part of us that, in time, would have brought greater rewards.

328

- *Careless errors.* In your rush to complete the exam, did you misread the question or directions, blacken the wrong box on the answer sheet, inadvertently skip a question, or use illegible handwriting?
- *Conceptual or factual errors.* Did you misunderstand a concept or never learn it in the first place? Did you fail to master certain facts? Did you skip part of the assigned text or miss important classes in which ideas were covered?

IF YOU HAVE TIME, TRY TO REWORK THE QUESTIONS YOU GOT WRONG. Based on the feedback from your instructor or other test administrator, try to rewrite an essay, recalculate a math problem by starting from the original question, or redo the questions that follow a reading selection. If you see patterns of careless errors, promise yourself that you'll be more careful in the future and that you'll save time to double-check your work. If you pick up conceptual and factual errors, rededicate yourself to better preparation.

AFTER REVIEWING YOUR MISTAKES, FILL IN YOUR KNOWLEDGE GAPS. If you made mistakes on questions because you didn't know or understand them, develop a plan to comprehensively learn the material. Solidifying your knowledge can help you in exams further down the road, as well as in life situations that involve the subject matter you're studying. You might even consider asking to retake the exam, if you have the time to do so. The score might not count, but you may find that focusing on learning rather than on grades can improve your knowledge and build self-respect.

TALK TO YOUR INSTRUCTORS. You can learn a lot from consulting an instructor about specific mistakes you made or about subjective essays on which you were marked down. Respectfully ask the instructor who graded the test for an explanation of grades or comments. In the case of a subjective test where the answers are often not clearly right or wrong, ask for specifics about what you could have done to have earned a better grade. Take advantage of this opportunity to find out solid details about how you can do better next time.

IF YOU FAIL A TEST COMPLETELY, DON'T THROW IT AWAY. First, know that many students have been in your shoes and that you have room to grow and improve. Then, try to understand why you failed by reviewing and analyzing your errors. This is especially important for an essay test. Whereas most objective questions are fact-based and clearly right or wrong, subjective questions are in large part subject to the opinion of the grader.

Sine qua non

Although the Latin language is no longer commonly used, it is one of the most dominant ancestors of modern English, and many Latin words and phrases have a place in the English language. The Latin phrase *sine qua non* (pronounced sihn-ay kwa nahn) means, literally, "without which not." Translated into everyday language, a *sine qua non* is "an absolutely indispensable or essential thing."

Think of true learning as the *sine qua non* of test taking. When you have worked hard to learn ideas and information, taking it in and using different techniques to review and retain it, you will be more able to take tests successfully, confident that you have the knowledge necessary to answer the required questions. Focus on knowledge so that test taking becomes not an intimidating challenge but an opportunity to show what you know.

IMPORTANT POINTS *to remember*

1. How can preparation help improve test scores?

Preparation is one key to test success. Strategies that can help improve your approach include identifying test type and coverage, choosing appropriate study materials, setting a study plan and schedule, reviewing (using SQ3R, notes, and critical thinking), taking a pretest, getting enough sleep and eating well, making the most of last-minute studying, and working through test anxiety (through effective preparation and a positive attitude).

2. What general strategies can help you succeed on tests?

Although all tests are different, there are methods that will help improve your performance on almost every test. These include writing down key information as soon as the test begins, taking time to skim the exam and get an overview, reading the directions, working from the easiest questions to the hardest, keeping track of time as you work, learning to guess intelligently, knowing how to fill out machine-scored tests, and using critical thinking to avoid errors.

3. How can you master different types of test questions?

Learning how to approach different types of test questions is important to your success. Objective questions are short-answer questions that test your ability to recall, compare, and contrast information—such questions include multiple-choice, true-or-false, matching, and fill-in-the-blank. Subjective questions—essay questions—require you to express your answer in terms of your own personal knowledge and perspective. There are different skills for each kind of objective question. For subjective questions, use an abbreviated version of the writing process. Oral exams require a combination of subjective question skills and public speaking skills.

4. How can you learn from test mistakes?

The purpose of a test is to see how much you know. Test mistakes can show you where you may need to strengthen your knowledge. When you get your test back, look for careless errors, as well as those that involve concepts and facts. Instead of taking your mistakes as a defeat, treat them as an opportunity to understand what happened and avoid making the same mistake in the future.

CRITICAL THINKING

APPLYING LEARNING TO LIFE

PREPARE FOR YOUR NEXT TEST AND EVALUATE YOUR PERFORMANCE. Use a textbook, review book, or study guide for a course you're currently taking. Focus on the part of your materials that you know will be covered in your next test in this course. In the space below, copy down four questions from your materials—two objective questions (any kind) and two subjective questions (essay questions). For each question, name a strategy or strategies from this chapter that will help you solve it and tell why.

Objective Question:

_____

Strategy:

_____

Objective Question:

_____

Strategy:

_____

Essay Question:

_____

Strategy:

_____

Essay Question:

_____

Strategy:

_____

Next, when you are tested on this material and you receive the corrected test, take a detailed look at your performance.

1. Write what you think of your test performance and grade. Were you pleased or disappointed? If you made mistakes, were they careless errors or did you lack the facts and concepts?

_____

_____

_____

2. Next, list the test preparation activities that helped you do well on the exam and the activities you wish you had done—and intend to do—for the next exam.

Positive things I did:

_____

_____

_____

Positive actions I intend to take next time:

_____

_____

_____

3. Finally, list the activities you are not likely to repeat when studying for the next test.

_____

_____

_____

TEAMWORK
COMBINING FORCES

STUDY PARTNERS. Choose a study partner in one of your classes. Work together to learn the material for a particular test. Use the following checklist to quiz each other and measure how well you prepare.

Go through the entire checklist before the exam. Evaluate each statement and decide together what needs to be done in order to check off that statement. Assign tasks to each other and share information (e.g., one person might research old exams, and the other might prepare a pretest based on class notes for both of you to take). Set specific times and dates to study together and go through your checklist.

After the exam, meet with your partner to evaluate the checklist. If you like, rewrite it according to your needs, adding new questions that you think should be included or crossing out questions that didn't seem to be necessary. Your improved checklist will help you do even better on the next exam.

- [ ] I asked the instructor what will be covered on the exam and the format of the test questions.
- [ ] I tried to learn as much as I could about the kinds of tests the instructor gives by talking to former students and getting copies of old exams.
- [ ] I used critical thinking to explore difficult concepts that might be on the test.
- [ ] I took a pretest.
- [ ] I tried to prepare my body and mind to perform at their best.
- [ ] I focused on preparation and attitude in order to combat test anxiety that might affect my performance.
- [ ] I have gotten my personal life under control so I can focus on the exam.
- [ ] I have a plan of action that I will follow when I see the test for the first time. I'll try to get an overview of the test, learn the ground rules, schedule my time, and evaluate questions and choices in case I have to guess.
- [ ] I reviewed strategies for handling multiple-choice, true-or-false, and essay questions and feel comfortable with these strategies.

WRITING

DISCOVERY THROUGH JOURNALING

To record your thoughts, use a separate journal or the lined page at the end of the chapter.

TESTS. Do you experience test anxiety? Describe how tests generally make you feel (you might include an example of a specific test situation and what happened). Identify your specific test-taking fears and write out your plan to overcome fears and self-defeating behaviors.

CAREER PORTFOLIO

CHARTING YOUR COURSE

TEST TAKING AND CAREER INVESTIGATION. Depending on what careers you are considering, you may encounter one or more tests—tests for entry into the field (such as the medical boards), tests on particular equipment (such as a proficiency test on Microsoft Word), or tests that are necessary to move you to the next level of employment (such as a technical certification test). This portfolio exercise has two parts. If for any reason no potential career of yours involves tests, complete Part Two only.

Part One: Choose one career you are thinking about and investigate what tests are involved in entering this particular field. Be sure to look for tests in any of the areas described previously. On a separate piece of paper, write down everything you find out about each test involved.

- What it tests you on.

- When, in the course of pursuing this career, you would need to take the test.
- What preparation is necessary for the test (including course work).
- Whether the test will need to be retaken at any time (e.g., airline pilots usually need to be recertified every few years).

Once you have recorded your information, see if there is any possibility of looking at, or even taking, any of the tests you will face if you pursue this particular career. For example, if you will need to be tested on a computer program, your career center or computer center may have the test available. As a practice, look at or take any test that you can track down.

Part Two: Your school's career center will have one or more "tests" that investigate your interests and abilities and make suggestions about what careers may be suitable for you. Explore the possibilities by taking one or more of these tests at the center. You may end up with results that match what you already want to do—or you may be surprised. Keep an open mind and take time to consider any surprises you encounter. Even if you do not want to follow any of the career areas suggested by the test, think about what the results say about you.

UGGESTED READINGS

Browning, William G., Ph.D. *Cliffs Memory Power for Exams.* Lincoln, NE: Cliffs Notes Inc. (1990).

Fry, Ron. *"Ace" Any Test,* 3rd ed. Franklin Lakes, NJ: Career Press (1996).

Kesselman, Judy Kesselman-Turkel and Franklynn Peterson. *Test Taking Strategies.* Chicago: NTC/Contemporary Publishing (1981).

Meyers, Judith N. *The Secrets of Taking Any Test,* 2d ed. New York: Learning Express (2000).

NTERNET RESOURCES

Grizzly Peak—information on test strategies and how to combat test anxiety: www.grizpeak.com/test1.htm

NetStudyAids.com—Study Aids, Skills, Guides, and Techniques: www.netstudyaids.com/

Florida State University—list of sites offering information on test taking skills: http://osi.fsu.edu/hot/testtaking/skills.htm

NDNOTES

1. Steven Frank. *The Everything Study Book.* Holbrook, MA: Adams Media Corporation (1996), p. 208.
2. Many of the examples of objective questions used in this chapter are from Gary W. Piggrem, Test Item File for Charles G. Morris, *Understanding Psychology,* 3rd ed. Upper Saddle River, NJ: Prentice Hall (1996).

Journal

NAME

DATE

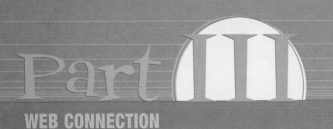
First, on the Prentice Hall Supersite at www.prenhall.com/success, locate the Note-Taking tab in the Study Skills section. Read the introduction about Online Olivia. Answer the following questions on a separate sheet of paper.

1. Do you use outlines when you take notes? If you do, describe the positive and negative effects, for you, of using an outline. If you don't, describe the note-taking technique you most frequently use.

2. Name the four note-taking techniques suggested by the article. Which do you think you would be most likely to enjoy using? For what course would you use it, and why?

3. Use a search engine to generate a list of sites that have information on note-taking skills. Write the site names and URLs. Look at one particular site and briefly discuss a helpful idea that you gained from reading that site's material.

Next, click on the Test-Taking section in the Study Skills tab. Read the material, then answer these questions.

1. What are the two things you do best under the three headings Preparation, Test taking, and Test analysis? What are the two things under each heading that are toughest for you?

2. Take the quiz—and be honest in your answers. Do you agree with the assessment of your test-taking skills? Describe your reaction to the assessment—and what advice, if anything, seems helpful to you.

3. Explore the test-taking links. Write down some test-taking ideas from the link you felt was most helpful and interesting.

Creating Life Success

PART FOUR

IV

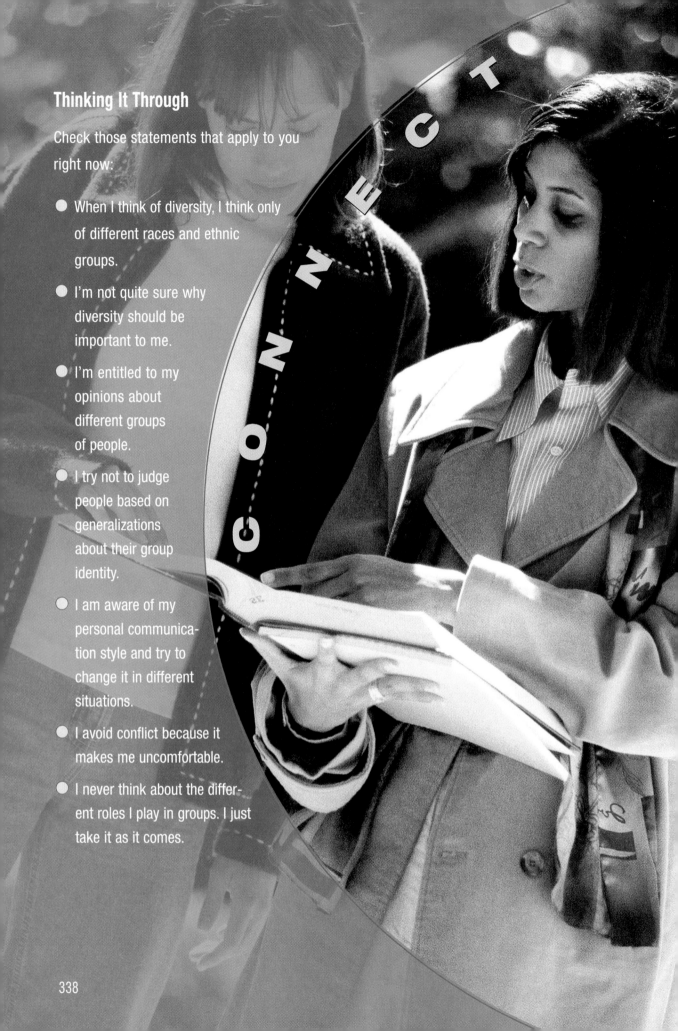

Thinking It Through

Check those statements that apply to you right now:

- When I think of diversity, I think only of different races and ethnic groups.

- I'm not quite sure why diversity should be important to me.

- I'm entitled to my opinions about different groups of people.

- I try not to judge people based on generalizations about their group identity.

- I am aware of my personal communication style and try to change it in different situations.

- I avoid conflict because it makes me uncomfortable.

- I never think about the different roles I play in groups. I just take it as it comes.

IN THIS CHAPTER,

you will explore answers to the following

questions:

- Why is it important to understand and accept others?
- How can you think critically about diversity?
- How can you express yourself effectively?
- How do your personal relationships define you?
- How can you handle conflict and criticism?
- What role do you play in groups?

The greater part of your waking life involves interacting with people—family and friends, fellow students, coworkers, instructors, and others. Having a strong network of relationships can help you feel good about yourself and your place in the world, grow as a person, and progress toward your goals. In this

Relating to Others

chapter, you will explore how your ability to open your mind can positively affect the way in which you perceive and relate to others. You will also explore communication styles, personal relationships, and the roles you play in groups and teams. Finally, you will learn to handle conflict and criticism so that you can learn from your points of vulnerability as well as your strengths.

HY IS IT IMPORTANT TO UNDERSTAND AND ACCEPT OTHERS?

As your world becomes increasingly diverse, you will encounter people who may be different from anyone you have ever met. Accepting differences—through an open mind and a willingness to learn—will allow you to expand your horizons and create more options in all areas of your life.

Diversity in Your World

DIVERSITY

The variety that occurs in every aspect of humanity, involving both visible and invisible characteristics.

More and more, **diversity** is part of your community, on your television, on the Internet, at your school, in your workplace, and in your family. Immigration and intermarriage will continue to increase the ethnic diversity of the United States, as shown in Figure 11.1, which compares the current population with what is projected for the year 2050. Diversity in age is also on the rise. Whereas in 1994 only 1 in 25 people was older than 65, it is projected that 1 in 5 will be over 65 by the year 2050 and that the elderly population will have more than doubled.[1]

Our society has changed dramatically in the last 50 years. Although in 1950 most communities, schools, and workplaces were comprised of people from similar backgrounds, today differences are interwoven into everyday life. You may encounter examples of diversity like these:

FIGURE 11.1   Growing diversity.

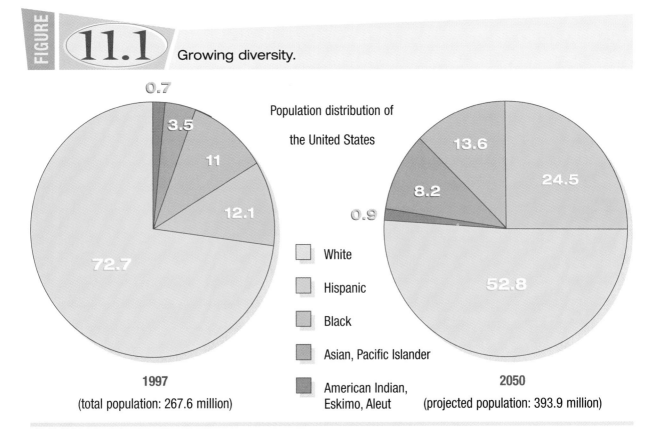

Population distribution of the United States

□ White
□ Hispanic
□ Black
□ Asian, Pacific Islander
□ American Indian, Eskimo, Aleut

1997
(total population: 267.6 million)

2050
(projected population: 393.9 million)

Source: U. S. Bureau of the Census, *Statistical Abstract of the United States 1998,* 118th Ed. (Washington, D.C.: U.S. Government Printing Office, 1998).

Source: U. S. Bureau of the Census, *Current Population Reports,* Series P25-1092 (Washington, D.C.: Government Printing Office, 1992), and *Statistical Abstracts of the United States 1994* (Washington, D.C.: U.S. Government Printing Office, 1994).

- Communities that include people in every life stage—from the very young to the very old
- Coworkers from different ethnic backgrounds
- Classmates who speak different languages and who consider English their second language
- Social situations that include people from various cultures, with various religions and sexual orientations
- Spouses or partners from different racial or religious backgrounds
- Parents who adopt children from different cultures and backgrounds than their own
- People with disabilities (physical or emotional) who are students and coworkers

Each person has a choice about how to relate to others—or even whether to relate to them. No one can force you to interact with any other person, or to adopt a particular attitude as being "right." Considering two important responsibilities may help you analyze your options.

YOUR RESPONSIBILITY TO YOURSELF IS TO MAKE SURE YOUR FEELINGS ARE HONEST AND WELL CONSIDERED. Observe your reactions to ideas. Consider their sources. Through critical thinking you can arrive at decisions about your diverse world that feel comfortable and fair.

YOUR RESPONSIBILITY TO OTHERS LIES IN TREATING PEOPLE WITH TOLERANCE AND RESPECT, EVEN IN THE FACE OF DIFFERENCES. No one will like everyone he or she meets, but acknowledging that others deserve respect for who they are and have the right to see things in different ways will help you build understanding.

The Positive Effects of Diversity

Acceptance and respect are the foundation for all successful relationships. As you meet people from different backgrounds, your ability to communicate and connect with them will depend on your willingness to accept them for whom they are, without judgment. When acceptance and respect become givens in your personal relationships, your communication with friends, classmates, and coworkers will improve immeasurably. And, in turn, the strength of these personal relationships will support you as you work toward goals and bring you a sense of peace and connection to the world around you.

Reactions to diversity can be troubling, but with changes in attitude, solutions are possible. The following examples illustrate this point. Although both situations focus on the reaction of one person, it's important to note that both parties need to work together to establish mutual trust and openness.

A STUDENT WITH A LEARNING DISABILITY HAS AN ASIAN INSTRUCTOR. If the student assumes that Asian people are intellectually superior, expecting a perfect performance, she may resist the instructor's advice and directions

STEREOTYPE

A standardized mental picture that represents an oversimplified opinion or uncritical judgment.

and do poorly in the class or drop it. On the other hand, if the student rejects racial **stereotypes** about Asians and talks to the instructor about the specific accommodations she needs to succeed in class, the instructor may feel respected and be more encouraging. The student may then be more likely to pay attention in class, work hard, and advance in her education.

A CAUCASIAN MAN HAS A SISTER WHO ADOPTS A BIRACIAL CHILD. If the man cuts off contact with his sister because he fears racial differences and doesn't approve of racial mixing, he may deny himself her support and create a rift in the family. On the other hand, if the man can respect his sister's choice, seeing the child as a new family member regardless of color, she may feel more supported and continue to support him in turn. The situation may help to build a close and rewarding family relationship.

Accepting others isn't always easy. Following are some barriers that can hinder your ability to accept and understand others and suggestions for how your problem-solving skills can help you overcome them.

HOW CAN YOU THINK CRITICALLY ABOUT DIVERSITY?

You deserve to feel positive about who you are, where you come from, what you believe, and those with whom you identify. However, problems arise when people use the power of group identity to put others down or cut themselves off from others. Table 11.1 shows how an open-minded approach when encountering people from different cultures, with different lifestyles, and at different life stages differs from an approach that is characterized by barriers. Thinking critically can help you understand and break down the barriers that prevent successful communication.

Prejudice

PREJUDICE

A preconceived judgment or opinion, formed without just grounds or sufficient knowledge.

Prejudice occurs when people prejudge (make a judgment before they have sufficient knowledge on which to base that judgment). People often form prejudiced opinions on the basis of a particular characteristic—gender, race, sexual orientation, religion, language, and so on. You may be familiar with the labels for particular prejudices, such as racism (prejudice based on race), ageism (prejudice based on age), and sexism (prejudice based on gender).

Why do people prejudge? Sources of prejudice include the following:

- *Family and culture.* You learn the attitudes of those with whom you grow up.
- *Individual experience.* Judging others because of a bad experience is human, especially when a particular characteristic raises strong emotions.
- *Jealousy, insecurity, and fear of failure.* When people feel insecure about their own abilities and lack self-esteem, they may find it easier to devalue the abilities of others than to focus on the problems inside themselves.

Approaches to diversity.

YOUR ROLE	SITUATION	CLOSED-MINDED APPROACH	OPEN-MINDED APPROACH
Fellow student	For an assignment, you are paired with a student old enough to be your mother.	You assume the student will be closed to the modern world. You think she might preach to you about how to do the assignment.	You get to know the student as an individual. You stay open to what you can learn from her experiences and knowledge.
Friend	You are invited to dinner at a friend's house. When he introduces you to his partner, you realize that he is gay.	You are turned off by the idea of two men in a relationship. You make an excuse to leave early. You avoid your friend after that evening.	You have dinner with the two men and make an effort to get to know more about what their lives are like and who they are individually and as a couple.
Employee	Your new boss is Japanese American, hired from a competing company.	You assume that your new boss is very hard-working, has demanding expectations, and doesn't take time to socialize.	You rein in your assumptions, knowing they are based on stereotypes, and approach your new boss with an open mind.

The many faces of prejudice often show on college campuses. A student may not want to work with students of another race. Members of campus clubs may reject prospective members who do not share their background. Such attitudes block attempts at mutual understanding.

Prejudice Causes Discrimination

Prejudice can lead to disrespect, avoidance, and even harassment. In some cases, prejudice may lead to unrealistic expectations of others that aren't necessarily negative, but that have a negative impact. For example, those who believe that all Jewish people excel in business are also likely to see Jews as interested only in money, and this may plant the seeds of anti-Semitism. The most destructive effect of prejudice is discrimination.

Discrimination occurs when people deny others opportunities because of their perceived differences in gender, language, race, culture, weight, physical ability, and other factors. Victims of discrimination suffer when they are denied equal employment, educational, and housing opportunities and when they are treated as second-class citizens in their access to goods and services. Sheryl McCarthy, an African American columnist for *New York Newsday,* says: "Nothing is quite so basic and clear as having a cab go right past your furiously waving body and pick up the white person next to you."[2]

Federal law states that it is unlawful for you to be denied an education, work, or the chance to apply for work, housing, or basic rights because of your race, creed, color, age, gender, national or ethnic origin, religion, marital status, potential or actual pregnancy, or potential or actual illness or disability (unless the illness or disability prevents you from performing required tasks and unless accommodations for the disability are not possible). Unfortunately, the law is often broken; the result is that many people suffer the impact of discrimination. Some people don't report violations, fearing trouble from those they accuse. Others aren't aware that discrimination has occurred.

I have a dream that one day on the red hills of Georgia the sons of former slaves and the sons of former slave owners will be able to sit down together at the table of brotherhood.

MARTIN LUTHER KING, JR.

Addressing Prejudice and Discrimination

The best and most lasting solutions come from addressing the cause rather than the effect (see Chapter 4). Therefore, fight discrimination by working to eliminate prejudice. First and foremost, be responsible for your own behavior. For example, if you go out of your way to avoid asking a classmate who uses a wheelchair to become part of your study group, ask yourself: Am I prejudiced against people with disabilities? If so, where did I get this prejudice? What are the effects of this prejudice on me and others? How can I reverse this negative thought pattern? Use problem-solving steps to make an adjustment if necessary.

When someone you know displays prejudice or discriminates, what can you do? It can be hard to stand up to someone and risk a relationship or, if the person is your employer, a job. Evaluate the situation and decide what choice is most suitable. You can decide not to address it at all. You may drop a humorous hint. You may test the waters with a small comment. Whatever you do, express your opinion respectfully. Whether or not the other person makes a change, you have taken an important stand.

Stereotyping

An assumption is an idea that is accepted without looking for proof. A stereotype is a kind of assumption, made about a person or group of people based on one or more characteristics. You may have heard stereotypical assumptions such as these: "Women are too emotional for business"; "Gay people sleep around"; or "People with learning disabilities can't hold down jobs." Stereotypes are as common as they are destructive.

What are some sources of stereotypes?

LACK OF UNDERSTANDING. People often look for easy answers and make these answers the foundation for their stereotypes. They refuse to seek out answers that are more complex and often less clear. Over the centuries, for example, Jews became money lenders because they were denied access to other occupations, not because their culture focused on money. The stereotype of the "money hungry" Jew misses this point of Jews' adaptation to anti-Semitism as a means of survival.

A DESIRE FOR PATTERNS AND LOGIC. People often try to make sense of a complex world by using the labels and categories that stereotypes provide.

THE MEDIA. The more people see stereotypical images—the unintelligent blonde or the funny overweight person—the easier it is to believe that such stereotypes are universal.

LAZINESS. Making assumptions from observing external characteristics is easier than trying to know people as individuals.

The "ease" of stereotypes comes at a high price. First and foremost, stereotypes can perpetuate harmful generalizations and falsehoods about others. Second, stereotypes communicate the message that you don't respect others enough to discover who they really are. This may encourage others to stereotype you in return.

Stereotyping Causes Stereotype Vulnerability

When people identify themselves as part of a particular group, they may want to distance themselves from stereotypical qualities associated with that group. Stereotype vulnerability occurs when people avoid facing a problem because they think that admitting it will just perpetuate a stereotype.[3] For example, an immigrant to the United States may resist tutoring in English for fear of seeming like just another foreigner. Such avoidance cuts people off from assistance and communication that could connect them with others and thus improve their lives.

Another side of stereotype vulnerability occurs when people refuse help because they believe that others want to help them out of pity: "She considers me disadvantaged because I'm African American"; "He only wants to help because he looks down on me because of my learning disability." These refusals are based on assumptions. Sometimes, such assumptions may contain a grain of truth. Frequently, though, the person who offers help just wants to help another human being, and the person who refuses it loses out on what may be valuable assistance.

Addressing Stereotypes and Stereotype Vulnerability

You can ask questions about an assumption to examine its validity. Apply these questions to stereotypes:

- In what cases is this stereotype true, if ever? In what cases is it not true?
- Has stereotyping others benefited me? Has it hurt me? In what ways? How would I feel if I were on the receiving end of this stereotype?
- What is the source of this stereotype, and why?
- What harm could be done by always accepting this stereotype as true?

Using these questions, think about the stereotypes that you assume are true, and curb your tendencies to judge according to such stereotypes. When you hear someone use a stereotype and you know something that disproves it, volunteer that information. Encourage others to think through stereotypes and to reject them if they don't hold up under examination. Approach every person as a unique individual who deserves respect.

Furthermore, if you find yourself avoiding help because you don't want to be labeled, don't let stereotypes prevent you from getting assistance.

Approach someone who can help you and give that person a chance to get to know your individual needs and problems. Perhaps she will see you not as a representative of a group but as an individual who needs and deserves specific attention.

Fear of Differences

It's human instinct to fear the unknown. Many people allow their fears to prevent them from finding out about what's outside their known world. As cozy as that world can be, it is also limiting as it cuts off communication with people who are perceived as different. Fear of differences may motivate a Christian from befriending a Muslim, for example, and it may be reason enough for a straight couple with children to decide not to buy a house because the next door neighbor is gay. In both cases, the person has denied himself a chance to learn a new perspective, communicate with new individuals, and grow from new experiences.

Fear of Differences Causes Hate Crimes

A hate crime is the most extreme effect of the fear of differences. Unfortunately, recent years have brought many unwelcome examples, such as the following:

- In June 1998, an African American named James Byrd, Jr. was chained to the back of a pickup truck and dragged along the road until he died. One of his convicted murderers is an admitted white supremacist.
- In Wyoming in the fall of 1998, a gay college student named Matthew Shepard was kidnapped and tied to a fence where his captors beat him and abandoned him. He died as a result of the injuries he sustained.
- In April 1999, Eric Harris and Dylan Klebold opened fire in Columbine High School in Littleton, Colorado, killing 12 students and 1 teacher and wounding others. Their writings revealed their intention to harm minorities, athletes, and others different from them.
- In May 1999 in Victor, Colorado, a white man named Mark Dale Butts was beaten by a group of African American men until he died. The incident started with some racially charged comments made in a bar.
- In August 1999, Buford O. Furrow entered the North Valley Jewish Community Center near Los Angeles, California, and shot three preschool children and two adults because they were Jewish. He then shot and killed a Filipino-American letter carrier because he was not white.

The increase in hate crimes in recent years has prompted a great deal of concern. Organized groups based on hate of a particular race or culture are growing, and many have Internet sites dedicated to their prejudiced ideas. Other Internet sites are developed and maintained by individuals who want to express their racism, anti-Semitism, hatred of gays, misogyny (hatred of women), or other prejudices. Some sites even promote prejudices to kids through games and other interactive formats. Figure 11.2 shows statistics on what motivates people to commit hate crimes.

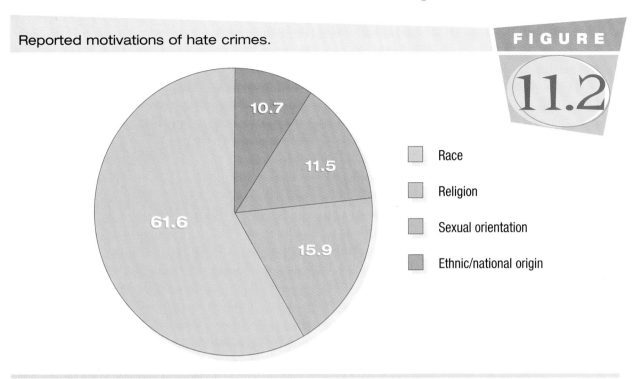

Reported motivations of hate crimes.

FIGURE 11.2

10.7

11.5

61.6

15.9

- Race
- Religion
- Sexual orientation
- Ethnic/national origin

Source: Federal Bureau of Investigation, *1996 Hate Crimes Statistics Press Release* (Washington, D.C.: FBI National Press Office, January 1998).

All of the causes of this devastating trend are not completely understood. What is important are an awareness of the problem and a willingness to face it.

Addressing Fear of Differences and Hate Crimes

Diversity doesn't mean that you have to feel comfortable with everyone and their beliefs. If you can gradually broaden your horizons, however, you may avoid limiting your growth through fear. Today's world increasingly presents opportunities for such exposure. You can choose a study partner who has a different ethnic background, expand your knowledge through books or magazines, or attend an unfamiliar religious service with a friend. If you are uncomfortable with even this level of exploration, you can start by respecting people who are different from you and allowing them to live peacefully and privately.

In addition, do whatever you can to promote the lessening of the kind of fear and anger that can lead to hate crimes. Step up your awareness, add your voice to those in protest, and treat people of all cultures and lifestyles with respect. Anything that you do to promote and encourage the positive effects of diversity—including all of the strategies in the following section—will combat the kind of irrational hatred that can lead to violence.

Accepting and Dealing with Differences

Successful interaction with the people around you depends upon your ability to accept differences. The opinions of family, friends, the media, and any group with which you identify may sometimes lead you to adopt attitudes that you haven't completely thought through. Ask yourself questions about the actions you want to take, and make a choice that feels right.

What can you do to accept and deal with differences?

AVOID JUDGMENTS BASED ON EXTERNAL CHARACTERISTICS. These include skin color, weight, facial features, physical disability, or gender.

CULTIVATE RELATIONSHIPS WITH DIVERSE PEOPLE. Find out how other people live and think, and see what you can learn from them. Acknowledge that everyone has a right to her opinion, whether or not you agree with it.

EDUCATE YOURSELF AND OTHERS. Read about other cultures and people. "Take advantage of books and people to teach you about other cultures," say Tamera Trotter and Joycelyn Allen in *Talking Justice: 602 Ways to Build and Promote Racial Harmony.* "Empowerment comes through education."[4] Be sensitive to the needs of others at school and on the job. Ask yourself questions about what you would feel and do if you were in another person's shoes.

> *Minds are like parachutes. They only function when they are open.*
>
> SIR JAMES DEWAR

HELP OTHER PEOPLE, NO MATTER HOW DIFFERENT THEY MAY BE. Sheryl McCarthy writes about an African American who, in the midst of the 1992 Los Angeles riots, saw a man being beaten and helped him to safety. "When asked why he risked grievous harm to save an Asian man he didn't even know, Williams said, 'Because if I'm not there to help someone else, when the mob comes for me, will there be someone there to save me?'"[5] Continue the cycle of kindness.

EXPLORE YOUR OWN BACKGROUND, BELIEFS, AND IDENTITY. Respect and explore your heritage. Share what you learn with others.

TAKE RESPONSIBILITY FOR MAKING CHANGES. Avoid blaming problems in your life on certain groups of people.

LOOK FOR COMMON GROUND. You might share parenting goals, classes, personal challenges, or interests.

RECOGNIZE THAT PEOPLE EVERYWHERE HAVE THE SAME BASIC NEEDS. Everyone loves, thinks, hurts, hopes, fears, and plans. People are united through their essential humanity.

At the forefront of the list of ways to deal with differences is mutual respect. Respect for yourself and others is essential. Knowing that other people's cultures, behaviors, races, religions, appearances, and ideas deserve as much respect as your own promotes communication and learning.

Expressing your ideas clearly and interpreting what others believe are two crucial keys to communicating in a diverse world. Particular strategies can help you communicate effectively with those around you.

Using a separate sheet of paper, complete the following.

Thinking Back

1. If you were writing a dictionary entry, how would you define the word *diversity?*

2. What are three diversity-related barriers that can block communication between people?

3. What are some reasons people tend to stereotype others?

4. Of the ways a person can accept and deal with differences, what three seem most important to you? Why?

Thinking Ahead

1. How would you describe yourself as a communicator? How do you prefer to get your message across?

2. What actions do you take to strengthen your personal relationships?

3. How does conflict make you feel? How do you tend to deal with it?

4. In a group situation at school, work, or with friends or family, what role do you tend to play?

OW CAN YOU EXPRESS YOURSELF EFFECTIVELY?

Every person has a different communication style. Your personal style—and the styles of your family members, friends, classmates, and coworkers—can enhance or obstruct the success of your relationships. Understanding the different styles, particularly your own, will help you express yourself more effectively.

Explore Communication Styles

Communication is an exchange between two or more people. The speaker's goal is for the listener (or listeners) to receive the message exactly as the speaker intended. Problems arise when one person has trouble "translating" a message that comes from someone who uses a different style.

Your knowledge of multiple intelligences (see Chapter 3) will help you understand different styles of communication. Particular communication styles tend to accompany dominance in particular intelligences. Recognizing specific styles in yourself and in others will help you communicate more clearly.

The Styles

Following are the communication styles that tend to accompany dominance in six of the eight intelligences.

BODILY–KINESTHETIC COMMUNICATORS ARE TUNED IN TO THE PHYSICAL. They often use body language to send messages and may be likewise adept at reading the body language of others. They may experience more communication success when speaking in person than when talking on the phone or reading e-mail because being physically present can help them read a situation comprehensively.

VISUAL–SPATIAL COMMUNICATORS BENEFIT FROM VISUAL AIDS TO COMMUNICATION. Reinforcing a message with a visual—for example, accompanying a spoken presentation at work with slides or transparencies—may boost their ability to listen and understand. Visual–spatial communicators may find it helpful to use visual images or aids when communicating to others.

VERBAL–LINGUISTIC COMMUNICATORS GRAVITATE TOWARD ANY KIND OF VERBAL COMMUNICATION. Whether spoken (oral) or written, they tend to put their messages across in words. They receive best those messages that are communicated verbally. As for their studies, verbal people process reading material well.

LOGICAL–MATHEMATICAL COMMUNICATORS FAVOR COMMUNICATION THAT FOLLOWS A STRUCTURE OR A SYSTEM. They often explain information in a manner focused more on logic or measurable quantities and less on emotion or other more vague concepts. They are also best at receiving any communication that has clear structure and a logical emphasis.

INTERPERSONAL COMMUNICATORS PREFER PERSONAL CONTACT. They tend to receive information most effectively and communicate information most clearly when interacting directly with others. Interpersonal communicators also tend to focus on, and respond to, emotion in their interactions.

INTRAPERSONAL COMMUNICATORS OFTEN NEED ADDITIONAL TIME TO PROCESS COMMUNICATION. They may prefer to spend time alone thinking through information before communicating it. They may also need similar processing time after receiving communication, whether written on paper or spoken in person.

You may shift from style to style according to the situation, particularly when trying to communicate with someone who prefers a style different from yours. Shifting, however, is not always easy or possible. The most important task is to try to understand the different styles and to help others understand yours. No one style is any better than another. Each has its own positive effects that enhance communication and negative effects that can hinder it, depending on the situation.

Identifying Your Styles

As with the intelligences themselves, people may possess characteristics from more than one category or may shift dominance depending on the situation, but for most people one, two, or perhaps three styles are most prominent. Thinking about your dominant intelligences will help you to determine your most comfortable communication style or styles. Consider which settings or strategies seem to have positive or negative effects on your ability to give or receive communication.

When you know what works best for you, try to create the best situation for you and for those with whom you communicate. Step back from your emotions and try to be as objective as possible. You can make adjustments both as the communicator and as the receiver.

Adjusting to the Receiver's Style

When you are the speaker, you will benefit from an understanding of both your own style and the styles of your receivers or listeners. It doesn't matter how clear you think you are being if the person you are speaking to can't "translate" your message due to a difficulty in understanding your style. Try to take your listener's style into consideration when you communicate.

Following is an example of how adjusting to the listener can aid communication.

> *An interpersonal instructor to a logical–mathematical student:* "I didn't get any sense of your individual writing voice from your essay." The student's reply: "What do you mean?"

- *Without adjustment:* If the interpersonal instructor doesn't take note of the logical student's need for detail and examples, she may continue with a string of general or emotion-focused ideas that might further confuse or turn off the student. "You need to elaborate more. Try writing from the heart. You're not considering your audience."
- *With adjustment:* If the instructor shifts toward a focus on detail, the student may begin to understand, and the lines of communication can open. "You've supported your central idea clearly, but you didn't move beyond the facts into your personal interpretation of what they mean. Your essay reads like a research paper—the language is technical and doesn't sound like it is coming directly from you. I've seen you put more of yourself into your work before."

Adjusting to the Communicator's Style

As a facet of communication, listening is just as important as speaking. When you are the listener, try to stay aware of the communication style of the speaker. Observe how that style satisfies or fails to meet your needs. Work to understand the speaker in the context of his style and translate the message into one that makes sense to you.

Following is an example of how adjusting to the communicator can boost understanding.

> *A bodily–kinesthetic/interpersonal employee to a verbal–linguistic supervisor:* "I'm really upset about the e-mail memo you sent to me. I don't think you've been fair in not addressing the situation with me in person. I don't feel I've had a chance to defend myself."

- *Without adjustment:* If the supervisor becomes annoyed with the employee's focus on direct personal contact, she may put up an even stronger barrier. "I told you clearly and specifically what needs to be done, and my language wasn't hurtful. I don't know what else there is to discuss."

- *With adjustment:* If the supervisor considers that a different approach will help the employee better understand the situation, she could respond in a way that incorporates the in-person communication that the employee understands best. "Let's meet after lunch so you can explain to me why you're upset and how we can improve the situation."

Styles are only one aspect of communication. Following are other issues that arise.

Address Communication Issues

Communication can be complicated; people filter information through their own perspectives and interpret it in different ways. Some of the most common communication issues follow, along with strategies to help you address them.

Issue: Unclear or incomplete explanation

Solution: Support ideas with examples

When you clarify a general idea with supporting examples that illustrate how it works and what effects it causes, you will help your receiver understand what you mean, and therefore, you will have a better chance to hold his attention. Be clear, precise, and to the point as you link your ideas to examples.

For example, if you tell a friend to take a certain class, that person might not take you seriously until you explain why. If you then communicate the positive effects of taking that class (progress toward a major, an excellent instructor, and friendly study sessions), you may get your message across. If at work you assign a task without explanation, you might get a delayed response or find mistakes in an employee's work. If, however, you explain potential positive effects of the task, you'll have better results.

Issue: Attacking the receiver

Solution: Send "I" messages

When a conflict arises, often the first instinct is to pinpoint what someone else did wrong: "You didn't lock the door!" "You never called last night!" Making an accusation, especially without proof, puts the other person on the defensive and shuts down the lines of communication.

Using "I" messages will help you communicate your own needs rather than focusing on what you think someone else should do differently: "I felt uneasy when I came to work and the door was unlocked." "I became worried about you when I didn't hear from you last night." "I" statements soften the conflict by highlighting the effects that the other person's actions have had on you, rather than the person or the actions themselves. When you focus on your own response and needs, your receiver may feel more free to respond, perhaps offering help and even acknowledging mistakes.

Issue: Passive or aggressive communication styles

Solution: Become assertive

Among the three major communication styles—aggressive, passive, and **assertive**—the one that conveys a message in the clearest, most productive way is the assertive style. The other two, although commonly used, throw the communication out of balance. Assertive behavior strikes a balance between aggression and passivity. If you can be an assertive communicator, you will be more likely to get your message across while assuring that others have a chance to speak as well. Table 11.2 compares some characteristics of each kind of communicator.

Aggressive communicators focus primarily on their own needs. They can become angry and impatient when those needs are not immediately satisfied. To become more assertive, aggressive communicators might try to take time to think before speaking, avoid ordering people around, use "I" statements, and focus on listening to what the other person has to say.

Passive communicators deny themselves the power that aggressive people grab. They focus almost exclusively on the needs of others instead of on their own needs, often experiencing unexpressed frustration and tension. To become more assertive, passive communicators might try to acknowledge anger or hurt more often, speak up when they feel strongly about something, realize that they have a right to make requests, and know that their ideas and feelings are as important as anyone else's.

Good communication skills will come in handy when you have to communicate in more formal situations. Remember these communication strategies as you read the next section on public speaking.

> **ASSERTIVE**
>
> Able to declare and affirm one's own opinions while respecting the right of others to do the same.

11.2 TABLE

Aggressive, passive, and assertive styles.

AGGRESSIVE	PASSIVE	ASSERTIVE
Loud, heated arguing	Concealing one's own feelings	Expressing feelings without being nasty or overbearing
Physically violent encounters	Denying one's own anger	Acknowledging emotions but staying open to discussion
Blaming, name-calling, and verbal insults	Feeling that one has no right to express anger	Expressing self and giving others the chance to express themselves equally
Walking out of arguments before they are resolved	Avoiding arguments	Using "I" statements to defuse arguments
Being demanding: "Do this"	Being noncommittal: "You don't have to do this unless you really want to"	Asking and giving reasons: "I would appreciate it if you would do this, and here's why . . ."

Speaking/Oral Presentations

Speaking in front of others involves special preparation, strategy, and confidence. Whether you are giving group project results to your class or making a presentation to coworkers, think critically in order to make your communication as effective as it can be. Use the strategies that follow.

THINK THROUGH WHAT YOU WANT TO SAY AND WHY. What is your purpose—to make or refute an argument, present information, entertain? Have a goal for your speech.

PLAN. Get organized beforehand. Brainstorm your topic—narrow it with prewriting strategies, determine your central idea or argument, and write an outline. Do research if you need to.

DRAFT YOUR THOUGHTS. It's important to get your thoughts organized for both speaking and writing. Instead of writing out complete sentences, make a draft using "trigger" words or phrases that will remind you of what you want to say.

USE CLEAR THINKING. Illustrate ideas with examples, and show how examples lead to ideas. As in writing, have a clear beginning and end. Begin with an attention getter and end with a wrap-up that summarizes your thoughts and leaves your audience with something to remember.

KNOW THE PARAMETERS. How long do you have? What topics do you have to choose from? Make sure you stick to the guidelines that your instructor gives you. Where will you be speaking? Be aware of the physical setting—where your audience will be, where you will be, and what you may have around you to use (e.g., a podium, table, chair, or blackboard).

USE INDEX CARDS OR NOTES. It's helpful to have notes to refer to. However, keep them out of your face; it's tempting to hide behind them. Use visuals if they help you to illustrate ideas.

PAY ATTENTION TO THE PHYSICAL. Your body positioning, your voice, and what you wear contribute to the impression you make. Look good and sound good. Walk around if you like to talk that way. Above all, make eye contact with your audience. You are speaking to them—be sure to look at them.

PRACTICE AHEAD OF TIME. Do a test run with friends or alone. If you can, practice in the room where you will speak. Audiotape or videotape yourself practicing, and use the tapes to evaluate yourself. Give yourself a positive image—envision yourself delivering the speech successfully and skillfully.

BE YOURSELF. When you speak, you express your personality through your words and your presence. First of all, if you have a choice of topic, choose something that moves or interests you. Then, don't be afraid to add your own bits of humor or style to the presentation. Finally, take deep breaths. Smile. Know that you can communicate successfully and that, in most situations, your audience has the very same hope for you.

Knowing who you are and being yourself isn't just useful for making oral presentations. It will also help you make the most of your personal relationships.

HOW DO YOUR PERSONAL RELATIONSHIPS DEFINE YOU?

The relationships you have with friends, family members, and significant others help to define who you are and can affect other areas of your life. On one hand, you may have experienced conflict that caused you to be unable to sleep, eat, or get work done. On the other hand, a successful relationship can have positive effects on your life, increasing your success at work or at school.

If you can feel good about your personal relationships, other areas of your life will benefit. Here are some strategies for improving your personal relationships.

MAKE PERSONAL RELATIONSHIPS A HIGH PRIORITY. Nurture the ones you have and be open to new ones. Life is meant to be shared. In some marriage ceremonies, the bride and groom share a cup of wine, symbolizing that the sweetness of life is doubled by tasting it together and the bitterness is cut in half when shared by two. Any personal relationship can benefit from the experience of this kind of sharing.

INVEST TIME. You devote time to education, work, and the other priorities in your life. Relationships need the same investment of attention. In addition, spending time with people you like can relieve everyday stress and strain. When you make time for others, everyone benefits.

SPEND TIME WITH PEOPLE YOU RESPECT AND ADMIRE. Life is too short to hang out with people who bring you down, encourage you to participate in activities you don't approve of, or behave in ways that upset you. Develop relationships with people who you respect, whose choices you admire, and who inspire you to fulfill your potential.

WORK THROUGH TENSIONS. Negative feelings can multiply when left unspoken. Unexpressed feelings about other issues may cause you to become disproportionately angry over a small issue. Get to the root of the problem. Discuss it, deal with it, and move on.

REFUSE TO TOLERATE VIOLENCE. People may tolerate violence out of a belief that it will end, a desire to keep their families together, a self-esteem so low that they believe they deserve what they get, or a fear that trying to leave may lead to greater violence. No level of violence is acceptable. If you find that you are either an aggressor or a victim, do your best to get help.

SHOW APPRECIATION. In this fast-moving world, people don't thank each other often enough. If you think of something positive, say it. Thank someone for a service or express your affection with a smile. A little positive reinforcement goes a long way toward nurturing a relationship.

IF YOU WANT A FRIEND, BE A FRIEND. If you treat a friend with the kind of loyalty and support that you appreciate yourself, you are more likely to receive the same in return.

TAKE RISKS. It can be frightening to reveal your deepest dreams and frustrations, to devote yourself to a friend, or to fall in love. However, if you take the plunge, you stand to gain the incredible benefits of companionship, which for most people outweigh the risks.

DON'T FORCE YOURSELF INTO A PATTERN THAT DOESN'T SUIT YOU. Some students date exclusively and commit early. Some students prefer to socialize in groups. Some students date casually and like to maintain a distance from the people they date. Be honest with yourself—and with those with whom you socialize—about what is right for you at any given time.

KEEP PERSONAL PROBLEMS IN THEIR PLACE. Solve personal problems with the people directly involved. If at all possible, try not to bring your emotions into class or work. Doing so may hurt your performance while doing nothing to help your problem.

IF A RELATIONSHIP DOESN'T WORK OUT, FIND WAYS TO COPE. Be kind to yourself, and use coping strategies that help you move on. Some people need time alone; others need to spend time with friends and family. Some seek counseling. Some people throw their energy into a project, job, class, or a new workout regimen. Some just need to cry it out. Some write in a journal. Do what's right for you, and believe that sooner or later you can emerge from the experience stronger and with new perspective.

Now and again, your relationships will be in conflict. Following are ideas for how to deal with conflict and criticism in a productive and positive way.

HOW CAN YOU HANDLE CONFLICT AND CRITICISM?

Conflict and criticism, as unpleasant as they can be, are natural elements in the dynamic of getting along with others. It's normal to want to avoid people or situations that cause distress. However, if you can face your fears and think about them critically, you can gain valuable insight into human nature—your own and that of others. You may be able to make important changes in your life based on what you learn.

Conflict Strategies

Conflicts, both large and small, arise when there is a clash of ideas or interests. You may have small conflicts with a housemate over a door left unlocked or a bill that needs paying. On the other end of the spectrum, you

Windows on the World

How can I deal with diversity?

Richard Pan, *Columbia University-New York City, Engineering Major*

I was born in Taiwan and came to the United States when I was 12. At my high school in Santa Barbara, CA, everyone mingled well. Caucasian kids hung out with Asians and African Americans and we all got along fine. Then, when I started college at Columbia University, I noticed a difference. The Asian kids hung out only with other Asians, and the Caucasians did the same. I'm used to hanging out with all sorts of people, and I like that. Now I feel this tension. It's as if the Asian kids are thinking, "Why is he bothering to hang out with them?"

During a summer work program at Harvard, I roomed with a Chinese-American who advised me to avoid being friends with people from different ethnic groups. Although I don't feel comfortable with his advice, I do think you get judged by both sides when you try to be friends with everybody. Sometimes if I'm with a Caucasian person and other Caucasian people approach us, they aren't as friendly, talking only to the other Caucasian kid like I'm not there. Whenever I've tried to talk to my Asian friends about this problem, they respond jokingly, saying something like, "Rich, you're just better at doing that [mingling with other groups] than I am."

Sometimes I feel like I'm having an identity crisis. I ask myself, "Which side am I on?" I'm not really Asian-American because I wasn't born here, but I have become accustomed to America and I like living here. I think overall I've handled the situation pretty well, but I am open to suggestions. Do you have any ideas about how I could do a better job managing this problem?

Jo Anne Roe, *Spanish Instructor, Oak Park-River Forest High School*

It is wonderful that you have developed the ability to mingle with and enjoy the company of people from diverse backgrounds. This is a skill that many people do not possess, a skill that will be immensely valuable for your personal and professional future. Your comfort in a multicultural setting reflects self-assurance, maturity, and a clearly defined sense of identity.

The problem that you face—prejudice—does not originate within you, but rather is being imposed upon you. To accuse one specific group of having a monopoly on this practice would be a denial of the truth. Misunderstanding of, apprehension toward, and nonacceptance of others who are different are facets of an elemental and, sadly, universal flaw in the human psyche. And because it is so painful, it is natural for people to guard themselves against its damage.

Perhaps your Caucasian friends display insensitivity out of a fear of being rejected by their peers.

Perhaps these same students believe they accept you so completely that not to show that they are aware of your presence is evidence that you are "one of the guys." I imagine that the other Asians are advising you out of a sincere concern for you not to be hurt by those with whom they have had negative encounters in the past. The bottom line is that you are not at fault!

The best advice that I can offer to you is the Golden Rule. Treat other people the way you want them to treat you. In following the wisdom of this refrain, you neither compromise your own outlook on life nor give in to the fears and insecurities of other people, and you maintain human dignity in general. Eventually you will begin to see gradual and positive changes in the actions of your friends and family, due to the impact you will have made on them through your positive, accepting attitude.

357

might encounter major conflicts with your partner about finances or with an instructor about a failing grade.

Conflict can create anger and frustration, shutting down communication. If calmly and intelligently handled, however, conflict can shed light on new ideas and help to strengthen bonds between those involved. The primary keys to conflict resolution are calm communication and critical-thinking skills. Think through any conflict, using what you know about problem solving.

1. *Identify and analyze the problem.* Determine the severity of the problem by looking at its effects on everyone involved. Then, find and analyze its causes.

2. *Brainstorm possible solutions.* Consider as many angles as you can, without judgment. Explore what ideas you can come up with from what you or others have done in a similar situation.

3. *Explore each solution.* Evaluate the positive and negative effects of each solution. Why might each work, not work, or work partially? What would take into account everyone's needs? What would cause the least stress? Make sure everyone has a chance to express an opinion.

4. *Choose, carry out, and evaluate the solution you decide is best.* When you have implemented your choice, evaluate its effects. Decide whether you feel it was a good choice.

One more hint: Use "I" statements. Focus on the effects the problem has had on you rather than focusing on someone who caused it.

Dealing with Criticism and Feedback

FEEDBACK

Evaluative or corrective information about an action or process.

No one gets everything right all the time. People use constructive criticism and **feedback** to communicate what went wrong and to suggest improvements. Consider any criticism carefully. If you always interpret criticism as a threat, you will close yourself off from learning. Even if you eventually decide that you disagree, you can still learn from exploring the possibility.

Criticism can be either **constructive** or nonconstructive. Criticism is considered constructive when it is offered supportively and contains useful suggestions for improvement. In contrast, nonconstructive criticism focuses on what went wrong, doesn't offer alternatives or help, and is often delivered in a negative or harsh manner. Whereas constructive criticism can promote a sense of hope for improvement in the future, nonconstructive criticism can create tension, bad feelings, and defensiveness.

CONSTRUCTIVE

Promoting improvement or development.

Any criticism can be offered constructively or nonconstructively. Consider a case in which someone has continually been late to work. A supervisor can offer criticism in either of these ways:

Constructive. The supervisor talks privately with the employee: "I've noticed that you have been late to work a lot. Other people have had to do some of your work. Is there a problem that is keeping you from being on time? Is it something that I or someone else can help you with?"

Nonconstructive. The supervisor watches the employee slip into work late. The supervisor says, in front of other employees, "Nice to see you could make it. If you can't start getting here on time, I might look for someone else who can."

How might you react? Think about which situation you consider to have more positive effects. If you can learn to give constructive criticism and deal with whatever criticism comes your way from others, you will improve your relationships and your productivity. When offered constructively and carefully considered, criticism can bring about important changes.

> *Do not use a hatchet to remove a fly from your friend's forehead.*
>
> **CHINESE PROVERB**

Giving Constructive Criticism

When you offer criticism, use the following strategies to communicate clearly and effectively:

- *Criticize the behavior rather than the person.* Make sure the behavior you intend to criticize is changeable. Chronic lateness can be changed; a physical inability to perform a task cannot.
- *Define specifically the behavior you want to change.* Try not to drag any side issues into the conversation.
- *Limit the behaviors you will criticize to one.* If you have others, discuss them later, one at a time. People can hear criticism better if they are not hit with several issues at once.
- *Balance criticism with positive words.* Alternate critical comments with praise in other areas.
- *Stay calm and be brief.* Avoid threats, ultimatums, or accusations. Use "I" messages; choose positive, nonthreatening words so the person knows that your intentions are positive.
- *Explain the effects caused by the behavior.* Talk about options in detail. Compare and contrast the effects of the current behavior with the effects of a potential change.
- *Offer help in changing the behavior.* Lead by example.

Receiving Criticism

When you find yourself on the receiving end of criticism, use the following coping techniques:

- *Listen to the criticism first.* Resist the desire to defend yourself until you've heard all the details. Decide if the criticism is offered in a constructive or nonconstructive manner.
- *Think the criticism through critically.* Evaluate it carefully. Is it constructive? Does it come from a desire to help, or has it emerged from a place of jealousy or frustration? It may be best to let nonconstructive criticism go without a response.
- *If the criticism is constructive, ask for suggestions on how to change the criticized behavior.* You could ask, "How would you handle this if you were in my place?"
- *Summarize the criticism and your response to it.* Repeat it back to the person who offered it. Make sure both of you understand the situation in the same way.
- *Plan a specific strategy.* Think over how you might change your behavior and what you might learn from the change.

Remember that the most important feedback you will receive in school is from your instructors, and the most important on-the-job feedback will come from your supervisors, more experienced peers, and occasionally clients. Making a special effort to take in this feedback and consider it carefully will help you learn many important lessons. Furthermore, knowing how to handle conflict and criticism will help you define your role and communicate with others when you work in groups.

WHAT ROLES DO YOU PLAY IN GROUPS?

Group interaction is an important part of your educational, personal, and working life. With a team project at work or a cooperative learning exercise in school, for example, being able to work well together is necessary to accomplish a goal.

A group or team can be coworkers, fellow students, a family, or other people who need to accomplish a goal together. Because everyone has a vested interest in the outcome, all group members should have the opportunity

to voice opinions and to participate in reaching the desired goal.

The two major roles in the group experience are those of participant and leader. Any group needs both to function successfully. Become aware of the role you tend to play, and try different roles to evaluate where you can be most effective. The following strategies are linked to either participating or leading.[6]

Being an Effective Participant

Some people are happiest when participating in group activities that someone else leads and designs. They don't feel comfortable in a position of control. They prefer to take on an assigned role in the project. Participants need to remember that they are "part owners" of the process. Each team member has a responsibility for, and a stake in, the outcome. The following strategies will help a participant to be effective.

Participation Strategies

- *Get involved.* If the rest of the group makes a decision you don't like and you don't speak up, you have no one to blame but yourself for the group's poor choice. Let people know your views.
- *Be organized.* When you participate, stay focused and organized. The more organized your ideas are, the more people will listen, take them into consideration, and be willing to try them.
- *Be willing to discuss.* Everyone has an equal right to express his ideas. Even as you enthusiastically present your opinions, be willing to consider those of others.

- *Keep your word.* Do what you say you're going to do. Let people know what you have accomplished. If you bring little or nothing to the process, your team members may feel as if you weigh them down rather than pulling your own weight.
- *Focus on ideas, not people.* One of the easiest ways to start an argument is for participants to attack people instead of discussing their ideas. Separate the person from the idea, and keep the idea in focus.
- *Play fairly.* Give everyone a chance to participate. Be respectful of other people's ideas. Don't dominate the discussion or try to control or manipulate others.

Being an Effective Leader

Some people prefer to initiate the action, make decisions, and control how things proceed. They have ideas they want to put into practice and enjoy explaining them to others. They are comfortable giving directions to people and guiding group outcomes. Leaders often have a "big picture" perspective; it allows them to see how all of the different aspects of a group project can come together. In any group the following strategies will help a leader succeed.

Leadership Strategies

- *Define and limit projects.* The leader should define the purpose of the gathering and limit tasks so the group doesn't take on too much. Some common purposes are giving and exchanging information, brainstorming, making a decision, delegating tasks, or collaborating on a project.
- *Map out who will perform which tasks.* A group functions best when everyone has a particular contribution to make. You can help different personalities work together by exploring who can do what best. Give people specific responsibilities, trusting that they will do their jobs.
- *Set the agenda.* The leader is responsible for establishing and communicating the goal of the project and how it will proceed. Having a written agenda to which group members can refer is helpful. A good leader invites advice from others when determining group direction.
- *Focus progress.* Even when everyone knows the plan, it's still natural to wander off the topic. The leader should do her best to keep everyone to the topic at hand. When challenges arise midstream, the leader may need to help the team change direction.
- *Set the tone.* Setting a positive tone helps to bring the group together and motivate people. When a leader values diversity in ideas and backgrounds and sets a tone of fairness, respect, and encouragement, group members may feel more comfortable contributing their ideas.
- *Evaluate results.* The leader should determine whether the team is accomplishing its goals. If the team is not moving ahead, the leader needs to make changes and decisions.

If you don't believe that you fit into the traditional definition of a leader, remember that there are other ways to lead that don't involve taking charge of a group. You can lead others by setting an honorable example in your actions, choices, or words. You can lead by putting forth an idea that takes a group in a new direction. You can lead by being the kind of person who others would like to be.

It takes the equal participation of all group members to achieve a goal. Whatever role works best for you, know that your contribution is essential. You may even play different roles with different groups. You might be a participator at school and a leader in a self-help group. You could enjoy leading a religious group but prefer to take a backseat at work. Find a role that feels comfortable. The happier each group member is, the more effectively the group as a whole will function.

Kente

The African word *kente* means "that which will not tear under any condition." *Kente* cloth is worn by men and women in African countries such as Ghana, Ivory Coast, and Togo. There are many brightly colored patterns of *kente,* each beautiful, unique, and special.

Think of how this concept applies to being human. Like the cloth, all people are unique, with brilliant and subdued aspects. Despite any mistreatment or misunderstanding by the people you encounter in your life, you need to remain strong so that you don't tear and give way to disrespectful behavior. This strength can help you to endure, stand up against any injustice, and fight peacefully but relentlessly for the rights of all people.

IMPORTANT POINTS *to remember*

1. Why is it important to understand and accept others?

In a world that is becoming increasingly diverse, your success in school, work, and in your personal life may depend on how well you interact with people from diverse backgrounds. Understanding and respectful communication are the keys to interaction. Stereotypes, prejudice, discrimination, and fear of differences can block understanding. Keep an open mind and work to overcome those blocks. If you can accept and promote differences, you will have the greatest chance of broadening your knowledge and relating successfully.

2. How can you think critically about diversity?

Thinking critically about diversity will help you break down the barriers that prevent successful communication. Critical thinking will help you confront prejudice and avoid personal acts of discrimination and making assumptions that are at the core of stereotypes. If you are a minority group member, an awareness of the problems associated with diversity will help you avoid stereotype vulnerability. Hate crimes, caused by a fear of differ- ences, are prevalent on college campuses and throughout the country. Overcoming prejudice and the hate it engenders is possible if you accept individual difference and respect the equal rights of others.

3. How can you express yourself effectively?

Effective communication is one important key to successful relationships. Addressing communication issues—such as different communication styles, body language, unclear explanations, assumptions, and passive or aggres- sive communication styles—will help. You can apply your understanding of effective communication to oral presentations. Your goal is to speak with confidence and poise in front of others.

4. How do your personal relationships define you?

Successful relationships with the important people around you, including your family members, friends, fellow students, instructors, and others, depend on strategies such as investing time, working through tensions, showing appreciation, taking risks, and keeping problems in their place.

5. How can you handle conflict and criticism?

Conflict and criticism are a natural part of human relationships. Conflicts arise when there is a clash of ideas or interests. Successful conflict resolution requires that you stay assertive, think critically, and use "I" statements. Constructive criticism can help you learn and improve. When giving criti- cism, avoid accusations and be specific about the behavior you want to criticize. When receiving criticism, listen before you judge and think criti- cally about the criticism. If you agree with it, ask for suggestions of how to change and plan a strategy for doing so.

6. What role do you play in groups?

Individuals play particular roles in groups. The two primary roles are those of leader and participant. Leadership strategies include defining and limit- ing tasks, setting the agenda and tone, and focusing on progress. Participant strategies include getting involved, being organized, being willing to discuss, and focusing on ideas. The more efficient each group member is, the more effectively the group will function.

CRITICAL THINKING
APPLYING LEARNING TO LIFE

DIVERSITY DISCOVERY. Express your own personal diversity. Describe yourself in response to the following questions.

How would you identify yourself? Write words or short phrases that describe you.

Name one or more facts about yourself that would not be obvious to someone who has just met you.

Name two values or beliefs that govern how you live, what you pursue, or with whom you associate.

Name a personal choice you have made that tells something about who you are.

Now, join with a partner in your class. Try to choose someone you don't know well. Your goal is to communicate what you have written to your partner and for your partner to communicate to you in the same way. Talk to each other for 10 minutes and take notes on what the other person says. At the end of that period, join together as a class. Each person will describe his or her partner to the class.

What is the most surprising thing you learned about your partner? Did what you learned contradict any assumptions you may have made about that person based on his or her appearance, background, or behavior?

TEAMWORK

COMBINING FORCES

PROBLEM SOLVING CLOSE TO HOME. Divide into small groups of two to five. Assign one group member to take notes. Discuss the following questions, one by one:

1. What are the three largest problems our school faces with regard to how people get along with and accept others?
2. What could our school do to deal with these three problems?
3. What can each individual student do to deal with these three problems? (Talk about what *you* specifically feel that you can do.)

When you are finished, gather as a class and hear each group's responses. Observe the variety of problems and solutions. Notice whether more than one group came up with one or more of the same problems. You may want to assign one person in the class to gather all of the responses together. That person, together with your instructor, could put these responses into an organized document that you can give to the upper-level administrators at your school.

WRITING

DISCOVERY THROUGH JOURNALING

To record your thoughts, use a separate journal or the lined page at the end of the chapter.

NEW PERSPECTIVE.[7] Imagine that you have no choice but to change either your gender or your racial, ethnic, or religious group. Which would you change, and why? What do you anticipate would be the positive and negative effects of the change—in your social life, in your family life, on the job, and at school? How would what you know and experience before the change affect how you would behave after it?

CAREER PORTFOLIO

CHARTING YOUR COURSE

LEADERSHIP AND PARTICIPATION. What you have accomplished as a leader or participant in various groups will be important for you to emphasize as you strive to land your ideal job. Whether on the job, in school, in the community, or at home, your roles help you gain knowledge and experience.

Use two pieces of paper. On one, list leadership roles. On the other, list participation experience. Consider workplace, school, community, and home situations. Record both your job title and the tasks that the job entailed (if the job had no particular title, come up with one yourself). Be as detailed as possible—it's best to write down everything you remember. Later, you can make this material more concise for purposes of writing a résumé. For example:

Production Assistant for WBAL-TV
• Coordinated personnel on location shoots (was in charge of making sure everyone got there on time and performed tasks on time)
• Coordinated food services (ordered lunch, made sure it got delivered, made sure everyone was fed, cleaned up)
• Maintained communications equipment (was in charge of transporting, distributing, and collecting walkie-talkies, and making sure they worked properly)
• Assisted director (performed last-minute tasks for director as needed)

Keep this list current by adding experiences and accomplishments to it as you go along. It will come in handy when you need to create a comprehensive résumé and prepare for an impressive interview.

UGGESTED READINGS

Stephen D. Bertholf. *What Every College Age Woman Should Know About Relationships*. Wichita, KS: Abbey House Books (1999).

Blank, Rennee and Sandra Slipp. *Voices of Diversity: Real People Talk About Problems and Solutions in a Workplace Where Everyone is Not Alike*. New York: American Management Association (1994).

Dublin, Thomas, ed. *Becoming American, Becoming Ethnic: College Students Explore Their Roots*. Philadelphia, PA: Temple University Press (1996).

Feagin, Joe R., Hernan Vera, and Nikitah O. Imani. *The Agony of Education: Black Students at White Colleges and Universities*. New York: Routledge (1996).

Gonzales, Juan L., Jr. *The Lives of Ethnic Americans,* 2nd ed. Dubuque, IA: Kendall/Hunt (1994).

Hockenberry, John. *Moving Violations*. New York: Hyperion (1996).

Levey, Marc, Michael Blanco, and W. Terrell Jones. *How To Succeed on a Majority Campus: A Guide for Minority Students*. Belmont, CA: Wadsworth Publishing Co. (1997).

Qubein, Nido R. *How to Be a Great Communicator: In Person, on Paper, and at the Podium*. New York: John Wiley (1996).

Schuman, David and Dick W. Olufs. *Diversity on Campus.* Boston, MA: Allyn & Bacon (1994).

Suskind, Ron. *A Hope in the Unseen: An American Odyssey from the Inner City to the Ivy League.* New York: Broadway Books (1998).

Takaki, Ronald. *A Different Mirror: A History of Multicultural America.* Boston: Little, Brown (1994).

Tannen, Deborah. *You Just Don't Understand: Women and Men in Conversation.* New York: Ballantine Books (1991).

Terkel, Studs. *Race: How Blacks and Whites Think and Feel About the American Obsession.* New York: Free Press (1995).

Trotter, Tamera and Joycelyn Allen. *Talking Justice: 602 Ways to Build and Promote Racial Harmony.* Saratoga, CA: R & E Publishers (1993).

 INTERNET RESOURCES

Asian-American Resources: www.ai.mit.edu/people/irie/aar/

Britannica Guide to Black History: http://blackhistory.eb.com

Diversity Web: www.diversityweb.org/text/index.html

Latino USA: www.latinousa.org

Latino Website Pathfinder: www.sscnet.ucla.edu.csrc/library/pathfind.htm

The Sociology of Race and Ethnicity: www.trinity.edu/~mkearl/race.html

 ENDNOTES

1. Bureau of the Census Statistical Brief "Sixty-Five Plus in the United States," SB/95-8, Issued May 1995, Washington, D.C., U.S. Department of Commerce, Economics and Statistics Administration, Bureau of the Census.

2. Sheryl McCarthy. *Why Are the Heroes Always White?* Kansas City, MO: Andrews and McMeel (1995), p. 188.

3. Claude Steele, Ph.D., Professor of Psychology, Stanford University.

4. Tamera Trotter and Joycelyn Allen. *Talking Justice: 602 Ways to Build and Promote Racial Harmony.* Saratoga, CA: R & E Publishers (1993), p. 51.

5. Sheryl McCarthy. *Why Are the Heroes Always White?* p. 137.

6. Louis E. Boone, David L. Kurtz, and Judy R. Block. *Contemporary Business Communication,* 2nd ed. Upper Saddle River, NJ: Prentice Hall (1997), pp. 460–469.

7. Adapted by Richard Bucher, Professor of Sociology, Baltimore City Community College, from Paula Rothenberg, William Paterson College of New Jersey.

Journal

NAME

DATE

Thinking It Through

Check those statements that apply to you right now:

- I have no idea what I want to do for a career.

- I don't know how to be marketable in the workplace if I don't have experience.

- I have a job that I like but I struggle to fit everything in with my classes.

- I can't pay for my education on my own.

- It's a drag to save money for the future when I need it now.

- I've run into trouble with credit cards, but I need them.

12

IN THIS CHAPTER,

you will explore answers to the

following questions:

- How can you plan your career?
- How can you juggle work and school?
- How can you explore career opportunities?
- What should you know about financial aid?
- How can strategic planning help you manage money?
- How can you create a budget that works?

Managing Career and Money

Many people either love their jobs but don't make much money or dislike their jobs but are paid well. Still others have neither job satisfaction nor a good paycheck to show for their work. The ideal career inspires passion and motivation and pays well. Career exploration and job-hunting skills can help you find your ideal career, whether it is being a teacher in Minnesota, an attorney in Manhattan, an archaeologist in northern Africa, or anything else that fits your dreams. Solid money-management skills can help you use your money effectively to meet your short- and long-term financial goals.

In this chapter, you will first look at career exploration and how to balance work and school. Then, you will explore how to bring in money with financial aid and how to manage the money you have.

OW CAN YOU PLAN YOUR CAREER?

Students are in different stages when it comes to thinking about careers. You may have already had a career for years and are looking for a change. You may have decided on a particular career but are now having second thoughts. Or, like many people, you may not have thought too much about it yet. Regardless of your starting point, now is the time to make progress.

Define a Career Path

Aiming for a job in a particular area requires planning the steps that can get you there. Whether these steps take months or years, they help you focus your energies on your goal. Defining a career path involves investigating yourself, exploring potential careers, staying current on the state of the working world, and building knowledge and experience.

Investigate Yourself

When you explore your learning style in Chapter 3, evaluate your ideal note-taking system in Chapter 7, or look at how you relate to others in Chapter 11, you build self-knowledge. Gather everything that you know about yourself, from this class or from life experiences. Ask the following questions:

- What do you know best, do best, and enjoy best?
- Out of all of the jobs you've had, what did you like and not like to do?
- How would you describe your learning style and personality?
- What kinds of careers could make the most of everything you are?

If you don't know exactly what you want to do, you are not alone. Many students who have not been in the workplace—and even some who have—don't know what career they want to pursue. Give yourself permission to change your mind as you take courses and find out more about different careers.

Explore Potential Careers

Career possibilities extend far beyond what you can imagine. Brainstorm about career areas. Ask instructors, relatives, and fellow students about careers that they have or know about. Check your library for books on careers or biographies of people who worked in fields that interest you. Explore careers you discover through movies, newspapers, novels, or nonfiction.

Use your critical-thinking skills to broaden your questions beyond just what tasks you perform for any given job. Many other factors will be important to you. Look at Table 12.1 for some of the kinds of questions you might ask as you talk to people or investigate materials. You may discover that:

Critical-thinking questions for career exploration.

What can I do in this area that I like or do well?	Do I respect the company and the industry?
What are the educational requirements (certificates or degrees, courses)?	Does this company or industry accommodate special needs (child care, sick days, flex time)?
What skills are necessary?	Do I need to belong to a union?
What wage or salary and benefits can I expect?	Are there opportunities near where I live (or want to live)?
What kinds of personalities are best suited to this kind of work?	What other expectations exist (travel, overtime, etc.)?
What are the prospects for moving up to higher-level positions?	Do I prefer the service or production end of this industry?

A WIDE ARRAY OF JOB POSSIBILITIES EXISTS FOR MOST CAREER FIELDS. For example, the medical world consists of more than doctors and nurses. Emergency medical technicians respond to emergencies, administrators run hospitals, researchers test new drugs, lab technicians administer procedures such as X rays, pharmacists prepare prescriptions, retirement community employees work with the elderly, and more.

WITHIN EACH JOB, THERE IS A VARIETY OF TASKS AND SKILLS. You may know that an instructor teaches, but you may not see that instructors also often write, research, study, design courses, give presentations, and counsel. Push past your first impression of any career and explore what else it entails.

COMMON ASSUMPTIONS ABOUT SALARIES DON'T ALWAYS HOLD. Medicine, the law, and computer science aren't the only sources of careers with good income. According to data gathered by the U.S. Labor Department, examples of other careers with high weekly earnings include electricians, public administrators, aircraft mechanics, and more.[1] Even if you work in a job that earns you an extraordinary salary, you may not be happy unless you truly enjoy and learn from what you are doing.

Your school's career center may offer job listings, occupation lists, assessments of skills and personality types, questionnaires to help you pinpoint areas that may suit you, and information about different careers and companies. Visit the center early in your college career and work with a counselor there to develop a solid career game plan.

Stay Current

The working world is always adjusting to the needs of workers, new technologies, and other changes. Reading newspapers and magazines, watching television news programs, and searching the Internet will help you keep abreast of what you face as you make career decisions. Following are two current workplace trends that may be important for you in your career investigation.

MORE TEMPORARY EMPLOYMENT. To save money, corporations are hiring more temporary employees (temps) and fewer full-time employees (the number of temps has increased from 800,000 in 1986 to over 2.5 million in 1997).[2] When considering whether to take a permanent job or a temporary job, consider the effects of each. Permanent jobs offer benefits (e.g., employer contribution to pension plan and health insurance) and stability, but may be less flexible. Temporary jobs offer flexibility, few obligations, and often more take-home pay, but few or no benefits.

NEW VARIETY IN BENEFITS. Companies are beginning to respond to the changing needs of the modern workforce, where workers often have to care for children or aging parents, need to plan for the financial and medical demands of a longer life span, and want to take measures to reduce life stress. This response often involves "quality of life" benefits such as the following:

- *telecommuting* (working from home via telephone, fax, and Internet access)
- *job sharing* (two employees working part-time to fulfill the duties of one full-time position)
- *personal services* such as counseling and financial planning
- *flextime* (the ability to adjust work time in response to school or family needs)
- *child care* on-site or nearby, often at reduced rates

Both workers and companies benefit from offering alternatives to traditional work arrangements. Workers enjoy greater quality of life, and companies are able to promote loyalty and keep employee turnover low in an age where job changing is on the increase. Offerings of these kinds of benefits will most likely continue to increase—see Figure 12.1 for projected growth of particular benefits.

Build Knowledge and Experience

Having knowledge and experience specific to the career you want to pursue will be valuable on the job hunt. Courses, internships, jobs, and volunteering are four great ways to build both.

COURSES. When you narrow your career exploration to a couple of areas that interest you, take a course or two in those areas. How you react to these courses will give you clues to how you feel about the area in general. Be careful to evaluate your experience according to how you feel about the subject matter rather than other factors.

In addition, interview an instructor who teaches a subject related to a career field that interests you. Find out what courses you have to take to major in the field, the grade point average you'll need to pursue a major, what jobs are available in the field, what credentials (degrees or training) you need for particular jobs, and so on.

Modern benefits.

FIGURE 12.1

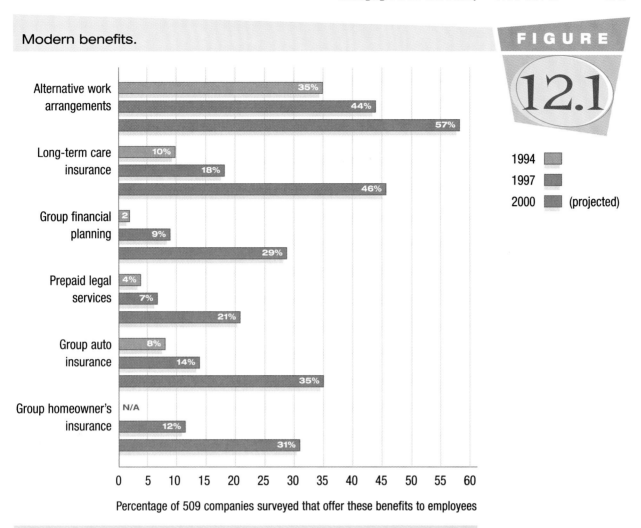

1994
1997
2000   (projected)

Percentage of 509 companies surveyed that offer these benefits to employees

Source: "Perks That Work," *Time,* Nov. 9, 1998. © 1998 Time Inc. Reprinted by permission. Research by Hewitt Associates.

INTERNSHIPS. An internship may or may not offer pay. Although this may be a financial drawback, the experience and new acquaintances may be worth the work. Many internships take place during the summer, but some are available during the school year. Companies that offer internships are looking for people who will work hard in exchange for experience they can't get in the classroom.

Your career center may be able to help you explore internship opportunities. If you discover a career worth pursuing, you'll have the internship experience behind you when you go job hunting. An internship is an excellent way to demonstrate real-world experience and initiative to a prospective employer.

JOBS. No matter what you do for money while you are in college, whether it is in your area of interest or not, you may discover career opportunities that appeal to you. Someone who takes a third-shift legal proofreading job to make extra cash might discover an interest in law. Someone who answers phones for a newspaper company might be drawn into journalism. Be aware of the possibilities around you.

> **INTERNSHIP**
>
> A temporary work program in which a student can gain supervised practical experience in a particular professional field.

VOLUNTEERING. Offering your services in the community or at your school can introduce you to careers and increase your experience. Some schools have programs that can help you find volunteering opportunities. Find out what services your school offers. Volunteer activities are important to note on your résumé. Many employers seek candidates who have shown commitment through volunteering.

No matter how you gather your career knowledge and experience, the key is to focus on continual improvement. You're not "done" when you complete a college degree, training program, course, book, or job. You need to continually build on what you know. With the world's fast-paced changes in mind, today's employers value those who seek continual improvement in their skills and knowledge.

Map Out Your Strategy

After you've gathered enough information to narrow your career goals, plan strategically to achieve them. Make a career time line that illustrates the steps toward your goal, as shown in Figure 12.2. Mark years and half-year points (and months for the first year), and write in the steps when you think they should happen. If your plan is five years long, indicate what you plan to do by the fourth, third, and second years, and then the first year, including a six-month goal and a one-month goal for that first year.

FIGURE 12.2

Career time line.

1 month	Enter community college on a part-time schedule
3 months	Meet with advisor to discuss desired major and
6 months	required courses
1 year	Declare major in secondary education
2 years	Switch to full-time class schedule
3 years	Graduate with associate's degree Transfer to 4-year college
4 years	Work part-time as a classroom aide
5 years	Student teaching
6 years	Graduate with bachelor's degree and teaching certificate Have a job teaching high school

Using what you know about strategic planning, fill in the details about what you will do throughout your plan. Set goals that establish who you will talk to, what courses you will take, what skills you will work on, what jobs or internships you will investigate, and any other research you need to do. Your path may change, of course; use your time line as a guide rather than as an inflexible plan.

The road to a truly satisfying career can be long. Seek support as you work toward goals. Confide in supportive people, talk positively to yourself, and read books about career planning, such as those listed at the end of this chapter.

Seek Mentors

Among the people you go to for career advice, you may find a true mentor. A mentor takes a special interest in helping you to reach your goals. People often seek a mentor who has excelled in a career area or specific skill in which they also wish to excel. You may also be drawn to a person who, no matter what their skills or specialty, has ideas and makes choices that you admire and want to emulate.

A mentoring relationship often evolves from a special personal relationship. A relative, instructor, friend, supervisor, or anyone else who you admire and respect may become your mentor. Think about whom you go to when you need guidance or support. Also, consider who may know a lot about a skill or career area you want to pursue. Some schools have faculty or peer mentoring programs to help match students with people who can help them.

Know What Employers Want

When you look for a job in a particular career area, your technical skills, work experience, and academic credentials that apply to that career will be important. Beyond those basics, though, other skills will make you an excellent job candidate in any career.

Important Skills

Particular skills and qualities, to an employer, signify an efficient and effective employee. You can continue to develop them as you work in current and future jobs. Table 12.2 describes these skills.

These skills appear throughout this book, and they are as much a part of your school success as they are of your work success. The more you develop them now, the more employable and promotable you will prove yourself to be. You may already use them on the job if you are a student who works.

Emotional Intelligence

One other quality in demand in the workplace is emotional intelligence. Daniel Goleman, in his book *Working with Emotional Intelligence,* discusses his findings that emotional intelligence can be even more important than IQ and information knowledge when it comes to success on the job. He defines emotional intelligence as a combination of these factors:[3]

Skills employers look for.

SKILLS	WHY?
Communication	Listening and self-expression are keys to workplace success, as is being able to adjust to different communication styles.
Critical thinking	An employee who can assess workplace choices and challenges critically and recommend appropriate actions will stand out.
Teamwork	All workers interact with others on the job. Working well with others is essential for achieving work goals.
Goal setting	Teams fail if goals are unclear or unreasonable. Benefit is gained from setting realistic, specific goals and achieving them reliably.
Tolerance	The workplace is becoming increasingly diverse. A valuable employee will be able to work with, and respect, a great diversity of people.
Leadership	The ability to influence others in a positive way will earn you respect and help advance your career.
Creativity	The ability to come up with new concepts, plans, and products will be valuable in the workplace.
Positive attitude	If you show that you have a high level of commitment to all tasks, you may earn the right to tackle more challenging projects.
Integrity	Acting with integrity at work—communicating promptly, following rules, giving proper notice, respecting others—will enhance your value.
Flexibility	The most valuable employees understand the constancy of change and have developed the skills to adapt to its challenge.
Continual learning	The most valuable employees stay current on changes and trends by reading up-to-the-minute media and taking workshops and seminars.

- *Personal Competence.* This includes self-awareness (knowing your internal states, preferences, resources, intuitions), self-regulation (being able to manage your internal states, impulses, and resources), and motivation (the factors that help you reach your goals).
- *Social Competence.* This includes empathy (being aware of the feelings, needs, and concerns of others) and social skills (your ability to create desirable responses in those with whom you interact).

The current emphasis on teamwork has made emotional intelligence important in the workplace. The more adept you are at working comfortably and productively with others (i.e., the more you have and use emotional intelligence), the more likely you will be to succeed.

Many students need to work and take classes at the same time to fund the education that they hope will move them into better careers. Although you may not necessarily work in a career that interests you, you can hold a job that helps you pay the bills and still make the most of your school time.

Trust in yourself. Your perceptions are often far more accurate than you are willing to believe.

CLAUDIA BLACK

OW CAN YOU JUGGLE WORK AND SCHOOL?

What you are studying today can prepare you to find a job when you graduate. In the meantime, though, you can make work a part of your student life to make money, explore a career, and increase your future employability through contacts or résumé building.

As the cost of education continues to rise, more and more students are working and taking classes at the same time. In the school year 1995–96, 79 percent of undergraduates—four out of five—reported working while in school. Most student workers 23 years of age or younger held part-time jobs (about 36 percent). Of students over the age of 23, the majority had full-time jobs (nearly 55 percent).[4] Figure 12.3 shows statistics related to working for both community college and four-year college students.

Being an employed student isn't for everyone. Adding a job to the list of demands on your time and energy may create problems if it sharply reduces study time or family time. However, many people want to work and many need to work to pay for school. Weigh the potential positive and negative effects of working so that you can make the most beneficial choice.

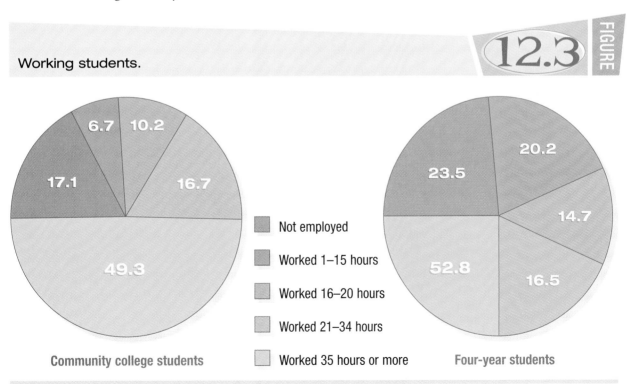

Working students.

FIGURE **12.3**

6.7 | 10.2
17.1
16.7
49.3

20.2
23.5
14.7
52.8
16.5

Not employed

Worked 1–15 hours

Worked 16–20 hours

Worked 21–34 hours

Community college students | Worked 35 hours or more | Four-year students

Source: U. S. Department of Education, National Center for Education Statistics, *Profile of Undergraduates in U. S. Postsecondary Education Institutions: 1995–96* (NCES 98-084), May 1998.

Effects of Working While in School

Working while in school has many different positive and negative effects, depending on the situation. Evaluate any job opportunity by looking at these effects. Potential positive effects include:

- money earned
- general and career-specific experience
- being able to keep a job you currently hold
- enhanced school and work performance (working up to 15 hours a week may encourage students to manage time more effectively and build confidence)

Potential negative effects include:

- demanding time commitment
- reduced opportunity for social and extracurricular activities
- having to shift gears mentally from work to classroom

If you consider the effects and decide that working makes sense, consider what you need from a job.

Establishing Your Needs

Think about what you need from a job before you begin your job hunt. Table 12.3 shows questions you may want to consider. Evaluate any potential job in terms of your needs.

In addition, be sure to consider how any special needs you have might be accommodated. If you have a hearing or vision impairment, reduced mobility, children for whom you need day care, or any other particular need, you may want to find an employer who can and will accommodate them.

Whether you are hunting for a job you need while in school or thinking about the bigger picture of your career, the strategies in the next section will help you find what's right for you.

HOW CAN YOU EXPLORE CAREER OPPORTUNITIES?

Many different routes can lead to satisfying jobs and careers. When you take the time to explore what's out there, you give yourself the chance to make an educated decision. The more you know about what's possible, the more you will be able to select the choice that suits you best. Plus, the information you gather will help you evaluate the positive and negative effects that any choice might have for you. Maximize your opportunities by using the resources available to you and making a strategic search plan.

Use Available Resources

Use your school's career planning and placement office, your networking skills, classified ads, online services, and employment agencies to help you

Evaluate job needs.

NEED	EVALUATION QUESTIONS
Salary/wage level	How much do I need to make for the year? How much during the months when I am paying tuition? What amount of money justifies the time my job takes?
Time of day	When is best for me? If I take classes at night, can I handle a day job? If I take day classes, would I prefer night or weekend work?
Hours per week (Part-time vs. full-time)	If I take classes part-time, can I handle a full-time job? If I am a full-time student, is part-time best?
Duties performed	Do I want hands-on experience in my chosen field? Is the paycheck the priority over choosing what I do? What do I like and dislike doing?
Location	Does location matter? Will a job near school save me a great deal of time? What does my commute involve?
Flexibility	Do I need a job that offers flexibility, allowing me to shift my working time when I have an academic or family responsibility?
Affiliation with school or financial aid program	Does my financial aid package require me to take work at the school or a federal organization?

explore possibilities for jobs you need right away and postgraduation career opportunities.

Your School's Career Planning and Placement Office

Generally, the career planning and placement office deals with postgraduation job placements, whereas the student employment office, along with the financial aid office, has more information about working while in school. At either location you might find general workplace information, listings of job opportunities, sign-up sheets for interviews, and contact information for companies.

The career office may hold frequent informational sessions on different topics. Your school may also sponsor job or career fairs that give you a chance to explore job opportunities. Start exploring your school's career office early in your university life. The people and resources there can help you at every stage of your career and job exploration process.

Networking

Networking is one of the most important job-hunting strategies. With each person you get to know, you build your network and tap into someone else's.

NETWORKING

The exchange of information or services between individuals, groups, or institutions.

Of course, not everyone with whom you network will be helpful. Keep in contact with as many people as possible in the hope that someone will. You never know who that person might be. With whom can you network?

- friends and family members
- instructors, administrators, or counselors
- people at employment or career offices
- alumni
- employers or coworkers
- former employers

> **CONTACT**
>
> A person who serves as a carrier or source of information.

The **contacts** with whom you network aren't just sources of job opportunities. They are people with whom you can develop lasting, valuable relationships. They may be willing to talk to you about how to get established, the challenges on the job, what they do each day, how much salary you can expect, or any other questions you have (similar to those in Table 12.1).

Remember this important point: Don't burn your bridges because anyone with whom you network has equal potential to help or harm you. If you maintain positive relationships, you will be more likely to earn help and references from those who know you. Thank your contacts and be ready to extend yourself to others who may need help and advice from you.

Whatever you think you can do or believe you can do, begin it. Action has magic, grace, and power in it.

JOHANN WOLFGANG VON GOETHE

Classified Ads

Some of the best job listings are in newspapers. Most papers print help wanted sections in each issue, organized according to career categories. At the beginning of most help wanted sections, you will find an index that lists the categories and their page numbers. Individual ads describe the kind of position available and give a telephone number or post office box for you to contact. Some ads include additional information such as job requirements, a contact person, and the salary or wages offered. You can also run your own classified ads if you have a skill to advertise.

Online Services

The Internet is growing as a source of job listings. You can access job search databases such as the Career Placement Registry and U.S. Employment Opportunities. Career-focused websites, such as CareerBuilder.com and Monster .com, list all kinds of positions. Individual associations and companies may also post job listings and descriptions, often as part of their World Wide Web pages.

Employment Agencies

Employment agencies are organizations that help people find work. Most employment agencies will put you through a screening process that consists of an interview and one or more tests in your area of expertise. For example, someone looking for secretarial work may take a word-processing test and a spelling test. If you pass the tests and interview well, the agency will try to place you in a job.

Most employment agencies specialize in particular careers or skills, such as accounting, medicine, legal, computer operation, graphic arts, child care, and food services. Agencies may place job seekers in either part-time or full-time employment. Many agencies also place people in temporary jobs, which can work well for students who are available from time to time.

Employment agencies are a great way to hook into job networks. However, they usually require a fee that either you or the employer has to pay. Ask questions so that you know as much as possible about how the agency operates.

Make a Strategic Search Plan

When you have gathered information on the jobs or careers that have piqued your interest, formulate a plan for pursuing them. Organize your approach according to what you need to do and how much time you have to do it. Do you plan to make three phone calls per day? Will you fill out three job applications a week for a month? Keep a record—on 3-by-5-inch cards, in a computer file, or in a notebook—of the following:

- people you contact
- companies to which you apply
- jobs you rule out (e.g., jobs that become unavailable or which you find don't suit your needs)
- response from your communications (phone calls to you, interviews, written communications), information about the person who contacted you (name, title), and the time and the dates of the contact

Keeping accurate records will enable you to both chart your progress and maintain a clear picture of the process. You never know when the information might come in handy again. If you don't get a job now, another one could open up at the same company in a couple of months. In that case, well-kept records would enable you to contact key personnel quickly and efficiently. See Figure 12.4 for a sample file card.

Your Résumé and Interview

Information on résumés and interviews fills many books. Therefore, your best bet is to consult some that go into more detail, such as *The Resume Kit* by Richard H. Beatty or *Job Interviews for Dummies* by Joyce Lain Kennedy. You'll find these sources and other suggestions listed at the end of the chapter.

Here are a few basic tips to get you started on giving yourself the best possible chance at a job.

RÉSUMÉ. Your résumé should always be typed or printed on a computer. Design your résumé neatly, using an acceptable format (books or your career office can show you some standard formats). Proofread it for errors, and have someone else proofread it as well. Type or print it on a heavier bond paper than is used for ordinary copies. Use white or off-white paper and black ink.

INTERVIEW. Be clean, neat, and appropriately dressed. Choose a nice pair of shoes—people notice. Bring an extra copy of your résumé and any other materials that you want to show the interviewer, even if you have already

FIGURE

Sample file card.

> Job/company: Child-care worker at Morningside Day Care
> Contact: Sally Wheeler, Morningside Day Care,
>   17 Parkside Rd, Silver Spring, MD 20910
> Phone/fax/e-mail: (301) 555-3353 phone, (301) 555-3354 fax,
>   no e-mail
> Communication: Saw ad in paper, sent résumé & cover letter on Oct. 7
> Response: Call from Sally to set up interview
>   —Interview on Oct. 15 at 2 p.m., seemed to get a positive
>   response, said she would contact me again by end of the week
>
> Follow-up: Sent thank-you note on Oct. 16

sent a copy ahead of time. Avoid chewing gum or smoking. Offer a confident handshake. Make eye contact. Show your integrity by speaking honestly about yourself. After the interview is over, no matter what the outcome, send a formal but pleasant thank-you note right away as a follow-up.

Earning the money you need is hard, especially if you work part-time so that your job will interfere with school less than a full-time job would. Financial aid can take some of the burden off your shoulders. If you can gather one or more loans, grants, or scholarships, they may help make up for what you don't have time to earn.

Using a separate sheet of paper, complete the following.

Thinking Back

1. What four areas help you build the knowledge and experience with which you can define a career path? Of those four, circle the two that for you demand the most energy and focus.

2. Name the skills that employers currently seek in their applicants. Check off the ones you consider your strengths, and circle the ones where you feel you need work.

3. Why has emotional intelligence become an important workplace factor—and a valuable asset for any employee?

4. Name three job-search resources and where you can find them.

Thinking Ahead

1. How do you finance your education—personal funds, financial aid, assistance from family members, etc.? If you would like to change how you gather the money for your tuition, discuss what kind of change you would like to make.

2. What is your philosophy about how much money you save and how much you spend?

3. Do you monitor your incoming and outgoing money? If so, how? What kinds of day-to-day strategies help you save money?

4. Do you use credit cards not at all, just enough, or too much? Do you pay on time, or do you fall behind?

WHAT SHOULD YOU KNOW ABOUT FINANCIAL AID?

Seeking financial help has become a way of life for many students. The average cost in the United States for a year's full-time tuition only (not including room and board) in 1997–98 ranged from approximately $1,318 for two-year public institutions to over $17,000 for four-year private ones.[5] In fact, the total cost for an undergraduate's yearly tuition, room, and board increased 23 percent at public colleges and 36 percent at private colleges in the 10-year span between 1985–86 and 1995–96, far outpacing the rate of inflation.[6] Not many people can pay for tuition in full without aid. In fact, according to data compiled in the academic year 1995–96, 49.7 percent of students enrolled received some kind of aid.[7]

Most sources of financial aid don't seek out recipients. Do some research to learn how you (or you and your parents, if they currently help to support you) can finance your education. Find the people on campus who can help you with your finances. Find out what's available, weigh the pros and cons of each option, and decide what would work best for you. Try to apply as early as you can.

Above all, think critically. Never assume that you are not eligible for aid. You don't know what you might receive until you ask. The types of aid available are student loans, grants, and scholarships.

Student Loans

A loan is given to you by a person, bank, or other lending agency, usually for a specific purchase. You, as the recipient of the loan, must then pay back the amount of the loan, plus interest, in regular payments that stretch over a particular period of time. Interest is the fee that you pay for the privilege of using money that belongs to someone else.

Types of Student Loans

The federal government administers or oversees most student loans. To receive aid from any federal program, you must be a citizen or eligible noncitizen and be enrolled in a program of study that the government has determined is eligible. Individual states may differ in their aid programs. Check with your campus financial aid office to find out details about your state and your school in particular.

Table 12.4 describes the main student loan programs to which you can apply if you are eligible. Amounts vary according to individual circumstances. Contact your school or federal student aid office for further information. In most cases, the amount is limited to the cost of your education minus any other financial aid you are receiving. All the information here on federal loans and grants comes from *The 2000–2001 Student Guide to Financial Aid*, published by the U.S. Department of Education.[8]

Grants and Scholarships

Both grants and scholarships require no repayment and therefore give your finances a major boost. Grants, funded by the government, are awarded to students who show financial need. Scholarships are awarded to students who show talent or ability in the area specified by the scholarship. They may be financed by government or private organizations, schools, or individuals. Table 12.5 describes federal grant programs.

There is much more to say about these financial aid opportunities than can be touched on here. Many other important details about federal grants and loans are available in *The 2000–2001 Student Guide to Financial Aid*. You might find this information at your school's financial aid office, or you can request it by mail, phone, or online service:

Address: Federal Student Aid Information Center
            P.O. Box 84
            Washington, DC 20044-0084
Phone: 1-800-4-FED-AID (1-800-433-3243)
            TDD for the hearing impaired: 1-800-730-8913
Internet address: www.ed.gov/prog_info/SFA/StudentGuide

Scholarships

Scholarships are given for various abilities and talents. They may reward academic achievement, exceptional abilities in sports or the arts, citizenship, or leadership. Certain scholarships are sponsored by federal agencies. If you display exceptional ability and are disabled, female, of an ethnic background classified as a minority (e.g., African American or American Indian), or a child of someone who draws benefits from a state agency (e.g., the spouse of a POW, prisoner of war, or MIA, missing in action), you might find federal scholarship opportunities geared toward you.

All kinds of organizations offer scholarships. You may receive scholarships from individual departments at your school or your school's independent scholarship funds, local organizations such as the Rotary Club, or privately operated aid foundations. Labor unions and companies may offer scholarships for children of their employees. Membership groups such as scouting organizations or the YMCA/YWCA might offer scholarships, and religious organizations such as the Knights of Columbus or the Council of Jewish Federations might be another source.

Federal student loan programs.

LOAN	DESCRIPTION
Perkins	Low, fixed rate of interest. Available to those with exceptional financial need (determined by a government formula). Issued by schools from their allotment of federal funds. Grace period of up to nine months after graduation before repayment, in monthly installments, must begin.
Stafford	Available to students enrolled at least half-time. Exceptional need not required, although students who prove need can qualify for a subsidized Stafford loan (the government pays interest until repayment begins). Two types of Staffords: the direct loan comes from federal funds, and the FFEL (Federal Family Education Loan) comes from a bank or credit union. Repayment begins six months after you graduate, leave school, or drop below half-time enrollment.
PLUS	Available to students enrolled at least half-time and claimed as dependents by their parents. Parents must undergo a credit check to be eligible, or applicants may be sponsored through a relative or friend who passes the check. Loan comes from government or a bank or credit union. Sponsor must begin repayment 60 days after receiving the last loan payment.

Federal grant programs.

GRANT	DESCRIPTION
Pell	Need-based; the government evaluates your reported financial information and determines eligibility from that "score" (called an expected family contribution, or EFC). Available to undergraduates who have earned no other degrees. Amount varies according to education cost and EFC. Adding other aid sources is allowed.
Federal Supplemental Educational Opportunity Grant (FSEOG)	Need-based; administered by the financial aid administrator at participating schools. Each participating school receives a limited amount of federal funds for FSEOGs and sets its own application deadlines.
Work-study	Need-based; encourages community service work or work related to your course of study. Pays by the hour, at least the federal minimum wage. Jobs may be on-campus (usually for your school) or off (often with a nonprofit organization or a public agency).

How can I handle my credit cards?

Maxine Deverney, *Truman College, Chicago, Illinois, Accounting Major*

Several years ago my husband and I divorced, and I became a single mother. I was responsible for raising three children on my own as well as working a full-time job. Four years ago my daughter died at age 21 in a car accident. I took custody of her son until he was five. During this traumatic and stressful time was when I began to use credit cards. They make spending so easy. I had four, and I used them to buy school clothes for my own children. Then, as they grew older and had children of their own, I helped financially with the grandchildren. I have 10 grandchildren.

I have been working steadily for many years. Although I have managed to pay off most of the

debt, and I am down to one credit card, I don't want to fall into that trap again. I have worked for four years in financial aid to help students receive grants from their tribes. I am also a secretary. Prior to this I worked as a director for a health clinic at a Chippewa reservation in Michigan. I am of the Potawatomi tribe of Wisconsin. When I graduate from Truman, I will have an Associate Degree in accounting. My goal is to open my own accounting business one day. I would like to do some accounting for small firms and businesses. Can you offer steps I can take to stay debt free?

Vernon Nash, *Business & Housing Development, Chicago, Illinois*

I know the challenges of using a credit card to ease the burden while being a working spouse, parent, and student. My challenge was with my son, Anthony, who was shot and had to have his leg amputated. This was devastating to me, my wife, and my other sons. So, we used credit cards to get ourselves through and to compensate for

the loss we all felt. I quickly found out that the interest and bills were mounting fast.

The problem with credit cards is that after your trying time has come and gone you are faced with a high credit card bill and can feel trapped in a cycle that seems impossible to stop. But it can be done. If you can pay additional money above what the credit card company is asking, you distance yourself from the debt. There are also a few things you can do to avoid this happening to you again:

1. Determine that you will only buy what you can pay for within 30 days.

2. Pay your credit card bill on time, at least 5 days before the due date, so that you don't rack up more interest payments.

3. Maintain a credit card balance of no more than 7 percent of your annual income.

4. Maintain a one card limit.

When you graduate and want to start your small business, one of the best places to go for assistance is the Small Business Administration in your area. They can give you information about financing your business. Best of luck to you!

Researching Grants and Scholarships

It can take work to locate scholarships and work-study programs because many of them aren't widely advertised. Ask at your school's financial aid office. Visit your library or bookstore and look in the sections on college and financial aid. Guides to funding sources, such as Richard Black's *The Complete Family Guide to College Financial Aid* and others listed at the end of the chapter, catalog thousands of organizations. Check out online scholarship search services such as Fresch! Free Scholarship Search at **www.freschinfo.com.** Use common sense when applying for aid—fill out the application as neatly as possible and send it in on time or even early. In addition, be wary of scholarship scam artists who ask you to first pay a fee for them to find aid for you.

No matter where your money comes from—financial aid or paychecks from one or more jobs—you can take steps to help it stretch as far as it can go. The next sections concentrate on developing a philosophy about your money and budgeting effectively. Using those skills, you can more efficiently cover your expenses and still have some left over for savings and fun.

HOW CAN STRATEGIC PLANNING HELP YOU MANAGE MONEY?

So you work hard to earn your wages and study hard to hold on to your grants and loans. What do you do with that money? Popular culture tells you to buy. You are surrounded by commercials, magazine and Internet ads, and notices in the mail that tell you how wonderful you'll feel if you indulge in some serious spending. On the other hand, there are some definite advantages to not taking that advice. Making some short-term sacrifices in order to save money can help you a great deal in the long run.

Sacrifice in the Short Term to Create Long-Term Gain

When you think about your money, take your values and your ability to plan strategically into account. Ask yourself what goals you value most and what steps you will have to take over time to achieve those goals. You are already planning ahead by being in school. You may be scrimping now, but you are planning for a career that may reward you with job security and financial stability.

Critical thinking is the key to smart money planning. Impulsive spending usually happens when you don't take time to think through your decision before you buy. To use your hard-earned money to your greatest benefit, take time to think about your finances using what you know about decision making.

1. *Establish your needs.* Be honest about what you truly need and what you just want. Do you really need a new bike? Or can the old one serve while you pay off some credit card debt?

2. *Brainstorm available options.* Think about what you can do with your money and evaluate the positive and negative effects of each option.

3. *Choose an option and carry it out.* Spend it—save it—invest it—whatever you decide.

4. *Evaluate the result.* This crucial step will build knowledge that you can use in the future. What were the positive and negative effects of what you chose? Would you make that choice again?

This section doesn't imply that you should never spend money on things that won't bring you long-term satisfaction. The goal is to make choices that give short-term satisfaction while still providing for long-term money growth. For example, you could buy a less expensive sound system instead of a state-of-the-art one that will test the limits of your credit card. When you spend wisely now, you will appreciate it later.

Develop a Financial Philosophy

You can develop your own personal philosophy about spending, saving, and planning. Following are a couple of strategies that you might want to incorporate into that philosophy.

LIVE BENEATH YOUR MEANS. If you spend less than you make, you can create savings. Any amount of savings will give you a buffer zone that can help with emergencies or bigger expenditures. Sometimes your basic needs will cost more than you make, in which case living beneath your means becomes very difficult. If you find, however, that extras are putting your spending over your earnings, cut back.

PAY YOURSELF. After you pay your monthly bills, put whatever you can save in an account. That savings could be your security when you grow older, money for your children's college education, help with a financial crisis, or a down payment on a large purchase. Don't think of the money left after paying bills as automatically available for spending. Make your payment to yourself a high priority so that you honor it as you do your other bills.

HOW CAN YOU CREATE A BUDGET THAT WORKS?

Every time you have to figure out whether the money in your pocket will pay for what you want at a store, you are **budgeting** your money. It takes thought and energy to budget efficiently. Consider your resources (money coming in) and expenditures (money flowing out). The most effective budget adjusts the money flow so that what comes in will be more than what goes out.

> **BUDGETING**
>
> Making a plan for the coordination of resources and expenditures; setting goals with regard to money.

The Art of Budgeting

Budgeting involves following a few basic steps: determining how much money you make, determining how much money you spend, subtracting what you spend from what you make, evaluating the result, and making decisions about how to adjust your spending or earning based on that result. Budgeting regularly, using a specified time frame, is easiest. Most people budget on a month-by-month basis.

Determine How Much You Make

Add up all your money receipts for the month. If you currently have a regular full-time or part-time job, add your pay stubs. If you have received any financial aid, loan funding, or scholarship money, determine how much of that you can allow for each month's income and add it to your total. For example, if you received a $1,200 grant for the year, each month would have an income of $100. Be sure when you are figuring your income to use the amounts that remain after taxes have been taken out.

Figure Out How Much You Spend

Many people don't have a good idea of how much they spend. If you have never paid much attention to how you spend money, examine your spending patterns (you will have a chance to do this at the end of the chapter). Over a month's time, record expenditures in a small notebook. Indicate any expenditures over five dollars, making sure to count smaller expenditures if they are frequent (a bus pass for a month, soda or newspaper purchases per week). In your list, include an estimate of the following:

- rent, mortgage, or room and board fees
- tuition or student loan payments (divide your annual total by 12 to arrive at a monthly figure)
- books, lab fees, and other educational expenses
- regular bills (heat, gas, electric, phone, and water)
- credit card or other payments on credit (car payment)
- food, clothing, toiletries, and household supplies
- child care
- entertainment and related items (eating out, books and publications, and movies)
- health, auto, and homeowners' or renters' insurance
- transportation and auto expenses

Subtract what you spend from what you make. Ideally, you will have a positive number. You may end up with a negative number, however, that indicates that you are spending more than you make. Over a long period of time this can create debt.

Evaluate the Result

It is thrifty to prepare today for the wants of tomorrow.

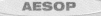
AESOP

If you have a positive number, decide how to save it if you can. If you end up with a negative number, ask questions about what is causing the deficit. Where might you be spending too much or earning too little? Of course, surprise expenses during some months may cause you to spend more than usual, such as a car repair or equipment fees for a particular course. However, when a negative number comes up for what seems to be a typical month, you may need to adjust your budget over the long term.

Make Decisions About How to Adjust Spending or Earning

Looking at what may cause you to overspend, brainstorm possible solutions that address those causes. Solutions can involve either increasing resources or decreasing spending. To deal with spending, prioritize your expenditures and trim the ones you really don't need to make. Cut out unaffordable extras. As for resources, investigate ways to take in more money. Taking a part-time job, hunting down scholarships or grants, or increasing hours at a current job may help.

A Sample Budget

Table 12.6 shows a sample budget of an unmarried student living with two other students. It will give you an idea of how to budget (all expenditures are general estimates, based on averages).

TABLE 12.6　A student's sample budget.

- Wages: $10 an hour, 20 hours a week:
  10 x 20 = $200 a week x 4 1/3 weeks (one month) = $866

- Student loan from school's financial aid office: $2,000 divided by 12 months = $166

- Total income per month: $1,032

MONTHLY EXPENDITURES	AMOUNT
Tuition ($6,500 per year)	$ 542
Public transportation	$ 90
Phone	$ 40
Food	$ 130
Medical insurance	$ 120
Rent (including utilities)	$ 200
Entertainment/miscellaneous	$ 100
Total spending	$ 1,222

$1,032 (income) − $1,222 (spending) = $ − 190 ($190 over budget).

To make up the $190 the student is over budget, he can adjust his spending. He could rent movies instead of going to the cinema. He could buy used CDs or borrow them. He could go to a warehouse supermarket. He could make lunch instead of buying it and walk instead of taking public transportation.

Not everyone likes the work involved in keeping a budget. For example, whereas logical–mathematical learners may take to it more easily, visual learners may resist the structure and detail (see Chapter 3). Visual learners may want to create a budget chart such as the one shown in the example, or use strategies that make budgeting more tangible, such as dumping all of your receipts into a big jar and tallying them at the end of the month. Even if you have to force yourself to do it, you will discover that budgeting can reduce stress and help you take control of your finances and your life.

Savings Strategies

You can save money and still enjoy life. Make your fun less expensive, or save up to splurge on a special occasion. Small amounts can eventually add up to big savings. Here are some savings suggestions.

- rent movies
- avoid buying basics at high-priced convenience stores
- walk
- trade clothing with friends
- use your local library
- buy display models
- buy household items in bulk
- bring your lunch from home
- shop in secondhand stores
- use e-mail or write letters
- use coupons

    Add your own suggestions here:

_____

_____

_____

    You can maximize savings and minimize spending by using credit cards wisely.

Managing Credit Cards

A credit card can be a lifesaver or a black hole of debt. Credit card companies make money in two ways.

INTEREST RATES. You are charged interest on the amount you carry as a balance. Interest rates can be fixed (guaranteed to always stay the same) or variable (able to be changed by the credit card company, often in response to economic change). A variable rate of 12 percent may shoot up to 18 percent when the economy slows down.

ANNUAL FEE. You may be charged an annual fee for usage of the card. Some cards have no annual fee; others may charge a flat rate of $10 to $70 per year.

Today's student body is more debt-ridden than ever, and credit card companies know it. Companies solicit students on campus or through the mail; it's up to you to sort through the offers and make smart choices. Pay attention to annual fees and interest rates. What looks like a low interest rate—for example, 6.9 percent—may only be a temporary rate designed to lure you into applying, and may skyrocket 10 or more percentage points after a few months. Following are some potential effects of using credit.

Positive Effects

Establishing a good credit history. If you use your credit card moderately and pay your bills on time, you will make a positive impression on your **creditors.** Your *credit history* (the record of your credit use, including positive actions such as paying on time and negative actions such as going over your credit limit) and *credit rating* (your score, based on your history) can make or break your ability to take out a loan or mortgage.

CREDITORS

People to whom debts are owed, usually money.

EMERGENCIES. Few people carry enough cash to handle unexpected expenses. Your credit card can help you in emergencies such as when you need a tow.

RECORD OF PURCHASES. Credit card statements give you a monthly record of purchases made, where they were made, and exactly how much was paid. Using your credit card for purchases that you want to track, such as work expenses, can help you keep records for tax purposes.

Negative Effects

CREDIT CAN BE ADDICTIVE. Credit can be like a drug because the pain of paying is put off until later. If you get hooked, you can wind up thousands of dollars in debt. The high interest will enlarge your debt; your credit rating may fall, possibly hurting your loan or mortgage eligibility; and you may lose your cards altogether.

CREDIT SPENDING CAN BE HARD TO MONITOR. Paying with a credit card can seem so easy that you don't realize how much you are spending. When the bill comes at the end of the month, the total can hit you hard.

YOU ARE TAKING OUT A HIGH-INTEREST LOAN. Credit is not cash. Buying on credit is similar to taking out a high-interest loan—you are using the credit company's money with the promise to pay it back. Loan rates, however, especially on fixed-interest loans, are often much lower than the 11 percent to 23 percent on credit card debt.

BAD CREDIT RATINGS CAN HAUNT YOU. Any time you are late with a payment, default on a payment, or in any way misuse your card, a record of that

Credit help resources.

FIGURE

12.5

occurrence will be entered onto your credit history, lowering your credit rating. If a prospective employer or loan officer discovers a low rating, you will seem less trustworthy and may lose the chance for a job or a loan.

Managing Debt

The most basic way to stay in control is to pay bills regularly and on time. On credit card bills, pay at least the minimum amount due. If you get into trouble, deal with it in three steps. First, admit that you made a mistake. Then, address the problem immediately to minimize damages. Call the creditor and see if you can pay your debt gradually using a payment plan. Finally, examine what got you into trouble and avoid it in the future if you can. Figure 12.5 offers some resources that can help you solve credit problems.

In Italy, parents often use the term *sacrifici,* meaning "sacrifices," to refer to tough choices that they make to improve the lives of their children and family members. They may sacrifice a larger home so that they can afford to pay for their children's sports and after-school activities. They may sacrifice a higher-paying job so that they can live close to where they work. They give up something in exchange for something else that they have decided is more important to them.

Think of the concept of *sacrifici* as you analyze the sacrifices you can make to get out of debt, reach your savings goals, and prepare for a career that you find satisfying. Many of the short-term sacrifices you are making today will help you do and have what you want in the future.

IMPORTANT POINTS *to remember*

1. How can you plan your career?

Begin to define a career path by investigating your self and looking at careers that might suit your needs, interests, and learning style. Then, build knowledge and experience by taking courses, jobs, and internships in areas that interest you. Think critically about what you want out of a career, and construct a strategic plan that will help you achieve your goal. As you follow your plan, prepare yourself to stay up-to-date on your field and to fulfill the expectations of today's employers.

2. How can you juggle work and school?

The rising cost of education has prompted over 40 percent of students to work while in school. Weigh the pros and cons of working to decide if it's right for you. Positive effects may include income, experience, and connections. Negative effects may include the time commitment, adjusting priorities, and shifting gears from school to work. Establish your needs before you begin a job hunt.

3. How can you explore career opportunities?

The more you know about what's out there, the better your chance of finding what suits you best. Use available resources (your school's career planning and placement offices, networking, classified ads, online services, and employment agencies) to explore possibilities. Use a strategic search plan as you investigate these possibilities, and keep accurate records of your search. Create an impressive résumé, know how to interview well, and follow up soon after an interview.

4. What should you know about financial aid?

You can find information about financial aid opportunities through your school's financial aid office, books and pamphlets, and private organizations that may offer scholarships. Different sources of aid include bank and student loans, grants, and scholarships. The federal government sponsors many loans and grants; each one has different requirements. Contact the Federal Student Aid Information Center for details on federal grants and loans.

5. How can strategic planning help you manage money?

Making smart choices in the short term can help you a great deal in the long run. First, consider sacrificing in the short term to create long-term gain. For any money issue, use your decision-making skills: Establish your needs; brainstorm and evaluate available options; choose an option, carry it out, and evaluate the result. Secondly, develop a financial philosophy—a blueprint for how you deal with your finances. Consider living beneath your means and paying yourself as part of your blueprint.

6. How can you create a budget that works?

Budgeting means setting goals with your money. Consider resources (money in) and needs (money out) when budgeting. The basic steps are determining what you make, determining what you spend, subtracting what you spend from what you make, evaluating the result, and basing a decision about how to adjust spending or earning on that result. Budgeting regularly, such as once a month, works for many people. Managing your credit cards will help you stay on track.

CRITICAL THINKING

APPLYING LEARNING TO LIFE

CAREER POSSIBILITIES. Name a career area that interests you.

_____

Research job possibilities in that area. For each of the following types of leads, list one contact or job possibility and name the source.

Help wanted listings (in newspapers, magazines, or Internet databases):

_____

_____

Listings of job opportunities and company contact information at your career center or student employment office:

_____

_____

Contacts from friends or family members:

_____

_____

Contacts from instructors, administrators, or counselors:

_____

_____

Finally, look back at Table 12.3 and think about your needs for a job in this career area. List your three most important priorities and write down any particular jobs or niches in this career area that you think might suit your priority list.

_____

_____

_____

TEAMWORK
COMBINING FORCES

SAVINGS BRAINSTORM. As a class, brainstorm areas that require financial management (e.g., funding an education, running a household, or putting savings away for the future) and write them on the board. Divide into small groups. Each group should choose one area to discuss (make sure all areas are chosen). In your group, brainstorm strategies that can help with the area you have chosen. Think of savings ideas, ways to control spending, ways to earn more money, and any other methods of relieving financial stress. Agree on a list of possible ideas for your area and share it with the class.

WRITING
DISCOVERY THROUGH JOURNALING

To record your thoughts, use a separate journal or the lined page at the end of the chapter.

CREDIT CARDS. Describe how you use credit cards. What do you buy? How much, on average, do you spend using your card each month? Do you pay in full each month or run a balance? How does using a credit card make you feel? If you would like to change how you use credit, discuss changes you want to make and what effects you would want those changes to have.

CAREER PORTFOLIO
CHARTING YOUR COURSE

FINANCIAL HISTORY. Create for yourself a detailed picture of your financial history. First, put copies of your budget exercises in your portfolio so that you have a record of your spending habits. Then, answer the following questions on a separate sheet and keep your work. Keeping accurate financial records is vital in making intelligent financial decisions.

1. *Financial aid.* List school, federal, and personal loans; scholarship funds; grants; and the amount that you pay out of pocket. Indicate all account numbers; payment plans; and records of payment, including dates and check numbers if applicable.

2. *Bank accounts.* For any account to which you have access, list all names on the accounts, bank name, type of account, and account number. Include any restrictions on the accounts such as minimum balances or time frames during which you will receive a penalty for removing funds.

3. *Loans.* List any nonacademic loans you are currently repaying, noting bank names, account numbers, loan types, repayment schedule, payment amounts, and dates of payments made.

4. *Credit cards.* List major credit cards (American Express, Visa, MasterCard, Discover, etc.), as well as cards for gas stations or department stores. For each card, include the following:

   • name on the card, card number, and expiration date

   • payment style (pay in full, pay minimum each month, etc.)

   • problems (late payments, lost cards, card fraud, etc.)

   • current balance and date

   Keep a copy of important credit card numbers separate from your wallet or purse so that you have records should you lose your cards. For your protection, any record of personal identification numbers (PINs) should be kept separate from credit cards or credit card numbers.

5. *Earning history.* List the jobs you have had or currently have. Include the following for each:

   • name of the company or business

   • job title

   • wages or salary

   • dates of your employment

   Store this information in your portfolio. Update it when you have new entries.

6. *References.* First, create a list of people who have served or could serve as references for you. Brainstorm names from all areas of your human resources:

• instructors	• fellow students	• friends
• administrators	• present/former employers	• mentors
• counselors	• present/former coworkers	• family members

For each potential reference, list the name, contact information (phone number and address), and how you know the person. Update the information as you meet potential references or lose touch with old ones. Keep it on hand for the time that you need a new letter or want to cite a reference on a résumé. When references write letters of recommendation for you, be sure to thank them right away for their help and to keep them up-to-date on your activities. Always let a reference know when you have sent a letter out, so that he or she may be prepared to receive a call from the person/company/program to which you have applied.

 UGGESTED READINGS

Adams, Robert Lang et al. *The Complete Résumé and Job Search Book for College Students.* Holbrook, MA: Adams Publishing (1999).

Beatty, Richard H. *The Resume Kit,* 4th ed. New York: John Wiley (2000).

Beckham, Barry, ed. *The Black Student's Guide to Scholarships—700+ Private Money Sources for Black and Minority Students,* 5th ed. Lanham, MD: Madison Books (1999).

Boldt, Laurence G. *Zen and the Art of Making a Living: A Practical Guide to Creative Career Design.* New York: Arkana (1999).

Bolles, Richard Nelson. *What Color Is Your Parachute? 2001: A Practical Manual for Job Hunters and Career Changers.* Berkeley, CA: Ten Speed Press (2000).

Cassidy, Daniel J. *The Scholarship Book 2001: The Complete Guide to Private-Sector Scholarships, Fellowships, Grants, and Loans for the Undergraduate.* Englewood Cliffs, NJ: Prentice Hall (2000).

Detweiler, Gerri. *The Ultimate Credit Handbook.* New York: Plume (1997).

FastWeb.com, ed. *The Complete Scholarship Book: The Biggest, Easiest Guide for Getting the Most Money for College.* Sourcebooks Trade (2000).

Goleman, Daniel. *Emotional Intelligence.* New York: Bantam Books (1997).

Goleman, Daniel. *Working With Emotional Intelligence.* New York: Bantam Books (1998).

Kennedy, Joyce Lain. *Job Interviews for Dummies.* Foster City, CA: IDG Books Worldwide, Inc. (2000).

McKee, Cynthia Ruiz and Phillip C. McKee, Jr. *Cash for College: The Ultimate Guide to College Scholarships.* New York: Hearst Books (1999).

Tyson, Eric. *Personal Finance for Dummies.* Foster City, CA: IDG Books Worldwide, Inc. (2000).

 INTERNET RESOURCES

Student Advantage—information on discounts: www.studentadvantage.com

Monster.com (online job search): **www.monster.com**

Tripod—Money/Business (financial and career advice, budget counseling): **www.tripod.com/money_business/**

1st Steps in the Hunt: Daily News for Online Job Hunters (advice on finding a job via an online search): **www.interbiznet.com/hunt/**

College Grad Job Hunter (advice on resumes, interviews, and a database of entry-level jobs): **www.collegegrad.com**

Women's Wire (helping women target a career and juggle work and family): **www.womenswire.com/work**

JobWeb (career information site for college students): **www.jobweb.org**

 NDNOTES

1. Peter Passell. "Royal Blue Collars," *The New York Times,* March 22, 1998, p. 12.

2. Steven Greenhouse. "Equal Work, Less-Equal Perks," *The New York Times,* March 30, 1998, pp. D1, D6.

3. Daniel Goleman. *Working with Emotional Intelligence*. New York: Bantam Books (1998), pp. 26–27.

4. U. S. Department of Education, National Center for Education Statistics. *Profile of Undergraduates in U.S. Postsecondary Education Institutions: 1995–96,* NCES 98-084. Washington, DC: U. S. Government Printing Office (1998), pp. 4, 31.

5. U. S. Department of Education, National Center for Education Statistics. *Digest of Education Statistics 1998,* NCES 1999-036. Washington, DC: U. S. Government Printing Office (1999), pp. 334–335.

6. Figures are adjusted for inflation. U. S. department of Education, National Center for Education Statistics, *Digest of Education Statistics 1996,* NCES 96-133. Washington, DC: U. S. Government Printing Office (1996), tables 37 and 309.

7. U. S. Department of Education. *The 1999–2000 Student Guide to Financial Aid.* Washington, DC: U. S. Department of Education (1999).

8. Ibid.

NAME

DATE

Thinking It Through

Check those statements that apply to you right now:

- I want to keep learning even after I graduate.

- Every time I think I've got my life under control, something new happens.

- I have a hard time shifting gears when I can't achieve my goals.

- When I fail or have a setback, I can't keep it in perspective.

- I tend to lose sight of my mission in life.

GROW

IN THIS CHAPTER,

you will explore answers to the following questions:

- Why is college just the beginning of lifelong learning?
- How can you adjust to change?
- What will help you handle success and failure?
- Why is it important to focus on wellness?
- How can you live your mission?

Moving Ahead

As you come to the end of your work in this course, you have built up a wealth of knowledge. Now you have more power to decide what directions you want your life to take and how you can make a difference in your corner of the world. This chapter will explore how to develop the kind of flexibility that can help you adjust goals, make the most of successes, and work through failures. You will consider what is important about life-long learning, wellness, and giving back to your community. Finally, you will revisit your personal mission, exploring how to keep it in sync with life's changes.

BUILDING A FLEXIBLE FUTURE

WHY IS COLLEGE JUST THE BEGINNING OF LIFELONG LEARNING?

Today's world favors the student and worker who doesn't stop learning at graduation. Rapidly changing industries demand that workers keep up with new developments. The focus on information requires a constant effort to learn more each day. Increasing numbers of workers changing jobs means that people must retrain frequently.

There is more to lifelong learning than taking college-level courses. In a general sense, lifelong learning means continually asking questions and exploring new ideas. As you change and the world changes, new knowledge and ideas continually emerge. Absorb them so that you can become a student of life who learns something new every single day. Here are some lifelong learning strategies that can encourage you.

INVESTIGATE NEW INTERESTS. When information and events catch your attention, take your interest one step further and find out more. If you are fascinated by politics, find out if your school has political clubs. If a friend of yours starts to take yoga, try a class. If you really like one portion of a particular class, see if there are other classes that focus on that topic.

READ BOOKS, NEWSPAPERS, MAGAZINES, AND OTHER WRITINGS. Reading opens a world of new perspectives. Check out what's on the best-seller list. Ask your friends about books that have changed their lives. Stay current about your community, state, country, and the world by reading newspapers and magazines. A newspaper that has a broad scope, such as *The New York Times* or *Washington Post,* can be an education in itself. Explore religious literature, family letters, and Internet news groups and Web pages.

PURSUE IMPROVEMENT IN YOUR STUDIES AND IN YOUR CAREER. When at school, take classes outside of your major if you have time. After graduation, continue your education both in your field and in the realm of general knowledge. Stay on top of ideas, developments, and new technology in your field by seeking out **continuing education** courses. Sign up for career-related seminars. Take single courses at a local college or community learning center. Some companies offer additional on-the-job training or pay for their employees to take courses that will improve their knowledge and skills.

FIND A MENTOR. A mentor is a trusted advisor who will help you make academic and career decisions that are right for you. He will point you to important information and courses and introduce you to people who may help you reach your goal. Finding a mentor and nurturing the mentoring relationship can have an important influence on your entire life.

DELVE INTO OTHER CULTURES. Visit the home of a friend who has grown up in a culture different from your own. Invite him or her to your home. Eat food from a country you've never seen. Initiate conversations with people of different races, religions, values, and ethnic backgrounds. Travel to different countries. Travel nearby to different neighborhoods or cities near you—they may seem as foreign as another country. Take a course that deals with some aspect of cultural diversity.

CONTINUING EDUCATION

Courses that students can take without having to be part of a degree program.

NURTURE A SPIRITUAL LIFE. You don't have to attend a house of worship to be spiritual, although that may be part of your spiritual life. "A spiritual life of some kind is absolutely necessary for psychological 'health,'" says psychologist and author Thomas Moore in his book, *The Care of the Soul.* "We live in a time of deep division, in which mind is separated from body and spirituality is at odds with materialism."[1] The words *soul* and *spirituality* hold different meanings for each individual. Whether you discover them in music, organized religion, friendship, nature, cooking, sports, or anything else, making them a priority will help you find a greater sense of balance and meaning.

A finished person is a boring person.

ANNA QUINDLEN

EXPERIENCE WHAT OTHERS CREATE. Art is "an adventure of the mind" (Eugène Ionesco, playwright); "a means of knowing the world" (Angela Carter, author); "a lie that makes us realize truth" (Pablo Picasso, painter); a revealer of "our most secret self" (Jean-Luc Godard, filmmaker). Through art you can discover new ideas and shed new light on old ones. Explore all kinds of art. Seek out whatever moves you— music, visual arts, theater, photography, dance, domestic arts, performance art, film and television, poetry, prose, and more.

MAKE YOUR OWN CREATIONS. Bring out the creative artist in you. Take a class in drawing, in writing, or in quilting. Learn to play an instrument. Write poems for your favorite people or stories to read to your children. Invent a recipe. Design and build a set of shelves for your home. Create a memoir of your life. You are a creative being. Express yourself, and learn more about yourself, through art.

Lifelong learning is the master key that unlocks every door you will encounter on your journey. If you keep it firmly in your hand, you will discover worlds of knowledge—and a place for yourself within them.

HOW CAN YOU ADJUST TO CHANGE?

Even the most carefully constructed plans can be turned upside down by change. Two ways to make change a manageable part of your life are maintaining flexibility and adjusting your goals. These actions, which were introduced in Chapters 1 and 2, are at the heart of your successful adjustment throughout life.

Maintain Flexibility

The fear of change is as inevitable as change itself. When you become comfortable with something, you tend to want it to stay the way it is, whether it is a place you live, a job, or the racial and cultural mix of people with whom you interact. Change may seem to have negative effects, and consistency pos-

FIGURE 13.1   Examples of changes people experience.

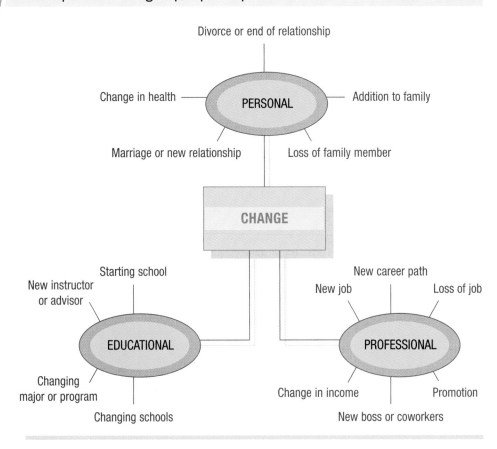

itive effects. Think about your life right now. What do you wish would always stay the same? What changes have upset you and thrown you off balance?

You may have encountered any number of changes in your life to date, many of them unexpected—see Figure 13.1 for some examples. All of these changes, whether they seem good or bad, cause a certain level of stress. They also cause a shift in your personal needs, which may lead to changing priorities.

Change Brings Different Needs

Your needs can change from day to day, year to year, and situation to situation. Although you may know about some changes—such as school starting—ahead of time, others may take you completely by surprise, such as job loss. Even the different times of year bring different needs, for example, a need for extra cash around the holidays or additional child care when your children are home for the summer.

Some changes that shift your needs occur within a week or even a day. For example, an instructor may inform you that you have an end-of-week quiz, or your work supervisor may give you an additional goal. Such changes lead to new priorities. For example, if you lose a job, your loss of income may lead to priorities such as job hunting, reduction in spending, or training in a new career area.

Flexibility Versus Inflexibility

When change affects your needs, flexibility will help you shift your priorities so that you address those needs. You can react to change with either inflexibility or flexibility, each with its resulting effects.

INFLEXIBILITY. Not acknowledging a shift in needs and circumstance can cause trouble. For example, if you lose your job and refuse to take courses to update your skills, ignoring the need to remain competitive in an ever-changing job market, you can drive yourself into chronic under- or unemployment.

FLEXIBILITY. Being flexible means acknowledging the change, examining your different needs, and addressing them in any way you can. Discovering what change brings may help you uncover positive effects. For example, a loss of a job can lead you to reevaluate your abilities and look for a job that suits you better. In other words, a crisis can spur opportunity, and you may learn that you want to adjust your goals in order to pursue it.

Sometimes you need time before you react to a major change. When you do decide you are ready, being flexible will help you cope with the negative effects and benefit from the positive effects.

Adjust Your Goals

Your changing life may result in the need to adjust goals accordingly. For example, a goal to graduate in four years may not be reasonable if economic constraints take you out of school for a while. Sometimes goals must change because they weren't appropriate in the first place. Some turn out to be unreachable; some don't pose enough of a challenge; others may be unhealthy for the goal setter or harmful to others.

Step One: Reevaluate

Before making adjustments in response to change, take time to reevaluate both the goals themselves and your progress toward them.

THE GOALS. First, determine whether your goals still fit the person you have become in the past week or month or year. Circumstances can change quickly. For example, dissatisfaction with a current major may result in some different ideas about educational goals.

YOUR PROGRESS. If you feel you haven't gotten far, determine whether the goal is out of your range or simply requires more stamina than you had anticipated. As you work toward any goal, you will experience alternating periods of progress and stagnation. You may want to seek the support and perspective of a friend or counselor as you evaluate your progress.

Step Two: Modify

If after your best efforts it becomes clear that a goal is out of reach, modifying your goal may bring success. Perhaps the goal doesn't suit you. For example, an active interpersonal learner might become frustrated while pursuing a detail-oriented, sedentary career such as computer programming.

Based on your reevaluation, you can modify a goal in two ways.

ADJUST THE EXISTING GOAL. To adjust a goal, change one or more aspects that define it—the time frame, due dates, or expectations. For example, a student adding a second major could adjust the anticipated graduation date, taking an extra year to complete her course work.

REPLACE IT WITH A MORE COMPATIBLE GOAL. If you find that a particular goal does not make sense, try to find another that works better for you at this time. For example, a student could change a major entirely, redesigning his educational plan to fit the new goal. You and your circumstances never stop changing—your goals should reflect those changes.

The course of your life, and your progress toward goals, will often be unpredictable. When you stay open to unpredictability, you will be more aware of life's moments as they go by. Be an explorer: Focus on what is rather than what is supposed to be, and be willing to be surprised. Having the awareness and flexibility of an explorer will help you understand that both successes and failures are a natural part of your exploration.

WHAT WILL HELP YOU HANDLE SUCCESS AND FAILURE?

The perfect, trouble-free life is only a myth. The most wonderful, challenging, fulfilling life is full of problems to be solved and difficult decisions to be made. If you want to handle the bumps and bruises without losing your self-esteem, you should prepare to encounter setbacks along with your successes.

Dealing with Failure

Things don't always go the way you want them to go. You may face difficult obstacles, let yourself down or disappoint others, make mistakes, or lose your motivation, as all people do. What is important is how you choose to deal with what goes wrong. If you can arrive at reasonable definitions of failure and success, accept failure as part of being human, and examine failure so that you can learn from it, you will have the confidence to pick yourself up and keep improving.

Measuring Failure and Success

Most people measure failure by comparing where they are to where they believe they should be. Because individual circumstances vary widely, so do definitions of failure. What you consider a failure may seem like a positive step for someone else. Here are some examples:

- Imagine that your native language is Spanish. You have learned to speak English well, but you still have trouble writing it. Making writing mistakes may seem like failure to you, but to a recent immigrant from the Dominican Republic who knows limited English, your command of the language will seem like a success story.

Ways to approach failure.

- Having a job that doesn't pay you as much as you want may seem like a failure, but to someone who is having trouble finding any job, your job spells success.

Approach Failure Productively

No one escapes failure. Many an otherwise successful individual has had a problematic relationship, a failing grade in a course, or a job that didn't work out.

Figure 13.2 shows the choices you have when deciding how to view a failure or mistake. Pretending it didn't happen can deny you valuable lessons and may create more serious problems. Blaming someone else falsely assigns responsibility, stifling opportunities to learn. Blaming yourself can result in feeling incapable of success and perhaps becoming afraid to try.

By far the best way to survive a failure is to forgive yourself. Your value as a human being does not diminish when you make a mistake. Expect that you will do the best that you can within the circumstances of your life, knowing that getting through another day as a student, employee, or parent is a success in and of itself. Forgiving yourself opens you up to the possibilities of what you can learn from your experience.

Learning from Failure

Learning from your failures and mistakes involves thinking critically about what happened. First, evaluate what occurred and decide if it was within your control. It could have had nothing to do with you at all. You could have failed to get a job because someone else with equal qualifications was in line for it ahead of you. A family crisis could have interrupted your studying, resulting in a low test grade. These are unfortunate circumstances, but they are not failures.

On the other hand, something you did or didn't do may have contributed to the failure. If you decide that you have made a mistake, your next steps are to analyze the causes and effects of what happened, make any improvements that you can, and decide how to change your action or approach in the future.

For example, imagine that after a long night of studying, you forgot your part-time work-study commitment the next day.

ANALYZE CAUSES AND EFFECTS. *Causes:* Your exhaustion and concern about the test caused you to forget to check your work schedule. *Effects:* Because you weren't there, a crucial curriculum project wasn't completed. An entire class and instructor who needed the project have been affected by your mistake.

MAKE ANY POSSIBLE IMPROVEMENTS ON THE SITUATION. You could apologize to the instructor and see if there is still a chance to finish up part of the work that day.

MAKE CHANGES FOR THE FUTURE. You could set a goal to note your work schedule regularly in your date book—maybe in a bright color—and to check it more often. You could also arrange your future study schedule so that you will be less exhausted.

> *If you have made mistakes, even serious ones, there is always another chance for you. What we call failure is not the falling down, but the staying down.*
>
> **MARY PICKFORD**

Think about the people you consider exceptionally successful. They have built much of their success on their willingness to take risks, make mistakes, and learn from them. You, too, can benefit from staying open to this kind of hard-won education. Let what you learn from falling short of your goals inspire new and better ideas.

Think Positively About Failure

When you feel you have failed, how can you boost your outlook?

REMEMBER THAT YOU ARE A CAPABLE, VALUABLE PERSON. Remind yourself of your successes, focusing your energy on your best abilities and knowing that you have the strength to try again. Realize that your failure isn't a setback as long as you learn from it and rededicate yourself to excellence.

SHARE YOUR THOUGHTS AND DISAPPOINTMENT WITH OTHERS. Everybody fails. When you confide in others, you may be surprised to hear them exchange stories that rival your own. Listen to one another's stories and come up with ideas about changes you can make in the future. Exchanging creative energy that can help you learn from failures is more productive than having a mutual gripe session.

LOOK ON THE BRIGHT SIDE. At worst, you at least have learned a lesson that will help you avoid similar situations in the future. At best, there may be some positive results. What you learn from a failure may, in an unexpected way, bring you around to where you want to be.

Dealing with Success

Success is the continual process of being who you want to be and doing what you want to do. Success is within your reach. Pay attention to the small things when measuring success. Although you may not feel successful until you reach an important goal you have set for yourself, each step along the way is a success. When you are trying to stop procrastinating on your papers, each time you complete a part of an assignment on schedule is positive. If you received a C on a paper and then earned a B on the next one, your advancement is successful.

Remember that success is a process. If you deny yourself the label of success until you reach the top of where you want to be, you will have a much harder time getting there. Just moving ahead toward improvement and growth, however fast or slow the movement, equals success.

Here are some techniques to manage your successes.

APPRECIATE YOURSELF. You deserve it. Take time to congratulate yourself for a job well done—whether it be a good grade, an important step in learning a new language, a job offer, a promotion, or graduation. Praise can give you a terrific vote of confidence.

TAKE YOUR CONFIDENCE ON THE ROAD. This victory can lead to others. Based on this success, you may be expected to prove to yourself and others that you are capable of growth, of continuing your successes and building on them. Show yourself and others that the confidence is well founded.

STAY SENSITIVE TO OTHERS. There could be people around you who may not have been so successful. Remember that you have been in their place and they in yours, and the positions may change many times over in the future. Enjoy what you have and support others as they need it.

You are a unique human being with unique capabilities. If you can define both failure and success in terms of your own goals and abilities, not those of others, you will develop the kind of positive and realistic attitude that will help you manage stress. Following are other important ways to maintain both your physical and mental health, in college and beyond.

Using a separate sheet of paper, complete the following.

Thinking Back

1. Thinking about the suggestions for how to continue learning throughout your life, name the three that suit you best and describe your personal plan for how to implement them.

2. Name three ways to manage your life in the face of change.

3. What are four ways in which you can react to a failure or mistake? Circle the one that seems most beneficial. Underline the one you tend toward most often.

4. Define success in your own words. What is one way that you might celebrate your successes?

Thinking Ahead

1. How well do you feel you manage stress? What causes you the most stress, and why? What are your best stress-busting strategies?

2. Do you feel that you live in a healthy way? Why or why not?

3. How do you define integrity? What role does integrity play in your life?

4. Do you predict that your life's mission might change? In what ways?

WHY IS IT IMPORTANT TO FOCUS ON WELLNESS?

Your health affects your ability to succeed in school. It doesn't matter how great your classes are if you aren't physically healthy enough to get to them or mentally healthy enough to focus and learn while you're there. Part of moving ahead successfully means looking at how to cope with stress, identify and work through particular health problems that many students face, and deal with substance use and abuse.

Stress

When you hear the word stress, you may think of tension, hardship, problems, anger, and other negative thoughts and emotions. However, stress can have positive results as well as negative. *Stress* is an effect of life change. Stress is not the change itself, but how you react to the change. Reactions vary with individual people. An event that causes one person great anxiety may cause only a mild reaction in another.

Almost any change in your life can create some level of stress. Although people most often associate stress with difficult or negative experiences (e.g., a death in the family, financial trouble), stress can also come from experiences most people perceive as positive (e.g., getting married, moving to a bigger and better home). How you cope with stress can have positive or negative effects on your life.

Positive Effects of Stress

What you feel in a stressful situation, such as the time before a test—increased energy, perhaps, and a heightened awareness that may make you feel on edge—can have positive effects. In fact, moderate levels of stress can actually improve performance and efficiency, while too little stress may result in boredom or inactivity, and too much stress may cause an unproductive anxiety level. Figure 13.3, based on research by Drs. Robert M. Yerkes and John D. Dodson, illustrates this concept.

Control over your responses is essential to maintaining a helpful level of stress. You can exercise some level of control by attempting to respond to

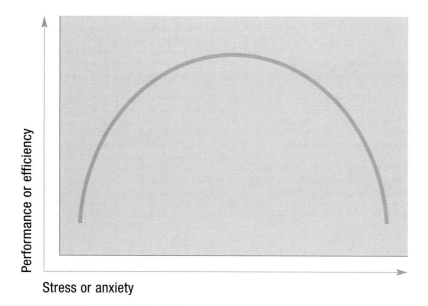

Yerkes-Dodson law.

FIGURE

13.1

stressful situations as positively as possible. Perceiving stress as good encourages you to push the boundaries of your abilities. For example, a student who responds positively to the expectations of college instructors might be encouraged to improve study skills and to work on time management in order to have more study time.

Being able to control how you respond will help you deal with the negative effects of stress as well.

Negative Effects of Stress

If you perceive stress as bad, you may pour your energy into unproductive anxiety rather than problem solving. For example, a student who responds negatively to instructor expectations may become distracted and may skip class or avoid studying. Negative stress may have dangerous physical and psychological effects. Physically, you may experience a change in appetite, body aches, or increased vulnerability to illnesses. Psychologically, you may feel depressed, unable to study or focus in class, unhappy, or anxious. Both kinds of problems may affect your relationships and responsibilities.

Negative reactions to excessive stress are an increasing phenomenon on the job. The American Institute of Stress and the American Psychological Association report that job stress costs companies an estimated $200 billion a year.[2] Pressure to succeed, **downsizing** with its resulting layoffs, and increasing two-career households all contribute to job stress.

Managing Stress

Thinking critically, you can use your problem-solving skills to cope with stressful life changes. First, try to adjust the cause of the stress. For example, if increased socializing is causing your grades to slip, consider how you

DOWNSIZING

Reducing in size; streamlining (usually referring to a business).

can refocus on your schoolwork and make better decisions about how to manage your time. Here are some strategies for determining and adjusting the cause in a stressful situation.

ADDRESS ISSUES SPECIFICALLY. When a situation at school or work is causing stress, think through the details and decide on a plan of attack. For example, if you have a problem with course work, set up a meeting with the instructor. If your work environment is stressful, brainstorm ways to change it.

BREAK JOBS INTO SMALLER PIECES. Goals will appear more manageable when approached as a series of smaller steps. Perform a smaller task well rather than a larger one not so well.

SET REASONABLE, MANAGEABLE GOALS. Trying to achieve something that is out of your reach will cause more stress than success.

AVOID PROCRASTINATION. The longer you wait to do something, the more difficulty you may have doing it. However distasteful the task, it will be much worse when time runs short and the expectations of others hang over your head.

SET BOUNDARIES AND LEARN TO SAY "NO." Don't take responsibility for everyone and everything. Stop stress before it starts by delegating what can be or should be taken care of by someone else.

Sometimes a cause lies beyond your control. In these cases, address its effect on you. For example, if the flu keeps you in bed for a week, you can reduce the negative effects of stress by contacting your instructors or classmates to see what schoolwork you can accomplish while you're sick.

The following are techniques that can help you adjust to the effects of a stressful situation.

EAT RIGHT, EXERCISE, AND GET ADEQUATE SLEEP. Physical health promotes clear thinking. Make healthy food choices and eat in moderation; make some type of exercise a regular part of life; figure out how much sleep you need and do your best to get it.

DO SOMETHING RELAXING. Take breaks regularly: Play music, take a nap, read a book, go for a drive, take a walk outside, or see a movie. Recreation restores your mind and body.

CHANGE YOUR SURROUNDINGS. Getting away from situations and locations you associate with stress can lighten the effect it has on you and help you place problems in perspective.

Positive thinking and taking action can help you control stress. In some cases, however, a disorder or situation may make stress difficult to handle without special treatment. If you experience any of the following, consult people who can help you.

Important information about depression.

POSSIBLE CAUSES OF DEPRESSION

- A genetic disposition toward depression

- A chemical imbalance in the brain

- Seasonal Affective Disorder (depression occurring in reaction to reduced daylight in autumn/winter)

- Highly stressful situations such as financial trouble, academic failure, death in the family

- Illnesses, injuries, lack of exercise, poor diet

- Reactions to medications

HELPFUL STRATEGIES IF YOU FEEL DEPRESSED

- Do the best you can and don't have unreasonable expectations of yourself.

- Try to be with others rather than alone.

- Don't expect your mood to change right away; feeling better will take time.

- Try to avoid making major life decisions until your condition improves.

- Remember not to blame yourself for your condition.

Source: National Institutes of Health Publication No. 94-3561, National Institutes of Health, 1994.

DEPRESSION. As many as 10 percent of Americans will experience a major depression at some point in their lives. More than just temporary blues, this illness requires medical evaluation and is treatable. Symptoms include constant sadness or anxiety, loss of interest in activities that you normally like, eating too much or too little, low motivation, constant fatigue, and low self-esteem. Table 13.1 describes causes of depression along with other depression strategies.

ANOREXIA NERVOSA. Some people develop such a strong desire to be thin that it creates unnatural self-starvation. This condition—anorexia nervosa—occurs mainly in young women. People with anorexia lose an extreme amount of weight and look painfully thin, although they often feel that they are overweight. They refuse to eat, exercise constantly, use laxatives, and develop obsessive rituals around food. An estimated 5 to 7 percent of college undergraduates in the United States suffer from anorexia.[3] Effects of anorexia-induced starvation may include organ damage, heart failure, and death.

BULIMIA. People who binge on excessive amounts of food, usually sweets and fattening foods, and then purge through self-induced vomiting have bulimia. They may also use laxatives or exercise obsessively. Effects of bulimia include damage to the digestive tract, stomach rupture, and even heart failure due to the loss of important minerals.

OBESITY. Being significantly overweight can be related to a number of different factors from serious medical problems to stressful life situations to a sedentary lifestyle to ignorance about proper nutrition and poor eating habits. Whatever the cause, the effects can be dangerous—high blood pressure, diabetes, high cholesterol, heart problems, and other physical ailments. Obesity also has a negative effect on self-image, especially if friends and family are normal weight. Despite the problems associated with obesity, its incidence is rising alarmingly among children, adolescents, and adults.

BINGE EATING. Like bulimics, people with a binge eating disorder eat large amounts of food and have a hard time stopping. However, they do not purge afterwards. Binge eaters often are overweight and feel that they cannot control their eating. The effects are similar to the effects of obesity.

Responding to stress in a self-destructive manner may also include abuse of substances. Knowing as much as you can about substance use and abuse will help you make the best choices for your life.

Substance Use and Abuse

Alcohol, tobacco, and drug users comprise men and women from all socioeconomic levels, racial and cultural groups, and areas of the country. Carefully consider the potential positive and negative effects before considering the use of these substances. Although some users prefer to ignore the statistics, the fact remains that the use or abuse of alcohol, tobacco, and drugs can cause problems and even destroy lives. Think critically and take the time to make decisions that are best for you.

Alcohol

Alcohol is a drug as much as it is a beverage. Of all alcohol consumption, **binge drinking** has the most problematic effects. Here are the statistics:

BINGE DRINKING

Having five or more drinks at one sitting.

- From a survey of a random sampling of students, 43 percent said they are binge drinkers, and 21 percent said that they binge drink frequently.[4]
- Of students who do not binge drink, 80 percent surveyed reported experiencing one or more second-hand effects of binge drinking (e.g., vandalism, sexual assault or unwanted sexual advances, interrupted sleep or study).[5]
- Students who binge drink are more likely to miss classes, are less able to work, have hangovers, become depressed, engage in unplanned sexual activity, and ignore safer sex practices.[6]

The bottom line is that heavy drinking causes severe problems. The NIAAA estimates that alcohol contributes to the deaths of 100,000 people every year through both alcohol-related illnesses and accidents involving drunk drivers.[7] Heavy drinking can damage the liver, the digestive system, and brain cells, and can impair the central nervous system. Indeed, as *The New Wellness Encyclopedia* states, "chronic, excessive use of alcohol can seriously damage every function and organ of the body."[8] Prolonged use also can cause addiction, making it seem impossibly painful for the user to stop drinking.

> **ADDICTION**
>
> Compulsive physiological need for a habit-forming substance.

Tobacco

College students do their share of smoking. The National Institute on Drug Abuse (NIDA) found that 38.8 percent of college students reported smoking at least once in the year before they were surveyed, and 24.5 percent had smoked once within the month before. Nationally, about 60 million people are habitual smokers.[9] The choice to smoke—often influenced by advertising directed at young people—shortly may turn into a harmful addiction.

When people smoke, they inhale nicotine, a highly addictive drug found in all tobacco products. Long-term effects of nicotine may include high blood pressure, bronchitis, emphysema, stomach ulcers, lung cancer, and heart conditions. Pregnant women who smoke run an increased risk of babies with low birth weight, premature births, or stillbirths.

Quitting smoking is extremely difficult and should be attempted gradually. However, the positive effects of quitting—increased life expectancy, greater lung capacity, and more energy—may inspire any smoker to consider making a lifestyle change. Weigh your options and make a responsible choice.

Drugs

NIDA reports that 31.4 percent of college students had used illicit drugs at least once in the year before being surveyed, and 16 percent in the month before.[10] Drug users rarely think through the possible effects when choosing to take a drug. However, many of the so-called "rewards" of drug abuse are empty. Drug-using peers may accept you for your drug use and not for who you are. Problems and responsibilities may multiply when you emerge from a high. The pain of withdrawal may not compare to the pain of the damage that long-term drug use can do to your body.

> **WITHDRAWAL**
>
> The discontinuance of the use of a drug, including attendant side effects.

You are responsible for choosing what you want to introduce into your body. If you think critically about drugs and ask important questions, you can draw your own conclusions. Ask questions like the following: Why do I want to do this? What are the positive and negative effects it might have? If others want me to do it, why? Do I respect the people who want me to do this? How does it affect other drug users I know of? How would my drug use affect the people in my life? The more informed you are, the better able you will be to make choices that benefit you and avoid choices that harm you.

Identifying and Overcoming Addiction

People with addictions have lost their control for any number of reasons, including chemical imbalances in the brain, hereditary tendencies, or stressful life circumstances. If you think you may be addicted, look carefully at your situation. Compare the positive and negative effects of your habits and decide if they are worth it. Although others can tell you how they feel and make suggestions, you are the only one who can truly take the initiative to change.

How do I become employable and promotable?

Titus Dillard, Jr., *Embry-Riddle Aeronautical University, Daytona Beach, Florida, Aviation/Business Management Major*

I transferred from a junior college to Embry-Riddle on a basketball scholarship, without which I probably wouldn't have been able to afford school. I've enjoyed it, but collegiate sports take up a lot of time. We practice six days a week for 2 1/2 hours a day. Game days, especially away games, require even more time. Coaches tell you to bring books  on the road, but there are too many interruptions to really focus on studying. To help pay the bills, I also work 10 hours a week as a Student Assistant for our business academic advisor. It's been a great experience, but again it takes away from my time to study. I'm the first in my family to graduate from college, and my mother is proud of me. But she still has four children at home, so I don't like to ask for anything.

Because I haven't been able to focus on academics, my grade point average has suffered. I am a senior now, so I have very little time to bring it up. There's a naval intelligence program sponsored by the U.S. government that I would like to apply for, but one of the requirements is a GPA of 3.45 or higher. Right now mine is only 2.5.

Last week we had a career exposition at my school and one of the first questions recruiters asked was, "What's your GPA?" I'm thinking about asking my basketball coach for a letter of recommendation to help show that I've been responsible, but I wonder if that will do any good. I want to make a good impression. Do you have any suggestions for how I can become employable and promotable after school?

Cherie Andrade, *Hawaii Pacific University, Honolulu, Associate Director of Admissions*

It's understandable that you worry about your future. First of all, although you are feeling discouraged about your GPA, try not to dwell on it. I don't think companies look primarily at GPA when considering a candidate. That's only one component of your profile. You have many things going for you. For one, you have an interesting background. The fact that you are the first generation to graduate shows your drive to succeed. Your experiences, such as playing basketball and working part-time, have built character and a work ethic. These are important to employers. Remember: Don't judge yourself. Let the people looking at the applications be the judges.

I have three suggestions for your interviews. First, make an appointment to talk with the director of the Career Services Center on your campus. This person  often knows what companies are looking for. Second, if you want to enter the naval intelligence program, you definitely should apply even though one of their qualifications is a high GPA. Career counselors often tell students to apply for what seems far-fetched because you might just be exactly what they're looking for. Third, do get a letter of recommendation from your coach, but don't stop there. Try to also get a letter from one of your instructors or the business advisor you work for. Explain to them what you want to accomplish so that they can give you a more focused recommendation.

To land the job or the training you want, you have to step out and take risks. If you pursue your career goals with the same determination and skills you've used to finish four years of college and juggle all your other commitments, I have no doubt you'll find work you love and that you'll continue to develop in your area of expertise.

Because substance use often causes physical and chemical changes, quitting often requires guiding your body through a painful withdrawal. If you determine that you need to make changes, many resources are available to help you along the way. Seek out any combination of the following:

- *Counseling and medical care.* Check with your school's counseling or health center, your personal physician, or a local hospital.
- *Detoxification ("detox") centers.* If you have a severe addiction, you may need a controlled environment in which to separate yourself completely from the substance that you abuse.
- *Support groups.* You can derive help and comfort from sharing your experiences with others. Alcoholics Anonymous is the premier support group for alcoholics.

When people address their problems directly instead of avoiding them through substance abuse, they can begin to grow and improve. Working through substance-abuse problems can lead to a restoration of both health and self-respect.

Your body and mind are connected. One important way to reduce stress is to focus on achieving the goals that are most important to you. Striving to live according to your personal mission can bring your stress level down and actually improve your health.

HOW CAN YOU LIVE YOUR MISSION?

Whatever changes occur in your life, your continued learning will give you a greater sense of security in your choices. Recall your mission statement from Chapter 2. Think about how it may change as you develop. It will continue to reflect your goals, values, and strengths if you live with integrity, create personal change, broaden your perspective, and work to achieve your personal best.

Live with Integrity

You've spent time exploring who you are, how you learn, and what you value. **Integrity** is about being true to that self-portrait you have drawn while also considering the needs of others. Living with integrity will bring you great personal and professional rewards.

INTEGRITY
Adherence to a code of moral values; incorruptibility, honesty.

Having integrity puts your ethics—your sense of what is right and wrong—into day-to-day action. Figure 13.4 shows the building blocks of integrity—the principles by which a person of integrity strives to live. When you act with integrity, you earn trust and respect from yourself and from others. If people can trust you to be honest, to be sincere in what you say and do, and to consider the needs of others, they will be more likely to encourage you, support your goals, and reward your work. Integrity is a must for workplace success.

Think of situations in which a decision made with integrity has had a positive effect. Have you ever confessed to an instructor that your paper is late without a good excuse, only to find that despite your mistake you have earned the instructor's respect? Have extra efforts in the workplace ever

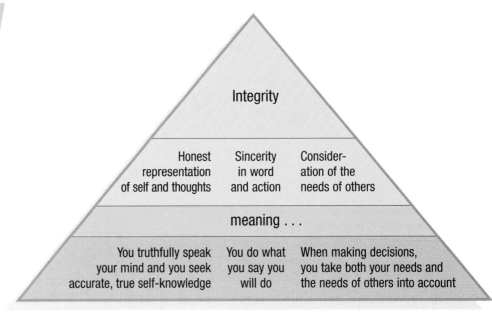

FIGURE 13.4 Building blocks of integrity.

helped you gain a promotion or a raise? Have your kindnesses toward a friend or spouse moved the relationship to a deeper level? When you decide to act with integrity, you can improve your life and the lives of others.

One specific kind of integrity—academic integrity—means being an honorable student and adhering to school rules such as the prohibition of plagiarism, cheating, or providing unethical aid to other students. Explore your school's specific requirements. Your school's code of honor, or academic integrity policy, should be printed in your student handbook. Read it to be sure you know what is expected of you. As a student enrolled in your school, you have agreed to abide by that policy.

And life is what we make it, always has been, always will be.

GRANDMA MOSES

Most important, living with integrity helps you believe in yourself and in your ability to make good choices. A person of integrity isn't a perfect person but one who makes the effort to live according to values and principles, continually striving to learn from mistakes and to improve. Take responsibility for making the right moves, and you will follow your mission with strength and conviction.

Create Personal Change

How has your idea of who you are and where you want to be changed since you first opened this book? What have you learned about your values, your goals, and your styles of communication and learning? Consider how your goals have changed. As you continue to grow and develop, keep adjusting your goals to your changes and discoveries.

Stephen Covey, in *The Seven Habits of Highly Effective People,* says: "Change—real change—comes from the inside out. It doesn't come from hacking at the leaves of attitude and behavior with quick fix personality ethic techniques. It comes from striking at the root—the fabric of our thought, the fundamental essential **paradigms** which give definition to our character and create the lens through which we see the world."[11]

Examining yourself deeply in that way is a real risk, demanding courage and strength of will. Questioning your established beliefs and facing the unknown are much more difficult than staying with how things are. When you face the consequences of trying something unfamiliar, admitting failure, or challenging what you thought you knew, you open yourself to learning opportunities. When you foster personal changes and make new choices based on those changes, you grow.

> **PARADIGM**
>
> An especially clear pattern or typical example.

Broaden Your Perspective

Look wide, beyond the scope of your daily life. You are part of an international community and a global economy. In today's interconnected and media-saturated world, people are becoming more aware of, and dependent on, each other. What happens to the Japanese economy affects the price of automobiles and electronic equipment sold in your neighborhood. A music trend that starts in New York spreads to Europe. When human rights are violated in one nation, other nations become involved. You are as important a link in this worldwide chain of human connection as any other person. Together, all people share an interest in creating a better world for future generations.

The twentieth century was marked by intense change. The industrial revolution transformed the face of farming, and inventions such as the telephone and television fostered greater communication. Labor unions organized, the civil rights movement struggled against inequality, and women fought for the right to vote.

Now, at the beginning of this century, major shifts are happening once again. Computer technology is drastically changing every industry. The Internet and cable news networks spread information to people all over the world at a rapid rate. Many people continue to strive for equal rights. You are part of a world that is responsible for making the most of these developments. In making the choices that allow you to achieve your potential, you will make the world a better place.

Aim for Your Personal Best

Your personal best is simply the best that you can do, in any situation. It may not be the best you have ever done. It may include mistakes, for nothing significant is ever accomplished without making mistakes and taking risks. It may shift from situation to situation. As long as you aim to do your best, though, you are inviting growth and success.

Aim for your personal best in everything you do. As a lifelong learner, you will always have a new direction in which to grow and a new challenge to face. Seek constant improvement in your personal,

educational, and professional life, knowing that you are capable of such improvement. Enjoy the richness of life by living each day to the fullest, developing your talents and potential into the achievement of your most valued goals.

Kaizen is the Japanese word for "continual improvement." Striving for excellence, always finding ways to improve on what already exists, and believing that you can impact change are at the heart of the industrious Japanese spirit. The drive to improve who you are and what you do will help to provide the foundation of a successful future.

Think of this concept as you reflect on yourself, your goals, your lifelong education, your career, and your personal pursuits. Create excellence and quality by continually asking yourself, "How can I improve?" Living by *kaizen* will help you to be a respected friend and family member, a productive and valued employee, and a truly contributing member of society. You can change the world.

IMPORTANT POINTS *to remember*

1. Why is college just the beginning of lifelong learning?

College is a golden opportunity to focus on learning. However, keeping a focus on learning even after college will help you continue to move ahead both at work and in your personal life. Learning brings change, and change causes growth. Continually taking in new knowledge and ideas will fuel your improvement and progress. Strategies for lifelong learning include investigating new interests, reading, pursuing career improvement, investigating human differences, and exploring your spiritual and artistic sides.

2. How can you adjust to change?

Rapid change is a reality of modern life. People often resist change because they fear its negative effects. However, being flexible—shifting priorities as change affects your needs—will help you handle change and experience its positive effects. You may need to adjust your goals, either because life changes or because the first goal wasn't appropriate. First reevaluate your goals and your progress toward them. Then, modify your goals by either adjusting or replacing them.

3. What will help you handle success and failure?

A perfect, trouble-free life isn't possible, but that doesn't mean life can't be challenging and wonderful. Accepting failures and successes along the way will help you stay afloat without losing your self-esteem. Deal with failure by defining failure and success, accepting failure as human, and approaching failure productively by thinking critically about what you can learn from what happened. Deal with success with celebration and confidence, and encourage others to keep working toward their goals.

4. Why is it important to focus on wellness?

Your success in school depends in large part on your physical and mental health. Many students feel stress—an effect of life change, experienced as positive or negative—on a fairly regular basis. Use problem-solving skills to cope with life changes that cause negative stress. Seek help with mental health issues such as depression and eating disorders. The use and abuse of alcohol, tobacco, and drugs also has an effect on the body and mind. Use critical thinking to evaluate your habits and determine whether they are taking too much of a toll. Seek help from school resources and support groups if you need to make a change.

5. How can you live your mission?

Your life's mission is as subject to change as the rest of your life. As goals, personal life, and the world change, your mission must adjust to reflect those developments. Put your sense of right and wrong into daily action by living with integrity: Be honest about your self and thoughts, be sincere in word and action, and consider the needs of others. Create personal change by having the courage to question your beliefs, face the unknown, and take risks. Broaden your perspective to understand how your actions cause ripples in the world. Aim for your personal best in everything you do. Live each day to the fullest and take your mission into the future as you work toward your most valued goals.

CRITICAL THINKING

APPLYING LEARNING TO LIFE

CHANGE AND LIFELONG LEARNING. What are the three biggest changes that have occurred in your life this year?

1. _____

2. _____

3. _____

Choose one that you feel you handled well. What shifts in priorities or goals did you make?

_____

_____

_____

Thinking ahead to the next year of your life, what change is coming up for you? Name the change and briefly discuss the strategy you plan to use to face it.

_____

_____

_____

_____

_____

Of the strategies for lifelong learning that you learned, which do you think you can do, or plan to do, in your life now? Name the three that mean the most to you.

1. _____

2. _____

3. _____

Choose one of these strategies and discuss how you will make it part of your life.

TEAMWORK

COMBINING FORCES

ACTIVELY DEALING WITH STRESS. By yourself, make a list of things that cause stress in your life. As a class, discuss the causes you have listed. Choose the five most common. Divide the class into five groups according to who would choose what cause as his or her most important (redistribute some people if the group sizes are unbalanced). Each group should discuss its assigned cause, brainstorming solutions, and strategies. List your best coping strategies and present it to the class. You may want to make copies of the lists so that every member of the class has five, one for each cause of stress.

WRITING

DISCOVERY THROUGH JOURNALING

To record your thoughts, use a separate journal or the lined page at the end of the chapter.

FIFTY POSITIVE THOUGHTS. Make a list. The first 25 items should be things you like about yourself. You can name anything—things you can do, things you think, things you've accomplished, things you like about your physical self, and so on. The second 25 items should be things you'd like to do in your life. These can be of any magnitude—anything from trying Vietnamese food to traveling to the Grand Canyon to keeping your room neat to getting to know someone. They can be things you'd like to do tomorrow or things that you plan to do in 20 years. Be creative. Let everything be possible.

CAREER PORTFOLIO

CHARTING YOUR COURSE

REVISED MISSION STATEMENT. Retrieve the mission statement you wrote at the end of Chapter 2. Give yourself a day or so to read it over and think about it. Then, revise it according to the changes that have occurred in you. Add new priorities and goals and delete those that are no longer valid. Continue to update your mission statement so that it reflects your growth and development, helping to guide you through the changes that await you in the future.

UGGESTED READINGS

Benson, Herbert, M.D. and Eileen M. Stuart, R.N., C.M.S. *The Wellness Book: The Comprehensive Guide to Maintaining Health and Treating Stress-Related Illness.* New York: Simon & Schuster (1993).

Boenisch, Ed, Ph.D. and C. Michele Haney, Ph.D. *The Stress Owner's Manual: Meaning, Balance, and Health in Your Life.* San Luis Obispo, CA: Impact Publishers (1996).

Delany, Sarah and Elizabeth Delany, with Amy Hill Hearth. *Book of Everyday Wisdom.* New York: Kodansha International (1994).

Editors of the University of California at Berkeley Wellness Letter. *The New Wellness Encyclopedia.* New York: Houghton Mifflin (1995).

Greene, Bob and Oprah Winfrey. *Make the Connection: Ten Steps to a Better Body and a Better Life.* New York: Hyperion (1999).

Moore, Thomas. *Care of the Soul: How to Add Depth and Meaning to Your Everyday Life.* New York: HarperCollins (1998).

McMahon, Susanna, Ph.D. *The Portable Problem Solver: Coping With Life's Stressors.* New York: Dell Publishing (1996).

Radcliffe, Rebecca Ruggles. *Dance Naked in Your Living Room: Handling Stress and Finding Joy!* Minneapolis, MN: EASE (1997).

Schuckit, Marc Alan, M.D. *Educating Yourself about Alcohol and Drugs: A People's Primer.* New York: Plenum Press (1995).

 NTERNET RESOURCES

ThriveOnline (health and fitness): **www.thriveonline.com**

Health.com (sections on stress management, conditions, and personal health): **www.health.com**

Queendom.com Soul Search (self-tests, personal exploration and growth): **www.queendom.com/portals/soulsearch.html**

 NDNOTES

1. Thomas Moore. *The Care of the Soul.* New York: Harper Perennial (1992), pp. xi–xx.

2. Stephanie Armour. "Workplace Hazard Gets Attention," *USA Today,* May 5 1998, p. B1.

3. Kim Hubbard, Anne-Marie O'Neill, and Christina Cheakalos. "Out of Control," *People,* April 12, 1999, p. 54.

4. H. Wechsler et al. "Changes in Binge Drinking and Related Problems Among American College Students Between 1993 and 1997," *Journal of American College Health,* Vol. 47, 9/98, p. 57.

5. Ibid., pp. 63–64.

6. National Institute on Alcohol Abuse and Alcoholism. "Alcohol Alert," Publication No. 29 PH 357, Bethesda, MD, July 1995.

7. J. McGinnis and W. Foege. "Actual Causes of Death in the United States," *Journal of the American Medical Association (JAMA)* 270.18, 1993, p. 2208.

8. The Editors of the University of California at Berkeley Wellness Letter, *The New Wellness Encyclopedia.* Boston: Houghton Mifflin Company (1995), p. 72.

9. National Institute on Drug Abuse, Capsule Series C-83-08. "Cigarette Smoking." Bethesda, MD: National Institutes of Health (1994).

10. National Institute on Drug Abuse. "National Survey Results on Drug Abuse from Monitoring the Future Study." Bethesda, MD: National Institutes of Health (1994).

11. Stephen Covey. *The Seven Habits of Highly Effective People.* New York: Simon & Schuster (1989), pp. 70–144, 309–318.

Journal

NAME

DATE

The Prentice Hall Supersite www.prenhall.com/success has a Career Path tab. Click on it and take the quiz to see what it says about your career possibilities.

1. What group number did you most closely associate with? What in the description of that group describes you well?

2. Which group would be your second choice, and what about that description suits you?

3. Select two professions that interest you from the ones listed as suiting your group type. Use a search engine to find career sites on the web that might have information about those professions. Write down the URLs for those sites so that you can return to them again.

Next, visit the Career Assessments section and click on the "What are my values?" assessment. Copy or print the value lists and complete the assessment as directed.

1. What are your most important terminal values?

2. What are your most important instrumental values?

3. Think about it—what careers do you think suit the values that are most important to you? If you are already involved with or interested in one or more particular careers, how well do you think those careers suit your values?

Index